17.30

P9-EDQ-882

CREATIVE MANAGEMENT TECHNIQUES IN INTERSCHOLASTIC ATHLETICS

CREATIVE MANAGEMENT TECHNIQUES IN INTERSCHOLASTIC ATHLETICS

Donald E. Fuoss
Professor of Physical Education and
formerly Athletic Director,
California State University
Sacramento, California

Robert J. Troppmann
Director of Physical Education and
formerly Athletic Director,
Redwood High School
Larkspur, California

John Wiley & Sons
New York ● Santa Barbara ● London ● Sydney ● Toronto

Copyright © 1977, by John Wiley & Sons, Inc.

All rights reserved. Published simultaneously in Canada.

No part of this book may be reproduced by any means, nor
transmitted, nor translated into a machine language without the written permission of the publisher.

Library of Congress Cataloging in Publication Data:

Fuoss, Donald E.
  Creative management techniques in interscholastic athletics

  Includes bibliographies and index.
  1. School sports—Management.   I. Troppmann, Robert,
joint author.   II. Title.
GV346.F86   375'.6137   76-465000
ISBN 0-471-28815-2

Printed in the United States of America

10 9 8 7 6 5 4 3 2 1

CAMROSE LUTHERAN COLLEGE
LIBRARY

GV
346
F86 / 20,065

Preface

Most people dislike change. Many people resist it, and some refuse to accept it. Change often forces us to give up something we value, tangible or intangible, that we have possessed and cherished for years. Change forces us to reexamine, reevaluate, and to readjust to what is occurring around us. To fail to do this means that one is not knowledgeable and is not with the times. To resist change or to fail to recognize it, to continue utilizing methods and techniques that are outdated, for whatever reason, means that one has a closed mind, considers change a threat, and may be merely existing but not living in modern times. Change takes place with or without us. The field of education is no exception, nor are administrators, faculty members, and students. Everyone experiences change and continues to experience the effects of change.

The management concept applied to athletic administration necessitates change. The management concept, relevant to the administration of athletic programs, and the business concept, important in conducting these programs, were first introduced at the collegiate level. In recent years, these concepts have started to be used at the scholastic level of athletic administration, although today their acceptance has not been as universal at the high school level as at the collegiate level. Many athletic administrators are just now becoming aware that there is a different way to do the job. This book stresses a new managerial approach to athletic administration.

Up to now, many educators have philosophically resisted the connection between the "make money" concept of business and the purpose and objectives of education. Changing times have brought about a different viewpoint in recent years. Recession and inflation have seriously threatened the survival of athletic programs. Insufficient funding for athletic programs is likely to be a fact of life for an indeterminable number of years. As a result, athletic administrators, first at the college level and more recently at the scholastic level, have begun to recognize that the economic law of efficiency, "Be efficient or die!" is as harsh as Darwin's law of evolution, "Adapt to survive!" Athletic directors at all levels now want to know how to administer efficient programs and how to adapt in order to retain viable, ongoing athletic programs and survive financial crises. Adherence to the principles, suggestions, and tenets discussed in this book should be an invaluable aid to athletic administrators, especially to those who administer interscholastic athletic programs, where we have placed our main emphasis.

This book was written for institutions offering professional preparation classes in physical education and sports administration. It is intended to serve as an essential guide and usable reference for the inservice education of administrators. Although we recognize the "as is" situation in scholastic athletics and realistically emphasize the present nature of athletics in high schools, we encourage athletic administrators and coaches to recognize the possibility of achieving the "should be" or "could be" situation. We stress the new managerial approach, which necessitates change.

Whereas the "could-should be" situation is goal oriented, the "as is" situation continues to be task oriented. This necessitates a change in the thinking of the athletic director and his associates. They must review their positions and work and the role and functions of the athletic director.

By applying the principles of management to administering the athletic program, coaches act as managerial supervisors in the hierarchy; the athletic director is middle management; and the principal is executive management. All are managers and all perform the same basic management function since management is a universal process. The managerial process at each level is different. The focus in this book is mostly on the middle manager's (athletic director's) role and functions. Note that in this book, where the masculine pronoun is used, the feminine term is also applicable, as the athletic director can be of either sex. This avoids the use of he/she, him and her, and other awkward constructions.

This book consists of 32 chapters divided into 8 parts. We discuss all of the managerial functions that the athletic director, as a middle manager, performs. Chapters are organized under functions performed rather than in a traditional sequence, which makes this book unique. At the conclusion of each chapter are questions for discussion, most of which deal with the material in the chapter. Other questions deal with case studies that require problem solving. Although not identified as such, they give the instructor and students the opportunity to make judgments relevant to codes of conduct, professional ethics, training rules, discipline, and other debatable subjects. Also at the end of most chapters are references and suggested readings; the readings refer to athletic as well as management publications.

Part I, "Managerial Role of the Interscholastic Athletic Director," consists of three chapters. The opening chapter identifies the problems, forces, and issues shaping interscholastic athletics today and probably for the future. The other two chapters deal with the organization of the interscholastic athletic program and the middle management responsibilities of the athletic director.

Parts II to VII deal with the specific functions that a manager performs, regardless of the managerial level, or the trade, business, or profession. Part II consists of five chapters dealing with goals and objectives, policy development, financing and budgetary problems or solutions, scheduling procedures and facilities, planning, scheduling, and the management of athletic contests at the secondary school level.

Part III, consisting of four chapters, deals with the management functions of organizing, staffing, coordinating, and communicating. Separate chapters are devoted to the certification of coaches and administrators, the screening, assigning, and evaluating of coaching personnel and methods of compensation for coaching assignments. The concluding chapter is on staff relations.

Part IV deals with the management functions of directing and delegating and has seven chapters. The major topics discussed are eligibility regulations governing interscholastic athletics, disciplinary responsibilities of the coach and the student-athlete, the courts and liability in interscholastic athletics, medical aspects, athletic awards, and the administration of interscholastic athletic events. There is a chapter on the selection, assignment, and evaluation of game officials.

Part V, consisting of six chapters, is concerned with the management functions of controlling and reporting. Two chapters discuss the purchase, care, storage, and inventory of athletic equipment.

There are separate chapters on safety considerations in interscholastic athletics, the transportation of athletes and athletic teams, effective office management and recordkeeping, and a concluding chapter on the evaluation of the interscholastic athletic program.

Part VI deals with the athletic director's managerial functions of innovating and consists of two chapters: The rapidly changing role, for girls' athletic competition and the leadership of creativity, innovation, and motivation.

Part VII is the concluding management function presented and consists of four chapters dealing with the national and state athletic associations, counseling and guidance of the student-athlete, public and community relations and crowd accommodations, and the management in interscholastic athletics.

Part VIII consists of a single chapter summarizing implications for the future of interscholastic athletics.

The material for this publication has been obtained from many diverse sources too numerous to mention. It is an accumulation of over more than 50 years of professional experience in coaching, administrative, and teaching experience at the high school and collegiate levels. This book is limited in scope to the administration of interscholastic athletic programs and excludes reference to junior high school, intramural, collegiate, and professional athletic programs per se. Needless to say we have been influenced in our thinking, philosophy, and writing by professionals at all levels; professional organizations and publications. For brevity only professional organizations are listed: National Association of Collegiate Directors of Athletics (NACDA) and Management Institute; National Collegiate Athletic Association (NCAA); Association of Athletics for Women (AIAW); National Federation of State High School Athletic Associations (NFSHSAA); National Council of Secondary High School Athletic Directors (NCSSAD); National Association for Girls and Women in Sports (NAGWS); National Association for Sports and Physical Education and Recreation (NASPE); American Alliance for Health, Physical Education and Recreation (AAHPER); and others.

Donald E. Fuoss
Robert J. Troppmann

Acknowledgments

We thank everyone who shared in the preparation of this book. No claim of originality is made for much of the material. The interpretation and applications, however, are our responsibility.

We are grateful to the authors and their publishers who granted us permission to quote from their publications, as shown in the credit line in the references or in the legends. We appreciate the help of the many high school athletic directors, coaches, and physical educators who responded to our questionnaire and who made available to us informational forms and related materials. Although response was overwhelming, we regret not being able to incorporate into the manuscript all of the voluminous material we received. However, a grateful "thank you", while inadequate, is expressed with much appreciation to all. Where materials were utilized, regardless of the source of information, we have attempted to give proper credit.

We appreciate the comments and suggestions of the professionals in the field of physical education and sports administration who reviewed our proposal, outline, and manuscript initially. We particularly wish to thank Dr. Harry Fritz, formerly Athletic Director and Dean of the School of Health Education and Professor of Physical Education State University of New York at Buffalo and presently Executive Secretary, National Association of Intercollegiate Athletics, for his many suggestions and detailed analytical comments on our manuscript throughout its various stages of development. Finally, without the assistance, encouragement, and unfailing support of our wives, Frances Fuoss and Marilyn Troppman, the project would have not become a reality.

D.E.F.
R.J.T.

Contents

PART III ORGANIZING, STAFFING, COORDINATING,
COMMUNTICATING

PART I
MANAGERIAL ROLE OF THE INTERSCHOLASTIC ATHLETIC DIRECTOR

Chapter 1

Problems Forces and Issues Shaping Interscholastic Athletics Today and for the Future

THE NEED FOR NEW APPROACHES AND DIRECTIONS

The issues, forces, and problems of the 1970s that confront present-day educators including athletic directors and coaches are, for the most part, different from those confronting educators from 1940 to the present. Different, too, are a number of today's concepts, methods, and practices for resolving current problems and issues in the field of education including the management and administration of interscholastic athletic programs.

There is no implication in this discussion, which is focused on the scope of the administration of secondary school athletic programs, that all previous concepts, philosophies, and methods are invalid merely because they were initiated in an earlier era. No claim is made that all previous ideas for resolving interscholastic athletic problems and issues should be discarded because they did not originate with the present generation. It is implied, however, that times, interests, and needs have changed and that the concepts, methods and practices currently being used by educators and administrators must constantly be examined, evaluated, and updated to resolve current concerns and problems. The management and administration of interscholastic athletic programs are not excluded. Dealing with today's problems by blindly adhering to yesterday's practices,

2

standards, and methods may not be acceptable or feasible because of the changing values and interests of today's society and, in particular, of this generation's youth.

Before outlining the methods, practices, and techniques best suited to administering a modern-day interscholastic athletics program, it is first necessary to identify certain current problems.

We initially identify the problems that confronted interscholastic athletics in the fifties and sixties, since some of them have not been resolved and still confront educators and athletic administrators today. They appear to be indigenous to athletics generally and very likely will be with us even after the seventies and eighties. In addition to some unresolved problems the field of education is confronted with new issues that are both a threat and a challenge to educators in all disciplines.

INTERSCHOLASTIC ATHLETIC PROBLEMS, FORCES, AND ISSUES IN THE 1950s AND 1960s

In the pilot study of school athletics intiated in March, 1951, the members of the Educational Policies Commission[1] expressed grave concern over "emphasis on false values" and "bad athletic practices" that were marring athletics in many American schools. The Commission identified the following emphasis on these false values:

1. Overemphasis on winning
2. Glorifying star athletes
3. Disparaging the nonathlete
4. School games as public spectacles

The commission also noted and discussed bad athletic practices that they felt stemmed from unthinking acceptance of false values and were thought to be detrimental to the participants, school, and community:[2]

1. Overemphasis on the varsity
2. Distortions in the educational program
3. Financial woes
4. Recruiting by colleges
5. Involving younger children
6. Coaches under pressure
7. Neglecting the girls
8. Distorting school organizations

SOURCES OF DATA USED TO IDENTIFY CURRENT
PROBLEMS, FORCES, AND ISSUES

In an effort to idenfity the problems, forces, and issues prevalent in interscholastic athletics today, we employed the following techniques in collecting pertinent data:

1. A questionnaire mail survey of a selected number of male athletic directors, many of whom are past or present members of the National Council of Secondary School Athletic Directors, who are or have been administering interscholastic athletic programs throughout a cross section of the United States. These NCSSAD members responded in writing to the following request: "From your position and view point, would you please enumerate, identify and discuss briefly current critical problems, issues and trends which have a direct bearing on interscholastic athletics today."

2. At the termination of the 1974 joint meeting of the California Coaches Association and the California Association for Health, Physical Education and Recreation, 247 male and female athletic coaches, athletic directors, or physical educators responded in writing by identifying and briefly analyzing problems, issues and trends facing interscholastic athletics and physical education.

3. A perusal of the available literature, including professional journals and magazines, books, and selected newspapers dealing specifically with interscholastic athletics.

4. Opinions were also secured, both solicited and unsolicited, on an informal discussion and data collecting basis from colleagues and other interested individuals, men and women athletic administrators, coaches and physical education teachers and faculty members at professional meetings of the California Athletic Directors Association, California Coaches Association, San Francisco Coach of the Year Clinics, California Association for Health, Physical Education and Recreation, and the National Association of Collegiate Directors of Athletics.

5. Gallup poll results on school problems.

We have made every effort to isolate secondary school athletic problems from those of the collegiate level. Although much data and materials have been collected from those involved in administering or coaching interscholastic athletics in California, there is sufficient evidence from all sources to indicate that the trends noted are nationwide and pertinent to all interscholastic programs and to most administrators of secondary school athletic programs.

Although researchers may question the rather random and un-structured method by which the current problems, forces, and issues were identified, we do not feel this is a weakness.

CURRENT INTERSCHOLASTIC ATHLETIC PROBLEMS, FORCES, AND ISSUES

No effort has been made to rank the problems, forces, and issues in the order of priority, notoriety, or importance, other than to in-dicate the rapid emergence of girls' athletics, which was cited most frequently.

Our research was commenced more than two years prior to the passage of Title IX regulation (July 21, 1975), which now prohibits sex discrimination in education and which requires that schools must provide equal opportunity for both sexes to participate in intramural, interscholastic, and intercollegiate athletic competition. Prior to the passage of Title IX implementing education amendments of 1972, there was much speculation and conjecture about the effect such legislation would have on existing boys' athletic programs. Although some problems are more common to the boys' program and some that relate only to the girls' athletic program, since the passage of Title IX there have emerged problems that are now common to and affect the interscholastic athletic programs of both sexes. Here are common issues, beneficial and detrimental to interscholastic athletic programs for both boys and girls:

□ The lack of funding or inadequate funding
□ The lack of adequate facilities and conflicts in scheduling
□ Expanded programs and greater number of participants
□ The lack of adequate equipment
□ The lack of qualified and properly credentialed coaches

Additional problems indigenous to the girls' athletic program are:

□ Inadequate coaching salaries for women
□ Inadequate transportation for girls' athletic teams
□ The lack of qualified officials for girls' athletic contests

Male respondents cited the following problems pertaining specifically to the boys' athletic programs:

- The lack of support and the decrease in attendance were viewed as financial threats
- The lack of discipline and administrative support to enforce discipline
- Drugs in the schools
- Apathy in and for athletic programs in some schools
- The recruiting of high school athletes
- Crowd control or crowd accommodation

Other athletic problems that were mentioned less frequently in the survey results are listed later in this chapter but will not be discussed. The results of a recent Gallup poll on the critical problems facing American's public schools today will also be included. Each of the above identified problems, issues, and forces are discussed in the ensuing portions of this chapter.

CURRENT PROBLEMS, ISSUES, AND FORCES AFFECTING BOYS' AND GIRLS' INTERSCHOLASTIC ATHLETIC PROGRAMS

Expanding Programs and Greater Numbers of Participants

Although there appears to be a shift in the number of participants from some of the so-called traditional sports in the boys' programs, there are great increases in numbers of young people participating in interscholastic athletics, especially females, according to the 1975 Sports Participation Survey released by the National Federation of State High School Associations.[3] These increases in the number of participants and in the additional sports that are now available to student-athletes of high school age obviously have a direct bearing on boys' and girls' interscholastic programs and the problems and issues that will be discussed in this text. The rapidly changing role for girls' athletic competition is discussed at length in Chapter 26.

Participation in High School Athletics Will Exceed the Five Million Mark

More than 4 million male participants and 1.3 million female participants were involved in interscholastic athletic programs during 1974-1975 according to the 1975 Sports Participation Survey. The survey counts individuals once for each sport in which they participate, which is the most accurate measure of the size of secondary school athletic programs.

Boys participation, which grew by approximately 100,000 participants between 1971 and 1973, increased nearly 300,000 during the past two years. Still, this increase is overshadowed by the continuing explosion in girls' athletics.

Girls' interscolastic athletic programs have increased by approximately 483,000 participants during the past four years. While boys' participation grew 11 percent in the past four years, girls' participation has increased 34 percent.

Football continues to attract more male participants, 1,071,000, than any other high school sport. Basketball is the most popular girls' sport with 307,607 participating annually.

Most Popular High School Sports[4]

BOYS		GIRLS	
1. Football	1,071,000	1. Basketball	307,607
2. Basketball	688,690	2. Track and Field	299,215
3. Track and Field	667,974	3. Volleyball	198,313
4. Baseball	409,510	4. Softball	110,140
5. Wrestling	319,048	5. Tennis	84,495
6. Cross-country	214,840	6. Swimming and diving	73,946
7. Golf	135,813	7. Gymnastics	61,424
8. Tennis	124,645	8. Field hockey	59,106
9. Swimming and diving	114,645	9. Badminton	24,071
10. Soccer	98,482	10. Golf	17,956

The Growth of the Interscholastic Athletic Program 1973-1975

BOYS		GIRLS	
1. Football	45,930	1. Track and field	121,013
2. Wrestling	40,024	2. Basketball	104,401
3. Baseball	37,727	3. Volleyball	90,015
4. Cross-country	34,166	4. Swimming and diving	32,126
5. Track and field	27,630	5. Tennis	30,555

Title IX Legislation

Some male respondents who participated in our survey preferred not to recognize the emergent legislation relevant to sex discrimination as a problem, but responded "that the girls deserve time and attention." Most male and female respondents recognized that the girls' athletics program have a direct bearing or effect upon the boys' programs. Interestingly enough, the 1975 survey reveals that while the girls' programs expanded in numbers of participants, so did the boys'. There has been three times as great an increase since 1973 as there was between 1971 and 1973. This may indicate that the rapid emergence of the girls' programs is serving as a stimulus to the boys' programs, particularly in some of the lesser known sports.

From our survey, it appears that the girls essentially desire to participate on their own teams. There appears to be little integration of girls on boys' teams where there is already an established girls' team. The consensus of coaches and athletic directors, both male and female, indicated each sex prefers to participate on its own teams in their own sports.

The hue and cry are not as prevalent today as they were several years ago when girls reported for boys' teams because of recent new legislation on sex discrimination in interscholastic athletics. The effects of Title IX on interscholastic athletics may not have the impact many people believe because most schools are now establishing comparable programs for boys and girls, and schools that have not done so may take up to three years to provide boys and girls equal opportunities to participate in interscholastic athletics.

Contact Sports

A number of respondents prior to the passage of Title IX, expressed concern about the physical well-being of girls if they were to participate in such contact sports as football and wrestling. Title IX clarifies this concern:[5] "Where a recipient operates or sponsors a team in a particular sport for members of one sex but operates or sponsors no such team for members of the other sex, the athletic opportunities for members of that sex have been previously limited, members of the excluded sex must be allowed to try-out for the team offered unless the sport involved is a contact sport. For the purposes of this part, contact sports include boxing, wrestling, rugby, ice hockey, football, basketball, and other sports the purpose of major activity of which involves bodily contact."

The Lack of Funding, or Inadequate Funding for
Interscholastic Athletics

Most athletic directors and coaches, male and female, emphatically cited the lack of funding and the need for more adequate funding by local school districts, as the most critical problem facing interscholastic athletics today.

Inflation, recession, increased taxation, and the devaluation of the dollar have all created a monstrous problem and the matter has reached crisis proportions across the country.

Pertaining to financial difficulties, the *COMPASS* (Competitive Athletics in Service to Society) survey revealed the following:[6]

1. More than one out of every four primary and secondary schools have cut back athletic programs or may soon do so.
2. An additional anxiety is a nationwide tendency toward taxpayer rejection of local bond issues and tax levies that include support for school athletic programs. In 1973, the bond issues and tax referendums reported in the COMPASS survey had a success rate of only 54.4 percent compared to a national average of 74 percent in 1964-1965.
3. More than 61 percent of the athletic directors whose programs face difficulties expressed a need for help to preserve their programs in the face of shrinking gate receipts and taxpayer's rejection of bond issues.
4. Of directors who itemized the activities being curtailed or eliminated, 20.6 percent said reserve teams in various sports, B Teams, freshman and junior varsity teams, and, at the junior high level, seventh grade teams were the first programs cut.
5. The COMPASS survey shows a marked increase in organized athletic activity for girls, even in schools with athletic budget problems.

The Lack of Adequate Facilities and Conflict
in Scheduling Activities

The available funds for improving athletic facilities, or building new ones in many instances, are simply nonexistent. Also, in most instances, existing athletic facilities are simply inadequate. Mutually sharing these facilities and the resultant scheduling conflict have created unexpected problems.

Some of the female athletic directors and coaches mentioned that in some boys' programs such as basketball, there may be three or more levels of teams while the girls can afford only one. These respondents previously expressed concern about utilizing facilities because, in practice, the boys most frequently received top priority. Now the girls expect to receive more funding, have more levels of teams, and have a legal basis for sharing the facilities on a more equitable basis.

Obviously scheduling priorities must be reexamined (Chapter 8) and there must be closer cooperation between the boys' and girls' programs. This problem must be shared with the coordinator of facilities, in high schools often a vice principal, so that new programs are not initiated in situations where funds and facilities are already inadequate for the existing girls' and boys' programs. Such a non-athletic administrator cannot dismiss the problem after it has been compounded, merely by admonishing athletic personnel, "You will have to work it out." Our survey indicated this sort of problem solving technique was not infrequent and many respondents commented on the lack of leadership by nonathletic administrators. Herein lies a chief argument for the establishment of the position of Director and Coordinator of Interscholastic Athletics.

The community's use of the school's facilities was listed frequently as a prevalent problem. Athletic facilities: planning, use of Facilities, and maintenance is discussed in Chapter 8.

The Lack of Adequate Equipment

The lack of adequate equipment is related to inadequate funding, which was discussed in detail previously. The problem is probably not as critical in the boys' programs as in the girls'. In the former, where there have usually been well established athletic programs of long standing, athletic directors and coaches have generally been able to build up their equipment inventory over the years. Yet, many of the male respondents listed the lack of athletic equipment as a ciritcal problem. This is probably due to the replacement factor, especially in the contact sports where a health and safety factor is involved and where there are annual rules and safety standards changes.

The new rule regarding football helmets, for example, (Chapter 22) will have a definite effect on the purchase of athletic equipment. In essence, the rule states that football helmets will only be worn for a specified limited period of time. The helmets will be stamped by the manufacturer and must be replaced in a given period of time. Safety standards are specified.

On the other hand, with the rapid emergence of the girls' program and the great increases in numbers of participants, the female participants need adequate athletic equipment immediately. A frequent complaint of girls and women is that girls' teams have no uniforms or one set of uniforms for several sports, while the boys have uniforms for each sport and at several sport levels.

A common problem to both men and women is the lack of funding plus the fact that the cost of athletic equipment has skyrocketed in recent years.

The purchase of athletic equipment is discussed in Chapter 20. The inventory, care, and storage of athletic equipment are presented in Chapter 21.

The Lack of Qualified and Properly Certified Coaches

It is unfortunate that as the interscholastic athletic program in schools broadens, no nationally uniform licensing or certification procedure is available for those individuals assuming coaching responsibilities. Although a number of professions and most trades, such as the electricians and plumbers, have developed certification training programs and examinations for their membership, there is no nationally required credential for the individual wanting to or assigned to coaching an athletic team. The controversy continues. There is a sporadic activity on a state-by-state basis, but there is no national effort to legislate coaching credentialing. The National Association for Sport and Physical Education (of AAHPER) has a Task Force on Coaching Certification that directs its efforts toward implementation at the state level.

Here again, as in funding and the use of facilities, the burden for this responsibility is on the administrator in charge. The administrator must realize that it is beneficial and desirable to have as many teams and participants as possible; however, the administrator may need to curtail the athletic program when adequate funding, facilities, and properly trained coaching personnel are not available.

Most states are in the process of developing educational requirements and inservice training programs leading to certification of coaches who are not physical education majors or minors (Chapter 9).

There is the implied feeling that the men should coach boys' teams and the women, the girls' teams. Obviously, there are some exceptions. This is not to imply that only male coaches are qualified or that female coaches are unqualified. Rather than expose students to an unqualified coach of the same sex, it is preferable to use qualified coaches of the opposite sex. There is some evidence to support the fact that both sexes have unqualified members coaching athletic teams.

Many colleges and universities are not encouraging men and women to enroll in a coaching major or minor, and many recent physical education graduates from some professional preparation programs are not actually qualified to coach. Their experiences for coaching may be limited to having only participated in a particular sport, which does not necessarily qualify an individual for coaching. Because of the present oversupply of physical educators in relation to employment opportunities, coaching positions are often being filled by teachers in other academic disciplines. One may accept a teaching position where coaching is required as part of the job, yet have little or no real interest in coaching. Many individuals will relinquish opportunities when they are granted tenure as a teacher. Many of the young teachers accept a coaching assignment for the supplemental pay. Once they move up on the regular pay scale or achieve tenure, they will abandon the coaching assignment and possibly seek other forms of gaining additional income.

Many women are content to teach in the classroom and do not have the interest and background to coach girls' athletic teams. Women coaches may not wish to put in long hours and the night and weekend work necessary to build successful athletic teams. Some women have been thrust into the role of coach as a result of girls' programs having more participants and teams, greater funding and, recently, a more equitable use of available facilities. It is too soon to determine whether women coaches will have the same interest and coach with the same intensity as most male coaches. This is not to say women cannot or will not do it. Many women recently given coaching assignments in schools and colleges have not been exposed to the athletic experience for which they now have supervisory responsibilities. It is a matter of conjecture at this point whether they want to follow the pattern common among male coaches.

CURRENT PROBLEMS, ISSUES, AND FORCES AFFECTING THE GIRLS' INTERSCHOLASTIC ATHLETIC PROGRAM

Inadequate Coaching Salaries for Women

Although male coaches may feel their financial compensation for coaching athletic teams is inadequate for the amount of time they put in their jobs and the extra duties and responsibilities involved, the women feel their coaching compensation is grossly inadequate, compared to that of men. Presently the trend toward equalizing of salaries for female coaches has not resulted in salaries commensurate with those of their male counterparts. Unless there is an equalizing of coaching salaries, supplements, or increments for female coaches, it is highly questionable whether an adequate number of women will devote their time and energy to a demanding task for which they feel they are not being adequately compensated. Although many women, including physical educators, have accepted coaching assignments in order to help establish programs of women's interscholastic athletics, their continuance in a career coaching role will be partially predicated upon adequate compensation. Methods of compensation for coaching assignments are discussed in Chapter 11.

Inadequate Transportation for Athletic Teams

When funding is provided, it may be that the girls' teams will travel in the buses and the boys' teams will travel on their own. In some instances, male coaches and athletic directors indicated that the lack of funds has caused the transportation of athletic teams to be a major problem. The practice has been to allocate available funds for the transportation of athletes, giving this a higher priority than the expenditures of funds for other items and services. Because of budgetary problems, transportation may not be provided for student-athletes when scheduled competition is in the same town or nearby. The funds are not expended for transportation and may be used for other purposes; however the practice can create numerous other problems, much more serious than one of budget. Aside from being detrimental to morale and not being educationally sound, there is the possibility of serious legal implications for school administrators if a student-athlete is injured in getting to a game site on his own, the game having been officially scheduled by authorized school personnel. Administrators who are held responsible for scheduling must resolve the lack of funds for transportation in some other manner.

Obviously, funds must be made available and/or schedules limited or curtailed. Nevertheless, transportation should be provided for student-athletes. Parents and friends driving student-athletes to contests, a practice frequently utilized, has certain little known legal implications and is not the answer to the problem. The transportation of athletic teams is discussed in Chapter 23 and the question of liability in Chapter 15.

The Lack of Qualified Officials for Girls' Contests

This particular problem is two-pronged. Considering the recent emergence of the program, there is an obvious lack of qualified officials for girls' contests. Although women coaches and athletic directors prefer to use female officials, the need for qualified officials far exceeds the present supply. Currently, game officials for girls' contests are paid substantially less than male officials. This is a source of irritation to the women coaches, athletic directors, and officials. Chapter 18, "Game Officials, Selection, Assignment, and Evaluation," deals with this problem.

CURRENT PROBLEMS, ISSUES, AND FORCES AFFECTING THE BOYS' INTERSCHOLASTIC ATHLETIC PROGRAM

In addition to the previously enumerated and discussed problems, issues, and forces affecting both boys' and girls' programs, there are certain problems and issues that particularly affect the boys' program.

Decrease in Attendance and Lack of Support of Athletic Contests

There appears to be at least two facets to this trend and the resultant problem. One is positive and the other negative.

In today's affluent, highly mobile society there is more for teenagers to do and many students simply do not attend their school's athletic contests. They are involved in other activities and many have interests other than athletics. If the activities are considered to be beneficial, such as desirable leisure time activities of life-time sports, this is a positive sign. Athletic directors and school officials normally feel that athletic events are for the students. If students are involved in "doing" instead of merely "watching," this is considered to be beneficial. Participating in such wholesome activities as golf, tennis, bowling, and fishing, instead of merely watching others participate, must be commended. If the students are engaged in unwholesome activities, obviously this has a negative impact.

Professional or collegiate sports events that take place in the area, or the possibility of viewing professional and collegiate teams and performers on television have a deleterious effect on the attendance at interscholastic athletic contests. Where admission is charged, the lack of attendance at interscholastic athletic events may also affect the funding for sports that rely on the "gate" as a means of generating income.

At one time, people rallied around their high school teams as a part of community pride and culture. Now fans can apparently satisfy their athletic identification needs through television. The great exposure of professional sports, which is entertainment, not education, has filled this need for many people. Scholastic sports, which are primarily educational in concept, have suffered.

In the search for interest and financial support for the program, several athletic directors and coaches asked, "How do you get the public to support your high school program?" The previously mentioned COMPASS Survey[6] pointed out that about 44 percent of the high school athletic directors who reported their programs in financial trouble cited a lack of public interest as the major obstacle to continued organized athletic activities.

A decline in public interest was also reported by 16.6 percent of the athletic directors whose programs were not encountering financial difficulties.

The survey indicates that many of the athletic directors who are faced with decreasing morale and financial support do not have a strategy for rebuilding support. Whereas 27.8 percent said they are working with local groups such as booster clubs and Jaycees to encourage community support for athletic programs, 26 percent reported that no local group or organization is spearheading such efforts. Another 10 percent said that they and their staffs are the community's sole voice in support of organized athletics. One out of every seven athletic directors stated he was unaware of any locally generated ideas to boost public support of athletic programs.

Lack of Discipline and the Failure of Administrative Support to Enforce Discipline[7]

Several athletic directors and coaches noted a liberalization of behavioral standards by parents, the community, school administration, and other coaches with the result that it is difficult today to impose rules, standards, and discipline on student-athletes. As a result of a liberalization of values, today's athlete questions almost everything and everyone, including his coaches and parents. Many older male coaches and athletic directors consider this a threat to their authority. There is inconclusive evidence to indicate whether or not women coaches and athletic directors have encountered this problem and to clarify their reaction to the male coaches' viewpoint in this area.

Athletes should be willing to sacrifice to compete and to achieve excellence. Rules without reason are highly questionable and lack validity. Some rules have been accepted on a hand-me-down basis with no thought as to their merit or relevance. These rules deserve questioning. This does not imply that athletes have the preogative of refusing to comply with all the rules, merely because they disagree with them. It appears that an increasing number of faculty members, school administrators, and others are criticizing sport as sport, and there is a belief that they are encouraging student-athletes to question the validity and necessity of rules imposed on them by the coaching fraternity and the athletic administration. As for the lack of administrative support in the enforcement of discipline, there has been a change in the traditional pattern of administration on the secondary school level. Until approximately the mid-sixties, the typical pattern of administration in high schools was for a coach to be elevated to vice principal, to principal, and not infrequently, to superintendent of schools. As a rule, these individuals, because of their athletic background and previous coaching experience, saw the inherent values of interscholastic athletics and believed in a strong discipline-oriented program. The trend in the seventies, as evidenced by the response to our survey, indicates that many recently appointed administrators have had little or no experience in coaching or athletic administration. Many of these administrators have shelved the traditional leadership role in favor of the committee-consensus type of leadership. The problem becomes one of philosophical differences between the nonathletic administrator and the coach or athletic director. Many times the community must act as a liaison between the two groups, which leads to unrest. Our survey revealed that the coaching profession would like to see a more positive leadership role taken by the administrator in charge. There should be an official posture concerning the conduct and educational worth of interscholastic athletics.

Many coaches and athletic directors feel that the lack of administrative support to enforce discipline creates innumerable problems. It is significant to point out here that a 1974 Gallup poll listed the lack of discipline as the number one problem facing America's public schools.[8]

Researchers Steinmentz and Bowen[9] reported in their study of economic considerations and social attitudes concerning competitive athletic programs that lack of discipline in schools, coupled with antiestablishment attitudes by young people, was one of eight reasons why taxpayers resisted or rejected bond issues and increased school spending.

Our survey indicated the need for answers to such questions as "How can we enforce training rules?" and "Is there a standard athletic code?"

Drug Problems

There appears to be widespread use of drugs in the high schools, although it is inconclusive to state that drugs are being used by student-athletes. According to our survey, probably fewer than one percent of the athletic directors and coaches who responded to the questionnaire reported the use of drugs by student—athletes. The results of the 1974 Gallup poll listed drugs fourth in the list of problems facing education today. It is believed that drug education and prevention represent one of the most formidable tasks of education today. Therefore, although the use of drugs by students generally may be widespread, our survey did not indicate specifically a concern about the use of drugs by student-athletes. Few respondents listed drugs as a problem. There have been newspaper and magazine articles reporting the use of drugs by collegiate and professional athletes and by high school and college students in general. We have no conclusive evidence of the use of drugs by high school athletes or that athletes use drugs to a proportionally greater degree than nonathletes. The use of drugs by high school athletes is speculation, conjecture, and inconclusive on our part.

OTHER CURRENT INTERSCHOLASTIC ATHLETIC PROBLEMS, FORCES, AND ISSUES

There were three "problems" that we anticipated would be cited frequently in the results of our survey. However, the feeling of apathy for the program, recruiting of student-athletes, and the problems of crowd accommodation were mentioned less frequently than anticipated. Yet, in talking with coaches and athletic directors, the general feeling of apathy toward the athletic program was mentioned frequently. The illegal recruiting of student-athletes has been mentioned on numerous occasions in newspapers, magazines, and some books as a critical interscholastic athletic problem. The importance and the need for crowd accommodation is always foremost in the minds of athletic directors.

Apathy in and for Athletic Programs in Some Schools

There is no reason to believe that apathy in and for the athletic program is shared by the administrators, faculty, students, student-athletes, and coaches. It appears to be manifested by a lack of direction, purpose, and helplessness; and by an attitude that "no one actually cares about the interscholastic athletic program." Perhaps it is the result of a general lack of discipline in the schools, a lack of administrative support, a lack of interest, a lack of adequate funding, a lack of adequate facilities, and the numerous other problems already enumerated and discussed.

The coaching profession must share part of the blame for the apathy that currently permeates the interscholastic athletic scene. Frequently the "new breed" of coaches are not carrying on in the aggressive, professional, and traditional manner of their predecessors of the fifties and sixties. This is evidenced by examining the rolls of the state coaches associations and attendance at state sponsored coaches' conferences. There appears to be a definite "coaching gap" between the old and the new and right now the gap has not narrowed. The "old timer" laments, "Young coaches are not as dedicated to their profession." Young coaches undoubtedly feel differently. Each is applying his or her own sense of values. Other professions are probably undergoing similar changes. Obviously, there is a change in coaches' philosophies and a change in philosophy in the conduct of interscholastic athletics. The program will continue but under a different format than the traditionalists would like to see.

In a study undertaken by Drs. Lawrence L. Steinmetz and David H. Bowen for the National Sporting Goods Association, the two university professors stated, "There is much evidence that many people are neither pro nor con with respect to athletics, but are indifferent. The research findings infer that a majority of citizens have never really given any serious thought to the financial and social pressures being applied to athletic programs." As Drs. Steinmetz and Bowen pointed out, "In many ways such a situation is more dangerous than widespread antagonism; it is often tougher to get people to care than to change their minds when they are negative. The biggest single reason for the current crisis facing organized athletics is that the silent majority is silently consenting to selling out organized athletics in order to receive tax relief."

The Recruiting of High School Athletes

It is most unusual that only a few athletic directors and coaches who responded to the authors' survey listed the recruiting of their high school athletes as a problem. From newspaper accounts of the illegal recruiting of high school athletes, it would appear the problem is even more serious than high athletic directors believe. On the other hand, despite the practice of illegal recruiting of high school athletes, it may not be as widespread as the reading public is led to believe. Information on guiding and counseling the college bound student-athlete is presented in Chapter 29.

Crowd Accommodation

Crowd accommodation is discussed at length in Chapter 31. However, our survey shows that this problem does not rate the importance that it did as recently as 1970-1971 when, for example, the militant demonstrations were prevalent. When interscholastic activities are properly planned, supervised, and administered, the problem seems to diminish. When discussing the crowd accommodation problem with athletic directors and coaches, the topic always leads to the "after game problems." One incident that appears in the papers regarding a spectator leaving the scene of a contest leads the public to believe that all interscholastic athletic events should be cancelled. In some areas of the country, the survey indicated that the respondents were more concerned about the lack of spectator interest and the lack of student and community support than they were in the problem of crowd control.

Other athletic problems that were mentioned in the questionnaire survey results but have not yet been discussed previously will merely be listed below and are discussed in the remaining chapters of this book.

- ☐ Problems of liability and legal responsibility (Chapter 15)
- ☐ Lack of Coaching positions
- ☐ Position description and responsibilities of the athletic director
- ☐ The place of club sports in the high school interscholastic program
- ☐ The issue of accountability of coaches and athletic directors
- ☐ Too much emphasis on winning
- ☐ Too much practice time; too many sports in one season; out of season practice; and the overlapping of sports seasons

SCHOOLS' TOP PROBLEMS: GALLUP POLL

A recent Gallup poll[8] indicated the lack of discipline was named by the nation's adults and students alike as the top problem facing America's public schools today. This finding coincides with reports from school administrators in many sections of the nation who say student violence and vandalism are increasing at an alarming rate. According to George Gallup, Princeton, New Jersey, "Discipline has been named as the number one problem of the schools in five of the last six years as determined by the annual surveys of the public." The following, in order of mention, are the leading problems faced by local schools, as determined by the 1974 survey:

1. Lack of discipline
2. Intergration-segragation problems
3. Lack of proper financial support
4. Use of drugs
5. Difficulty in getting "good" teachers

6. Size of school and classes
7. Parents' lack of interest
8. School board policies
9. Poor curriculum
10. Lack of proper facilities

Interestingly, more responses relate to student behavior than relate to those problems traditionally associated with education and the schools. The Gallup survey based on in-person interviews in 1974 with 1,702 adults, 18 years and older, in 535 sampling locations, which were selected by strict stratified random sampling techniques. "A separate survey was undertaken to gather views of high school junior and seniors based on a sample of 250 students," according to the Gallup survey.

SCHOOLS' TOP ATHLETIC PROBLEMS

It is interesting to note that four of the ten problems listed by the Gallup poll are listed in our survey of athletic directors, coaches, and physical educators. Specifically, lack of discipline, lack of proper financial support, lack of proper facilities, and difficulty getting "good" (qualified) teachers (coaches).

It is our opinion, borne out by survey data, that many of the athletic problems today stem from lack of strong support from the central administration for interscholastic athletics. The athletic director must delineate his role to his subordinates, and perhaps the athletic director must also "educate" those to whom he or she reports as to the inherent value of interscholastic athletics and the athletic director's role in administering a well-rounded, educationally sound athletic program.

Chapter 2 and 3 deal with the managerial aspects of the athletic program and the athletic director's duties and responsibilities. Chapters 4 to 31 outline, define, and discuss the responsibilities that are inherent in each phase of the interscholastic athletic programs.

Questions

1. Identify at least six different critical problems, forces, or issues shaping interscholastic athletics today and for the future.
2. How are the problems that affect interscholastic athletics today

different from those of the previous three decades?

3. Discuss why the lack of adequate funding or insufficient funds is considered by many as the most threatening force or critical problem facing interscholastic athletics.

4. Discuss what bearing and effect 1975 Title IX legislation has on interscholastic athletics generally and girls' athletics specifically

5. How does lack of discipline, which has been identified by several authoritative sources as the number one problem facing American public schools today, bear on interscholastic athletics?

REFERENCES

1. Education Policies Commission, *School Athletics and Policies*, National Educational Association of the United States, Washington, D.C., 1954, pp.5-7.
2. Ibid., pp. 7-10.
3. National Federation of State High School Associations, *Sports Participation Survey—1975;* 400 Leslie St., Elgin, Illinois 60120. By Permission.
4. Ibid.
5. Title IX, An Act to Amend the Educational Act of 1972, passed July 21, 1975. Director, Office of Civil Rights, HEW, Washington, D.C. 20024.
6. "Prognosis for School Athletics," *Scholastic Coach*, Vol. 43, No. 5, January 1974, pp. 92-93. Copyright j Scholastic Magazines, Inc., 50 West 44th St., New York, N.Y. 10036.
7. Keith, Dwight, Editor, *"Danger in Sports," Coach & Athlete*, Vol xxxii, No. 4 December 1974, p. 6, 200 South Hull St., Montogomery, Alabama 36104.
8. Gallup, George, *"Schools" Top Problem—Lack of Discipline,"* As reported in the *Sacramento Bee*, November 21, 1974, p. 49, Sacramento, California 95813.
9. Steinmetz, Lawrence L., and Bowen, David H., *Sports in Schools: Jeopardy and Uncertainty*, Copyright c 1971, National Sporting Goods Association, Chicago, Illinois, pp. 1-15, By permission.

SUGGESTED READINGS

Cratty, Bryant J., *Psychology In Contemporary Sport: Guidelines* for Coaches and Athletes, Prentice-Hall, Englewood Cliffs, N.J. 1973, pp. 304.

Drugs and the Coach, 1201 16th St., N.W., Washington D.C. 20036, 1971.

Jones, K.L., Shainberg, L.W., and Byer, C.O. *Drugs and Alcohol* Harper and Row, New York, 1969.

Kenyon, Gerald S., ed., *Sociology of Sport*, The Athletic Institute, Chicago, Illinois, 1969.

Lawther, John D., *Sport Psychology*, Prentice-Hall, Englewood Cliffs, N.J. 1972.

NASSP bulletin April 1973, No. 372, *Drug Abuse: Attitude to Prevent and Programs to Combat it*, pp. 49-91.

National Collegiate Athletic Association, *The Coach: Drugs Ergogenic Aids and the Athlete, 1971 NCAA*, Missouri.

Poindexter, Hally B.W., and Mushier, Carole, *Coaching Guides for Women's Sports 1973* W.B. Saunders, Philadelphia.

Sabock, Ralph J. *The Coach*, W.B. Saunders Company, West Washington Square, Philadelphia, Pa. 19105, 1974.

Women's Athletics: Coping with Controversy, AAHPER, 1974.

Singer, Robert N., *Coaching, Athletic and Psychology*, McGraw-Hill, New York, 1972.

Chapter 2

Management and Organization of Interscholastic Athletics

How the athletic director views his position in terms of duties and responsibilities and how subordinates, associates, superiors, and the public view his position is likely to be vastly different. A concept of the athletic administration may picture the director sitting in a swivel chair, feet on a desk, issuing orders in an authoritative manner. On the other extreme is the concept where the athletic director is expected to do everything. The latter includes lining the athletic fields, picking up towels in the locker rooms, selling tickets, and handling all such chores and tasks that must be done as part of an interscholastic athletic program. Neither concept is correct.

MANAGEMENT CONCEPT IN ATHLETIC ADMINISTRATION

In the former concept, the athletic director's position is viewed as the "boss" with complete control of the athletic empire. Since the actual work must be performed in order to have a successful athletic program, sufficient funding must be available to pay for that work. This concept is far from the typical situation in interscholastic athletics. If the athletic director views his job in this context, little is likely to be accomplished and much will remain undone.

Conversely, if the concept is that the athletic director should do everything, he may accomplish many chores and tasks; but it is likely that more important issues and matters will remain unsolved and unattended. The time factor alone will prohibit the athletic director from doing everything that must be done. It is a mistake for the athletic director to perpetuate the concept that he should do "every-thing." What then is the athletic director's role? The duties and re-sponsibilities of the athletic director are covered in Chapter 3. Our intention is to confine the topics to the management functions of interscholastic athletics rather than to include a philosophical dis-cussion of the value of athletics.

POSITION ANALYSIS

It is imperative that the athletic director know what his superiors expect of him. In turn, the supportive staff should know what the athletic director expects of them and what they may expect of him. A position analysis must be undertaken to assure an orderly and systematic assembling of all the facts about each person's position. The purpose of such an analysis is to study the individual elements and duties that will focus the formal organizational structure on the specific parts and eliminate gaps and overlaps of responsibilities of the total staff. Unless the athletic director paints a clear-cut picture for both his superiors and subordinates, there will be a vast differ-ence of opinion as to who does what and why.

It is paramount that a position description be prepared. This is a written statement that clarifies duties, relationships, and results expected of each member of the staff, including the athletic director. A position description usually includes a position title, the title of the person to whom the person in the position reports, the name of the person who prepared the description, a brief statement of the purpose of the position, and a list of duties and responsibilities. Position specifications should include the qualification requirements, educational experience, skill requirement, and health requirements.

The position evaluation process should be ongoing in an effort to study descriptions and specifications to determine levels of respon-sibilities and difficulties for evaluation, grading, and pay purposes.

The starting point for eliminating much confusion and clarifying who does what is a different viewpoint of the position of athletic director than has generally been expressed before. Succinctly, it is the concept that the athletic director is actually an administrator of a program and is a middle management person and must perform basic management functions. This is discussed in Chapter 3. This idea is entirely different from the two extremes previously expressed.

Basic Administrative Management Functions

It is the consensus that management is the accomplishment of goals and objectives through the efforts of other people. It means accomplishing the job through coaches, supportive staff, and subordinate personnel. The athletic director must recognize the "as is" situation, but work toward the "could be" or "should be" situation. The former is problem oriented while the latter is usually opportunity or result oriented. In *Management in Action*[1], Laurence A. Appley stated, "Management is guiding human and physical resources into a dynamic, hard hitting organizational unit that attains its objectives to the satisfaction of those served, and with a high degree of morale and sense of attainment on the part of those served." This means that the athletic director must perform certain managerial functions such as planning and budgeting, organizing, staffing, coordinating and communicating, directing and delegating, controlling and reporting, innovating and representing. In addition, the athletic director must become involved in problem solving, decision making, and motivation. Chart 2-1 gives a visual picture of the managerial functions and the correlated activities that must be performed by the athletic director.

Identifying Responsibilities

It is becoming more difficult to identify responsibilites and be certain they will be carried out, especially with the growth of the athletic program. There are more coaches involved, increased activities, and the problem of limited funding and the sharing of facilities. The athletic director must be innovative, creative, and imaginative and encourage others on the staff to follow this pattern. By involving the total staff in setting goals and objectives, everyone will understand how they are related to the total program and will be more willing to carry out their part. The ideal situation would be to have a staff that is creative, innovative, and imaginative, able to exercise self-supervision and self-appraisal. Before this can happen, staff personnel must know exactly what their jobs consist of, what authority they have to carry them out, and what results are acceptable. The staff must accept the same kind of responsibility for the results in their areas that the athletic director does for the staff as a whole.

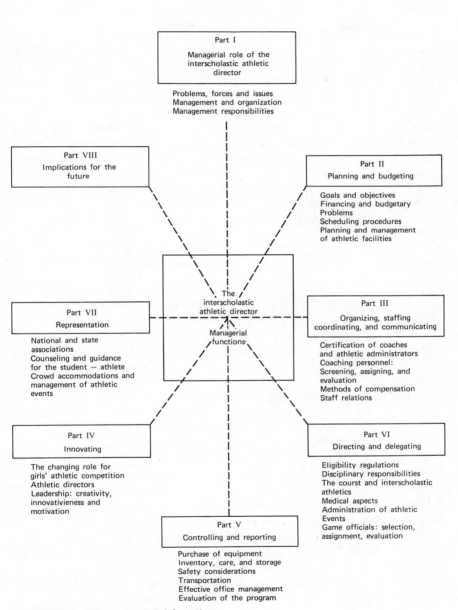

CHART 2-1 The managerial functions.

27

Athletic Director Leadership

Motivation and leadership are discussed in Chapter 27. It is important to mention here that the athletic director must first develop his potential to the fullest and then seek to reach the full potential in all his staff members. Leadership occurs when one person inspires others to work toward some predetermined objective. Some people are obviously better followers than leaders and it is desirable for the athletic director to encourage the staff to carry out their functions as if they held the ultimate authority. Leadership has to do with the dynamic quality of a relationship, the action-reaction phase of managing others. A team effort and a spirit of cooperation are called for. The athletic director must subordinate his own opinions and even his personal goals and aspirations for the good of the total staff and, in the case of interscholastic athletics, what is best educationally for the student-athlete.

The Successful Athletic Director

There is no guarantee that because a person has been a successful coach, the same individual will be a successful athletic director. The role that must be filled and the duties and responsibilities of the position are different from a coach's. Although the athletic director must draw from experiences gained as a coach, it is a mistake to revert to the role of coach in administering the interscholastic athletic program.

It is analogous to the situation of a lathe operator being promoted to shop foreman or supervisor. It would be a mistake to take the lathe into the office and continue to turn out pieces. The role is now that of a supervisor, not a lathe operator. Another mistake is to go out into the shop and show the workers how to turn out pieces on the lathe. The athletic director who was a former coach should think of the art and science of management, not of the techniques of coaching, and should not revert to telling or showing other coaches how it should be done.

The principal, who finds the interscholastic program becoming more complex, usually appoints the senior member of the staff to assume the position of athletic director. The newly appointed athletic director undoubtedly will find unfamiliar areas because prior training was a teacher-coach. The administrative assignment calls for the management of a complex athletic program and should be staffed by a person who has had training in management and administration.

Professional Preparation for the Athletic Director

More and more colleges and universities are offering courses in athletic administration to alleviate the situation of the nontrained athletic director. This thinking has obviously been brought about by the growth of athletics on the interscholastic athletic level, the expanded community interest, and the complex cultural aspect of athletics. Colleges and universities are also offering graduate courses for athletic directors who have been out in the field and who now find themselves in a position of management. Most athletic directors are either majors or minors in physical education and have the general qualifications as a player and coach. With the advent of a graduate program in athletic administration, the athletic director will be able to fill the gap within the areas indicated.

Course content varies for an athletic administration credential but the essential material would include: the role of athletics in education; historical, cultural, philsophical aspects; ethics in relationship to the athletic program; business procedures, accounting practices, budget and finance, purchase and inventory; equipment and supplies, purchase, design, renovation, maintenance, and inventory; planning, construction, maintenance, and use of facilities; school law and legal liability; administration of athletic events; community relations; medical aspects; transportation; effective office management and profession organizations. Professional preparation and certification of interscholastic athletic coaching personnel are discussed in Chapter 10.

The Time Element

In most secondary schools, the athletic director has to assume the new role as athletic director and still carry out a daily teaching and, perhaps, coaching assignment. This may cause problems if the untrained athletic director does not know how to "get things done through the efforts of other people." If they try to do everything personally, they frequently find themselves in a mind-bogling situation. The athletic director must quickly learn to enlist the help of the staff in carrying out many details that must be taken care of if the program is to succeed. The athletic director must give leadership in setting objectives, goals, and targets through the efforts of subordinates. Standards of performance are then set through which these objectives, goals, or targets shall be reached by each individual staff member. It becomes obvious that the sum of all the staff members' performance should equal the group's objectives.

Responsibility to the School

One of the first problems the athletic director must face, especially if still a member of the coaching staff, is that of an administrator. In all probability, the philosophy that he applied to coaching will have to be modified when he assumes responsibility for the total athletic program. If the athletic director is still coaching a sport, it will make it more difficult, especially when it comes to budget allocations or when a decision must be made for the total athletic program. The athletic director will sometimes have to make decisions not advantageous to his own sport.

More high school principals are realizing that the ideal situation exists when the athletic director is a full-time administrator. To justify this status, the athletic director has to assume responsibilities such as student body liaison, finance, total supervision of the athletic program, and probably some added administrative duties. High school principals and superintendents could make a real contribution to athletics by making the athletic director a bona-fide administrator with appropriate designation. With Title IX a reality, the problems of finance and facilities have made the athletic director's position more complex.

The administrative format sometimes provides for the individual director for the boys' and girls' programs. In other situations, a man or woman, with an assistant or coordinator of the opposite sex, will administer both programs.

Dr. Dean W. Stoakes, Superintendent of Glenbard, Illinois High School District[2] stated, "If we believe the place of athletics is one that enhances the total educational program, then it is imperative the athletic director must sit as a regular member at all discussions that are held between the chairmen of all departments. We must be realistic in recognizing that the athletic director is more needed and more important to the total system than ever before."

Responsibilities to the Profession

A problem confronting the athletic director may be the principal's lack of understanding of the values of interscholastic athletics. It is the athletic director's obligation to "educate" the principal in this regard. Otherwise, the interscholastic athletic program may be diluted to a mere recreation or intramural program because the principal does not understand the philosophy of interscholastic athletics and specialized management techniques. The principal may be aware that it is highly desirable to give all students the opportunity to participate in athletics. However, his knowledge may not encompass an educationally sound philosophy that provides for different levels of competition with interscholastic athletics at the top of the pyramid, intramural sports in the middle, and the basic instructional program in physical education at the base.

The athletic director must seek to keep each program in its proper perspective, that is, physical education, intramurals, recreation, and athletics. The opportunity is present for all students. The school provides the opportunity. Whether the student takes advantage of this opportunity is an individual matter. The physical education programs are elective and intended for participation by the majority of students. Interscholastic athletics, however, are not necessarily for all students. They are actually for the accelerated student-athlete. While the opportunity is available to all student to participate in interscholastic athletics, on the basis of their skill, not all students are capable of participating in the program. Accelerated courses in mathematics or foreign languages, for example, are not for all students but for the gifted. The same applies to interscholastic athletics. The opportunity is there for all, the physical education basic instruction program, intramurals, or the interscholastic athletic program for boys and girls. The students will find their own level of competition.

The athletic director has definite responsibilities to the national and state athletic associations. These associations have worked diligently for many years to upgrade the interscholastic athletic program. The men and women who head these state organizations are dedicated to providing the safest most equitable conditions they possibly can for interscholastic athletics. The athletic director must have an up-to-date knowledge of all the rules and regulations in order to counter forces that are sometimes dedicated to eliminating interscholastic competition.

Management Functions of the Athletic Director

Managerial functions and responsibilites are discussed at length in Chapter 3. However, it is important at this point to emphasize some universal opinions on management functions. Authorities agree that management is a distinct type of work and that all true managers generally perform much the same functions regardless of what they are managing. Included are athletic directors who manage athletic programs. Although not all authorities agree on what these functions are, most of them agree that management deals with people, with decision making, and is a process of organizing and utilizing resources to accomplish predetermined objectives.

It is generally agreed that a manager should perform four basic functions: planning, organizing, directing, and controlling. These functions were probably first identified by Henri Fayol,[3] one of the early pioneers in the field of management. Luther Gulick,[4] another early pioneer and recognized authority in the field, coined the word POSDCORB from the initial letters of management functions: planning, organizing, staffing, directing, coordinating, reporting, and budgeting. Other authorities in the field have included innovation and representation as functions of management.

Every manager actually performs most of these functions as part of their duties, but the importance attached to each one may vary at different times and in different situations. The role of the athletic administrator or manager of interscholastic athletic program is no exception.

Equally important to the science of management is the human relations skill or aspect of management. It is important that the athletic director understand the people with whom he works and is associated. He must know their personal and professional goals and the satisfaction that each member of the staff seeks. The principle of human relations management deals with the psychological aspect, perceptions, learning processes, emotions, attitudes, and personalities. Any success the athletic director attains with the athletic program will depend primarily on how satisfactorily he deals with students, faculty, parents, superiors, coaches, staff personnel, and the community. The athletic director must remember that he is dealing with people first. The method used is as important as knowing what to do. Psychologists have proved that the manner in which we perceive another person has a definite effect on how we behave toward that person and also how that person responds to us.

These findings have great significance for athletic directors. This power of expectation is just as potent when dealing with the staff as it is with an individual. In interactions with people, we tend to force them to produce behavior that will fit our perception. The reason seems to be that whenever we make assumptions about people, we invariably perceive according to our own feelings and attitudes.

Obviously, an athletic director can fail simply because the job is too big for him or he lacks sufficient technical knowledge for the position. It is almost inevitable that the athletic director will fail if he does not have a good relationship with people, especially superiors and subordinates.

Questions

1. Why are there likely to be diverse opinions as to how the athletic director views his position in terms of duties and responsibilities and how subordinates, associates, superiors, and the public perceive the athletic director's role? What means may be utilized to clarify this dilemma and identify the athletic director's role, duties, and responsibilities?

2. Describe the athletic director's role as a middle manager in the hierarchy of management. Discuss his role in light of the definition "Management is the accomplishment of goals and objectives through the efforts of other people."

3. List at least five common basic management functions that all administrators should perform. This includes the athletic director, who is considered to be a middle manager.

4. While the successful athletic coach may perform many of the functions of management, why is there no guarantee that the same individual will be successful if elevated to the athletic directorship? How are the managerial roles different? How may there be a conflict of interest if an individual holds the dual position-assignment of head coach and athletic director? Would the dual role-assignment of athletic director and assistant coach pose any management problems? Identify and discuss.

5. What is meant by the statement, "The athletic director must recognize the 'as is' situation, but work toward the 'could be' or 'should be' situation." Give several pertinent illustrations.

REFERENCES

1. Appley, Lawrence, *Management in Action,* A collection of writings by the American Management Associations Board Chairman, AMACOM, 135 West 50 Street, New York, N.Y., 1973.
2. Stoakes, Dr. Dean W., Superintendent of Glenbard, Illinois High School Districts, *Athletics in Modern America,* National Conference of High School Athletic Directors, Columbus, Ohio, p. 3. By permission.
3. Fayol, Henri, *General and Industrial Management,* Pitman, London, 1949, p. 22.
4. Gulick, Luther, *Notes on the Theory of Organization,* Papers on the Science of Administration, Institute of Public Administration, New York, 1937.

SUGGESTED READINGS

Albers, Henry, *Principles of Management: A Modern Approach* 4th edition, Wiley, New York, 1974.

Forsythe, Charles E. and Keller, Irvin A., *Administration of High School Athletics,* Prentice-Hall, Englewood Cliffs, N.J., 1972.

Hersey, Paul and Blanchard, Kenneth H., *Management of Organizational Behavior,* Prentice-Hall, 1972.

Hodge, B. J. and Herbert J. Johnson, *Management and Organization Behavior,* Wiley, New York, 1970.

Lakein, Alan, *How to Get Control of Your Time and Your Life,* Wyden, New York, 1973.

Louden, Keith J., *Making it Happen* AMACOM, New York, 1973.

Massie, J. L. and John Douglas, *Managing: A Contemporary Introduction,* Prentice-Hall, Englewood Cliffs, N.J., 1973.

Purdy, Robert L., *The Successful High School Athletic Program,* Parker Publishing, West Nyack, N.Y. 10994.

Scanlan, Burt K., *Principles of Management and Organizational Behavior,* Wiley, New York, 1973.

Secondary School Athletic Administration: A New Look, AAHPER Publications-Sales, 1201 16th St., N.W., Washington D.D. 20036.

Chapter 3
An Overview of the Management Responsibilities of the Interscholastic Athletic Director

The athletic director is responsible for administering all aspects of the athletic program in accordance with the total school philosophy, objectives, and policy. The athletic director must comply with student association regulations and be in accord with the appropriate provisions of the constitution and by-laws of league, section, state, and national athletic regulations.

The athletic director may delegate various assignments but is still held accountable to the chief administrator of his educational unit for the ultimate fulfillment of those assignments and responsibilities. The athletic director must possess sufficient knowledge of the total athletic program in order to work effectively with students and faculty.

As mentioned previously, there are definite managerial functions that the efficient athletic director must perform. These managerial functions are discussed briefly in this chapter and are discussed in detail in the parts indicated.

MANAGEMENT FUNCTIONS: PLANNING AND BUDGETING
(Part II)

Planning must preceed performance, and the athletic director must involve the group process and give leadership to the planning and setting of goals, objectives, and policy for the interscholastic athletic program. These goals, objectives, and policies must be determined by participating members of the school community. Once they are defined and agreed upon, the athletic director must recognize that the accomplishment of goals, objectives, and policies can only result through the efforts of subordinate personnel. The athletic director's function is to give guidance, direction, recognition, and motivation to other people's efforts. The athletic director must decide what has to be done, set short and long range goals for the program, and decide on the means by which they will meet good standards of performance. In measuring standards of performance, the goals should be attainable and they should be worded to prevent misinterpretation.

The athletic director must forecast, in light of the monetary and other resources available, what has to be accomplished to achieve the objectives. Planning may be said to encompass budgeting since a budget is a plan to obtain and spend a certain amount of money to accomplish goals and objectives.

The athletic director's managerial function is as follows: to set goals and objectives for the interscholastic athletic program; to set schedule procedures and contracts; to be concerned with athletic facilities layout, scheduling, and maintenance.

Checklist to Aid the Athletic Director with Planning and Budgeting

1. Aid in setting goals and objectives, long and short range, for the interscholastic athletic program.
2. Develop, through a group process, policies for the program.
3. Discuss and promote necessary means for financing the athletic program.
4. Prepare, justify, and present annual budgets to the student council and other appropriate budget review bodies.
5. Schedule and coordinate the use of athletic facilities.
6. Discuss and plan the maintenance and upkeep of athletic facilities.
7. Schedule all athletic contests and events.
8. Set up means of communication to disseminate to school officials current pertinent information relevant to athletic affairs and trends.
9. Disseminate information and instructions to the coaching staff for budgeting and financial arrangements for each sport.

MANAGEMENT FUNCTIONS: ORGANIZING, STAFFING, COORDINATING, AND COMMUNICATING (Part III)

In organizing, the director of athletics decides the positions to be filled and the duties and responsibilities attached to each one. Since the work performed by various members of the athletic department will be interrelated, a means to coordinate their efforts must be provided. Coordinating is, in fact, an essential part of organization rather than a function in itself.

In staffing, the athletic director attempts to find the right person for each job. Organization and staffing are likely to be continuing functions because changes in the department occasionally necessitate a complete reorganization. Staffing obviously cannot be accomplished permanently because coaches frequently leave or change jobs. The managerial functions of the athletic director in organizing, staffing, coordinating, and communicating are: professional preparation and certification of the staff; responsibility for the hiring and assigning of all coaching personnel; encouragement for supplemental pay for coaching assignments; and the furtherance of good staff relations through proper communications.

Checklist to Aid the Athletic Director in Organizing, Staffing, Coordinating, and Communicating

1. Consult with the principal in making recommendations to the superintendent for the employment of all coaching personnel.
2. Prepare a position description for all coaching positions.
3. Consult with the principal in assigning personnel.
4. Arrange for and work toward supplemental pay for coaching personnel.*
5. Supervise all personnel employed to coach athletic teams.
6. Set up an evaluation procedure for coaching personnel.
7. Encourage "inservice" training programs to insure professional preparation for nonphysical education majors or minors who are assigned to a coaching position and for other coaches who are

---

*This is not necessarily the goal of all school systems and athletic programs. Some people consider it better educational practice for coaches to be assigned coaching duties as a part of their load. Coaching is perceived as an educational experience; coaching assignments are made much as other class assignments.

ineffectual or who have not kept abreast of new techniques.
8. Provide and maintain unity to create a unified coaching staff in all interscholastic sports.
9. Provide a method to disseminate information to the coaching staff in regard to objectives, goals, policy, rules, regulations, and philosophy of the total athletic department.
10. Work in harmony with the director or coordinator of the interscholastic athletic program. The athletic director may have administrative responsibilities for both the boys' and girls' program.

MANAGEMENT FUNCTION: DIRECTION AND DELEGATION (Part IV)

Direction and delegation refer to the manager's inherent responsibility to face problems and make decisions. The athletic director's responsibility is to put into action the plans, decisions, and programs through the people being supervised. Authority should be commensurate with responsibility. If the athletic director is responsible for maintaining an efficient athletic program, he should have authority to take the steps to attain the objective. Two of the main reasons for greater financial or load compensation for any athletic administrator are the unavoidable decision making and delegating responsibilities of the position. Unless the athletic director can make prudent decisions, the planning and organizational concepts will not function.

Checklist to Aid the Athletic Director in Direction and Delegation

1. Coordinate and monitor the preparation of eligibility forms to assure availability of eligibility decisions prior to the first regularly scheduled contest in each sport to which will protect the integrity of the school and the future eligibility of all participants.
2. Implement the policy regarding training rules and discipline regarding the student-athlete.
3. Implement the policy regarding the legal aspects of interscholastic athletics including those that have legal or liability implications.
4. Arrange for and organize all medical aspects of the interscholastic athletic program, such as physical examinations, insurance, and availability of physicians.*

*Student and faculty members who are assigned teams should be appropriately trained in emergency care procedures to function in the role of athletic trainer.

5. Be responsible for the administration of all athletic contests including any state or local tournaments that are held in conjunction with the athletics program.
6. Establish or maintain policies and procedures for the assignment and evaluation of officials in athletic contests.
7. Serve as advisor or member of the grievance committee and interpret and investigate questionable practices in regard to athletic policy and make recommendations.

MANAGEMENT FUNCTIONS: CONTROLLING AND REPORTING (Part V)

Controlling, as a management function, means measuring performance and guiding actions toward some predetermined target. The essentials of controlling are: setting a target, measuring performance, making comparisons, and taking corrective action. In control, the athletic director is primarily responsible for the evaluation of the coaches' performance.

Reporting is a means of control rather than a separate function. Reports are made so that the athletic director, administration, or members of the department may see what is happening and if necessary, change course. For example, budget is not only a plan, it is also a means of control. The athletic director must formulate a control system that is generally acceptable to the members of his staff.

Checklist to Aid the Athletic Director in Controlling and Reporting

1. Approve the purchase, inventory, care, storage, and maintenance of all athletic equipment.
2. Approve the payment of all purchases of athletic equipment initiated or incurred by any member of the coaching staff.
3. Arrange for maintenance, replacement, or repair of all athletic facilities.
4. Be responsible for following through faculty eligibility reports as received from the principal's office.
5. Supervise the total athletic program in regard to monies spent or collected.
6. Arrange for the payment of game officials.
7. Establish a method of control and clear-cut procedures for news releases and publicity.

8. Arrange for all transportation for athletes or athletic teams and ascertain vehicular insurance coverage and appropriate driver licensing.
9. Maintain an efficient record keeping system for all athletic events.
10. Act as liaison between the athletic department and the community especially in regard to the local booster club.
11. Set up a framework upon which an evaluation of goals and objectives may be based.
12. Continually evaluate the progress of the program to determine the effectiveness in meeting the needs of the students.
13. Establish control for the use of facilities in regard to student activities and community use.
14. Organize a system of certification, issuance, and purchase of athletic awards.
15. Develop and maintain a system of historical and statistical records of participation of students and teams in interscholastic competition.
16. Coordinate class release for athletes who are required to miss school or class for an athletic event.

MANAGEMENT FUNCTION: INNOVATION (Part VI)

Innovation is the development and introduction of new ideas, new ways of doing things, or the implementation of new programs, facilities, teaching, or coaching methods. The successful athletic director must be an innovator and develop a climate of creativity within the department to insure that the program will not decline from lack of ideas. The athletic director may innovate in several ways; personally present new ideas, combine old procedures with new ones, stimulate others to develop and carry out innovations, and be creative.

The athletic director may desire to incorporate an inservice program for members of the staff to keep them abreast of the current problems and solutions to activities related to sports. A critical function of the director is to retool, renew, and reeducate older department members through a variety of inservice and motivational techniques. Many faculties grow stale and unproductive if conscious efforts are not made to upgrade skills and utilize new approaches.

Checklist to Aid the Athletic Director in Being Innovative and Creative

1. Keep abreast of trends and changes in athletic facilities and equipment.
2. Develop articulation among the feeder schools in the district and between these schools and the secondary schools.
3. Work with student committees in planning activities for the inter-scholastic athletic program.
4. Assume leadership in aiding the coach in the performance of his duties.
5. Encourage each coach to conduct himself in accordance with the coaches' code of ethics.
6. Encourage the coaching staff to give diligent attention to each athlete with regard to physical condition before, during, and after each contest.
7. Encourage the coaching staff in continuous effort to adhere to the principles of good teaching and good coaching methods.
8. Stimulate the motivation of the staff in being creative by offering new ideas to the program.
9. Work to establish compatibility and cooperation between the girls' and boys' athletic department in the light of Title IX and the changing role for girls' athletic competition.

MANAGEMENT FUNCTION: REPRESENTATION (Part VII)

Representing the athletic program to outside groups, agencies, and individuals is a management function. The athletic program is constantly on display, and it is a responsibility of the athletic director to serve as liaison between the community and the interscholastic program. The athletic director must become involved in local and state professional organizations, assist in guidance and counseling for the student-athlete in regard to attending a college or university, be conscious of good crowd accommodations and sportsmanship at all athletic contests, be conscious of public relations and be ready to attend all civic meetings upon request.

Checklist to Aid the Athletic Director in Representation

1. Represent the school at all league, district, section and, state meetings concerned with the interscholastic athletic program.
2. Act as a liaison between the athletic department and the community.
3. Regularly attend all coaching clinics, state conferences, and national athletic directors meetings, if possible.
4. Develop good public relations with the press, radio, and television. Cooperate with other schoolwide news service agencies.
5. Be responsible for crowd accommodation at athletic contests. Any incident that could have been avoided and was not properly planned for will leave a bad impression on the community and jeopardize the continuance and future development of the program.
6. Work with college recruiters in the guidance and counseling of student-athletes.
7. Help in the establishment and control of parent or community booster clubs. Such organizations must be oriented toward a positive enhancement of the program and must officially and ethically comply with requirements of state high school associations as well as with collegiate regulatory agencies such as NCAA, NAIA, and JJCAA.
8. Prepare and distribute various sports brochures, schedules, and other information to members of the media and the athletic community.
9. Work with the student-athlete, through the coach, to encourage all athletes to adhere to school and community rules and regulations and to show respect for individuals and property.
10. Assist athletes in the attainment of high school educational and athletic goals.
11. Establish criteria to determine whether the athletic program is in the mainstream of the total educational philosophy of the school.
12. Prepare an annual or periodic summary report for the administration. This report should include number of participants, cost factors, and recommendations for the coming year.

Questions

1. Why are "human relations" skills or the "human relations aspect of management" as important as the "science of management," or knowing what to do in the position? (Some management authorities maintain that human relations skills are more important!) Discuss.

SUGGESTED READINGS

Davis, Keith, *Human Behavior at Work: Human Relations and Organizational Behavior* 4th edition, McGraw-Hill, New York, 1972, Ch. 1, Ch. 4, Ch. 5, and Ch. 10.

McGregor, Douglas, *The Human Side of Enterprise*, reprinted in K. Davis and W. Scott, eds., *Human Relations and Organizational Behavior*, McGraw-Hill, New York, 1969, p. 8.

Strauss, G. and Sayles, L. R., *The Human Problems of Management*, Prentice-Hall, Englewood Cliffs, N.J., 1960, p. 62.

Vardaman, George T., *Dynamics of Managerial Leadership*, Auerbach Publishers, Philadelphia, 1973, Ch. 7, pp. 79-91.

Zeigler, Earle F. and Spaeth, Marcia J., *Administrative Theory and Practice in Physical Education and Athletics*, Prentice-Hall, Englewood Cliffs, N.J., 1975.

PART II
MANAGEMENT FUNCTIONS: PLANNING AND BUDGETING

Chapter 4
Goals and Objectives for the Interscholastic Athletic Program

In setting goals and objectives for the interscholastic athletic program, it should be noted that the program is primarily conducted for the student participants. Because athletics are a part of and fit harmoniously into the total curriculum, they must be controlled by school authorities and be directed by the rules and regulations of the local, state, and national athletic associations. It is paramount that athletic programs be conducted by members of the faculty who have been trained and credentialed in the field of physical education and athletics. The total interscholastic athletic program should be funded by the school district and not dependent upon special fund-raising activities and handouts. Funding will be discussed in detail in Chapter 6.

The goals of athletic participation should be to contribute to the health and well-being of the student-athlete as well as the development of physical skills, emotional maturity, social awareness, moral values, a sense of cooperation, a spirit of competition, self-discipline, and an understanding of the democratic processes.

Objectives must be in harmony with goals, attainable but challenging and, in reality, must cause participants to reach a little higher to achieve individual and program goals. Participants should be accountable, and understand how the individual relates to the broad major objectives of the athletic department and the total educational community.

Objectives should be periodically reconsidered and redefined. They should allow for creative methods and should not predetermine the means for achieving participants' goals. They should not be too numerous or too complex.

The essential elements of setting· goals and objectives requires a clear statement of purpose, a means of measuring performance, and a review of the accomplishments based on the agreed upon measures.

TESTING THE VALIDITY OF AN OBJECTIVE

If objectives are set to reach a desired end for the interscholastic athletic program, it is obvious that certain criteria must be applied to test the validity of the objective. What is the objective trying to accomplish? What is the desired result? The following suggestions might aid those who are setting objectives for a interscholastic athletic programs.

1. Is there a plan? Are the objectives specific enough to aid the athletic director and the staff in reaching the desired result?
2. Will the objectives serve as a guide, a plan of action, in developing the skills necessary to reach the desired results?
3. Are the objectives workable? Will they measure and control the effectiveness of the interscholastic athletic program?
4. Are the objectives attainable?
5. Are there outside forces that will hinder the achievement of the objectives?
6. Have the objectives been set with the total educational picture in mind or have they been designed solely for the benefit of the athletic department? Basically, objectives should be set so that each participant is accountable for attaining his goal. If each individual attains his goal, the goals and objectives of the athletic department, school, community will have achieved their goals and objectives.
7. Are the objectives ongoing? Will the objectives be explainable in the event of changes in the department? The athletic director, for example, who has been on the job for many years, knows the objectives or the plan but must be able to explain them to the new personnel who join the staff each year.

The athletic director will encourage the new people on the staff to modify the plan, but he must insist that the course of action, "the plan," be followed. With the rapid turnover that exists in coaching personnel, this can be a serious problem because personal goals may conflict with the overall goals of the department.

The goals and objectives of the athletic program serve as a common denominator by which individual members may cooperate within the program. There should be enough latitude within the objectives for an individual member to achieve his personal goals while at the same time working toward achieving the major goals that have been set for the interscholastic athletic program as a whole.

DEVELOPING OBJECTIVES AND GOALS. THE S.W.O.T.S.

The athletic director must meet with the athletic staff at the beginning of each school year to review and redefine existing goals and objectives. A method currently being used for reviewing the existing goals and objectives is called the S.W.O.T.S. methods. Strengths, Weaknesses, Opportunities, Threats, and Suggestions are reviewed prior to defining the goals and objectives for the coming year. Although each athletic director may have some definite thoughts for each of the above mentioned catagories, the following suggestions may serve as an aid:

1. *Strengths.* Quality of the staff, cooperation of the administration, facilities, variety of individual and team sports offered, flexibility in scheduling, success of the program over the years, support of the booster club, good community relations, a perspective in which the athletic program fits into the total program, excellent faculty support, and excellent student body support.
2. *Weaknesses.* Inadequate compensation for coaches, lack of qualified coaching personnel, limited budget, lack of upkeep and maintenance of facilities, implementation of Title IX in relation to budget and facilities, poor coordination of the assignment of faculty to the supervision of specific student-athletic contests, and unrealistic formulation and implementation of the student body budget.
3. *Opportunities.* Greater student participation, increased number of teams, greater student body support, greater faculty support, opportunity for more administrative support, recruiting, assignment and evaluation of all coaches and recommendations for

retention, implementation of programs of orientation for new coaches, and inservice programs for all coaches, coordination and supervision of student spirit activities including rallies, rooter busses, car parades, and other student spirit activities.

4. *Threats.* Implementation of Title IX without proper funding and improvement of facilities, decreasing funds in present inflationary times, teams being coached by noncredentialed personnel, specialization of athletics, youth group activities, administrative apathy toward interscholastic athletics, coaches' apathy toward joining professional organizations, increased liability suits, attitudes of professional athletes, and the trend toward recreational activities and away from more intensive varsity-type competition.

5. *Suggestions.* For improvement of the expanding opportunities for girls in the interscholastic athletic program, for the analysis of Title IX and methods for implementation of Title IX, inservice training for the purpose of certification of nonphysical education majors and minors, plans for staffing to include a trainer in the athletic program, and methods of scheduling of facilities to enhance the expanding program.

GENERAL ATHLETIC PROGRAM GOALS AND OBJECTIVES

The athletic staff, after reviewing the strengths, weaknesses, opportunities, threats, and suggestions that are related to the interscholastic athletic program, should review the program goals and set a list of priorities for the purpose of reaching the total goals for the overall athletic program.

An example of well-defined program goals appeared in the Kent School District (Kent, Washington) Administrators Athletic Department Manual,[1] and are included below to illustrate well-defined program goals.

1. To develop physical excellence and understanding of the value of competition in our society. This is accomplished through recognition of outstanding performance and by emphasizing the educational value of winning and learning to compete.

2. To keep the athletic program within the spectrum of the total educational program, objectives and goals for the participants should include: providing an opportunity for self assurance and determination and to know the deeper meaning of group loyalities and responsibilities; to provide experiences which are immediate in their effect and which are

therefore crucial and lasting; to provide an outlet for expression of student emotions; to provide opportunity to coordinate physical, emotional and intellectual powers into actions; to develop qualities of good citizenship by subscribing to the written and unwritten laws of sportsmanship; and to develop valuable personal qualities or responsibility and leadership.

3. One of the main objectives for the student body and the school is to capitalize on the potential of athletics as a educational force of great magnitude. Other objectives for the student body would include; to provide an opportunity for students to belong to group activities of their own choice; to provide an opportunity for students to release their competitive energy in constructive channels in the role of spectators; to develop the athletic program so that it is the medium for unity and school pride and morale; to develop a program of student interest by enlisting the student's aid in support of the program; to maintain a program broad in scope which includes activities that are interesting and beneficial to the greatest number of students; to provide an opportunity for a student to recognize the difference between work and play and to organize their day to meet responsibilities and yet include other interests.

MANAGEMENT BY OBJECTIVES

The athletic director and staff, in attempting to set goals for others, must set personal short range goals. Personal goals and accomplishments and the constant striving to improve are matters that all athletic administrators must be concerned with.

This encompasses the management-by-objectives theory to which each member of the staff is accountable and according to which each member has the freedom to select the method that will achieve his goals and objectives. In essence, if all staff members are working toward the same major goals of the department when they accomplish their personal goals, then the goals of the department will be met.

The strengths, weaknesses, opportunities, threats, and suggestions are reviewed by the athletic director. He will then design a goal list, relevant to the review. Once these goals have been accomplished, the department is on its way to reaching its designated target. Such a management by objective goal list might include:

1. By September 1 introduce an annual inservice training program to be held prior to the beginning of each school year for all

members of the athletic staff.

2. During the year, hold individual conferences monthly with the head coach of each sport.
3. During the year conduct staff conferences quarterly for planning and information sharing purposes that involve all athletic personnel.
4. Design an athletic department handbook with all pertinent information pertaining to the conduct of the school's athletic program.
5. By October 1 revive the student athletic Block Club and have a schedule of planned activities.
6. By November 1 meet with the faculty and report on the progress of the interscholastic athletic program.
7. By May 1 meet with the student body financial officers and present a budget for the coming year.
8. By May 15 complete the inventory of all athletic equipment.
9. By June 1 meet with the principal in regard to coaching assignments for the coming year.
10. Throughout the year continue to promote measurable program improvements and evaluation methods through management objectives.
11. Encourage the athletic department staff to continue a program of improvement by involvement in district, league, state, and national professional organizations.
12. Work to promote district approval of a formula for increasing the number of qualified coaches and adequate coaching compensation.
13. Prior to the first home football game, implement new procedures for providing game officials and for crowd accommodations.

It is obvious the athletic director's list of goals will include any and all duties and responsibilities that are inherent to the position. Unless the athletic director develops such a plan or list, the major goals of the department will not be accomplished.

Objectives Should be Based on Competitive Spirit and a Code of Ethics

Anyone in the teaching profession is in a position to help people. Our objectives then must include a competitive spirit, not only to win the game or to be the best person we can, but to help others grow and develop and to use their capacities to the fullest possible extent. The distinguishing characteristic of the coaching profession is that its members are dedicated to rendering service to others. Financial gain or personal reward must be of secondary consideration. In selecting the coaching profession, an individual assumes an obligation to conduct himself in accord with its ideals.

Competitive Spirit

The interscholastic athletic program is rapidly becoming one of the few places that the competitive attitude still exists. Charles B. "Bud" Wilkinson,[2] former Oklahoma University football coach and advisor on athletics and sports to two presidents stated,

> The competitive process, which is to demand the best, is in my opinion the best way to breed true excellence. Most people function only about as well as outside pressures force them to. This is what a coach is trying to do for the people who play for him. He first tries to have them understand their potential and next he presents a challenge to them to be as good as they can be. Then he hopes that this will carry over into other activities in life in which they may become involved. I honestly believe that most people are capable of doing somewhere between 30 percent and 40 percent better than their usual level of performance. The competitive process, without any question, is what has made America. As long as we preserve this attitude, I feel that we will maintain our position as the world's greatest nation. Very frankly, we coaches are guardians of a prime example of the competitive process. We are the one group that say simply, line it up and let's see who can win. Fair start, same course, and let's see who can win and to the victor belongs the glory. You simply cannot take the competitive element out of competition, as some people would like to do. If you are involved in a competitive game, the idea is to play the best you can, to make the sacrifices and give the dedication and devotion to insure your best possible performance. Anybody who wants to erode this factor is destroying the priceless contribution that we in competitive athletics can make to our society.

Code of Ethics

Coaches must be mindful of the history and evolution of the coaching profession if they are to serve effectively in the educational development of the young men and women who are participating in the interscholastic athletics program.

Essentially the program belongs to the students who participate in the athletic activities. Justification for including it in the school program rests upon the dual premise that it provides both physical and character values for those who participate. The burden of proof rests largely with the coaching profession.

It has become increasingly clear during recent years that because of the tremendous increase in the numbers of players, teams, and coaches, there is need for reviewing and perhaps updating an operating code of principles and ethics.

In dealing with goal setting and objective achievement, it is important that the people who are working with the student-athlete clarify and distinguish ethical and approved professional practices from those that are detrimental and harmful. Ethics has been defined as the basic principle of right action. It stresses the proper functions of the coaching profession in relationship to the school, athlete, and the community. Ethics imply a standard of character in which the public has trust and confidence. The ultimate success of any code of ethics rests primarily with the coaches.

Although there are many versions of a code of ethics, the basic premise is always the same. We have chosen the creed of the California Coaches Association[3] as an example of what statements or information should be included in such a document.

Creed of the California Coaches Association

I BELIEVE that athletics have an important place in the general education scheme and pledge myself to cooperate with others in the field of education to so administer it that its value never will be questioned.

I BELIEVE that my own actions should be so regulated that at all times I will be a credit to my profession.

I BELIEVE in the exercise of all the patience, tolerance, and diplomacy at my command in my relations with all players, co-workers, game officials, and spectators.

I BELIEVE that these admirable characteristics, properly instilled by me through teaching and demonstration, will have a long carry over and will aid each one connected with the sport to become a better citizen.

I BELIEVE in and will support all reasonable moves to improve athletic conditions, to provide for adequate equipment, and to promote the welfare of an increased number of participants.

I BELIEVE that the proper administration of these principles offers an effective laboratory method to develop in its adherents high ideals of sportsmanship, qualities of cooperation, courage, unselfishness and self control; desires for clean and healthful living, respect for wise discipline and authority.

Finally, it should be stressed that goal and objective formulation is a group process to which the director provides leadership.

There are four basic rules which together, make the effective administrator, according to Peter F. Drucher,[4] author of the 1974 best-seller, *Management: Tasks, Responsibilities, Practices.*

1. Think through what the really important contributions are which only you can make—and make sure you make them.
2. Know where your time goes and where it should go.
3. Set priorities and abide by your priority decisions.
4. Build on strength, and especially on the strength of people; look for strength, staff for strength.

Questions

1. What is the rationale and justification that the total interscholastic athletic program should be funded by the school district and not be dependent upon special fund-raising activities and hand-outs?
2. In embracing sound educational philosophy, why should interscholastic athletics be considered a part of not separate from the physical education program and curriculum?
3. List five educational objectives of interscholastic athletics.
4. What does M.B.O. mean? Can an athletic director apply the concept and principles of M.B.O. to administering the interscholastic athletic program? Discuss.
5. What does S.W.O.T.S. mean? How can S.W.O.T.S. be utilized to set goals and objectives and then evaluate if they have been met? Explain.

REFERENCES

1. Burrell, Jack, Athletic Director, Kent School District No. 415, King Count, Kent, Washington. *District Administrators Athletic Department Manual,* 1974. By permission.
2. Wilkinson, Charles B., *The Competitive Spirit,* San Francisco Coach of the Year Football Clinic Notes, San Francisco, 1972, p. 23. By permission.
3. "Creed for the California Coaches Association," *California Coaches Association Handbook,* 1975. By permission.
4. Drucher, Peter F., *Management: Tasks, Responsibilities, Practices.* Reprinted in Interscholastic Athletic Administration, Vol. 1, No. 2, Spring 1975 p. 26. National Federation of State High School Associations, Spencer Marketing Services; New York, N.Y. 10017.

SUGGESTED READINGS

Dessler, Gary, *Organization and Management: A Contingency Approach*, Prentice-Hall, Englewood Cliffs, N.J., 1976, Ch. 7, Leadership; Ch. 9, Motivation and Satisfaction; Ch. 11, Staffing and Performance Appraisal; Ch. 13, Decision Making; Ch. 14, Managerial Planning.

Forsythe, C. E., *Administration of High School Athletics*, 4th edition, Prentice-Hall, Englewood Cliffs, N.J., 1962, Ch. 1 History and Objectives of High School Athletics.

George, J. F. and Lehmann, H. A., *School Athletic Administration*, Harper and Row, New York, 1956. Ch. 2, Citizenship Aspects.

Grieve, A. W., *Directing High School Athletics*, Prentice-Hall, Englewood Cliffs, N.J., 1963, Ch. 1, Objectives and Principles.

Haimann, T. and Scott, William G., *Management in the Modern Organization*, Houghton Mifflin, Boston, 1974.

Hodge, B. J. and Johnson, H. J., *Management and Organizational Behavior* Wiley, New York, 1970, pp. 21-24, 175-177.

Massie, J. L. and Douglas, J., *Managing: A Contemporary Introduction* Prentice-Hall, Englewood Cliffs, N.J., 1973, Ch. 11, Setting Objectives, pp. 214-228.

Purdy, R.L., *The Successful High School Athletic Program*, Parker Publishing, West Nyack, N.Y., 1973, Ch. 1, Principles and Organization for Successful Athletic Administration.

Rogers, Rolf E., *Organization Theory*, Allyn and Bacon, Boston, 1975, pp. 182-183.

Chapter 5

Policy Development in Interscholastic Athletics

The high school interscholastic athletic program is justified by the contributions it makes to general educational objectives. The program should exist primarily to provide education experiences for the participants as a phase of the school's curriculum. Curriculum might be defined as all those activities carried on under the jurisdiction of the school. Therefore, athletics are part of the school's curriculum and should be viewed in this perspective and subject to the same kinds of administrative control.

The fundamental principle for competitive athletics is to serve the education of youth. Athletics provide a vehicle through which the school can accomplish the task of effectively meeting the needs and interests of students. Athletics should both promote and supplement the regular curriculum in the total educational picture. Interscholastic athletics must be able to withstand examination and justify every facet of its program. It must also strive to maintain the highest possible standards in the conduct of its program and as a worthwhile educational experience.

FORMULATION OF POLICY

Policies should be written in precise language that leaves no doubt about the intended meaning. A policy statement satisfies the need to be consistent when immediate action must be taken or a decision or judgment made in a number of similar cases. The availability of such a policy statement helps to prevent inconsistency in forming judgments. Policies should conform with relevant school, league, district, and state association regulations and should be complete in scope. Policies should not be so detailed, however, that they hamstring the administration in reacting to an emergent problem.

Policy Characteristics

The responsibility for development of policy is legally that of a local school board of education. It seems practical that the board look to the administration and director of athletics for relevant data, pertinent information, valid recommendations, and general administrative assistance in designing and implementing policies.

Presently, many school districts are losing court decisions because district policy is arbitrary, ambiguous, or nonexistent. Policy must be kept up to date and functional. Many policies fall into the catagory of being no longer relevant or legal.

Policy recommendations are the responsibility of the central school administration, the athletic director, and the entire coaching staff. It is their function to:

1. Review existing policies, education law, legislation, and other regulations pertaining to the athletic program.
2. Examine policies of other school districts.
3. Survey areas for which no policy exists.
4. Make recommendations to implement a policy statement.

Need for a Well-Developed Policy Statement[1]

"Besides averting calamitous dangers, there are some very positive and compelling reasons to have complete, updated board policy:

1. Properly prepared policies anticipate problems. An alert administration and a wise board, in foreseeing a potentially dangerous situation can formulate thoughtful policy before a crisis occurs. Developing policy in advance of problems insures a high degree of involvement, research, and subsequent acceptance. Policy developed quickly in reaction to an immediate circumstance, and probably based on expediency, is certain to cause difficulty.
2. Continuity in any complex organization is essential to optimal productivity. As school board members, administrators, and staff move in and out of a district, well-developed board policy allows smooth transitions and becomes basis for continuous decision making and problem solving.

3. Good policy enhances administration. Besides forming the basis for all administrative regulations, the administration is freed from dealing constantly with routine matters. Procedures that work smoothly release the board and administration to concentrate on major critical issues.
4. Comprehensive board policies provide an essential on-going communication bond among all parties in the educational community. As a public relations document any citizen can quickly find the board's position on important issues.
5. Attention should be given to the development of a policy manual for communication purposes. The policy manual should be well organized, clearly indexed and correctly catalogued. This implies a looseleaf notebook format with page replacement facilitated for a systematic method of replacing amended policy which insures a continous update by sending changes to all concerned.

Principles of Policymaking

Policies should be made with regard for the welfare of all students, not the win-loss record of the coach or the school. Policies reveal the purposes, goals, and ideas on which the fundamental organization of the athletic program is based and must be broad enough in scope and general enough in meaning to enhance the entire program.

Policies are guidelines, that give direction to the interscholastic athletics program. The school administration must be able to point with great pride at the activities and the procedure by which the program is being conducted. If the program is based on a sound educational philosophy, the conduct of the people involved will make it clear that the participant is more important than the game; the program will thus be able to withstand outside criticism and community pressure.

Facilities and Personnel Policy Criteria

Consideration must be given to the following criteria relevant to facilities and personnel determination:
1. The scope of the program. The number of sports that can be offered commensurate with proper teaching and coaching, adequate equipment, and satisfactory facilities.
2. The determination of athletic schedules, that is, travel, frequency of games, open or closed season, overlapping seasons, specialization or a broad concept of athletics. In a school, for example, with a small enrollment, an athlete will perhaps participate in two

CAMROSE LUTHERAN COLLEGE LIBRARY

or three sports; in a large school, he may participate in only one sport because of specialization and the increased number of participants. This will also determine the length of season, start of practice, and the number of coaches available.

3. How are programs financed? Do several of the spectator sports, such as football and basketball, finance the entire program with their gate receipts? How are other activities financed?
4. What effect has Title IX had on the interscholastic program?
5. Does the school or the individual participant pay for athletic insurance?

Policy Implementation

Policy, once established, should be the bylaws for the participant, faculty, administration, and the community in the conduct of the interscholastic athletic program. Once rules and regulations are accepted, they must be monitored and carried out under the existing policy, until this policy is changed.

The athletic director is responsible for implementing the policy and must conduct the interscholastic athletic program accordingly. The process of comprehensive policy development and the measure of success of the program is dependent upon the interest and integrity of the people responsible for the program. The final result is judged by the actual coach of a sport and his ability to work within the framework of the system. If the coach is allowed to conduct his program in a manner that conflicts with the general policy of the interscholastic athletic department, the program will suffer and break down from within. Many coaches like to operate in a very independent fashion and have great need for ego satisfaction. The athletic director is faced with the task of making "team players" of all coaches.

Administrative Responsibilities

The success or failure of any high school athletic program is determined by the administrators responsible for the program. Basically, the school athletic program, in most communities, is directly traceable as follows: (1) to the board of education that develops policies and a sound athletic philosophy for the schools of the community; (2) to the superintendent, the executive director for the schools, who implements the policies and philosophy of the board of education; (in some school districts the central administrator's office, attached to the superintendent's office, has an assistant superintendent or other official with administrative responsibilities for interscholastic athletics); (3) to the principal of a school in the district who implements the policies and philosophy for the schools.

Each group has certain responsibilites that are primarily delegated to them. Each school should have written policy distributed to all people involved in the athletic program, including the total faculty, which defines the delegation of duties and responsibilities. This policy should be approved and have the sanction of the board of education, the superintendent, the local school administration, the athletic director, the coaching staff, and the athletic board of control or athletic advisory committee.

SUGGESTED POLICY STATEMENT FOR THE INTERSCHOLASTIC ATHLETIC PROGRAM

The following policy statement is an example of the content that should be seriously considered when formulating a policy for your school.

Policy

The athletic director shall, at the beginning of each school year, confer with his coaching staff and define appropriate rules and regulations for all athletes participating in the interscholastic athletic program. Each rule and regulation shall clearly relate to one of the following criteria: (1) valid educational reason, (2) performance, (3) health or safety.

Once the rules are defined and approved by the coaching staff, athletic director, principal, superintendent, and the board of education, they may be questioned through the same administrative channels. While the rule is in effect, the burden will be upon the petitioner to demonstrate the unreasonableness of that rule under challenge and he shall be governed by that rule until such time as a final determination is made by the district.

Objectives of the Policy

1. To support and strengthen the role that secondary school athletic directors play in helping attain the educational objectives of the interscholastic athletic program.

2. To foster high standards of professional proficiency and ethics.
3. To improve understanding of interscholastic athletics throughout the total school community.
4. To establish a closer working relationship with related professional groups.
5. To demonstrate to the community that secondary school athletic staff and school administrators have a vital interest and responsibility in maintaining high standards for the interscholastic athletic program.

RESPONSIBILITIES OF PERSONNEL

The board of education, the superintendent or his delegate, the principal, the athletic director, and the coaching staff each have certain responsibilities. In an attempt to list these duties and responsibilities, only major areas, as they relate to the overall administration of a sound interscholastic athletic program are suggested. Here is a list of inherent and assigned responsibilities for the provision of maintenance, operation, and supervision of the interscholastic athletic program.

The Board of Education

1. Assume general overall responsibilities for the development of policies for the organization of the interscholastic athletic program.
2. Develop a philosophy for athletic competition to meet the needs of the students and the community.
3. Allocate funds for the operation of the athletic program with due regard for the needs of the total educational program.
4. Employ a professional educator, designated as the district superintendent, to direct and supervise the organization and operation of the athletic program in accordance with the policies as set by the board.
5. Provide for adequate funds, fields, courts, gymnasium, equipment, and transportation.
6. Implement Title IX in regard to equality in the athletic program.

The District Superintendent

1. Direct and supervise the athletic program of the district in accordance with the policies and regulations designed by the board of

education.
2. Interpret the policies of the board of education to the community and interpret to both the board and to the community the activites that are conducted as part of the athletic program.
3. Maintain a sound athletic philosophy of the athletic program as set forth by the board.

The Principal

1. Direct and supervise the athletic program in his school in accordance with policies of the board of education and the superintendent.
2. Interpret the policies of the board of education and the superintendent to both the faculty and the community.
3. Certify the eligibility of all athletes in accord with provisions of the school, the district, and the state organization.
4. Sign and validate all eligibility lists and other requests from state athletic associations.
5. Recommend to the superintendent all coaching assignments.
6. Sign all athletic game contracts.
7. Submit all athletic contracts with financial agreements to the superintendent.
8. Provide for supervision of all home athletic contests and provide for assistance in the supervision at contests played away from home.
9. Support the athletic department staff in organizing and maintaining a sound athletic program that is consistent with the objectives and the needs of the total educational program.
10. Represent the school or delegate a person to represent the school at all league meetings.
11. Regularly assess the athletic program and report the finding to the superintendent.
12. Appoint a person to be responsible for all financial aspects of the interscholastic athletic program.

The Athletic Director

The most efficient way to administer the interscholastic athletic program is to create an administrative position with full responsibility for the program. The day has passed, if it ever really existed, when the directorship of athletics provided a convenient landing spot into which an aging or losing coach is "retired." As it is normally constituted in our schools, the athletic director position requires full professional commitment, expertise, and competence in a variety of specialized areas and the diligence to pursue the most exacting and demanding tasks. The position cannot be satisfactorily filled by a school principal, concerned with the overall school administration.

The athletic director should be responsible directly to the principal and be prepared to fulfill all of the responsibilities of his position as a member of the administrative staff. The position should include administrative, supervisory, and coordinating responsibility and be so structured as to make it possible for the person to contribute to the school administrative policy.

The person appointed to such a position should be trained and fully qualified in athletic administration and must have competence in areas of program development, personnel management, business management and finance, development and utilization of facilities, and a good public relations manner. The athletic director must also have a thorough knowledge of laws (national, state, and local) and regulations of the state department of education.

Additional Responsibilities of the Athletic Director

Along with the responsibilities listed above and the position description discussed in Chapter 3, the athletic director should:
1. Cooperatively, with the administration and the athletic staff, develop well-defined goals and objectives for the interscholastic athletic department of the school (Chapter 6) including policy for combating outside influences that are detrimental to the program.
2. Plan joint meetings of faculty, administration, and athletic personnel for a better understanding of all school policies.
3. Formulate written policies and procedures as they pertain to each member of the coach staff.
4. Hold periodic personnel conferences with the athletic staff for review and evaluation of the program.
5. Work with the administration on the scheduling of faculty meetings and curriculum conferences so that teaching obligations can be held to a minimum and at a convenient time for coaches during their sport season.
6. Keep informed of planning of future facilities with careful attention given to the development of specifications so that the archi-

tectural and construction work fits the needs of the athletic
department.
7. Keep pace with all significant and feasible development in curriculum and techniques.
8. Be innovative and creative but practical toward program development and management.
9. Encourage promotion and development from within the system.
Selection should be made on the basis of competence.

DEVELOPMENT OF A CODE OF ETHICS FOR
THE INTERSCHOLASTIC ATHLETIC PROGRAM

In Chapter 4, we discussed the need for a Code of Ethics for the interscholastic athletic program. The Code of Ethics should be included in the policy manual as a guide for professional educators to
insure a high level of performance of anyone connected with the
program. Included in the code of ethics should be statements re-
flecting moral character, behavior, leadership, integrity, respect,
ethical relationships, responsibilities concerning health services,
safety hazards, health habits, and the establishment of sound training
rules.

The following code of ethics developed by the Interscholastic
Athletic Conference of Hawaii[2] sets forth a code for the administrators, athletic director, coach, game official, and spectator. It is
an excellent example of information that should be included in
almost any code that is being devised for the interscholastic athletic
program.

Code of Ethics for the Administrator

It is the duty of all concerned with the administration of high school
athletics to:
1. Emphasize the proper ideals of sportsmanship, ethical conduct,
and fair play.
2. Stress the values derived from playing the game fairly.
3. Show courtesy to all sports officials.
4. Establish friendly relationships with visiting teams and coaches.
5. Respect the integrity and judgment of sports officials.
6. Understand thoroughly and accept the rules of the game and the
standards of eligibility.

7. Encourage leadership, use of initiative, and good judgment by athletes.
8. Recognize that the purpose of athletics is to promote the athlete's physical, mental, moral, social, and emotional well-being.

Code of Ethics for the Athletic Director

1. He shall clearly understand his role in the athletic program of the school.
2. He shall include in the athletic schedule only those activities that are educationally sound.
3. He shall solicit the help and cooperation of the community to improve the quality of the athletic program.
4. He shall refuse admission to athletic contests to anyone who has shown chronic disregard for sportsmanlike behavior.
5. He shall secure game officials that are mutually agreed upon by both teams.
6. He shall formally contract game officials with respect to fees, expenses, and time and place of the game.
7. He shall adequately provide for the handling of crowds so there will be no disturbances and riotous behavior at athletic contests.

Code of Ethics for the Coach

1. He shall assist his superiors in their effort to make athletics a part of the total island program.
2. He shall insist upon high scholarship among the players and rigidly enforce all rules of eligibility.
3. He shall have a genuine and up-to-date knowledge of the game that he is to coach.
4. He shall be fair to all squad members.
5. He shall carefully attend to the physical condition of players.
6. He shall teach athletes to win by legitimate means only.
7. He shall counteract unfounded rumors of questionable practices of opposing players.
8. He shall prohibit gambling and the use of obscene language.

Code of Ethics for the Game Official

1. He shall have a thorough knowledge of the game rules.
2. He shall report for duty at least 30 minutes before the start of the game.

3. He shall neatly wear an authorized official's uniform.
4. He shall control the game at all times by warning crowds and inflicting penalties to players and coaches for unsportsmanlike conduct.
5. He shall respect the decisions of his fellow officials as well as aid in making decisions.
6. He shall clearly interpret and announce the rules governing his decisions to both teams.
7. He shall not discuss plays or players of a team in the presence of prospective opponents.
8. He shall not compensate for his errors in judgment against a team by overpenalizing the opposing team.
9. He shall not change his decision because of the disapproval of spectators.
10. The welfare of the participants shall be a paramount consideration at all times.

Code of Ethics for the Athlete

1. He shall play fairly and play hard.
2. He shall play for the joy of playing and for the success of the team.
3. He shall keep his head and play the game.
4. He shall respect officials and their decisions.
5. He shall conduct himself in an exemplary way on and off the field.
6. He shall faithfully complete all his school work.
7. He shall completely and faithfully observe all training rules.
8. He shall treat visiting teams and officials as guests and the extention of every courtesy to them.
9. He shall give opponents full credit when they win.
10. He shall be modest in victory.
11. He shall not "crow" when his team wins or blame the officials when it loses.
12. He shall not quit, cheat, bet, "grandstand," or abuse his body.

Code of Ethics for the Spectator

1. He shall practice sportsmanlike conduct as much as he demands it from the athlete.

2. He shall assist the proper development of the athletes and the athletic tradition of the community be making certain that both athletes and administration faithfully observe their respective codes.

Questions

1. What is a policy? What are the purposes of policies?
2. In policy determination and implementation, what is the hierarchy from the board of education downward to the athletic director?
3. What is the difference between policy and procedure? Give examples of each.
4. List some components of the code of ethics for the coach and for the athletic participant.

REFERENCES

1. Johnson-Monahan Administrative Services, *Map Management, Action Paper*, Vol. 4, No. 1, 1974, Cupertino, California 95014. By permission.
2. Interscholastic Conference of Hawaii, Office of Instructional Services, Department of Education, Honolulu, Hawaii, 1970. By permission.

SUGGESTED READINGS

Forsythe, C. E. and Keller, I. A., *Administration of High School Athletics* 5th edition, Prentice-Hall, Englewood Cliffs, N.J., 1972, Ch. 6, Policies and Administration Plans for Local Athletic Programs.

George, J. F. and Lehmann, H. A., *School Athletic Administration*, Harper and Row, New York, 1966, Ch. 11, Policies and Procedures.

Hixon, C. G., *The Administration of Interscholastic Athletics*, J. Lowell Pratt, New York, 1967, Ch. 1, Administration Control, Ch. 2, A Basic Point of View, and Ch. 3, Organization for Administrative Control.

Hodge B. J. and Johnson, H. J., *Management and Organization Behavior: A Multidimensional Approach*, Wiley, New York, 1970, pp. 357-360.

Massie J. L. and Douglas, John., *Managing: A Contemporary Introduction*, Prentice-Hall, Englewood Cliffs, N.J., 1973.

Chapter 6
Financing and Budgetary Problems and Solutions

Throughout the nation many boards of education are facing financial crises and are confronted with problems that are not easily resolved. In many instances, communities are not receptive to voting affirmatively for additional tax referendums, regardless of the reason. Viable athletic programs must be curtailed or eliminated from the physical educational curriculum because of insufficient funding. School boards are faced with an either/or situation, that is, which course offerings, activities, and programs to retain or drop. All educational endeavors have increased in cost and expenditures and athletic equipment, uniforms, transportation, and officials are not exceptions.

Ironically, during this period of financial crisis in the secondary schools, there has never been greater participation in interscholastic athletics, as pointed out in Chapter 1 in the National Federation of State High School Association's participation survey.[1] "Not only has the boys' program grown by more than 300,000 in the last two years, the girls' program has increased by approximately one million participants in the past four year period."

Federal legislators have enacted recent legislation, Title IX, which has had an immediate effect on the interscholastic programs throughout the United States.

TITLE IX REGULATIONS

School districts are currently trying to implement Title IX regulations, which became effective July 21, 1975. It is too early to determine what effect Title IX will have on the interscholastic athletic program. Title IX is discussed at length in Chapter 27. It should be mentioned at this point, however, that the regulations do not demand dollar for dollar matching expenditures. Expenditures may differ because of the nature of the sports within each program, provided the differences in expenditures do not affect the equal disbursement of equipment, supplies, facilities, and publicity, for example. It does require equity of opportunity and enhances opportunities for girls and women in athletics. It allows schools the flexibility they need to develop competitive comparable programs for girls.

Title IX provides equal opportunity in athletics in those sports and levels of competition offered by the school, and accommodates the interests and abilities of both sexes and equity in providing equipment and supplies, in scheduling games and practices, and in providing coaching.

The allocations for additional coaches, equipment, and facilities to comply with Title IX will have a definite budgetary effect on the school that has a fixed budget. If funds to comply with the regulation must come from the existing budget, there will be a serious problem in conducting a well-balanced interscholastic athletic program. As pointed out in Chapter 1, a hardship is caused in most schools if the school boards do not come to the aid of the interscholastic athletic program.

METHODS OF FINANCING THE INTERSCHOLASTIC ATHLETICS PROGRAM

Each school district is unique in solving its own financial problems; however, most general methods are applicable to all school districts. It is a fact that the interscholastic athletic program will face much competition in securing district funds with which to conduct the program. The interscholastic athletic program will be competing with every department in the school for tax funds. As of now, the profession holds a low priority for receiving such funds. This low priority has been established during the past decade by misinformed students, faculty, and the general public. The interscholastic athletic program, being an integral part of the total educational community, must meet the challenge in requesting funds from the district.

Allies in Financing the Program

The proponents of interscholastic athletics must rally the forces and "resell" the value of high school athletics and substantiate their worth if the program is to survive. The coaching profession has taken many things for granted and has not relied on one of its main assets, public relation to educate the public as to the goals, objectives, philosophy, and values that are gained from a well-conducted athletic program.

Public relations is an ongoing and critical phase of the athletic program, as stated in Chapter 33. The community must constantly be reminded of the variety of activities and the number of participants taking part if they are to be expected to help in the financing of the program. The public should be educated to recognize that the interscholastic athletic program is meeting the needs and interests of a large percentage of the school enrollment and is a part of a well-balanced educational system. As such, it should be funded as any other department in the school district.

MOST COMMON METHODS OF FUNDING THE INTERSCHOLASTIC ATHLETIC PROGRAM

In various states, methods of financing interscholastic athletics programs vary from complete district support from tax funds to complete student support with revenue from gate receipts and student fees. There are six commonly recognized methods of funding:

1. *Board of Education Funding.* The most desirable approach would be for the Board of Education to finance the interscholastic athletic program as it does other departments in the school. Gate receipts and other revenue are returned to the district to lighten the burden.

2. *Gate Receipts and Student Activity Cards.* The second approach would be to finance the program through gate receipts and student activity cards with additional support from the Board of Education for such items as insurance, transportation, game officials, protective equipment, medical supplies for the care and prevention of athletic injuries, and reconditioning of athletic equipment.

3. *Student Control Approach.* In this approach, all monies received from gate receipts, school plays, dances, and fund-raising activities are placed in a general fund and allocated on a need basis. Such a method of financing the interscholastic athletic program has many drawbacks. The main problem created by this method arises because only a few of the athletic activities bring in gate receipts and these activities are basically the sole support of the entire program. A misconception, rather common in the minds of many people, is that some of the activities are self-supporting. The connotation is that football and basketball *make* "x" number of dollars through gate receipts where in actuality football and basketball *take* in "x" number of dollars. There is quite a difference. In most cases the money that is received at the gate goes to defray a percentage of the expenses of the sport. Not many high school programs are self-supporting. The second drawback to the general fund approach is that it places the students in the role of fund raisers, which is not a sound method of financing the program. We do not ask history, chemistry, or language students to raise funds; nor should we ask this of student-athletes.

4. *The Booster or Parents' Club Method of Funding.* The booster or parents' club method of financing places the parents in an untenable position in that, if they are financing the program, they want to have a say in how the program should be conducted. The result is that the public may be running the program and not professionally trained educators. Booster club funds should only be accepted without obligations. The basic intent of the booster or parents' club organization should be to assist the athletic department in the purchase of items not provided by the school, such as awards, banquets, and film, and not the purchase of basic equipment for athletic teams. These clubs can provide valuable support services to the participants and coaches. Care must be taken so that their participation in the interscholastic program is within the scope of the educational philosophy of athletics.

5. *Physical Education Department Support.* Over the years, the physical education department and the athletic department have been synonymous. Through capital outlay expenditures, supplies, the sharing of facilities and equipment, the interscholastic athletic program has been able to remain within the existing budget

allotted to them. As the physical education budgets are undergoing the same cutbacks as the athletic budgets, this trend or aid from the physical education department is diminishing. State legislation in some areas has caused physical education to become optional in all or part of the program, and this affects not only the budget but the staffing.

6. *The Self-Supporting Method.* The self-support method of financing the interscholastic athletic program has become popular, out of necessity, in the past few years. Athletes are asked to purchase some of their equipment such as football practice and game jerseys, baseball bats, tennis balls, and other equipment not provided for by the school. The drawback to this method is that the cost to an individual to participate in a sport may exceed his desire to compete. The athletic department must be realistic in the amount it charges each athlete. If an athlete is asked to purchase football shoes, insurance, socks, supporters, mouth piece, and then additionally, his practice and game jersey, it may present a financial hardship. The self-supporting method of financing interscholastic athletics may also include the assessing of each athlete a fee for participation in the program. In Bloomington, Minnesota, for example, each participant in the athletic program is assessed a $7.50 fee. More than $6000 accrued from participants in the athletic program of Bloomington's three high schools in recent years. Participation and public opinion were unaffected.

Problem Must be Studied

School administrators and interscholastic athletic directors need to study the problem as it relates to their particular situation and decide upon a course of action that is best for their schools. The athletic director must establish himself as an expert in the field of athletic administration and have ready plans and alternatives when it is time to submit the budget for the coming year. Regardless of the type of funding that is used for the interscholastic athletic program, the athletic director must be fully informed about new equipment, innovative ideas, and methods of obtaining the best supplies and equipment for the least amount of money. The athletic director must educate the school board and the school administration to the degree that they will understand the problem that faces the program if adequate funds are not available.

The athletic director must correct any misinformation concerning the financial status of the athletic program and assure the community that with adequate funding, all students will have an unlimited, satisfying, and useful experience.

BUDGET PLANNING AND CONSIDERATIONS

Planning and budgeting for the interscholastic athletic program must be accomplished in accordance with the uniform policies and procedures established for the total school program. Prior to the preparation of the budget, there must be an assessment of changing attitudes and interests of the students. The students should be involved in the planning and programming. The needs and interests of the student body should determine the budget. The budget should never determine the program.

Analysis of Cost and Benefits

A budget is nothing more than a statement of anticipated income vs. anticipated expenditures, usually forecast for one school year. The program should be reevaluated periodically, depending on the need, with consideration for health, safety, sanitation, performance, and appearance. As a guideline for establishing the budget, the athletic director must consider such basic factors as the number of student participating in each sport, the number of contests, the extent of travel, the cost of officials, guarantees and other current expenses, supplies, repair of equipment, and general student interest and attitude toward the program.

Allocations for All Programs

In case of established activities, previous year budgets may be used in order to determine priorities. The athletic director, in order to stabilize the budget from year to year, has to set up a revolving system to assure each sport a fair share over a period of years. This may be accomplished by allocating a large sum one year to replace football helmets, and the following year, basketball uniforms. This practice should continue until the budget is rotated among all of the activities of the program. It is obvious that under this system, with the existing funds available, each sport will have to go through a period of time when only the necessities may be purchased. On the rotation basis, each sport will have a turn at a large sum purchase. A high priority should be given to new programs as they are added and until they are ready to become a part of the revolving process.

Standardization of uniforms and basic equipment to facilitate gradual rather than "wholesale" replacement spreads the cost over a period of years and develops a traditional style.

BUDGET PROCESS

In the preparation of the budget, the athletic director must outline a budget process for the coaching staff. Each varsity coach should be held responsible to prepare the budget for his sport and present it to the athletic director for adoption. The budget process should be undertaken in the following three steps:

1. *Collect Necessary Information.* The coach must have the beginning inventory count and the present inventory count. Some of the equipment will need repair. Some will have to be replace because it has been lost, stolen, unaccoutable, discarded, unsafe, or not usable. The coach will have to determine the number of participants needing equipment.
2. *Classify the Information.* In classifying the information, the coach will compile information on the total number of new articles needed for the next season and indicate the approximate cost of each item.
3. *Present the Budget to the Athletic Director.* The completed form must be presented to the athletic director on the prescribed date, usually the last day in March.

   The athletic director will compile a list of the total number of participants for the entire program during the coming year. He will submit this list along with the budget to the proper authorities for the final adoption. In the case of district funding, the athletic director will submit the budget to the district business manager. In the case of general school funding, the athletic director will submit the budget to the treasurer of the student body funds. The athletic director will be asked to meet with the student treasurer, the advisor, and the student committee for discussion and possible adoption of the budget.

The athletic director should present the budget with the following catagories: Personal services, administrative expenses, equipment, transportation, anticipated number of students who will participate, number of teams involved and whether these expenditures are for existing sports or for a new sport that is being added to the program.

The athletic director will also present a review of expected revenues from gate receipts, student activity cards, student assessment fees, or other sources of income.

Administration of the budget becomes possible when it is formally adopted. Appraisal of the budget is a continuous process. It is the responsibility of the athletic director to exercise control of all funds to insure proper expenditures and accounting. The close of the school years calls for an independent audit of the accounts and a critical appraisal of the entire program.

Budgetary management reflects the emphasis that is placed on certain activities that are considered important in long term planning and those activities that need developing. Budgeting and program planning go hand in hand as most administrative decisions of any interscholastic athletic program are related, in some way, to finances. The budget, therefore, is a documented plan that reflects the manner in which funds are allocated to achieve the goals and objectives of the total interscholastic athletic program.

Questions

1. Enumerate the various ways that interscholastic programs are funded presently.
2. Why is the most desirable way to have the board of education fund the entire interscholastic athletic program?
3. What do we mean when we say "no strings attached" in receiving money from booster clubs to support the interscholastic athletic program? Give illustrations.
4. What are the steps an athletic director would follow in compiling data and formulating a budget for presentation to the board of education, including validating the coaches' requests?
5. Enumerate the major categories that should be taken into consideration in preparing a master budget for the board of education for an interscholastic athletics program with 12 sports.

REFERENCES

1. Fagan, Clifford B., *Interscholastic Athletic Administration* Spring 1975 Vol. 1., No. 2 p. 5, Clifford B. Fagan, Executive Secretary, National Association of State High School Associations, Spencer Marketing Services, New York, N.Y. 10017. By permission.

SUGGESTED READINGS

Forsythe, C. E. and Keller I. A., *Administration of High School Athletics*, 4th edition, Prentice-Hall, Englewood Cliffs, N.J., 1972, Ch. 10, Athletic Finances and Budgets.

George, J. F. and Lehmann, H. A., *School Athletic Administration*, Harper & Row, New York, 1972, Ch. 6, Finances and Budget.

Grieve, A. W., *Directing High School Athletics*, Prentice-Hall, Englewood Cliffs, N.J., 1963, Ch. 8, Budget Problems and Their Solution.

Hixon, C. G., *The Administration of Interscholastic Athletics*, J. Lowell Pratt, New York, 1967, Ch. 6, Financing the Program.

Hodge, B. J. and Johnson, H. J., *Management and Organizational Behavior*, Wiley, 1970, pp. 357-360.

Massie, J. L. and Douglas, J., *Managing: A Contemporary Introduction*, Prentice-Hall, Englewood Cliffs, N.J., 1973, pp. 232-236.

Purdy, R. L., *The Successful High School Athletic Program*, Parker Publishing, West Nyack, N.Y., 1973, Ch. 5, Financing a Productive Interscholastic Program on any Budget.

Chapter 7
Scheduling Procedures: Facilities and Contests

In the management and administration of interscholastic athletics, a high priority should be given to scheduling the use of facilities and to the scheduling of athletic contests.

The scheduling of interscholastic athletic contests demands cooperation and planning on the part of all concerned. Conference or league contests are usually planned several years in advance by league commissioners or the league scheduling committee. The scheduling of nonleague contests or contest to fill bye dates, is the responsibility of the athletic director and should be planned for as far in advance as possible to avoid last minute confusion.

Probably the most difficult situation in scheduling contests, especially with the implementation of Title IX, is the lack of facilities with which to handle the expanding program. Conflicting demands for indoor and outdoor practice areas and game or meet facilities and schedule time for practice and games, illustrate the need for more and improved scheduled use of existing facilities. Until the procurement of new and better facilities is possible, it may be necessary to shift traditional time allotments by changing some sport seasons, combining practices, or by using the facilities more at night, early morning, and weekends to create equitable practice and game schedules.

SCHEDULING AND USE OF FACILITIES

Planning and building new facilities will not solve the immediate problem of the overcrowded conditions that exist in most secondary schools. Never before in the history of our profession has there been more demand on the use of high school plants for all types of physical activity with persons from six to sixty. Many high school facilities are used approximately 15 hours a day, six and seven days a week. This is as it should be. However, in order to run a well-balanced physical education, intramural, interscholastic athletic and recreation program, the activities must be coordinated and priorities established in order to avoid undue confusion and to obtain maximum use of the facilities.

In most instances, the physical education program will be operative from 7:30 a.m. until 3:00 p.m., five days a week; the interscholastic athletic program usually commands all the facilities for practice and contests from 3:00 to 6:00 p.m., with additional games and contest slated for some night and Saturday activity. The intramural and recreation activities are conducted during early morning hours, noontime, nights and on weekends, working their schedule in and around the physical education and interscholastic athletic programs. The priorities have been established by the nature of the activities and the ranking order would then be physical education, interscholastic athletics, intramural, school recreation, and community recreation programs.

Master Calendar

The ideal situation would be for the athletic director to coordinate all activities, working with and through the other department chairpersons who are responsible for the physical education, intramural, and recreation programs. Scheduling problems occur mainly during the nonphysical education hours, the physical education program having established priorities during the daily school hours.

A master calendar, located in the athletic director's office, would be a means of communication and eliminate any last minute confusion. A daily or weekly reminder from the athletic director to all concerned would keep everyone informed as to the activity and the facility in use each hour of the day. The calendar should be an ongoing schedule, planned by all people concerned with the various activities. No one except the athletic director should finalize schedules on the master calendar. This will eliminate the first come, first served procedure. If, for reason, the activity is cancelled or changed, all department chairpersons or area supervisors should be contacted to enable another group to use the facility. The calendar must be a working calendar and kept up-to-date by the athletic director. Form 7-1 is used as an example of a master calendar for the use of the swimming complex at Parway School District, Chesterfield, Missouri. Form 7-2 charts an alternate sports season plan. Although this is used for the junior high school students in Cedar Rapids, Iowa, it is an excellent "master schedule" for the complete use of facilities on a year round basis. Form 7-2 also shows an example of gymnasium utilization.

Flexibility in Utilizing Existing Space

Over the years coaches have been flexible in finding space for their various activities. One such way is "developing a mental flexibility toward locating space for our programs," says Coach Harry Chap-

FORM 7-1 Master calendar for the use of the swimming complex. (Don Sparks, Director of Athletics and Activities, Parkway School District, Chesterfield, Missouri. By permission.)

TIME	MONDAY	TUESDAY	WEDNESDAY	THURSDAY	FRIDAY	SATURDAY	SUNDAY
5:30-7:30 a.m.	COMMUNITY SCHOOL SWIM PROGRAM A.A.U. (Older age groups)					Community School Program 6:30-8:00 a.m.	NO scheduled program
7:30-2:30 p.m.	SENIOR HIGH PHYSICAL EDUCATION PROGRAM *Senior High Schools schedule practice sessions during the holidays in this time period.					Community School Learn-to-Swim Program 10:30-2:30 p.m.	Pool Maintenance & Filtering Time Parkway Handi-capped Program 12:30-2:00
2:30-5:30	SENIOR HIGH SCHOOL SWIM & WATER POLO PRACTICES Intramurals & School Programs					Community School Swim Program A.A.U. All Age 2:30-6:00	Community School Open Swim 2:00-5:00
5:30-7:30	COMMUNITY SCHOOL SWIM PROGRAM A.A.U. all age groups						
7:30-9:30	Community School Learn-to-Swim Programs	Junior & Senior Life-Saving	Adult Swim Lessons	Adult Swim Lessons	Community Family Swim	Recreation and Maintenance (no regular schedules)	Recreation & Mainte-nance (no regular schedules)

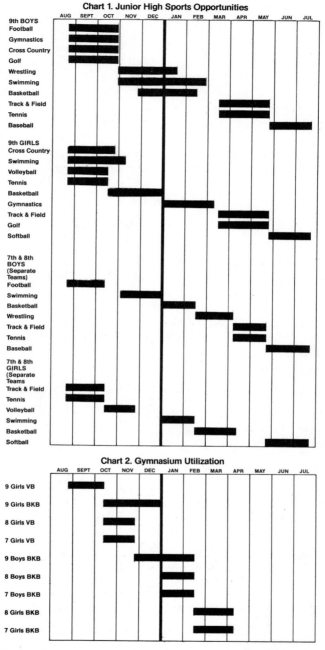

FORM 7-2 Alternate sports season plan. (Tom Ecker, Cedar Rapids (Iowa) Community Schools. By permission.)

man,[1] Cumberland Valley High School, Pennsylvania. "Our physical conditioning program utilizes four separate stations located in unusual areas around the school. The station for conventional weights is in the hallway outside the boys' physical education locker room. The station for quickness and agility is in the main gymnasium lobby. A weight machine constitutes the third station and is located in a converted storage room. The fourth station, the exergenie station, is tucked away behind the folding bleachers on the upper deck of the gymnasium.

SCHEDULING INTERSCHOLASTIC ATHLETIC CONTESTS

Before discussing the actual format for scheduling athletic contests or events and without debating the issue, the concept of "student" teams should be mentioned. It is likely to become a reality in the near future, if it is not already taking place, that there will be one team, called a "student" team, for many of the interscholastic athletic programs. As the implementation of Title IX progresses, there may be one track team or one golf team, one swimming team, one tennis team for all students, regardless of sex. This would indeed be beneficial in scheduling contest and practice facilities. There is also the possibility that there will be some coed mixed teams such as three girls and three boys on a volleyball team, a swim relay team, or mixed doubles in tennis. By law now, girls cannot be denied membership on a boys' team if they have the ability and there is no girls' interscholastic team in that sport. Although there is a time limit for the implementation of Title IX, the process will be slow. Any change that comes so rapidly creates many problems. For the present at least, there will be student teams for girls and boys and the scheduling of contest and facilities will still have its innate problems. If it develops that there is only one interscholastic team in a given sport, this will negate some participation that, in our opinion, is not the intent of Title IX.

Experimental Scheduling

Conferences and leagues are currently experimenting with various combinations of scheduling interscholastic athletic events and contests. One example is where boys and girls have the same season, such as track. In this situation, it has been found practical to have both teams practice at the same time and hold the meets simultaneously.

This type of scheduling is becoming popular in sports where there is a relation of similarity or analogy of activities for boys and girls. The scheduling of girls' and boys' basketball games on the same day or night is another example of better utilization of facilities. Another method of scheduling is the dove-tailing of seasons, such as boys' golf in the spring and girls' golf in the fall; girls' tennis in the fall and boys' tennis in the spring. As mentioned above, the advent of Title IX and the talk of "student" teams will bring about changes in the scheduling process.

Options for Scheduling Interscholastic Programs

There are many combinations and options for scheduling athletic programs. There are many variables, such as the number of teams, type or facilities, weather conditions, and other factors inherent in each school. The scheduling challenge has certainly become the number one concern, especially with the emergence of girls in the interscholastic athletic program, lack of funding, transportation problems, and lack of adequate facilities in which to hold the various events.

In order to achieve a high degree of success, there must be coordination, cooperation, and reasonableness between all parties concerned. Unless the athletic director is concerned with the total athletic program and is concerned with the welfare of all students, regardless of sex, there will be problems. The athletic director must hold regular staff meetings in order to maintain lines of communication and set scheduling objectives and priorities that are approved and adhered to by all.

ATHLETIC ASSOCIATION REGULATIONS

State athletic associations have specific regulations with respect to scheduling athletic contests to effect a relative equal distribution of sports participation throughout the school year. Factors that are used in developing seasons of sports might include:

□ Maximizing the use of school facilities.
□ Developing a season of sport that corresponds to state championship competition.

- Typical climatic conditions of a specific season.
- Maximizing the potential for gate receipts.
- Separating sports that appeal to the same students.
- Precedence of both boys' and girls' varsity competition over non-varsity competition.
- The number of participants involved.
- The traditional time of the year for a particular sport.
- Date for the first practice session; number of days prior to the first contest; date the first contest may be scheduled.
- The end of the season date, including section, state playoffs, and invitational tournaments.
- The maximum number of games or contests per season, per week.

Future factors that may influence the determination of sports seasons are:

- Title IX regulations
- Society's changing concept of sex role patterns, that is, changing concept of masculinity and femininity.
- Changes in student interest.
- Expanded intramural offerings.
- Constraints such as funding, facilities, coaching, transportation, officials, and supervisory personnel.
- Concurrent boys' and girls' sports seasons.
- Combined boys' and girls' practicies and concurrent seasons.
- Coed teams (requiring a specific number of boys and girls on each team).
- Mixed teams (student teams) consisting of both boys and girls, according to ability level.

Forms 7-3 and 7-4 from the California Interscholastic Federation, San Diego Section, are examples of regulations for the season of sport.

Forms 7-5 and 7-6 are a proposed season of sport model presented by the North Coast Section Board of Managers, California Interscholastic Federation, January 17, 1976.

Scheduling of Nonleague Contests

There are some definite guidelines in a scheduling nonleague contest that must be considered by the athletic director. In most cases, the coach of a particular sport, especially a veteran coach, will have de-

By Permission: Don Clarkson, Commissioner
San Diego Section, CIF
9449 Friars Road, San Diego, Ca 92120

California Interscholastic Federation, San Diego Section

Interscholastic Athletic Schedule—*Boys*

1975-1976

Season	Sport	Earliest Date for Beginning Practice	Earliest Date for First Game	Date for Last Game	Number of Weeks in Regular Schedule	Tentative Playoff Schedule
Fall	Football	September 1	September 19	November 14	9	November 21, 28 December 5, 12
Fall	Cross country	September 1	September 19	November 14	9	November 19, 26
Fall	Water polo	September 1	September 19	November 14	9	November 17 to 22
Winter	Rifle	November 17	December 2	February 20	10	February 23 to 28
Winter	Basketball	November 17	December 2	February 20	10	February 23 to 28
Winter	Wrestling	November 17	December 2	February 13 (League finishes February 20)	10	CIFSD February 27 to 28 State March 5, 6
Winter	Soccer	November 17	December 2	February 13	9	February 17 to 28
Spring	Track	February 23	March 5	May 7 (League finishes May 14)	9	CIFSDS Preliminary 5/22 CIFSD Finals 5/29 State June 5, 6
Spring	Baseball	February 23	March 5	May 21	10	May 25 to 29
Spring	Tennis	February 23	March 5	May 14	9	Team 5/17 to 5/21 Individual 5/25 to 5/29
Spring	Golf	February 23	March 5	May 14	9	Team May 21 Individual May 17
Spring	Swimming	February 23	March 5	May 7	8	May 11, 14
Spring	Gymnastics	March 8	March 26	May 21	8	Finals May 28

FORM 7-3 Regulations for the season of sport. (Don Clarkson, Commissioner, San Diego Section, California Interscholastic Federation. By permission.)

By Permission: Don Clarkson, Commissioner
San Diego Section, CIF
9449 Friars Road
San Diego, Ca 92120

Form 7-4

APPROVED   California Interscholastic Federation, San Diego Section

Interscholastic Athletic Schedule—*Girls*

1975-1976

Season	Sport	Earliest Date for Beginning Practice	Earliest Date for First Game	Date for Last Game	Number of Weeks in Regular Schedule	Tentative Playoff Schedule
Fall	Swimming	September 1	September 19	November 14	9	November 22
Fall	Tennis	September 1	September 19	November 14	9	Team 11/17 to 11/21 Individual 11/24 to 11/29
Fall	Volleyball	September 1	September 19	November 14	9	November 17 to 22
Fall	Badminton	September 1	September 19	November 14	9	November 17 to 22
Winter	Field hockey	November 17	December 5	February 20	9	February 23 to 27
Winter	Softball	November 17	December 5	February 20	9	February 23 to 27
Spring	Basketball	February 23	March 5	May 14	9	May 17 to 22
Spring	Gymnastics	February 23	March 5	May 14	9	May 21
Spring	Track	February 23	March 5	May 7 (League finals May 14-May 18)	9	CIFSDS Preliminaries 5/22 CIFSDS Finals 5/29 State June 5, 6

FORM 7-4 Regulations for the season of sport. (Don Clarkson, Commissioner, San Diego Section, California Interscholastic Federation. By permission.)

IV. Proposed Season of Sport model

	First Practice (Not Earlier Than)	First Game	Last Regular Season Game	Desirable Number of Games per Week	Final Post-season Competition	Maximum Number of Games per Season
Fall						
Cross country student and girls	Day after Labor Day	Third full week in September	First full week of November	2	Third full week in November	12
Girls tennis	Day after Labor Day	Third full week in September	Second full week of November	2	Third full week in November	14
Student water polo	Day after Labor Day	Third full week in September	Second full week of November	2	Third full week in November	14
Student football	Twenty-one calendar days Before first game	Third full week in September	Second full week of November	1	Last week-end in November	9
Girls volleyball	Day after Labor Day	Third full week in September	First full week of November	2	Second full week in November	16
Girls gymnastics	Day after Labor Day	Third full week in September	Second full week of November	1	Third full week of November	9

Winter

Student basketball	Third full week in November	Fifth Monday in November or first Monday in December	Third full week in February	2	Second full week in March	24
Girls basketball	Third full week of November	Fifth Monday in November or first Monday in December	Third full week in February	2	Second full week in March	24
Student wrestling	Fifth Monday in November or first Monday in December	Third full week in December	Second full week in February	2	First full week in March	20

FORM 7-5 North Coast Section, California Interscholastic Federation 1976.

87

IV. Proposed Season of Sport model (continued)

	First Practice (Not Earlier Than)	First Game	Last Regular Season Game	Desirable Number of Games per Week	Final Post-season Competition	Maximum Number of Games per Season
Spring						
Swimming student and girls	Third full week of February	Second full week in March	Second full week of May	1-2*	Third full week in May	14
Track student and girls	Third full week of February	First full week of March	Second full week of May	1-2*	First week-th end in June	14
Badminton girls	Second full week of March	Fourth full week of March	Third full week of May	2	Fourth full week in May	14
Softball girls	Third full week of February	First full week of March	Second full week of May	1-2*	Third full week in May	14
Baseball student	Third full week of February	First full week of March	Third full week of May	1-2*	First week-end of June	20
Golf student	Third full week in February	Second full week in March	Second full week of May	1-2*	Last full week of May	14

88

Sport						
Tennis student	Third full week in February	Second full week in March	Second full week of May	1-2*	Third full week of May	14
Nonvarsity Winter Seasons						
Student basketball	Second full week in November	Third full week in November	Third full week in January	2	None	16
Girls basketball	Third full week in January	Fifth Monday in January or first Monday in February	Second full week in March	2	None	16
Student wrestling	Fifth Monday in November or first Monday in December	Third full week in December	Second full week in February	2	None	16

Definitions and Notes:

Full week—starts on Monday and goes through Saturday.

Weekend—adjacent Friday and Saturday dates.

c—State championship dates determined by State CIF Federated Council.

*—in order to facilitate scheduling make-up games, it is suggested that only one interscholastic competition be scheduled per week late in the regular season.

FORM 7-6 North Coast Section, California Interscholastic Federation 1976.

finite ideas about who the opponents should be. The athletic director should consider the advice of the coach and try to schedule the suggested opponent. The coach should have the best knowledge of the caliber of team that will be returning and will want to adjust the schedule accordingly. The athletic director should, in some instances, advise the coach when it is not feasible to schedule a prospective opponent.

The scheduling of nonleague opponents, especially in football and basketball, may have a definite effect on the type of season a team may have. If a team is "overscheduled" and loses all of its practice or nonleague games, the morale may be so destroyed that it cannot get ready for league games.

If a team is "underscheduled," the team may feel it is better than it really is. This may have a disastrous effect on the coming season. The athletic director and the coach will know in advance, whether they have a veteran team or a young team returning and should schedule accordingly. The idea of playing out of one's class to upgrade the program has worked to the advantage and disadvantage of many coaches. There is no secret system to scheduling nonleague opponents other than a lot of thought and advance planning.

Home or Away Contests

The league schedule, facilities, and financial planning will be the determining factors in scheduling contests at home or at the opponent's school. To develop a home and home arrangement with a school that has a good following and reputation might prove to be wise scheduling. This could be a deciding factor when income from gate receipts is used to underwrite part or all of the athletic program. The prime factor, however, should be to select a team for equitable competition and not the gate receipts.

Loss of Class Time

League contests are usually scheduled to minimize the loss of class time. This same pattern should be followed with respect to nonleague contests also. The distance a team has to travel for a contest should be kept to a minimum whenever feasible. This is not only a deterent for athletes who have to be excused from school to make the trip, but for spectators alike.

How to Locate Suitable Opponents

Most coaching clinics have a games wanted or open-date information board for coaches who are looking for nonleague games. The information usually includes the team: varsity, junior varsity, sophomore or freshmen; date; school enrollment; coach's name and how he can be contacted.

The city newpapers also are a means of contacting opponents. Usually during the latter part of a season, newpapers will publish a "games wanted" list. The athletic director and the coach can then check the league standings and possibly obtain a game program to check the returning lettermen. If possible, the athletic director should make it a point to see the team in action to make a judgment on the caliber of the team and the program.

Another method is for the coaches to exchange game films at the conclusion of the season and decide whether the teams would be comparable. Finally, the state coaching association publication will publish a list of schools looking for games in their winter edition.

GAME POSTPONEMENT POLICY

In the case of a postponement of a contest, usually a football game due to inclement weather, for a night game the decision should be made by 1:00 p.m. on the day of the game. The opposing school should be contacted by the athletic director of the home school by 10:00 a.m. on the day of the game with notification that a postponement may be forthcoming.

The principal and the athletic director of the host school, after conferring with the athletic director and the principal of the opposing school, shall make the final decision. If feasible, the game should be rescheduled at the time of the postponement. For example, if a Friday game is postponed, it should be scheduled for the next day, Saturday, if at all possible. Any further delay, especially in football, would be disruptive to league play. Most states have a period of time in which a football team cannot play two games, usually a period of eight days. This obviously means that if a team cannot make the game up the next day, other arrangements will have to be made. In the case of a nonleague game, the contest may have to be cancelled.

The athletic director, once the game has been postponed, cancelled, or rescheduled, should immediately notify all parties concerned.

In considering a postponement, the coach, athletic director, and principal should consider the following items prior to making a decision:

1. Playing conditions of the field
2. Safe travel for opponents and participants
3. Safe travel for officials, game supervisors, students, and other spectators
4. Damage to playing surface and equipment
5. Safety to the spectators
6. Consideration of band members and uniforms, cheerleaders, and song leaders
7. In the case of a league game, the rescheduling factor

If at all possible, the game should be played if, in essence, the safety of the players is not at stake. Postponement of a contest is always a hardship because of the many factors involved.

CONTRACTUAL OBLIGATIONS

The staging of all athletic events should be preceded by a written contract ratified by the athletic directors and principals of each school. The contract should be concise but comprehensive enough to clarify all contractual agreements between the participating schools. Contracts should be rechecked to be certain that date, time, and location of contest are correct. The coaches should be familiar with the contracted obligations and have a copy of the contract on hand prior to the contest involved.

Contracts should be initiated by the host school and signed by the athletic directors and principals of the participating schools. Basic information should include classification of team, that is, varsity, junior varsity, sophomore; date, time, and place of contest. The financial arrangements should be spelled out in detail. For example: "The home team agrees to pay the visiting school the sum of $xxx.xx and make further provisions as stated herein." Form 7-7 is a sample contract used in interscholastic athletics.

Additional information on a more formal contract would state: that the rules of the state association of the home school apply; the names of officials who have been assigned to the contest; the service the home team will supply, such as supervisors, public address system, scoreboard, timer, etc.; the right of postponement and rescheduling of the contest; cancellation of the contract because of

AMOS ALONZO STAGG SENIOR HIGH SCHOOL
1621 Brookside Road
Stockton, California 95207
ATHLETIC CONTEST CONTRACT

Stockton, California _____, 19 ___

This AGREEMENT entered into on the _____ day of _____, 19 ___

between Stagg senior High School and _____ High School for

a _____ game to be played at _____ p.m.

at _____, California, on _____, 19 ___.

Each player must be eligible to compete in accordance with C.I.F. rules.

Both parties agree to the following terms:

1. If either team fails to appear at the scheduled time the school represented by that team shall pay $ _____ to the other school.

2. This contract can be changed only by mutual consent of the two parties concerned.

3. _____

_____

_____

Signed this _____ day of _____, 19 ___.

Stagg Senior High School vs. _____ High School.

STAGG HIGH SCHOOL   _____ HIGH SCHOOL

By _____   _____
         Principal   Principal

_____   _____
    Athletic Director   Athletic Director

_____   _____
       Coach   Coach

Please sign and return one copy to:
Stagg Senior High School
1621 Brookside Road
Stockton, California 95207
c/o C. T. Haan, Principal
                                      By Permission

FORM 7-7 Sample contract used in interscholastic athletics. (C. T. Haan, Principal, Stagg High School, Stockton California. By permission.)

disbandment of a team and the failure to agree upon officials.

Contracts throughout the states vary in content. For example, the Pennsylvania Interscholastic Athletic Association uses a very formal contract for its contest, which includes much of the above information (Form 7-8).

Easton Area High School, Easton, Pennsylvania uses a master chart (Form 7-9) for recording contracts. This form includes participating school, date, time, place, date contract was mailed, date copy was received and, in the case of a contest where the other school is the host school, the date their contract was received, and the date the signed copy was returned to the school.

Easton Area High School sends out copies to all concerned parties once the schedules have been confirmed.

SCHEDULING AND ENERGY CRISIS

Diane Morrill, Kendall Sports Research Analyst, writing in the *Kendall Sports Trail Magazine*[2] stated, "The energy crisis and the growing realization of the need to conserve resources has had a dramatic impact on the athletics programs at both high school and college levels."

In a survey conducted among *Sports Trail* readers it was found that "in addition to cut-backs in heat and light, many schools found it necessary to modify their athletic programs. Approximately 26 percent reported the necessity of re-scheduling games and 19 percent were forced to cancel some games altogether."

Some of the steps taken to relieve the problem according to the survey were, "Approximately 25 percent state that activities were combined to allow two or more teams to travel together. Seventeen percent were scheduling games closer to home." Although the energy crisis may not be permanent, it indicated to athletic directors and principals ways and means of conserving through proper and new methods of scheduling contests.

Questions

1. Enumerate factors or elements an athletic director should take into consideration in building schedules for the interscholastic athletic program.
2. How are priorities determined in the scheduling of activities so

Contract for Games Under P. I. A. A. Rules

(Revised September 1, 1961)

This contract made in duplicate this _____ day of _____ 19_____

between the Principal of the _____ High School

and the Principal of the _____ High School

WITNESSETH.

1. That the contracting parties agree that _____ game _____ , meet _____ , contest _____ of _____
   (Number)

held _____ Junior Varsity

shall be played between the _____ Varsity _____ teams of their respective High Schools under the following conditions:

(a) That the term of this contract shall be for _____

(b) That the date or dates of the game _____ , meet _____ , contest _____ shall be _____
_____ . Subject to provision for postponement set forth as an addenda to this
contract and incorporated herein by reference.

(c) That the time of game _____ , meet _____ , contest _____ shall be _____

(d) That the place of the game _____ , meet _____ , contest _____ shall be _____

(e) That the guarantee shall be as follows: _____

2. (a) That in accordance with P. I. A. A. By-Laws, Article XIV, Section 1:—

   MAJOR OFFICIALS MUST BE APPROVED BY P. I. A. A.
   All major officials, in all interscholastic athletic contests participated in by a member school of the P. I. A. A.,
   shall be persons who have been approved by the Board of Control.

   (b) In accordance with the provisions of P. I. A. A. By-Laws, Article XI, Section 7, the officials shall be agreed
   upon at least fifteen days prior to the date of the game _____ , meet _____ , contest _____ .

   (c) That the cost of the officials shall be borne by: _____

   (d) That the final decision of the major officials shall be accepted without protest by both contracting parties.

   (e) That in case of failure to agree upon officials fifteen days prior to the date or dates of the game _____ , meet _____ , contest _____ the provisions of the P. I. A. A. By-Laws, Article XI, Section 7, relative to the appointment of officials by
   the Chairman of the District Committee and the Executive Director of the P. I. A. A. shall apply.

3. That the following sections from the P. I. A. A. By-Laws, Article XI, Sections 4, 5, 6 and 7 are thoroughly understood
   by both contracting parties and apply to the game _____ , meet _____ , contest _____ designated in this contract.

   Article XI
   Section 4. **CONTRACTS OF SUSPENDED SCHOOLS NULL AND VOID.**
   A. The suspension of a school from the Association shall render its contracts with member schools null and void.
   B. The legal withdrawal of a school from the Association, approved by the Board of Control, shall render its contracts
   with member schools null and void.

   Section 5. **CANCELLATION OF CONTRACT.**
   In case of cancellation of contract or failure on the part of any one of the contracting parties to fulfill any of the terms
   of the contract, except by written mutual consent, or due to the suspension of one of the schools, the offending
   school shall be suspended from the P. I. A. A. for a period of one calendar year from the date of suspension.

   Section 6. **CANCELLATION OF CONTRACT DUE TO DISBANDMENT OF TEAM.**
   In case the failure to play a game as scheduled should be due to the disbandment of either team by the principal, the
   penalty may or may not be imposed, provided that the principal immediately notifies the District Committee, the Board
   of Control and the Faculty Manager of such teams as his team is scheduled to play, stating the reason for disbandment.

   Section 7. **FAILURE TO AGREE UPON OFFICIALS FOR GAMES.**
   In case of failure of the contracting schools to agree upon the officials fifteen days prior to the date of the game, it shall
   be the duty of the principals of the two contracting schools to notify the District Chairman of such failure. The District
   Chairman shall then appoint the officials for the game, and the fees of the said officials shall be borne by the schools as
   originally agreed in their mutual contract. In case, the game is scheduled between schools located in different districts,
   the Executive Director of the P. I. A. A. shall appoint the officials.

Signed:

_____ Principal _____ High School

_____ Principal _____ High School

Postscript:—(To be filled in at least fifteen days before the date set for game _____ , meet _____ , contest _____)

It is agreed that the following persons shall act as major officials in the game _____ , meet _____ , contest _____ scheduled above.

(1) _____ (2) _____

(3) _____ (4) _____

Signed _____ Principal _____ High School

Signed _____ Principal _____ High School

_____ 19_____

ADDENDA

"The home team reserves the right to postpone the game if weather conditions indicate that the playing of such game would
cause undue damage to the playing surface. A new date for the playing of the game will be set by mutual agreement of the
principals of the respective schools."

Signed _____ Principal _____ High School

Signed _____ Principal _____ High School

_____ 19_____

FORM 7-8 Formal contract for interscholastic competition. (Pennsylvania
Interscholastic Athletic Association. By permission.)

95

EASTON AREA HIGH SCHOOL ATHLETIC DEPARTMENT

GAME CONTRACTS

School	Date Assigned	Place	Time	Request Mailed	Received		Our Contracts		Their Contract	
					yes	no	sent	rec'd	rec'd	ret'd

By Permission:
John B. Maitland, Director
Health, Physical Education and Athletics
Easton Area School District
Easton, Pennsylvania 18042

FORM 7-9 Master chart for recording contracts. (John Maitland, Director of Health, Physical Education and Athletics, Easton Area School District, Easton, Pennsylvania. By permission.)

FRESHMAN WRESTLING 1973-1974

SHULL

Saturday	December 15	Bethlehem Catholic	Away	10:00 a.m.
Wednesday	December 19	Warren Hills	EJHS	3:30 p.m.
Thursday	January 3	Easton B	EJHS	3:30 p.m.
Wednesday	January 9	Easton A	EJHS	3:30 p.m.
Wednesday	January 16	Easton B	Shull	5:00 p.m.
Wednesday	January 23	Phillipsburg	EJHS	3:30 p.m.
Wednesday	January 30	Easton A	EJHS	3:30 p.m.
Wednesday	February 6	Phillipsburg	EJHS	5:00 p.m.
Wednesday	February 13	Saucon Valley	EJHS	5:00 p.m.

EASTON A

Friday	December 14	Warren Hills	Away	4:00 p.m.
Saturday	December 22	Bethlehem Catholic	EJHS	10:00 a.m.
Thursday	January 3	Phillipsburg	EJHS	5:00 p.m.
Wednesday	January 9	Shull	EJHS	3:30 p.m.
Wednesday	January 16	Phillipsburg	Shull	3:30 p.m.
Friday	January 18	Saucon Valley	EJHS	3:30 p.m.
Wednesday	January 30	Shull	EJHS	3:30 p.m.
Tuesday	February 6	North Hunterdon Regional	EJHS	3:30 p.m.
Wednesday	February 13	Warren Hills	EJHS	3:30 p.m.

EASTON B

Wednesday	December 12	Phillipsburg	EJHS	3:30 p.m.
Saturday	December 15	Nazareth	Away	10:00 a.m.
Thursday	January 3	Shull	EJHS	3:30 p.m.
Friday	January 4	North Hunterdon Regional	Away	3:45 p.m.
Wednesday	January 16	Shull	Shull	5:00 p.m.
Saturday	January 19	Bethlehem Catholic	Away	10:00 a.m.
Friday	January 25	Saucon Valley	Away	3:30 p.m.
Wednesday	January 30	Phillipsburg	EJHS	5:00 p.m.
Wednesday	February 6	Warren Hills	Away	4:00 p.m.

COACHES

Shull	Stephen Miller
Easton A	Gene Smith
Easton B	Thomas A. Bubba

RULES AND REGULATIONS

1. Except for the matches otherwise specified, all wrestling will be held in the Easton Junior High School gymnasium, 12th Street. When two matches are held on the same day, the first match is 3:30 p.m., the second match at 5:00 p.m. Wrestlers from the 5:00 p.m. match are expected to assist in putting mats away at the conclusion of that match.
2. Weigh In: At the respective schools at *lunchtime* under supervision of the coaches. A signed list of contestants and weight classes must be exchanged between coaches before the match. When a match is held on a Saturday, weigh in will be at the host school one hour before match time.
3. Weights shall be regular high school weights, that is, 88, 98, 105, 112, 119, 126, 132, 138, 145, 155, 167, 185, 250.
4. Time of periods shall be 2—2—2.
5. Parental permission slips and doctor's examinations are required.
6. Any ninth grade boy who did not attain his 16th birthday before November 1973, and who maintains a passing grade in three major subjects is eligible to compete.
7. Eligibility sheets are to be exchanged between contestant schools per NJIAA and PIAA rules.

By Permission John Maitland. See Form 7-10.

FORM 7-10 Confirmation of scheduled events. (Easton Area School District. Easton, Pennsylvania. By permission.)

97

that, as an illustration, basketball, gymnastics, and wrestling contests are not scheduled in the same facility at the same time?
3. Enumerate the factors you should take into consideration in
   building the athletic schedule for a contact team sport such as
   football; for a noncontact sport such as track and field.
4. Defend and justify your "overscheduling" in football and basketball, wherein your school receives sizable guarantees that benefit
   the overall athletic program.
5. Enumerate valid reasons for postponing and cancelling athletic
   contests other than for adverse inclement weather.

REFERENCES

1. Chapman, Harry, Cumberland Valley High School, Mechanicsburg, Pennsylvania, "*Idea Exchange-Flexibility,*" *Interscholastic* Athletic Administration
   Magazine, Vol. 1, Winter 1974.
2. National Federation of State High School Associations. Spencer Marketing
   Services, New York, N.Y., 10017. By permission.
3. Morrill, Diane, Kendall Sports Research Analyst, "*Athletics and the Energy
   Crisis,*" *Kendall Sports Trail Magazine*, September-October, 1974, p. 8.
   Kendall Company, Sports Division, 20 Walnut Street, Wellesley Hills, Massachusetts. By permission.

SUGGESTED READINGS

1. Forsythe, P.E. and Keller, I. A., *Administration of High School Athletics* 5th
   edition, p. 131, Prentice-Hall, Englewood Cliffs, N.J., 1972.
2. Grieve, A.W., *Directing High School Athletics*, Prentice-Hall, Englewood
   Cliffs, N.J., 1963, Ch. 5.
3. Long, Edwin, Phoenix Union High School System, *Athletic Manual* 12th
   ed., 1973.
4. Purdy, Robert L. *The Successful High School Athletic Program* Parker
   Publishing, West Nyack, N.Y., 1973, Ch. 9, Scheduling.
5. O'Dell, Griffith C., Director of Interschool Athletics (Retired) Minneapolis
   Public Schools, Minneapolis, Minnesota, *Department of Interschool Athletics
   Manual*, 1973-1974.

Chapter 8
Planning and Management of Athletic Facilities

The trend toward increased activities and participants has brought about the realization that in planning any new facilities or adding to the existing facilities, cooperative planning is necessary. The trend in school construction emphasizes that the Director of Athletics, Director of Physical Education, Director of Recreation and others vitally concerned should be members of the building planning committee.

Boards of education have come to realize that the original planning of facilities did not take into consideration the growth of activities and participants in physical education, athletics, and recreation. As emphasized in *Planning Areas and Facilities for Health, Physical Education and Recreation,*[1] "The widening impact of athletics, public recreation and physical education has aroused public consciousness to the importance of more and improved provision for programs and services in athletics, physical education and recreation. It has also directed attention to the unmistaken need for additional areas and facilities to meet the growing demand to enable these programs and services to function fully and effectively."

In regard to interscholastic athletics, the athletic director should participate in planning and procurement of facilities for the athletic program. All available resources should be used in promoting understanding and support for procurement of needed facilities. The athletic director should be the determining factor in the scheduling of all facilities in cooperation with the physical education department chairman, the recreation director, and proper administrative authorities. Once the program is in effect, the athletic director is responsible to see that the facilities are properly maintained.

THE COMMUNITY SCHOOL CONCEPT

In the early stages of planning a new facility or enlarging the existing facility, the subject always turns to the financial question. Where will the money come from? Local school finance issues have become increasingly difficult to pass. As the issues fail, school boards, in responding to the taxpayers, have been eliminating athletics and athletic facilities from the ballot with increasing frequency. In some cases, the ballot has two items, one for classrooms and one for athletic facilities. In effect, the voters have an option of cutting out the "frills"; they end up voting for the classroom and the needed school budget rather than for the much needed athletic facilities. This is another way for boards of education to satisfy the local taxpayers, yet a disservice is being done to physical education, interscholastic athletics and recreation.

One way to combat the possibility is the Community School concept in which all the facilities are developed for the total community. Dr. Robert T. Bronzan, Professor of Physical Education at California State University, San Jose, California, in his article, "Planning New Facilities," *Interscholastic Athletic Administration Magazine,* [2] says "Planning a school in the traditional way and concept assures several things: mediocrity, isolation from the community and failure to provide opportunities and experiences of the time. Planning schools for students only is a gross error. Schools should be planned for all, from the pre-school child to the retired worker or homemaker. Good modern school planning will provide all citizens with continuous learning and leisure opportunities. This requires the changing of a public school into a community school. The community school concept is to make the school extend itself from the more traditional role of merely providing educational services solely for the young, to one of being a total human resource center for all age groups."

Local tax issues and bond issues will have a better chance of passing with this concept because of the public's increased interest in its physical fitness image. The facilities will be used from early morning to late at night.

The emphasis on youth athletic and recreation programs, the modern physical education programs, the increased number of athletic teams for boys and girls, and the increased activity for adults in their leisure time make the need for new and expanded facilities a necessity in every community. The local taxpayers who realize that they will benefit from the facilities will have a more positive attitude when it comes time to vote for a tax increase or pass a school bond issue.

THE PARK-SCHOOL COMPLEX

Equally as adaptive as the Community School Complex is the Park-School Complex, which is part of the trend toward providing areas that serve the educational, athletic, and recreational needs of the community. The Park-School is a new concept that may be the most desirable type of facility in the local neighborhood. It combines the neighborhood recreational area and the elementary school site, the community recreational area and the secondary school site. As stated in the "Facility Planning Guide,"[3] "The Park-School is an example of cooperative action between school and municipal authorities. In addition to the resulting economy in land acquisition and use, construction, operation and maintenance, it represents a wholeness of environment in which integrated living in education, recreation and community life takes place."

PLANNING FACTORS

The "Facility Planning Guide"[4] outlines the guiding principles associated with total planning. They are as follows:

Every community needs areas and facilities for physical education, athletic and recreation programs. Every community requires a master plan based on a study of its needs. The type, location and size of essential areas and facilities should be planned in relation to the social and economic characteristics of the community. Areas and facilities should be planned with due regard for the full potential use of existing and available physical resources. Areas and facilities should make possible programs that serve the interests and needs of all the people.

Plans for areas and facilities must conform to state and local regulations and, as far as possible, to accepted standards and practice. Close cooperation among all public and private agencies concerned with the location acquisition, development and operation of areas and facilities designed for athletics, physical education and recreation is of the utmost importance. All interested organizations, individuals and groups should have an opportunity to share in the planning of areas and facilities intended for public use. Full use should be made of the knowledge and experience of individuals who are qualified to give expert advice and assistance in planning areas and facilities. Every available source of property of funds should be explored, evaluated and utilized whenever appropriate. Widespread publicity, sound interpretation and public discussion facilitate the implementation of area and facility plans.

The need for intelligent and cooperative planning by all those involved in the project is paramount at this time. If the needs of this and the following generations are to be met, long range and imaginative planning must begin now.

PLANNING AND FINANCING FACILITIES
FOR SECONDARY SCHOOLS

Dr. Robert T. Bronzan in his excellent book, *New Concepts in Planning and Funding Athletic, Physical Education and Recreation Facilities*,[5] gives some basic guidelines for planning and financing facilities for physical education, recreation, and athletics at the secondary level. Dr. Bronzan sites the superintendent of schools as the most vital person in planning and financing facilities, followed by the board of education, which must approve or disapprove proposals since they represent the taxpayers of a school community.

Dr. Bronzan details the specific objectives of each person in the building project. The following is a list of those people involved in a secondary school building project: "The school planner, instructions staff, a school or project architect, equipment planner, site finder, general contractor, citizen committee, planning agencies, commercial representatives, reference library, resources center, state, regional sources, State Department of Education, special facility consultants, federal sources."

It has only been during the last few years that our facilities have become outmoded. Today the facilities are used from early morning to late at night by the young and old alike, a prime consideration when planning begins for a new facility should refer to Dr. Bronzan's book. "Attention is given to planning, financing and justifying facilities; interrelationships of philosophies, policies, programs and facilities are clarified. Specifications and functional relationships relating to indoor and outdoor facilities are stressed. Color photographs and graphic materials are included along with an appendix format containing practical check lists for planning indoor facilities, natatoria and stadia."

A survey should be conducted prior to the appeal for funds for a building project. The survey will not only describe the goals and objectives of the programs involved, but will point out the lack of innovations in the program by the inadequate facilities. The survey will also allow the planning committee to meet the needs of the changing community and plan ahead for maximum use of the facilities.

Trends in Planning Modern Facilities

Currently there is an abundance of material available on trends in building modern physical education, interscholastic and recreation areas from the various types of artificial turf to the air-supported bubbles that encompass the entire physical education facility. The name geodesic dome is now synonymous with field house. A specialist must be consulted to determine what type of surface would be the best, whether it be the best, whether it be a synthetic turf such as Astrofurf, a monolithic poured Porturf surface, or one of the many other types now on the market. The University of Idaho has a "roll-on" football field, one that is laid down and removed mechanically. Desinged and engineered by 3M, the 200 by 370 foot unitized peice of Tartan Turf provides a surface for football, soccer, golf, baseball, and other sports normally played on grass. It is rolled out directly over an asphalt base and is rolled up afterwards on a 210 foot long cord of ten gauge steel, eight feet in diameter.

Surfaces for Tennis and Track.   Once it has been decided that there shall be tennis courts and an all-purpose track. the problem for the site engineer and the site planning committee is to decide what surface shall be used. The U.S. Tennis Court and Track Builders have a few suggestions to offer when constructing tennis courts or a track. Form 8-1 is a sample specification guide order form.

Synthetic Surfaces.   The athletic director who is a member of the building planning committee will be concerned with the type of surface to use. The athletic director will quickly realize that the newly developed synthetic surfaces are a wise investment because of their ease of maintenance and long-lasting wear. They will also learn that synthetic surfaces come in a variety of colors and have a resilience that is essential to the health, safety, and welfare of the athlete.

The two most common types of synthetic surfaces are polyvinyl chloride and polyurethane. Polyvinyl chloride is usually manufactured in wide strips and applied to concrete flooring with adhesive or it may be stored in rolls and rolled out when needed. Polyurethanes are either premanufactured or may be poured in place. It would be wise for the athletic director to call on an expert in the field of synthetic surfaces and discuss such items as tensile strength, compression, rebound resilience, and the maintenance factor.

Richard Theibert, University Administrator and member of the

BUILDERS ASSOCIATION

<u>TENNIS</u>

_____Type   I   Fastdry

_____Type   II   Clay

_____Type   V   Portland Cement Concrete

_____Type   VI   Hot Plant Mix

_____Type   VII   Emulsified Asphalt Mix

_____Type   VIII   Combination Hot Plant and Emulsified Asphalt Mix

_____Type   IX   Penetration Macadam

_____Type   XI   Hot Leveling Course & Hot Cushion Course

_____Type   XII   Hot Leveling Course & Cold Cushion Course

_____Type   XIII   Cold Leveling Course & Cold Cushion Course

<u>TENNIS COURT FENCING</u>

_____Type   I   Vinyl Clad Chain Link

_____Type   II   Galvanized Chain Link

<u>TENNIS COURT LIGHTING</u>

_____Type   I   Lighting Outdoor Tennis Courts

_____Type   II   Lighting Indoor Tennis Courts

_____<u>TENNIS COURT REPAIR GUIDE</u>

<u>TRACK</u>

_____Type   I   Cinder

_____Type   II   Natural Clay Running Tracks

_____Type   III   Decomposed Granite

_____Type   VI   Expanded Shale

_____Type   VIII   Fired Clay

_____Type   X   Hot Leveling Course & Hot Cushion Course

_____Type   XI   Hot Leveling Course & Cold Cushion Course

_____Type   XII   Cold Leveling Course & Cold Cushion Course

_____Type   XV   Conversion of Existing Pervious to Impervious All Weather Track

FORM 8-1 Specification guide order form. (U.S. Tennis Court and Track Builders Association, Glenview, Illinois. By permission.)

Education Facilities Laboratories team[6] said of synthetics, "One of the most underrated items of our time. They give you an acre of June every day."

EDUCATIONAL FACILITIES LABORATORIES

Harold B. Gores, President of the Education Facilities,[7] is in the business of helping schools and colleges with their facilities problems. EFL is a laboratory that does not give gifts but has made grants for studies in facilities and equipment. Over the years they have studied every facet of the modern physical plant and new equipment ranging from plastic ice for skating, artificial turf for field games, composition floors for track and basketball, all weather facilities for physical education and athletics, buildings that open and close, the use of roof tops for additional facilities, and studied the original aluminum bat that is now commonly used in physical education and athletic activities.

General Gores definitely agrees that "schools should be built not just for children but for people. To be sure, the school must serve the children well, but especially if the school is in the central city, it must serve people of all ages. It is especially incumbent on physical education, health and recreation that this plant and program operate year-round, day and night."

TOTAL UTILIZATION OF FACILITIES

Dr. Dean Stoakes, Superintendent of Glenbard, Illinois High School, (Columbus, Ohio Conference, p.1)[8] offers the following in regard to planning facilities. "The gym or the field house do not belong to the athletic director or a given coach, they are part of the total educational plan and we must cooperate in developing facilities so they can receive total utilization. The athletic director must be concerned as we develop educational facilities and plan future expansion and he must thoroughly understand that if we attempt to totally utilize a building there are such things as music, drama, girl's athletics and other functions that always must be considered."

Robert L. Conklin, Director of Athletics and Student Activities for the Denver Public Schools,[9] comments that, "An active complex is the answer to the facilities squeeze. Under a complex committee the following components were suggested for Denver Schools: Enlargement of present stadiums; installation of all-weather track; construction of arena-field house; construction of activities building; construction of a natatorium. Such a mulitple use facility is considered the panacea to these problems: Lack of facilities for large audience activities; poor crowd control at existing facilities; scheduling difficulties; transportation and parking problems."

A county athletic facility committee was established by Superintendent of Broward County Public Schools, Florida, Dr. William C. Drainer. The committee is composed of lawyers, investment brokers, insurance personnel, parents, coaches, athletic directors. principals and newspaper writer. As a result of this broad-based committee, reports Broward County's Director of Athletics, Clarence Noe,[10] "Upgrading of grading of football stadiums and practice fields is meeting little opposition."

Charles R. Dyer, Assistant Director for Athletics, The Dallas Independent School District,[11] "The assessed value of our facilities would be exorbitant if the facilities weren't used constantly, but the posture of the Dallas Superintendent, Dr. Nolan Estes, is to utilize all facilities to their utmost twelve months a year. The main goal of coordinating our athletics program is to assure a lower cost per capita. If this is the mark to measure by, then keep the stadia open, plan activities with an open mind, and sooner or later a bond election will be the proof that what you're doing is right."

THE YEAR-ROUND SCHOOL

Paul D. Rice, Director of the National Council on Year-Round Education,[12] writing on the effect of the year-round school on athletics, states, "If you would consider several recent major changes affecting athletics, the point will start to become clear. First, consider the rapidly expanding interscholastic program for girls. We must now provide sporting season, facilities, equipment and coaching for this area. The problem is enhanced in that these same problem areas already exist for our boy's program. Perhaps an additional three months of school operation will relieve pressures in all or some of the four areas mentioned. Second, the expanded operation time might also allow us to give more attention to intramural programs for all students."

Rice sites some areas of concern that athletic directors and the administration must be aware of:

- State and association eligibility rules related to school attendance during a particular sporting season
- The present structure for setting starting and ending dates for sporting seasons
- Academic requirements
- Provide leadership in cooperative efforts between community recreation organizations and local high schools
- Provide information on federal funding that the Bureau of Outdoor Recreation is making available for joint community/school use

The year-round school is becoming a reality in several states. Texas has passed legislation that makes it mandatory for all its school districts to operate on a quarter system by 1975-1976. The California State Assembly voted in 1973 that a teacher can be assigned to a school operating year around without asking the teacher for prior approval.

MANAGEMENT OF FACILITIES

The proper management, care, and maintenance of facilities is one of the major concerns of the athletic director. Once the planning has been accomplished, the facilities erected, the scheduling of activities completed, competent management must receive high priority.

Most secondary schools have a maintenance and operation department that cares for the cleanliness and safety of the total school plant. More than 50 percent of the total school plant is devoted to physical education, interscholastic sports, and recreation activities. Therefore, the scope of utilization, coordination, maintenance, and repair of the facilities is enormous.

The athletic director must act as a liaison between the maintenance and operation department and the departments of physical education, interscholastic athletics, and recreation. Priorities must be established for the assignment and utilization of facilities and the total program must be the number one priority. The facilities are for student and community use and the maintenance and repair should be so coordinated that maximum use of the facilities is obtained. It is poor management to water or reseed the field during prime use time. Even though the fields must be maintained, it must be realized that the program has priority. In many cases, the maintenance department assumes that its staff is more important and that the program is secondary.

It is beneficial for the athletic director to have a good working relationship with the head of the maintenance department to avoid thses problems .

The athletic director, working with the physical education department chairperson and the recreation director, must be constantly aware of the safety and upkeep of the total facility. This phase of the program should be on the agenda at each staff meeting to avoid the entire staff an opportunity to make suggestions not only for the safety and cleanliness aspect of the facility, but for facility change or expansion to accomodate the ever-expanding curriculam.

A major problem, especially in physical education, is that the students are demanding more elective offerings and do not realize that the existing facilities will not accommodate such a program. The administration of the school that acceded to the wishes of the students must place the expansion and addition of facilities high on the priority list. In the meantime, it is essential that the existing facilities get the maximum use and that the maintenance department must also be in full accord with this plan.

Financing the Maintenance Program

Every secondary school has the same problem. There is never adequate money to do all the things that need to be done. Priorities must be set up on a long range plan so that each area is optimally maintained. If the football field is reseeded one year, the basketball floor should be resurfaced the next year. This should be coordinated by the athletic director, physical education chairperson, and the director of the maintenance and operation department.

The recreation department may be of assistance in the financing of the maintenance since the community uses the facilities to a great extent. Money can be obtained by the local recreation override tax or civic center funds as it is described in some areas. The tax is usually 0.5 cents on the dollar of tax monies collected per capita, which in some communities raises enough money to purchase tennis courts, swimming pools, and share in the upkeep and maintenance of the total program. Most districts have a community committee set up for the distribution of such funds.

Records of Repair and Maintenance. It is highly desirable to keep a record of repair items and maintenance work, other than the daily routine items. Request forms or work order forms for smaller projects should be filed and recorded according to date requested and the item or facility to be repaired. The purpose of this is twofold. It may alleviate the liability factor in case of an accident due to faulty equipment or needed repair. Unfortunately, it is usually the case that two or three requests are necessary before the actual work is accomplished. In the case of a backlog of requests, the duplicate requests may be sent to the principal or superintendent for dispostion in order to inquire why the job has not been completed.

Coordination between the physical education department, interscholastic athletic department, recreation department, and the maintenance and operation department is essential. A detailed schedule for the custodian should be discussed and posted in order to assure harmony in this regard. A sample "Daily Duties" schedule (Form 8-2) has been submitted by Redwood High School, Larkspur, California.

Questions

1. Why is it imperative to maintain accurate records relevant to maintenance and improvement of facilities that are utilized for athletics, physical education, and recreation?
2. Why or why not is it desirable and advisable to involve the staff in planning facilities?
3. Where the Community School concept prevails and facilities are utilized from early morning until late at night, how are priorities determined so that there is no conflict between the school and community organization using the facilities?
4. If the athletic director has the responsibility of "facilities coordinator" in that he schedules all groups and organizations using school facilities, enumerates routine procedures and guidelines for handling all requests.
5. How would you handle this situation? A girls' basketball game has been scheduled in the high school gymnasium for months in advance at 7:00 p.m. on a specific night. A community civic organization telephones you less than a week before the girls' scheduled basketball game with a request they be permitted to use the school's gymnasium for a donkey basketball game for a money-making pro-

DAILY DUTIES

Route Number ___5___   School ___Redwood___

Hours ___8:30—5:00 PM___   Assigned to ___Manuel Nunes___

Lunch ___12:00—12:30___   Day ___Custodian___

On arrival, check pool readings, also during day and back wash when necessary.

Keep pool deck and scum gutters clean daily.

Vacuum pool when needed, brush pool daily, keep rest rooms in pool area clean.

Check boys locker room, coaches shower, and rest rooms clean if needed.

Help keep black doors at gym clean.

Keep curbing at gym and district office cleaned.

During break dust mop boys and girls gym floors, and multi-use rooms between periods.

Police grounds at field, district office, gym and pool area.

Help line athletic fields.

During lunch dust mop boys and girls gym floors and pick up locker room, police gym and pool area and empty trash cans at these areas and girls locker room and take to trash bin.

After last class dust mop boys and girls gym floors and multi-use rooms.

Help keep lockers and walls in locker room free from soil and writing.

Keep shower stalls filled with soap.

Replace lights when needed.

Let down bleachers as required and help with Civic Center and Student Body affairs.

Make minor repairs and report major repairs to the supervising custodian.

Dust mop gym floors before and at half time, between and after all A,B,C, Basketball games.

Other duties as assigned.

FORM 8-2 Custodians daily duties. (Redwood High School, Larkspur, California. By permission.)

ject. After you explain procedures and guidelines for handling the use of facilities, you answer, "No, it can't be done at this late date." Later the superintendent calls and asks why the civic organization's basketball game can't be scheduled in the school's gymnasium at this late date. How do you rationalize and justify your decision?

REFERENCES

1, 3, and 4. *Planning Facilities for Athletics, Physical Education and Recreation*, American Alliance for Health, Physical Education, and Recreation, 1201 16th Street, N.W. Washinton, D.C., 1974. By permission.

2. Bronzan, Robert T., *"Planning New Facilities,"* Interscholastic *Athletic Administration Magazine*, Vol. 1, No. 1, 1974, p. 6. National Federation of State High School Associations, Spencer Marketing Services, New York New York, 10017. By permission of the author.

5. Bronzan, Robert T., *New Concepts in Planning and Funding Athletic, Physical Education and Recreation Facilities.* Phoenix Intermedia Inc., 292 Cherokee Avenue, Saint Paul, Minnesota 55107, 1974. By permission.

6. Gores, H., *New Trends in Athletic Facilities*, Secondary School Administration, American Alliance for Health, Physical Education and Recreation, Washington, D. C., 1969, p. 123. By permission.

7. Theibert, Richard, *Educational Facilities Laboratory*, Secondary School Athletic Administration, American Alliance For Health, Physical Education and Recreation, Washington, D.C., 1969. By permission.

8, 9, 10, and 11. *Interscholastic Athletic Administration*, Vol. 1, No. 1, Winter 1974. National Federation of State High School Associations, Spencer Marketing Services, New York, New York 10017. By permission.

12. Rice, Paul D., Director National Council on Year-Round Education, *"Is the Year-Round Athletic Program Coming?"* 1974, p. 6—7, *Kendall Sports Trail Magazine*, Kendall Company, Sports Division, 20 Walnut Street, Wellesley Hills, Massechusetts.

Form 8-1 *Specification Guide Order Form, U.S. Tennis Court and Track Builders Association*, 1201 Waukegan Road, Glenview, Illinois 60025, 1976. By permission.

SUGGESTED READINGS

Athletic Institute, *Planning Areas and Facilities for Health, Physical Education and Recreation*, Athletic Institute and AAHPER, Chicago and National Education Association, Washington, D.C., 1965.

Bucher, Charles A., *Administration of Health and Physical Education Programs Including Athletics* 6th edition, C. V. Mosby, St. Louis.

Ezersky, Eugene and Theibert, Richard, *Facilities in Sports and Physical Education*, C. V. Mosby 3301 Washington Blvd, St. Louis, Missouri 63103, 1976.

George, J. F. and Lehmann, H. A., *School Athletic Administration*, Harper and Row, New York, 1966, Ch, 10, Facilities.

Purdy, R. L., *The Successful High School Athletic Program*, Parker Publishing, West Nyack, N.Y., 1973, Ch. 7.

PART III
Management Functions: Organizing, Staffing, Coordinating, and Communicating

113

Chapter 9
Certification of Coaches and Athletic Administrators

A major problem facing interscholastic athletes, as pointed out in our survey results in Chapter 1, is the lack of qualified coaches and competent, skilled athletic administrators at the secondary school level.

Arthur J. Gallon,[1] in his book *Coaching-Ideas and Ideals*, points out that,

> One fourth of the interscholastic athletic coaches currently serving in the United States have not had any form of professional training. One reason for this has been the growth in the number of sports currently being offered on the high school level. The obvious reason for the expansion of the number of teams and the number of activities is to provide a greater opportunity for more students to receive the educational benefits derived from an athletic experience. The impact of such expansion has resulted in the need for more coaches.

Dr. Harry Fritz,[2] Dean, School of Health Education, State University of New York, chairman of the task force that conducted the above survey, also pointed out, "Forty one of the states had no specific certification requirement for coaching, only that they be licensed teachers. Since this survey in 1971, most states have been moving toward some type of certification for non-physical education majors and minors."

PROFESSIONAL PREPARATION

It is administratively impossible to employ certified physical educators for every coaching assignment because of the number of men

114

and women coaches required to conduct a interscholastic athletic program properly in a secondary school. There is a definite need for professionally qualified and certified coaches, in addition to physical educators who coach, in the interscholastic athletic program. The nonphysical educator who is certified to coach should be certified to teach in an area other than physical education. This professional versatility is a valuable asset in the secondary school.

Task Force on Certification of High School Coaches[3]

Proposed standards for certification of coaches, who are nonphysical education majors or minors, are considered minimal essentials for certification and are not intended to be applicable for teacher certification in physical education. Suggested standards for coaching certification focus on five essential areas identified by the AAHPER-Division of Men's Athletics Task Force of Certification of High School Coaches.

The five areas are:
- Medical Aspects of Athletic Coaching
- Sociological and Psychological Aspects of Coaching
- Theory and Techniques of Coaching
- Kinesiological Foundations of Coaching
- Psysiological Foundations of Coaching

Concepts, competencies and experiences have been suggested for each of the above areas.

While such a program would not provide a comprehensive physical education background, it would aid in the safety and health protection of the athlete. Leaders of youth would realize and understand the socio-psychological implication of sports participation. It would provide for athletic programs conducted by men and women with properly structured technical information in athletics. Prospective coaches would obtain a thorough knowledge of human anatomy and the mechanics of movement. A knowledge ad understanding of the functioning of the human organism in addition to the above, would help make the coach a better counselor and a more effective leader.

Administrators are pursuing the certification of nonphysical education teachers to alleviate the problem of staffing interscholastic athletic programs. F. Gardner Gillen,[4] Principal, Schenley High School, Pittsburgh, Pennsylvania in his article, *The Principal Looks at Coaches and Their Qualifications*, discusses the dilemma that is occurring on the secondary school level.

It has been the custom over the years for the principals to assign teachers of physical education to various interscholastic coaching posts. The action was justified on the basis that such personnel received special training not only in physical and health education but also in coaching. In recent years, however, the high school principal has been confronted with the dilemma of not having a sufficient number of physical education teachers to cover the many coaching assignments. This situation is typical in high schools throughout the country.

This problem will be compounded in the near future as many of the states are eliminating mandatory physical education programs in the secondary schools and are offering physical education programs on an elective or optional basis. This will actually mean that the need for hiring physical education teachers will diminish as the number of students enrolling in physical education classes decreases. The end result will be that more interscholastic teams will be coached by teachers from other teaching disciplines and the need for certification of coaches will become even greater.

Legal Implications of Certification

The subject of the courts and interscholastic athletics is discussed in Chapter 15; however, it should be pointed out at this point that there are serious legal implications in the area of interscholastic athletics, especially when teams are coaching by noncertified personnel. Howard C. Leibee,[5] former Director of Physical Education, University of Michigan in his article, *Standard of Care in Coaching Sports*, stated:

In spite of the fact that many coaches and physical education instructors have little or no professional preparation in the prevention and care of athletic injuries, the judicial tendency is to measure their conduct against that of a hypothetical coach who has had thorough preparation in coaching techniques, the care and prevention of injuries, and the medical aspects of athletic coaching related to the sport which he coaches. It is established, too, that the employment or assignment of an incompetent individual to function in a specific area constitutes negligence on the part of the employer or assigner. School administrators hiring incompetent personnel as coaches are directly liable for any injury occurring as a result of their negligent choice.

Medical Implications

The medical aspect of interscholastic athletics is discussed in greater detail in Chapter 16. There are serious medical implications for persons who are assigned to coach a sport. Dr. Allan J. Ryan,[6] University of Wisconsin Medical Center States:

> The sports coach who has to depend entirely on others for the knowledge which he should have to promote the health and safety of athletes under his supervision, is in serious trouble.
>
> Most coaches today, however, are anxious to acquire whatever information they can use in this area and attend clinics and enroll in summer courses. Unfortunately, for some, the opportunity has come too late and worthwhile post graduate courses in this area, while increasing, are too few. Regrettably, many become involved in coaching who do not have a basic knowledge of health and safety problems in sports, a background which could have been acquired in the undergraduate professional preparation program. Courses in the care and prevention of athletic injuries and sports medicine must be made available to all those who intend to become coaches and those who become coaches by accident rather than design.

TEACHER PREPARATION INSTITUTIONS

Many of the colleges and universities are now producing some qualified coaches who have majored in a subject area other than physical education. The Southwest Missouri State University, Springfield, Missouri was one of the first universities to recognize the problem of certification of coaches and actually established coaching certification in 1969.

Wayne C. McKinney,[7] Head, Department of Health and Physical Education, Southwest Missouri State University states:

> A required coaching certification has not been adopted in Missouri by the State Board of Elementary and Secondary Education; however, each state college and state university in Missouri is also a legal certifying agency. Each of these institutions offer coaching certification for non-physical education majors who are pursuing Bachelor of Science in Education Degrees.
>
> The following minimum standards for certification of coaches who are

not certified in physical education were utilized in the Missouri State Universities and College to establish programs in the late 1960's and early 1970's.

	Semester Hours
Kinesiology	3
Athletic Injuries	2
Scientific Bases of Conditioning or Exercise Physiology	3
Coaching Theory and a minimum of one year of intercollegiate athletic experience (the latter is optional at each university)	2
Administration of Physical Education or Athletics	3
Sports Officiating	2
Total	15

These have been modified or updated in some universities. For example, Southwest Missouri State University deleted sports officiating in favor of giving the student a choice between Sociology of Sport, Psychology of the Athlete, or Sport in America.

An Ad Hoc Advisory Committee for Minimal Voluntary Coaching Certification Standards of the Missouri State Department of Elementary and Secondary Education passed the following coaching certification statement on April 19, 1974:

Teachers that are certificated in some area other than physical education may meet the standards for a coaching certificate by earning a minimum of 15 semester hours in the following five areas with at least two semester hours in each area:

1. *Medical Aspects:* Athletic Injuries, Sport Medicine (A Course in First Aid would not meet this competency requirement.)

2. *Sociological and Psychological Aspects:* Psychology of Sports, Motor Learning, Introduction and/or Principles of Physical Education and Athletics.

3. *Theory and Techniques of Coaching:* Organization and Administration of Athletics or Physical Education. (At least one sport theory course is required.)

4. *Kinesiological Foundations:* Analysis of Sport Skills, Kinesiology, Biomechanics.
5. *Physiological Aspects:* Exercise Physiology and/or Scientific Bases of Conditioning.

The above criteria were used to follow the recommendations made at the AAHPER's Professional Preparation Conference in 1973 at New Orleans.

An Ad Hoc Committee for Secondary Certification is now studying all extracurricular activity certification proposals, including coaching certification, in the State of Missouri. It is anticipated that coaching certification will also be available through Missouri's State Department of Elementary and Secondary Education in 1976. This organization only certificates approximately twenty percent of the teachers while the State Universities and Colleges award certification to the remaining graduates entering the teaching profession.

State of Oregon—Athletic Coaching Endorsement

Dr. Robert W. Bergstrom,[8] Assistant Dean, School of Health and Physical Education, Oregon State University reports:

The Oregon Legislature has assigned to the Oregon Teacher Standards and Practices Commission the responsibility for a) establishing rules for teacher certification, b) issuing teaching certificates, c) adopting standards for approved teacher education programs, and d) taking disciplinary action against teachers in violation of Oregon statues or performance standards.

In the fall of 1975, TSPC appointed a review committee to make recommendations on the proposal for certification of athletic coaches in Oregon. The involved groups including the Oregon Association for Health, Physical Education and Recreation, the Oregon Coaches Association, the Oregon Association of School Administrators and others comprised the review committee. The proposed certification would include a basic (4 year) and a standard (5 year) requirement. The endorsement would appear on the teaching certificate issued by TSPC.

It is anticipated that adoption by TSPC might occur some time in 1976, with certification becoming mandatory four years after the initial adoption. Teachers presently coaching athletic teams would not be required to achieve the coaching endorsement, but would probably be encouraged to do so. Those teachers who become certificated in 1980 or thereafter would be required to hold the athletic coaching endorsement on their teaching certificate in order to be assigned athletic coaching duties.

Oregon State University Athletic Coaching Minor—Fall 1974

	Semester Hours
Professional activities	4
Care and prevention of athletic injuries	2
Motor development	3
Kinesiology	3
Athletic coaching courses	4
Seminar: Psychology of coaching	3
Seminar: Sports in American culture	3
Physiology of exercise	3
Competitive athletics	3
Elementary human anatomy	6
Physiology	6
Physical education practicum	2
Total	42

ORGANIZATION OF STATE COMMITTEE
FOR CERTIFICATION

Many competent authorities in the field of physical education and athletics have studied the problem of coaching certification and have offered solution, endorsement, registration, or some form of competence requirement for coaches of secondary interscholastic athletic teams. Several states (two of which we have discusses, Missouri and Oregon) are in the process of establishing a program of certification. The problem of nonqualified personnel coaching interscholastic athletic teams must receive high priority. A program must be implemented in those states that have not done so at this time.

A state committee should be formed immediately to establish a program of certification for coaches.

Composition of the State Committee[9]

To insure a broad based representation and valuable input, it is suggested that the composition of the state committee include representatives from the following state organizations:

- State Director of Health, Physical Education, and Athletics
- President of the State Coaches Association
- President of the State Association for Health, Physical Education, and Recreation
- Member of the State High School Athletic Association
- Representative form colleges and universities that prepare majors or minors in health, physical education, and recreation or offer programs of coaching certification
- Member of the state medical association
- Member of the state teachers association
- Member of the state athletic trainers association
- Member of the National Association for Girls and Women in Sport
- Member of the state high school athletic directors association

Duties of the Committee

1. The President of the State Coaches Association will act as chairman and will gather all pertinent information regarding the certification of coaches in the secondary schools. This information should include programs that are now in existence, programs that are about to become effective, suggested programs of the AAHPER Task Force, examples of programs that have been established in colleges and universities, and the recommendations of the state department of education.
2. The chairperson should disseminate this material to committee members and set a date for the committee to meet.
3. At the first meeting, the committee should review the material and determine specific areas that should be included in the program. A final document offering professional preparation in coaching should be drafted; it should be distributed to selected chief administrative officers of colleges and universities, state department of education, and selected individual school districts.
4. Upon input from the key selected personnel as mentioned above, the program should be ready for implementation. Copies of the course content should be sent to all colleges and universities who offer degrees in physical education, with a resolution to the effect that by a given date complete certification plans would be in effect.
5. Resolutions should be drafted and sent to all associations represented on the committee stating that by a given date superinten-

dents or principals must have verification of a coaching credential prior to assigning a person to a coaching position. All head coaches who are not physical education majors or minors must complete approved courses in athletic coaching at a college or university appropriately approved by the state committee. (Usually states, Missouri for example, that implement a program of coaching certification do not make such programs retroactive.)
6. The State Department of Education must enforce certification after a given implementation date if violations occur.

MULTIDISCIPLINARY PROGRAM IN ATHLETIC ADMINISTRATION[10]

With the 1972 fall quarter, Western Illinois University, Macomb, Illinois, initiated a specialized program for those students who desire to become athletic administrators. Students successfully completing the program will graduate with a Master of Science in Physical Education degree with an emphasis in Athletic Administration.

The need for a specific program in Athletic Administration is a direct result of the growth in size and complexity of athletic programs in secondary schools, colleges, and universities. Secondary schools, both large and small, are expanding their athletic offerings in terms of sports and levels of competition. For those programs to be effective and continue to be of educational service, competent leadership is needed.

The major thrust of the Western Illinois University's program in Athletic Administration has been planned to train administrators for athletic programs in secondary schools, colleges and universities. The program represents a multidisciplinary approach involving a joint effort of the Department of Physical Education for Men and Women and the College of Business at Western Illinois University. In addition, numerous elective courses may be taken in various departments of the university.

The Master of Science in Physical Education degree program with an emphasis in Athletic Administration involved earning forty five quarter hours of graduate credit. A core of fifteen hours entails two courses in Physical Education and two courses in the College of Business. Nine to twelve additional hours of elective course work in Physical Education are needed while twelve to fifteen quarter hours of elective courses in the fields of business, education, sociology, speech and psychology are necessary to complete the course work.

OHIO UNIVERSITY'S SPORTS
ADMINISTRATION PROGRAM[11]

Ohio University was the first institution to offer a graduate program conceived to train athletic administrators.

With the expansion of both recreational and spectator sports, the need for capable, highly trained people in sports administration has greatly increased. Ohio University saw this need nine years ago and today is in its tenth year of training quality individuals for careers in administration of sports organizations. The original idea, from Walter O'Malley of the Los Angeles Dodgers, was to train people for professional sports administration, but through the years the program has been expanded. Since 1970 when Dr. William G. Steward became director of the program, the curriculum has been broadened to cover athletic administration at the interscholastic and intercollegiate levels as well as arena, auditorium and recreational management.

The Ohio University's Masters' Degree Porgram in Physical Education, with an emphasis in Sports Administration, is designed to prepare the student for a career in the administration of sports programs at the public school, college or professional level or in other sports related fields.

The program is flexible, interdisciplinary and planned to provide theoretical and practical experiences which meet the needs and interests of individual students. The program is designed so a student may complete the entire program in one calendar year, taking three quarters of class work on campus and spending a minimum of one quarter in an intership program.

ST JOHN'S BACCALAUREATE DEGREE IN
ATHLETIC ADMINISTRATION[12]

Many universities are now offering degrees in sports administration. We have cited two programs, Western Illinois University program in athletic administration and Ohio University's sports administration program and have included the St. John's University's baccalaureate degree program in athletic administration as a further example of the progress that has been made in this area.

The St. John's program is designed to prepare young men and women for challenging careers in the field of Athletic Administration at the community, secondary school, collegiate and professional levels. Sports, on all levels, is one of the most expanding activities in the United States today. The administration of athletic programs requires well educated, dynamic, intelligent and professional individuals with highly refined and sophisticated skills.

In order to insure that the St. John's program will stay abreast with professional developments and practices, the University has formed an Athletic Administration Advisory Council. This Council includes leading executives in all areas of athletic administration. It will provide guidelines on the operation of the program and will insure that the program is not only professional but also relevant to the needs of the athletic administration field. Another unique feature of the program is that it will provide cooperative internship programs to interested students. The internship will give students an opportunity to apply what is learned in class to practical problem solving situations in the field.

All professions, including the teaching profession, have a means of certification for its members. In this chapter we have researched the progress that has been made in some states in the area of coaching certification and professional preparation in sports administration. In our opinion, if athletic coaching and related areas are to attain recognition in the public's mind as a profession making a worthwhile and beneficial endeavor in the field of education, some uniform standards regarding professional preparation and certification of coaches and athletic directors must be adopted on a national basis.

REFERENCES

1. Gallon, Arthur J., *Coaching: Ideas and Ideals*, p.l, Copyright (c) by Houghton Mifflin Company, Boston, Massachusetts, 1974. By permission.
2. Fritz, Harry, *JOHPER (Journal of Health, Physical Education and Recreation)* September 1970. American Alliance for Health, Physical Education and Recreation, Washington, D.C. By permission.
3. Task Force, AAHPER, Division of Men's Athletics, *Certification of High School Coaches.* American Alliance for Health, Physical Education and Recreation, Washington D.C., 1969. By permission.
4. Gillen, F. Gardner, Principal, Schenley High School, Pittsburgh, *The Principal Looks at Coaches and Their Qualifications*, pamphlet, American Alliance of Health, Physical Education and Recreation, Washington D.C., 1971.
5. Leibee, Howard C., former Director of Physical Education for Men, University of Michigan, *Standard of Care in Coaching Sports*, pamphlet, American Alliance for Health, Physical Education and Recreation, Washington D.C., 1971, pp. 17-24. By permission.

6. Ryan, Allan J., M.C., University of Wisconsin Medical Center, Madison, Wisconsin, *What Coaches Should Know about Health and Safety in Sports*, pamphlet, American Alliance for Health, Physical Education and Recreation, Washington D.C., 1971, pp. 23-25.
7. McKinney, Dr. Wayne C. Head, Department of Health and Physical Education, Southwest Missouri State University, Springield, Mo. 65800, Coaching Certification in the State of Missouri, 1976. By permission.
8. Bergstrom, Robert W., Assistant Dean, School of Health and Physical Education, Oregon State University, *State of Oregon Athletic Coaching Endorsement*, 1976. By permission.
9. *California Committee on Safety in School Sports and Physical Education*, January 17, 1975, Los Anteles, California. Al Baeta, Chairman. By permission.
10. Hermann, Dr. George W., Western Illionis University, Macomb, Illinois, *Multidisciplinary Program in Athletic Administration*, 1975. By permission.
11. Steward, William G., *Sports Administration Program Ohio, University*, School of Health, Physical Education and Recreation, College of Education, Athens, Ohio 45701, 1976. By permission.
12. Geis, John F., Director, *Athletic Administration Program*, St. John's university, Jamaica, N.Y. 11439, 1976. By permission.

Chapter 10
Coaching Personnel: Screening, Assigning, and Evaluation

One of the main functions of the athletic director is to assist in the screening, assigning, and evaluation of personnel who are to be responsible for the program of interscholastic athletics.

To accomplish management by objectives, as discussed in Chapter 4 and to accept the responsibility for accountability and implementation, the athletic director must be involved in the process of preparing a position description, setting position specifications, screening applicants, assigning persons to coaching positions, and in the evaluation of the entire coaching staff.

SCREENING APPLICANTS

The trend toward certification of coaches will have a direct effect on the hiring process because the selection committee should be seeking persons who are qualified candidates for a classroom position and who also have a coaching certificate. It is imperative that the athletic director be involved in the selection or screening process and employ the best qualified coach who first must be the best available classroom teacher.

The athletic director must inform the members of the screening committee, prior to the interview of a candidate, of the type of person that is needed to fill the positions in the athletic program. The committee should have the following information:

1. Position description: A written statement that clarifies the duties, relationships, and results expected.
2. Position specifications: This sets the qualifications needed for a specific task, for example, football coach, track coach, basketball coach, etc.
3. Position evaluation: This is the process of studying the position description and position specifications to determine levels of responsibilities for placement on the extra service contract scale or for other methods of compensation.

The candidate for a coaching position and the selection or screening committee must realize that a program of interscholastic athletics presents a limitless opportunity for the coach to guide and develop the interests and abilities of young people.

The interscholastic athletic program furnishes the occasion, under competent leadership, for the molding of personality in a vivid, realistic, and competitive atmosphere. The values of the program of interscholastic athletics are in direct proportion to the quality of the leadership that gives direction to it. Not every person is suited to coaching athletics, and it is erroneous thinking to believe otherwise. Not everyone should be assigned to a coaching position. It is the function of the athletic director to state the guidelines during the screening of the candidate.

PERSONAL QUALITIES OF THE COACH

The selection committee, while seeking a candidate for a particular coaching position, must select a professional person with a sound educational background and personal qualities that will enable him to make a wholesome contribution to the total school community. This must be a person that can relate to the student body, community, administration, faculty and, obviously, to the participants. The selection committee is really looking for a person who will be able to perform with excellence in the classroom and be able to carry out a coaching assignment to the general welfare of all concerned.

Desirable Coaching Characteristics[1]

Should possess a strong interest in their teaching field equal to their coaching interests.

Should demonstrate a willingness to meet, or go beyond, the time demands associated with, but not limited to their sport interest.

Should be willing to commit time and help at the elementary school levels where program development occurs.

Should, since planning and organization are essential for maximum results during practice, pre- and post-season play, be well prepared; and since

Assistant coaches are under the supervision of head coaches, they should receive appropriate direction for maximum utilization of personnel.

Should not view their sport program as an end in itself, but rather as something compatible with youngsters' total educational objectives.

Should be flexible enough to accept new ideas, to alter, when appropriate, what may have been strengths in previous years.

Must be able to transmit knowledge of the sport to participants if execution toward perfection is a desired result.

Must put the athlete above the sport and winning or losing. (Building a program requires that youngsters maintain their enthusiasm. An egocentric coach will have it in reverse order and generally creates a poor learning situation for students. Coaches who recognize and identify this fault will usually have the interest at heart of all squad members, rather than a select few. Squad members are not necessarily team members unless they have been convinced of this by participation as a player.)

Regardless of the wealth of sports knowledge, should be able to maintain rapport with the teaching staff, administration, and most certainly with fellow coaches. (This is reflected in the coach's support of the total educational program, others sports' areas which they are not coaching, and their encouragement to youngsters to gain competitive experience by participation in another sports area.)

Seek and encourage youngsters to enter their sports activities (as opposed to waiting for opening date to handle those who show up).

Have a sports' background from high school and college as a participant, with class work related to coaching and first aid. (Tactical knowledge is important, but not considered the major criteria for selecting coaches).

TITLE IX AND THE HIRING PROCESS

Implementing Title IX regulations will have a definite effect on the screening, hiring, and assigning of coaches. In regard to employment, the Title IX regulations state specifically:[2] "All educational institutions or activities receiving federal assistance must comply with the employment provisions of the regulations. In general, the regulation prohibits: exclusion from participation in, denial of the benefits of or subjection to discrimination on the basis of sex of any person in employment." This essentially means that the best qualified person will be hired to coach a team, regardless of sex. Title IX further states, "In the absence of a finding of discrimination on the basis of sex in an education program or activity, a recipient may take affirmative action to overcome the effects of conditions which resulted in limited participation therein by persons of a particular sex. Nothing herein shall be interpreted to alter any affirmative action obligations which a recipient may have under Executive Order 11246."

AFFIRMATIVE ACTION

Affirmative action,[3] a relatively new concept in the hiring process that has been developed in recent years as the result of federal legislation states, "No discrimination of the basis or race, color, religion, sex, age or national origin will exist in any area of the school district."

It is the policy of school districts to maintain the highest quality. The plan for affirmative action is intended, in ways that are consistent with this premise, to increase the number and improve the relative position and acceptance of minority group members and women.

Goals of the Affirmative Action Program[3]

1. To obtain the commitment and active cooperation of all certificated and classified staff to achieve the goals of this affirmative action program for staff employees.
2. To modify and improve employment programs to assure the adequate representation of minority and female employees throughout the district at all levels of employment.
3. To provide for staff development and training programs with special attention to minority and female staff members.
4. To administer upgrading and promotion functions for all staff members and to provide special assistance to minority and female staff members in moving into positions that are identified as underutilizing women and members of identified minority groups.
5. To study and improve the means of hearing about, responding promptly to, and considering fairly the problems, complaints and grievances of minority, female, and all other staff members.

6. To utilize all appropriate channels of communication to keep all members of the faculty and staff informed of the goals, objectives, responsibilities, and implementation schedules and programs of this affirmative action program and to provide means by which all staff members may submit suggestions, comments, and questions regarding the program.

PROFESSIONAL GROWTH THROUGH INSERVICE TRAINING

The coach should be aware of and receptive to continuous professional growth. The athletic director must work with the coaching staff in developing clinics and inservice programs designed to improve competencies and to foster awareness of continuous change in coaching methods, philosophy, and procedures and to develop a new awareness of our sports environment.

Sources of continuing professional growth encompasses both individual and group endeavors and includes:[4]

1. The study of current physical education and sport literature
2. Professional writing and research
3. Active participation in professional organizations at local, state and national levels
4. Structured visitations to schools and colleges
5. Advanced study
6. In-service seminars and workshops stressing a competency approach
7. Participation in clinics and institutes which emphasize technical advancement in coaching
8. Participation in conferences which stress sports medicine, sport sociology and sport psychology
9. In-service planning sessions using local staff as well as outside consultants
10. Observational evaluation of selected sports contests
11. Self-evaluation through introspection and comparison
12. Coaching forums for the discussion and debate of ideas, experiences and theories
13. The use of instructional media, particularly television and radio
14. Travel study sport programs of national and international scope
15. Coaching material centers to induce personal, school, university and/ or association collections of a wide range of educational information

EVALUATION AND APPRAISAL OF PERFORMANCE

The main purpose of evaluation or appraisal of the coaches' performance is to improve coaching and learning. There are many instruments used to evaluate coaches, such as observation, checklists, and various types of rating charts.

Maxwell Ivey, Director of Athletics for the Atlanta Public Schools[5] states, "What we really need at this time is an acceptable accountability program which includes program goals, performance objectives, continuous supervisory development, evaluation interviewing for the purpose of improving present role performance, assistance to strengthen professional performance and provision for feedback."

There should be a preevaluation conference and a postevaluation conference, especially if corrective steps are to be prescribed. The post-conference dialogue should have a its main goal to lead to the improvement of instruction and should concern itself with the skills and responsibility of coaching duties. It should be prescriptive in nature and must be based on the mutual concerns of the evaluator and the evaluatee.

Observations must be recorded on an evaluation form that would give an accurate appraisal of the individual's efforts toward fulfilling requirements that relate to responsibility and effectiveness. The evaluation is intended to help the evaluator and evaluatee understand and improve coaching procedures.

Measuring Performance by Goals

Dr. Victor Lesch, Director of Physical Welfare for Addison Trail High School in Addison, Illinois[6] has developed a means (Form 10-1) for coaches to measure their performance by their major responsibilities, goals, and target dates for the accomplishment of these goals.

Coaching Appraisal

William Allen, Director of Physical Fitness for School District 27-J in Brighton, Colorado[7] uses the management support system to identify areas of responsibility, procedures that will be used to fulfill those responsibilities, who will be serviced by those responsibilities, and how to determine the extent in which those areas of responsibility are being met. Based on a needs assessment, a Coaches' Assessment (Form 10-2) was formed as a part of the total evaluation of coaches. "In this manner we point out more clearly where a coach needs assistance and improvement or where there is a total difference of opinion about the specific job within the total coaching assignment."

PERFORMANCE GOALS FOR MAJOR RESPONSIBILITIES

(Name) _____   (Date) _____   (position) _____

Major Responsibilities	Goals	Target Date	Measures of Performance
(1) — Recruitment and retention of athletes	— Encourage 50 boys to come out for *wrestling*	— November 15	— Number of athletes out
	— To retain until end of season 35 — To contact returning athletes from previous year	— March — Beginning of season	— Listing of students recorded
(2) — Junior high feeder school encouragement	— Visit and observe two junior high meets or games	— March	— Schedule turned in to Athletic director
— Promote tournaments	— Organize all star junior high basketball game at AT	— March	— Scheduled
(3) — Staff development/ Communication among staff — administration	— Hold minimum of three scheduled staff meetings per season	— March	— Minutes submitted to Athletic director
(4) — Self-development/	— Attend _2_ clinics: (1) N.W. (2) U. of Ill.	— Specific dates	— Material and information on return
— Keep up-to-date with latest professional improvements	— Join an active membership in Coaches Association	— Yearly	— Periodically
(5) — Skill Development/ Wrestling	— Observe wrestler by use of video tape replay	— Weekly	— Use video tape unit
— Gymnastics Team Improvement	— Team score _100_	— First dual meet	— Score increase
	Team score _120_	End of season	
(6) — Locker room supervision	— Establish rotation of locker room duty for each coach		— Master schedule distributed

What must the Athletic Director provide to meet these goals? How can we better improve your program?

By Permission:
Dr. Victor Lesch, Managing Athletic Programs by Goals,
Director of Physical Welfare
Addison Trails High School
Addison, Illinois 60101,
Spring 1975, Vol 1, No. 2, p 18.

FORM 10-1 Measurement of performance by major responsibilities. Goals and target date for the accomplishment of these goals. (Dr. Victor Lesch, Director of Physical Welfare, Addison Trail High School, Addison, Illinois. By permission.)

Form 10-3 was developed as an observation form; it is really a worksheet for the athletic director. The observation form may be filled out at any time during the season and then shared with the coach.

Form 10-4 is a composite of the observation and assessment form and is completed with statements on strength, areas for improvement, and recommendation for future employment as a coach.

Criteria for Evaluation/Appraisal of Coaches[8]

The following checklist may be used as a guideline for observation in evaluating the coaching staff:

1. Obligations to the administration: Supports administration's policy-rules; does not air differences outside department.
2. Obligations to the athletic board: Aware of conduct and promotion of his sport; accepts rulings when they do not concur with his.
3. Obligations to athletic director: Willingness of coach to contribute ideas for improvement of his sport; willingness to accept decisions and uphold them.
4. Obligations to the admissions office: Does not bring pressure on admission office, goes through proper channels.
5. Obligations for eligibilities: Knowledge of rules and regulations; responsible for enforcing rules; does not exert pressure on teachers for grades.
6. Responsibility to injured players: Injuries diagnosed by proper medical authority; accepts decision of doctor without coercion from staff.
7. Leadership example to athletes: Shows exemplary leadership traits: brings credit to his sport through his actions.
8. Statement in publications: Does not rely on newspaper coverage to apply pressure; no direct or implied pressure on administration or players.
9. Conduct during a game: Bench discipline; relationship with officials; relationship with opposing coach and team; control of the game.
10. Knowledge of rules: Knows the rules of his sport.
11. Application of rules: Applies rules in spirit of their intent.
12. Beating the rules: Does not circumvent rules to gain advantage of opponent.
13. Good sportsmanship: Teaches fair play and respect for opponent.
14. Treatment of officials: Respects officials' decisions with control during game.
15. Postgame comments: Does not alibi nor level criticism at players, opponents, or officials.
16. Public relations with sportswriters and sportscasters: Uses discretion in interviews; teaches players respect for information given to press.

Name of Coach _____   Sport Assignment _____   Level _____

Date: _____

		Critical Problem			No Improvement Needed	

I. Professional and Personal Relationships:

1.1 Cooperation with A.D. in regard to submitting participant lists, parent permission and physical slips, year-end reports, program information relative to your sport.   1   2   3   4   5

1.2 Rapport with the athletic coaching staff.   1   2   3   4   5

1.3 Appropriate dress at practices and games.   1   2   3   4   5

1.4 Participation in a reasonable number of professional and in-service meetings.   1   2   3   4   5

1.5 Public Relations: Cooperation with newspapers, radio, T.V., Booster Clubs, parents and interested spectators.   1   2   3   4   5

1.6 Understanding and cooperation with rules and regulations as set forth by all governing agencies of your sport.   1   2   3   4   5

1.7 Parent's night, banquets, pep club, pep assemblies, band, letters to colleges regarding players, and encouragement of students to enter sports for the benefits that can be obtained from participation.   1   2   3   4   5

1.8 Sideline conduct at games toward players, officials and other workers.   1   2   3   4   5

1.9 Works cooperatively with A.D. in budget matters, including coaching salary matters, contracts and related items.   1   2   3   4   5

II. Coaching Performance:

2.1 Develops respect by example in appearance, manners, behavior, language, interest.   1   2   3   4   5

2.2 Supervision and administration of locker and training rooms.   1   2   3   4   5

2.3 Is well versed and knowledgeable in matters pertaining to your sport.   1   2   3   4   5

2.4 Has individual and team discipline and control.   1   2   3   4   5

2.5 Prepares for daily practices with staff so maximum instruction is presented utilizing all opportunities for instruction and plans for contests.   1   2   3   4   5

FORM 10-2 Coaches' assessment. (By permission; see caption, Figure 10-4.)

			Critical Problem				No Improvement Needed
	2.6	Provides for individual as well as group instruction.	1	2	3	4	5
	2.7	Helps other coaches become better coaches.	1	2	3	4	5
	2.8	Develops integrity within the coaching staffs and among fellow coaches.	1	2	3	4	5
	2.9	Is fair, understanding, tolerant, sympathetic and patient with team members.	1	2	3	4	5
	2.10	Is innovative using new coaching techniques and ideas; in addition to using sound, already proven methods of coaching.	1	2	3	4	5
	2.11	Is prompt in meeting team for practices and games.	1	2	3	4	5
	2.12	Shows an interest in athletes in off-season activities and class-room efforts.	1	2	3	4	5
	2.13	Provides leadership and attitudes that produce winners and winning efforts by participants.	1	2	3	4	5
III.	Related Coaching Responsibilities:						
	3.1	Care of equipment, including issue, inventory and storage.	1	2	3	4	5
	3.2	Is cooperative in preparation of non-league scheduling.	1	2	3	4	5
	3.3	Is cooperative in sharing the use of facilities.	1	2	3	4	5
	3.4	Understands place in the line of authority in relationship to: 1. Head Coach—Athletic Director. 2. Head Coach—Assistant Coach.	1	2	3	4	5
	3.5	Shows self-control and poise in all areas related to coaching responsibilities.	1	2	3	4	5
	3.6	Displays enthusiasm and vitality in assignment as a coach.	1	2	3	4	5
	3.7	Keeps Athletic Director informed about unusual events within the sport activity.	1	2	3	4	5
IV.	Developing a Needs Assessment:						
	4.1	Shows a willingness to become involved in developing a Management Support System for the sport, including Task Procedures, and Task Evaluation.	1	2	3	4	5
	4.2	Shows a willingness to establish goals for each sport season and to evaluate whether those goals have been met.	1	2	3	4	5
	4.3	Is willing to conduct a Needs Assessment for the sport activity.	1	2	3	4	5

Coach is to mark "Coaching Assessment" with an "O".
A.D. will mark the "Coaching Assessment" with an "X".

17. Relations with alumni and booster organizations: Are such organizations encouraged to circumvent administrative control? Do coaches give in to alumni or booster club demands?
18. Organization of the sport: Are schedules made and adhered to? Are student-athletes being treated equally?
19. Preparation for practices: Are practices well organized and meaningful?
20. Teaching skill: Does the coach get across tactical as well as technical skills?
21. Enthusiasm and interest: Is the coach optimistic and enthusiastic? Does the coach alibi?
22. Pose and self-confidence: Does the coach possess these qualities?
23. Squad discipline: Does the coach demand and receive the respect of the players? Are rules enforced for all squad members on an equal basis?
24. Tolerance: Is the coach concerned with student problems?
25. Coach-athlete relations: Is there a good coach-athlete relationship?
26. Coaching responsibility: Does the coach accept responsibility along with authority?
27. Does the coach stay abreast of developments in the field by attendance at professional meetings, and by reading professional journals?
28. Does the coach have flexibility in accordance with necessary administrative changes?

BLUEPRINTING YOUR COACHING CAREER

For the individual seriously interested in pursuing or furthering their career in athletic coaching, we recomment reading *Blueprinting Your Coaching Career*. (See Suggested Reading.) This book shows how to take an accurate inventory of your competencies, how to find out about and apply for positions, how to prepare a resumé and prepare for the interview, how to guide an interview to get across your strongest assets, and how to follow up after the interview. It offers suggestions, tips, and techniques that may be utilized to aid you in attaining your professional goal more efficiently and rapidly.

COACH'S AGREEMENT . . . TERMS AND CONDITIONS[9]

Kurby Kyle, Supervisor of Activities/Athletics, Cherry Creek Schools, Colorado, has designed a very successful tool for communication between the coach and the district. "The Coaches' Agreement" is not a contract, but rather a guideline that allows both parties, the coach and the district, to know what is expected in a professional manner. Quite frequently we tell coaches what is expected of them but take much for granted. Without a written agreement, the administrator has nothing to fall back on to help him make necessary adjustments when things don't turn out well."

FORM 10-3   Observation form. (By permission; see caption, Figure 10-4.)

Date: _____

Coach: _____   Sport: _____

Position: _____   School: _____

The prime object of this Observation Form is to serve as a constructive means of helping coaches to improve their coaching competencies.

Where deemed necessary, appropriate assistance or follow-up will be provided by the Director of Physical Fitness.

√ = this item needs strengthening.

I.   **Teaching Personality**
Self control and poise.
Appropriate sense of humor.
Emotional stability.
Vitality and good health.
Enthusiasm in working with students.
Appearance.
Punctuality in attendance.
Voice quality.
English usage (grammar).

II.   **Professional Qualities**
Has harmonious relationship with other staff members.
Participates in staff meetings and discussions.
Upholds departmental and school policies, rules and regulations.
Follows planned prescribed program.
Cooperates with co-teachers.
Willingness to assume extra duties.
Relationship with parents.
Written reports (on time and organized).
Keeps administrative leader informed about sport activities.
Cooperates and develops good relations with other school coaching staffs.

III.   **Team Management**
Prompt in meeting team.
Supervises locker room before and after activity.
Makes maximum time available for instruction.
Utilizes every opportunity for instruction.
Demonstrates care of equipment and facilities.
Team discipline and control (based on respect not fear of reprisal).
Utilization of student leaders as assistants (not in place of the coach).
Commands respect by example in appearance, manners, behavior and language.

IV.   **Coaching Performance**
Well versed in sport matter content.
Provides for individual as well as group instruction.
Is sympathetic; fair, tolerant, and patient with athletes.
Is well versed in and practices safety procedures.
Shows interest in athletes in off-season activities and classroom efforts.

COACHES EVALUATION   Date: _____

Coach: _____   Assignment: _____

Season: _____   School: _____

Number of years coaching in this assignment in District 27-J: _____

Number of years coaching in School District 27-J: _____

Number of years in coaching at the high school level: _____

Strengths:

Areas Needed To Be Improved:

Suggested Recommendations:

General Evaluation of the Coach's performance in this assignment:

	Satisfactory	Probationary	Unsatisfactory

This page
completed by: Athletic Director's Signature: _____

                                         Head Coach's Signature: _____

_____   Coach's Signature: _____

Satisfactory: To be recommended for continued assignment.
Unsatisfactory: Not to be recommended for re-assignment.
Probationary: To be recommended for re-assignment, provided an understanding can be reached in areas where improvement
    is suggested.

FORM 10-4 Composite of the observation and assessment form. (William Allen, Director of Physical Fitness, School District 27-J, Brighton, Colorado. By permission.)

Form 10-5, the Coaches' Agreement, is signed by the coach and the school athletic administrator and filed in the local school athletic office and district activity/athletic office.

Form 10-6 contains the terms and conditions that are required for all coaching assignments.

CHERRY CREEK SCHOOLS

COACH'S AGREEMENT

Duties and Responsibilities

I understand that I will be assigned as the _____

coach at _____ for _____
         School   Period of Assignment
and that the compensation for such assignment will be the amount established

by the appropriate Supplemental Salary Schedule of the Board of Education of

the Cherry Creek School District.

I have been given a copy of, and have read and understand, the terms and

conditions governing assignment of Cherry Creek Schools' coaches and I agree

to abide by, and comply with, all terms and conditions set forth therein.

Agreed to this _____ day of _____, 197___

_____
                                    Coach

Witness:

_____
School Athletic Administrator

Board approved: _____
                  Date

Copies on file:
Local School Athletic Office
District Activity: Athletic Office

By Permission:

Kurby Lyle
Supervisor of Activities/Athletics
Cherry Creek Schools
Englewood, Colorado 80110

FORM 10-5   Coaches agreement. (By permission; see caption, Figure 10-6.)

All coaching assignments are conditional and the following requirements must be met without exception:

1. CERTIFICATION. Athletic coaches must be certificated teachers.

2. ANNUAL ASSIGNMENT. Athletic coaches in the Middle and Senior High Schools shall be assigned annually to coaching duties, which are in addition to other teaching duties, by the Principal, with the approval of the Supervisor of Student Activities and Athletics. Each coach assigned shall be informed by the Principal of the fact that the seasonal assignment(s) is (are) for one year only.

3. BASIS OF ASSIGNMENT. Athletic coaches may be selected and assigned to coaching duties for one or more sport seasons but not to exceed three (3) assignments per year. Renumeration for coaching duties shall be consistent with the Supplemental Pay Policy for the Cherry Creek Schools.

4. PERSONAL JOB DESCRIPTION. Keep an updated copy of the Job Description with the local building Athletic Administrator and attach to this agreement. Take the responsibility to review, correct, or change, with the Principal's approval prior to your activities first event.

5. REPORTING FOR DUTY. All coaches will report for duty on the opening practice dates for their respective sport(s) as set by the Colorado High School Activities Association and/or the Cherry Creek Schools and will perform duties throughout the season for which assigned.

6. PRACTICE TIMES AND SCHEDULES. Practice times and schedules will be submitted to the school Athletic Administrator for approval.

7. RELATED COACHING DUTIES. Related coaching duties must be assumed, that is, assisting with non-league officials, schedules, transportation arrangements, and all sports administrative work. Compensation for coaching also covers related coaching duties including, but not limited to, the following:

    a. Attendance at all meetings called by the League president.

    b. Attendance at all meetings called by the Building Administrator or Athletic Director relative to your position.

    c. Attendance at all pre-season planning meetings.

    d. Attendance at any Cherry Creek Schools' Coaching Clinic.

    Failure to perform these related coaching duties may result in appropriate penalties.

8. PROFESSIONAL ESPRIT DE CORPS. Cooperation is vital in the athletic program. Interference with other sports and activities or an unwillingness to assist fellow coaches can not be tolerated.

9. ORIENTATION FOR NEW COACHES. New coaches will attend any orientation meeting which is set-up by the Office of Activities/Athletics prior to, or during, the assumed duties.

10. CONFLICT OF INTEREST. A Head Coach's or Assistant' first responsibility is to his/her team. A coach will accompany the team and/or any athletes who are participating in any League, District, or State competition.

11. COMPLIANCE WITH SCHEDULE. Coaches must comply with all varsity, junior varsity, sopomore, and freshmen league schedules and make no alteration. The building Athletic Director should make all schedule changes and confirmations.

12. KNOWLEDGE OF, AND COMPLIANCE WITH, RULES AND REGULATIONS.

    a. Observe and follow all rules and regulations set forth by the Colorado High School Activities Association.

    b. Observe and follow all rules and regulations set forth by the Centennial League Board of Control.

    c. Observe and follow all rules and regulations set forth herein.

13. PENALTIES. Penalties for failure to comply with rules and regulations and for misconduct or unethical behavior inimical to the objectives of the athletic program which may be imposed by the school principal, the local school Athletic Board of Control or the District Supervisor of Activities/Athletics as the situation may warrant.

    No penalty will be assessed until a thorough investigation has been conducted in which the building Principal and the District Supervisor for Activities/Athletics are both involved.

14. APPEALS PROCEDURE. Appeals may be made as set forth by School District Policy No. 4116.1.

FORM 10-6 Terms and conditions that are required for all coaching positions. (Kurby Lyle, Supervisor of Activities/Athletics, Cherry Creek Schools, Englewood, Colorado. By permission.)

EVALUATION OF HIRING PROCESS UNDER TITLE IX

Each recipient education institution shall, within one year of the effective date of Title IX, evaluate in terms of the requirement, its current policies and practices and effects thereof concerning employment of both academic and non-academic personnel working in connection with the recipient's education program or activity; modify any of these policies which do not or may not meet the requirements; take appropriate steps to eliminate the effect of any discrimination which resulted from adherence to these policies and practices.

Questions

1. Discuss the following statement: "The values of the program of interscholastic athletics are in direct proportion to the quality of the leadership which give direction to it."
2. When hiring a person for a teaching-coaching position, enumerate desirable personal qualities that you think the individual should possess. Discuss how you arrived at your selection of personal attributes and why you feel they are important qualities.
3. Explain the meaning of affirmative action as it relates to the hiring process. Discuss.
4. Discuss the merits of inservice education.
5. Enumerate valid criteria for the evaluation-appraisal of athletic coaches.

REFERENCES

1. Lyle, Kurby, Supervisor of Activities/Athletics, Cherry Creek Schools, Englewood, Colorado, *Desirable Coaching Characteristics*, 1976. By permission.
2. Title IX of the Education Amendments 1972, Director, Office of Civil Rights, HEW, North Building, Washington, D.C. 20024.
3. Tamalpais Union High School District, Larkspur, California, *Affirmative Action Program Paper*, 1976. By permission.
4. *Coaches Manual*, National Association for Sport and Physical Education and Recreation, American Alliance for Health, Physical Education and Recreation, Washington, D.C. 20036. A reprint of *Coaches Manual, A Guide to Athletic Coaching in Florida Schools*, Bulletin 741, pp. 12-13. By permission.
5. Ivey, Maxwell, *Staff Management: An Overview*, Interscholastic Athletic Administration, Spring 1975, Vol. 1, No. 2, p. 7, National Federation of State High School Associations. Published by Spencer Marketing Services, New York, New York 10017. By permission.
6. Lesch, Dr. Victor, *Managing Athletic Programs by Goals*, Interscholastic Athletic Administration, Spring 1975, Vol. 1 No. 2, p. 18, National Federation

of State High School Associations. Published by Spencer Marketing Services, New York, New York 10017. By permission.

7. Allen, William, *Coaching Appraisal*, Interscholastic Athletic Administration, Spring 1975, Vol 1 No. 2. National Federation of State High School Associations. Published by Spencer Marketing Services, New York, New York 10017. By permission.

8. Lewis, Dr. Fred, Professor of Physical Education, *Criteria for Rating Coaches*, California State University, Sacramento, California, 1969. By permission.

9. Lyle, Kurby, Supervisor of Activities/Athletics, Cherry Creek Schools, *Coach's Agreement. Terms and Conditions*, Englewood, Colorado 80110. By permission.

SUGGESTED READING

Forsythe, C. E. and Keller, I. A. *Administration of High School Athletics*, 5th edition, Prentice-Hall, Englewood Cliffs, N.J., 1972.

Fuoss, Dr. Donald E., *Blueprinting Your Coaching Career*, Pilot Industries, New York, 1973, 64 pages.

George, Jack F. and Harry A. Lehman, *School Athletic Administration*, Harper and Row, New York, 1966 Ch. 12, Personnel.

Haney, William V., *Communication and Organizational Behavior* 3rd edition, Richard D. Irwin, Homewood, Ill., 1973.

Hixson, Chalmer G., *The Administration of Interscholastic Athletics*, J. Lowell Pratt and Co., New York, 1967, Ch. 5.

Massie, Joseph L. and Douglas, John, *Managing: A Contemporary Introduction*, Prentice-Hall, Englewood Cliffs, N.J., 1973.

Chapter 11

Methods of Compensations for Coaching Assignments

In a statistical research project conducted by the University of California[1] concerning methods of coaching compensation, 80 percent of these people surveyed favored additional pay beyond the regular salary schedule rather than released time from class assignments, or a combination of additional pay and released time.

In the summation of the findings regarding additional pay for coaching assignments, the report stated that 96.6 percent of the districts that provide additional pay for coaching assignments, compensate for all coaching assignments. Other districts that responded, pay for only selected assignments.

The report also noted that most districts that provide additional pay for coaching assignments pay their head coaches more than they pay their assistant coaches. Eleven percent of the districts pay equal amounts to all coaches.

METHODS OF ESTABLISHING COMPENSATION

Districts that provide coaches extra pay calculate the amount of pay by four methods:
1. Compensate on a flat season amount.
2. Compensate on an hourly basis.
3. Compensate on an increment plan similar to salary schedule.
4. Compensate on a percentage of the coaches' regular teaching salary.

Districts Providing Release Time

Of the districts surveyed that gave released time to coaches as compensation for extra services, the following was reported:

1. Released time was given only for selected sports in 5 percent of the districts.
2. Equal amounts of released time to both head and assistant coaches was given by 57.7 percent. The amount of released class time was one (1) hour per sport.

Summary and Recommendations of the California Survey

It was established that districts agree there should be compensation for coaching beyond that of the regular salary. The authors of the survey recommended that a coach receive a percentage of his annual salary rather than a flat sum. This method has various advantages to the district and to the coach:

1. It keeps pace with the rise in the cost of living.
2. It compensates the coach with more service, placing emphasis on experience.
3. It eliminates the necessity of reviewing the flat amount from year to year that is inconvenient to the district and to the employee.
4. A new employee does not start at the maximum salary during his first year of coaching and can look forward to rewards for experience.

The authors of the survey also recommended that the four sports of football, basketball, baseball, and track be paid a higher percentage than other sports in the program. However, it is the responsibility of the district to determine the sports of major emphasis. The head coach would receive a greater percentage than an assistant coach or the coach of a junior varsity, sophomore, or freshman team. It was suggested that head coaches of the selected sports receive a minimum of 6 percent and that coaches of other sports and assistants receive a minimum of 4 percent.

The survey pointed out that if a coach, by the nature of the sport, is obligated by the district to coach during vacation periods, he should be additionally compensated as any teacher or counselor would be if required to work during the vacation period. The survey recommended that the districts compensate their coaches for attendance at coaching clinics and workshops.

METHODS FOR DETERMINING
COMPENSATION FOR COACHING

Most studies favor a percentage rating as the basis for determining the compensation for coaching. James P. Thurston, consultant of teacher salaries and negotiations,[2] has developed a formula for extra duty pay. Thurston says, "The most common reason why no real relationship to basic salaries has been maintained is that supplements have normally been dollar amounts established without regard to basic salary and by arbitrary decisions usually made by boards of education and administrators without regard to practioner. Therefore, it is our responsibility to see that a relationship is developed which allows for all of these diverse relationships. It must be a relationship that grows and reflects change and improved proficiency."

Thurston proposes that an "index needs to be developed which reflects the time spent in activity as a ratio to the basic schedule rather than setting the index on pressure, public exposure, responsibility, experience and added training. The whole argument thus becomes parity for time spent in the activity in question as related to the basic schedule."

The Thurston Formula for Extra Duty Pay

Number of hours spent in activity		Length of activity per school year (days, weeks, months)	
_____	$\times$	_____	Equals basic time index
Number of hours in school day		Length of normal school year	

Example 1. High school basketball coach who spends two hours per day with his squad. The season lasts five months in a ten-month year with an eight-hour day.

$$2/8 \times 5/10 = \text{basic index } .125$$

Example 2. High school chemistry teacher spends one hour, twice a month with the science club. The school operates on an eight hour day, two hundred days a year.

$$1/8 \times 20/200 = \text{basic index } .0125$$

These time indices may be applied on a B.A. base, base of degree held, step on B.A. scale, or step on teacher's basic salary scale.

Kent School District Formula[3]

The Kent School District No. 415, King County, Kent, Washington has developed a unique system for supplemental pay (Form 11-1).

The amount to be added to the base pay of an individual who holds one of the following positions (Form 11-1) shall be determined by the point factors. In each case, the factor for a position is to be multiplied by the amount in the basic salary schedule on that experience step equal to the number of years' experience in that position by that individual. A maximum of five years' experience shall be allowed. The total salary for a coach or person during extra duties shall be the sum of the base salary and the time and responsibility factor.

The Houston Independent School District, Houston, Texas has an annual salary for coaching assignments. It also has a clause for extended time based on teacher's salary in addition to coaching salary (Form 11-2).

The Montclair Plan

The Department of Health, Physical Education, and Safety of the Montclair, New Jersey Public Schools made an effort to form an extra pay guide according to present practices in normal educational salary adjustment. Their project resulted in a plan to pay personnel a percentage of their teaching salary for performing extra duties. Harry Oestreich, writing in the *Journal of Health, Physical Education and Recreation*[4] said,

"The percentage plan of payment involves five related steps.

1. Evaluate and weigh all sports and related activities on the basis of:
   a. Community interest
   b. Student interest
   c. Number of participants, number of squads
   d. Number of games and related responsibilities for players and for players and for equipment

   e. Number and length of practices, including evening, weekends, and holiday activities

2. List all activites or sports according to responsibility assigning 100 percent value to activity with most responsibility.
3. Determine the maximum remuneration for most responsible assignment and divide this by the maximum on the teacher salary guide. (Example: if football is 15 percent stipend, then since basketball has 80 percent difficulty in assignment, the stipend would be 80 percent of 15 percent or 12 percent).
4. Translate the percentage rate in dollar figures.
5. Adjust dollar figures by comparing them with amount currently being paid for the assignment.

Developing a Single Salary Schedule for Coaches

Developing a salary schedule for coaching assignments has been a difficult and emotional assignment for the director of athletics and the administration. The situation has become more acute with the implementation of Title IX and the increasing number of women coaches. The answer lies in the development of a single salary schedule for all coaches, regardless of sex, with the only difference being in the nature of the coaching assignment.

Gordon Straley, Athletic Director, West Lafayette High School, West Lafayette, Indiana offers a step-by-step plan based on the West Lafayette School Corporation evaluation of the various coaching positions. The plan is as follows:[5]

Step I. In order to establish the number of hours for which a coach is to be paid, the Principal and the athletic director should establish a season for each sport.

Step II. Appoint a committee of eight to ten people to evaluate the coaching positions.

Step III. Require each coach to write a job analysis of his or her coaching position: exact duties and responsibilities, how performed, how much planning and preparation, how many students involved, etc. This will be helpful to the committee when the evaluation process begins.

Step IV. The committee should identify the criteria to be used in preparing a Job Analysis. The criteria used in West Lafayette is:

1. Total number of hours involved.
2. Number of students involved.
3. Experience necessary: specialization, quality and length of experience necessary to coach this activity.
4. Attention demand: amount of mental and visual concentration re-

KENT SCHOOL DISTRICT 1973 - 1974 COACHES SALARY SCHEDULE

Junior High Points

Sport	Points
Football	16
Basketball	14
Wrestling	12
Track	11
Boys' gymnastics	10
Girls' gymnastics	10
Baseball	9
Cross country	6 *
GAA**	6 *
Intramurals**	6 *
Golf	6 *
Girls' volleyball	6 *
Boys' swimming	7
Girls' swimming	6 *
Girls' track	6 *
Tennis	8

Junior High Points

Sport	Points
Football	12
Basketball	11
Wrestling	11
Track	10
Baseball	9
GAA**	6 *
Intramurals**	6 *
Softball	6 *
Co-ed swimming	6 *
Girls' volleyball	6 *

Elementary Points

Intramurals	3

*No head coach is to be paid less than the 6 point scale (which is imposed where the scale is less than 6), EXCEPT for the Elementary Intramurals positions.

**Carries two season responsibility.

PROCEDURES FOR IMPLEMENTATION

Experience Equivalents: An experience equivalent will be considered to be on satisfactory season experience in a sport or an equivalent determined by athletic director evaluation.

Experience Equivalent	Point Factor
0	.0088
1	.0095
2	.0102
3	.0109
4	.0116
5	.0123

Salary for Head Coach Assignments: Is determined by multiplying Point Factor × Base Salary × Scale Points (minimum of 6 points).

Salary for Assistant Coach Assignments: Is to be 60 percent of the head coach salary.

(For further explanation as to how points are arrived, refer to negotiated agreement book under KEA. This gives the full agreement.)

1973 — 1974
KENT SCHOOL DISTRICT
COACHES SALARY SCHEDULE

HEAD COACH						
	0	1	2	3	4	5
16	1099	1186	1274	1361	1449	1536
14	962	1038	1115	1191	1268	1344
12	824	890	955	1021	1086	1152
11	756	816	876	936	996	1056
10	687	741	796	851	905	960
9	618	667	716	766	815	864
8	549	593	637	681	724	768
7	481	519	557	596	634	672
6	412	445	478	510	543	576
3	206	223	239	255	272	288

ASSISTANT COACH @ 60%

16	659	712	764	816	869	922
14	577	623	669	715	761	806
12	494	534	573	613	652	691
11	454	490	526	562	598	634
10	412	445	478	511	543	576
9	371	400	430	460	489	518
8	329	356	382	409	434	461
7	287	311	334	358	380	403
6	247	267	287	306	326	346
3	124	134	144	153	163	173

FORM 11-1 Supplemental pay. (Kent School District 415, King County, Kent Washington. By permission.)

ATHLETIC PROGRAMS and SALARIES

September 1974

SENIOR HIGH SCHOOLS

Assignment	*Annual Salary*	
	Head Coach	*Assistant Coach*
Football (fall)	$1300.00	$900.00
Football (spring)	400.00	300.00
Basketball	950.00	400.00
Track	700.00	400.00
Baseball	700.00	400.00
Tennis	250.00	
Golf	250.00	
Swimming	250.00	

JUNIOR HIGH SCHOOLS

Football (fall)	650.00	500.00
Basketball	600.00	500.00
Track	350.00	250.00
Swimming	200.00	

SPONSORS FOR SENIOR HIGH SCHOOL GIRLS

Drill squad	900.00
Girls volleyball	600.00
Girls' tennis	250.00
Girls' archery	150.00
Girls' swimming	250.00

*EXTENDED TIME BASED ON TEACHER'S SALARY
IN ADDITION TO COACHING SALARY*

SENIOR HIGH SCHOOL		*JUNIOR HIGH SCHOOL*	
Head football coach	1 month	Head football coach	
Assistant football coach	1/2 month	and assistant coach	1/2 month

Head and assistant basketball
  coach   1/2 month
(Unless worked football—then 1/4 month)

SENIOR HIGH SCHOOL PLAYOFFS

Under this schedule, head high school football coaches would be paid for 11 months. Assistant high school football coaches, high school basketball coaches and junior high football coaches would be on 10½ months basis.

JCT mb

APPROVED:

Dr. Sylvester Rains
Coordinator, Regular Education Division

FORM 11-2 Annual salary for coaching assignments. (Joe Tusa, Assistant Superintendent for Athletics, Houston Independent School District, Houston, Texas. By permission.)

quired by the job.

5. Community and spectator reaction and pressures: what is the effect of the activity on spectators, on the community, and the resulting reflection on the coach.

6. Physical demands: nature and frequency of physical efforts required in performing the duty.

7. Working conditions: environmental factors, indoors, outdoors, noise, etc.

8. Weekend and vacation time necessary.

9. Public relations: extent to which the duty requires contact with people outside the school, the importance of those contacts in maintaining good will, community support, etc.

10. Supervisory responsibilities: extent to which the assignment requires administrative or supervisory duties involving other employees, such as assistant coaches, junior high coaches, custodians, etc.

11. Equipment and facility responsibilities: quantity, type, cost and care of equipment and facilities .

12. Complexity of duties: number, importance and frequency of decisions that must be made and problems dealth with.

13. Health and safety of students: injury element present in activity, degree of concern necessary in maintaining conditions conducive to good student welfare.

Step V. Once the criterions have been established, a weighted score should be given to each criterion. Some may seem more important than others. Our criterion were weighted on a scale of 1 to 4.

Step VI. The committee sets up ground rules that can be applied to all coaching positions during the evaluation. Number of hours for each practice session; how much time to allot for traveling to and from contests; for planning and preparation; for getting equipment ready before the season, and for storing it after the season, for locker room supervision.

Step VII. The evaluation committee then evaluates and rates each coaching position on a scale of 1 to 5, using the above criteria. Each head coach should be interviewed for input. The written job analysis of each coach will also be helpful.

Step VIII. The rating score for each criterion multiplied by the weighted score results in a weighted raw score for each criterion. The sum of the weighted raw scores for the position is obtained, and a committee average is computed. (Each member rates individually.)

Step IX. After all positions have been evaluated, they are then placed in final numerical order or rank, according to the Total Weighted Raw Score for each position.

From this ranking of coaching positions, a salary schedule for all coaches could be devised. For example, an index system with annual experience increments could be developed, or perhaps "X" number of dollars per point on the rating scale could be allotted to each position.

Exactly how it is done will depend on the experiences and ingenuity within the committee, existing philosophies and policies within the school corporation, the amount of money available, etc.

A method similar to the West Lafayette criterion for the establishment of compensation for coaches was submitted recently by the Tamalpais District Teachers' Association[6] in their collective bargaining agreement. The similarity of the two programs leads us to believe that the origin of the criterion was taken from the West Lafayette study, which is only our conjecture. However, it is presented in a concise package and entered here for the reader's perusal.

Criterion Used
A. HOURS INVOLVED—to include the total number of hours necessary to prepare for and to conduct the activity.
B. NUMBER OF STUDENTS PARTICIPATING—to include the number of students who remain in the activity throughout the major portion of the season a year.
C. TRAINING REQUIRED—to recognize the degree of specialization and extent of training judged essential for their extra assignment.
D. INJURY POTENTIAL—to acknowledge the responsibility for injury prevention and for injury care.
E. WEEKEND, HOLIDAY TIME—to identify the extent of "premium" time required in the supervision of the activity.
F. EQUIPMENT AND FACILITY—to identify the routine necessary in the care of equipment and facilities.
G. INDOORS, OUTDOORS—to consider the "environmental" factors as they relate to the supervisory responsibilities of an activity.
H. TRAVEL, BUS SUPERVISION—to recognize the extent of bus supervision involved in the supervisory responsibilities of an activity.
I. EXPERIENCE—to allow for the additional expertise gained through experience at this assignment.
Once the criterions are listed and defined, consideration has to be given to the weighing of each. Some criterion seem to be more important and

pertinent than others. The weighings listed below represent and average.

CRITERION	WEIGHING
A. Hours involved	4
B. Number of students participating	3
C. Training required	2
D. Injury potential	2
E. Weekend, holiday time	3
F. Equipment and facility	2
G. Indoors, outdoors	1
H. Travel, bus supervision	2
I. Experience	1/year

The next step is to rate each activity on each of the criterions. The rating scale used is on a numerical basis; one represented little and five extensive. The final step in the process is the development of a weighted score for each activity. Using the varsity football coach as an example, the weighted score could be developed as follows:

Criterion A—Hours involved:

Weighing of criterion 4

Rating for varsity football 5

Weighed rating . . . . 4 times 5 equals 20

This procedure would be followed for each of the other eight criterion listed. The rate of pay could be established in a negotiated rate per point.

Summation

We have presented various methods for determining coaching compensation. There does not seem to be a general agreement on the method to be used. There is general agreement that coaches should be compensated for extra services. The percentage plan seems to have the most merit in that it is an "ongoing" plan, that is, it is consistent with the general salary schedule of the school district and places emphasis on years of experience in coaching.

Boards of education must realize that as the program expands, the budget for coaching salaries must also be expanded proportionately. Boards will have to consider the implementation of Title IX, section 86.54. "A recipient shall not make or enforce a policy or practice which, on the basis of sex: (a) makes distinction in rates of pay or other compensation; (b) results in the payment of wages to employees of one sex at a rate less than that paid to employees of the opposite sex for equal skill, effort and responsibility which are performed under similar working conditions."

Questions

1. Discuss the pros and cons of compensation "released time" for an individual with a coaching assignment as compared to additional financial compensation for a coaching assignment.
2. Enumerate and discuss different methods that may be utilized to calculate the rate of additional financial compensation for coaching assignments.
3. Where a school district agrees there should be compensation beyond the regular teaching salary for coaching assignments, what are the advantages to the district and the coach if the individual receives a percentage of his annual salary rather than a flat sum of money for coaching?
4. Where the school district adheres to the philosophy and policy of "extra assignments means extra pay," which factors should be taken into consideration in order to determine the rate and extent of financial compensation?
5. Should sports be classified "major" and "minor" in respect to extra compensation?
6. Should head coaches receive greater compensation than assistant coaches?
7. Should consideration be given years of experience in coaching? Should an experienced coach receive greater compensation than an inexperienced coach? Discuss.

REFERENCES

1. California Coaches Association, *Coaching Compensation Survey*, Statistical Research by the University of California, Department of Education, Berkeley, California, 1967. By permission.
2. Thurston, James P., *Secondary School Athletic Administration—A New Look*, American Alliance of Health, Physical Education and Recreation, Washington D.C., 1969, pp. 82-83. By permission.
3. Burrell, Jack, Athletic Director, *Kent School District Formula*, Kent School District No. 415, King County, Kent, Washington. By permission.

4. Oestreich, Harry, *"Percentage Payment Plan for Extra Services," Journal of Health, Physical Education and Recreation,* November-December 1966, Vol. 37, pp. 40-42. American Alliance of Health, Physical Education and Recreation, Washington D.C. By permission.

5. Straley, Gordon, Athletic Director, West Lafayette High School, West Lafayette, Indiana, *"One Salary Schedule for Men and Women Coaches," The Athletic Director,* Vol. 7, No. 2, October 1975. American Alliance of Health, Physical Education and Recreation, Washington D.C.

6. Tamalpais Union High School District Teachers Association, Collective Bargaining Project. Criterion for Establishment of Compensation for Coaches, March 1976, Larkspur, Ca. 94939.

SUGGESTED READINGS

Bucher, Charles A., *Administration of Health and Physical Education Programs Including Athletics,* C. V. Mosby, St. Louis, Mo., 1971.

Forsythe, E. and Keller, I. A., *Administration of High School Athletics,* 5th edition, Englewood Cliffs, N.J., Prentice-Hall, 1972.

Chapter 12
Staff Relations

Staff relations is management by objectives through which members of the athletic department are motivated to the accomplishment of definite objectives or goals.

The athletic director must approach the task of staff relations with a positive attitude and must realize that, to be effective, the program must be result-oriented rather than task-oriented. Being in a position of management, the athletic director's success will lie in the ability to get things accomplished through other people. The athletic director must show leadership through his own personality and never try to emulate someone else or the staff will recognize his insincerity.

For the program to be a success, it is imperative that the athletic director and staff cultivate and maintain respect for one another. The athletic director should be a model figure and lead by example rather than by the authority of his position. John C. Youngblood, Athletic Director, Washington-Lee High School, Arlington, Virginia[1] states, "As the athletic administrator, it seems to be that one of my major responsibilities is to continually strive to attain the major qualities of an outstanding leader: integrity, reliability, industry, maturity, decisiveness, concern for other and organizational ability."

Mr. Youngblood continues, "Probably the next best way we, as athletic administrators, have to be a good effect on our staffs, to have excellent rapport and cooperation and to attain desired objectives, is by improving the 'self-image' of each coach by praising him for his good qualities and performances."

MOTIVATION BY OBJECTIVE TECHNIQUES

The basic philosophy of the motivation by objectives technique is to provide a process by which effective communication is developed among members of the athletic staff with reference to expectations, priorities, and accomplishments to be achieved in a given period of time. The more common methods are discussed below.

The S.W.O.T.S. Technique

This technique was discussed in Chapter 4 but it is reiterated at this point as a technique of communication between the athletic director and the staff.

At the beginning of the school year, the athletic director and the coaching staff should design and discuss the strengths, weaknesses, opportunities, threats, and suggestions (S.W.O.T.S.) for improvement of a particular sport. During the course of the academic year, individual conferences will be held to find out if the weaknesses and threats have been minimized and if the coach has capitalized on the strengths, opportunities, and suggestions. The athletic director and the coach together decide whether the objectives of S.W.O.T.S. are being realized. Perhaps they are too high or too low and the objectives need to be reassessed.

Self-Evaluation Technique

The coach should use a self-evaluation form and rate himself on items related to the major responsibilities of his position and, in addition, on items considered to be highly desirable personal and professional qualities, including the principles and practices of good coaching.

The athletic director also rates the coach on a similar form and the information is shared. Differences are discussed and methods for improvement, if needed, are mutually agreed upon.

Performance Goals for Major Responsibilities

Performance goals for major responsibilities were discussed in Chapter 10. Used in this context, the athletic director and the coach will be able to keep an ongoing account of the major responsibilities, goals, target dates, and current measure of performance. Form 10-1 indicates the material that may be included in such a form. Such a technique may also be utilized at the conclusion of the school year for a complete evaluation of the athletic staff members.

Job Description Technique

A coach is requested to write a job description for his sport. All responsibilities and duties should be included in the description (Form 11-3). The athletic director, through individual conferences with the coach, will be able to discuss the job description and offer suggestions and help, if requested. This is an excellent method for the coach to know exactly what is expected of him, by constantly referring to this form, he will be able to actively seek his goal.

Staff Handbook

A staff handbook, (Chapter 3) which is not difficult to prepare, provides information and a common ground of understanding for the entire athletic staff. All phases of the program must be covered in the handbook and no detail, however small, should be omitted. This should be the "bible" for the department, describing the standards, principles, and philosophy by which the members of the staff may work together to achieve a common goal.

By indicating the procedures and policies located in the handbook, the athletic director makes use of another motivational technique that may help guide the staff.

By indicating the procedures and policies located in the handbook the athletic director makes use of another motivational technique that may help guide the staff.

Counseling the Staff. Dr. Robert J. Waldorf, counselor at Fort Hunt High School, Fairfax County, Virginia,[2] in his aricle, "6 Ways to Improve the AD/Coach Relationship," posed this question, "What do you think makes you coaches tick?" Dr. Waldorf states, "There are many personality theories to choose from, but nobody knows for sure what makes people act, talk and believe the way they do." Dr. Waldorf offers some very definite concepts that are well accepted and worthy of consideration:

1. Emotion dominates thinking.
2. People act according to their self concept or self image.
3. Most people are egocentric.
4. Programs or policies have a much better chance of working when those who carry them out have a voice in their formation.
5. Seek out the positive in the people with whom you work.
6. Use the preventive idea or concept, employed so successfully in fields such as medicine and clinic psychology. Fire fighters or fire preventers?

Dr. Waldorf states, "Unfortunately most of us seem to be fire fighters rather than fire preventers."

To utilize the preventative concept, athletic directors could work with the coaches in the avoidance of problems. We might even call it counseling.

Dr. Waldorf continues, "For whatever counseling is, it can be roughly defined as helping others to solve, alleviate, to avoid or to endure difficulties. How good it must be for a coach to be able to turn to somebody who is concerned, who likes and accepts him or her, and who truly wants to help. Perhaps, this attitude, as well as the previously mentioned concepts is at the heart of improving relationships between people and in this case, between coach and athletic director."

Pitfalls in Good Staff Relations. The athletic director must avoid obstacles or pitfalls that inhibit good staff relations, which produce low self-esteem and loss of effectiveness in achieving the goals of the department. Here are some of the more common pitfalls.

1. Lack of democratic leadership tends to upset the staff. Each member of the staff must be able to offer suggestions for the betterment of the program and must feel they are contributing rather than just taking orders and acting as a robot. Coaches tend to be leadership oriented and accept that they have to follow orders. This is where the athletic director must use insight and tact in his democratic leadership. Coaches generally want to voice their opinions, yet they are generally, not adamant about the athletic director making the decision.
2. In the field of education generally, the athletic and physical education department members and their programs have not been universally accepted. Since numerous faculty members do

not look at coaches as teachers, this has a demeaning effect on staff relations. The athletic director should work toward remedying this unfortunate situation. The athletic staff must get into the "mainstream" of the school and become a viable part of the faculty by accepting membership on various school committees, attendance at all faculty meetings, and socializing with other faculty members.

3. The low man on the totem pole theory where the youngest man or the last man hired goes through a ritual of doing things because he is the junior member of the staff. Historically, people in education move up in stature through seniority. This approach takes the incentive away from a new member of the staff, and should be avoided where possible.

4. Athletic directors who move up from the coaching ranks, as is true in most cases, often have the attitude, "When I was a coach, I did it this way." Obviously, this is not a good way to offer constructive help.

5. The athletic director who creates the impression, "I will take care of all the details and you do just the coaching" will become so tied up in minutia that he will be unsuccessful in establishing the recognized management concept of getting things done through other people.

6. The athletic director who moves up from a staff of long standing seems to keep in a traditional pattern.

7. The difficulty of a coaching staff in establishing basic philosophies may be due to the individual nature of each coach. The tennis coach, for example, will probably have a different outlook on life than the football coach. It is the responsibility of the athletic director to develop a philosophy that each individual coach can live with.

8. The same problem with setting goals is also apparent. The new or young coach undoubtedly will set goals that differ from those of the athletic director who has been in the profession for many years. Although the athletic director will not want to inhibit the young coach and prevent him from achieving his personal and professional goals, it is the athletic director's responsibility to keep the individual's goals in perspective with the philosophy and goals of the department.

Resolution of Conflicts

The athletic director, in many cases, takes the position of moderator and has to make a concentrated effort to try and resolve the many conflicts that are likely to occur. The athletic director may be compared to a psychologist who becomes an "ear" for people to unload their problems. The conflict, regardless of how small it may seem, should be resolved if at all psssible.

One of the best methods of resolving a conflict is to come up with a new approach to the problem, one that both the athletic director and the coach can agree on. This method seems to work better than a definite opinion on the part of the athletic director or the compromising position where no one is completely satisfied.

The open door policy has a good effect on staff morale and keeps the lines of communication open between the athletic director and the staff. It is a truism that if the department is unorganized, it is usually because of lack of communication.

Summation

From the viewpoint of the athletic director in an administrative-managerial position, a role assignment is motivating staff members to develop teamwork that effectively fulfills their needs and achieves organizational objectives.

To accomplish this objective, anyone seriously interested in furthering a career in athletic administration and other areas, would do well to become familiar with the writings of Abraham H. Maslow and his needs-priority theory (see Suggested Reading) and other authors or publications dealing with the subjects of human relations and communications.

Human relations applies broadly to the interaction of people in all types of endeavor and in the specific instance of interscholastic athletics, of how people may be motivated to work together in greater harmony. In the area of communications, there is conclusive evidence to support the contention that much of the conflict that occurs in organizations, including athletic departments, is not due to the unwillingness of people to coordinate activities voluntarily, but is due to the lack of communciations or to miscommunication.

Questions

1. Why is it important for the athletic director to try and encourage and cultivate a "we" attitude among the coaches and staff members as compare to an "I" attitude?

2. What is the S.W.O.T.S. method of evaluation? How may it be utilized by the coaches, athletic director, and the principal for improving the interscholastic athletic program?

3. What is meant by the statement that a good administrator, including an athletic director, should be a firepreventer rather than a fire fighter? Give specific illustrations pertaining to interscholastic athletics and the role of the athletic director.

4. A leader motivates. Enumerate some ways an athletic director can motivate the physical education and athletic staff members.

Optional:

5. If you have read in Suggested Reading, Maslow's "Order of Priority of Human Needs," how does this apply to one in the coaching profession? How does it apply to the athletic director? What can you apply of Maslow's theory to yourself.

REFERENCES

1. Youngblood, John C., "Interview with John C. Youngblood," *Interscholastic Athletic Administration Magazine*, Vol. 1, No. 2, Spring 1975, pp. 28 National Federation of State High School Associations. Published by Spencer Marketing Services, New York, New York 10017. By permission.

2. Waldorf, Robert D., "6 Ways to Improve the AD/Coach Relationship," *Bike Sports Trail Magazine*, The Kendall Company, Sports Division, 20 Walnut Street, Wellesley Hills, Mass. 02181.

SUGGESTED READINGS

Davis, Keith, *Human Behavior at Work: Human Relations and Organizational Behavior* 4th edition, McGraw-Hill, New York, 1972.

Ewing, David W., *Writing for Results in Business, Government and the Professions*, Wiley-Interscience, Wiley, New York, 1974.

Forsythe, E. and Keller, I. A., *Administration of High School Athletics*, 5th edition, Prentice-Hall, Englewood Cliffs, N.J., 1972.

Gallon, Arthur J., *Coaching: Ideas and Ideals*, Houghton Mifflin, Boston, 1974.

Goble, Frank, *The Third Force (A Psychology of A. Maslow, A Revolutionary New View of Man)* Grossman, New York, 1970.

Haney, William V., *Communication and Organizational Behavior,* Richard D. Irwin, Homewood, Ill., 1972.

Maslow, A.H., "A Theory of Human Motivation," *Psychology Review,* Vol. 50, 1943, pp. 370-396.

Maslow, A.H., *Motivation and Personality,* Harper and Row, New York, 1954.

Maslow, A.H., *Toward a Psychology of Being* 2nd edition, Van Nostrand-Reinhold, New York, 1968.

Resick, Mathew and Erickson, Carl E., *Intercollegiate and Interscholastic Athletics for Men and Women,* Addison-Wesley, Reading, Mass., 1975.

PART IV
MANAGEMENT FUNCTIONS: DIRECTING AND DELEGATING

Chapter 13
Eligibility Regulations Governing Interscholastic Athletics

There are generally two major areas that require the athletic director's utmost attention and vigilance, eligibility, and finances. Eligibility of interscholastic athletics is discussed in this chapter. Budgeting and financing of the interscholastic athletics program were discussed in Chapter 6.

Interscholastic athletics are a significant educative force in meeting many of the needs of the secondary school youth. Competition and cooperation are prized in our culture and both can be fostered by well-conducted athletic programs under competent leadership.

The controlling forces of the interscholastic athletics program are national, state, and local athletic conferences and associations. The development of eligibility regulations and a commitment to sound administrative practices and optimal opportunities for students are some of the most important contributions that the various associations can offer.

The program is developed through a logical sequence in which the whole range of sports activities should be initially taught in classes of physical education. Provisions are made for pupils to compete individually or as team members in a program of intramural athletics. There should be an extensive well-balanced interscholastic athletic program for those who develop a high level of athletic skill.

INTERSCHOLASTIC ATHLETIC PROGRAMS

John Klumb, State Department of Education, California,[1] said, "School athletics under approved and properly supervised regulations can provide major educational benefits ot participating pupils. Some of these follow: Developing a physical well-being; learning imposed and self-discipline vital to adult life; providing a wholesome release of physical energy; learning loyalty to a team, a group or a cause; acquiring emotional control during times of stress; and gaining an appreciation for life long physical fitness."

To fully utilize the educational potential of athletics, state athletic programs are organized and conducted in accordance with the following basic principles, as voiced by William Russell, Commissioner, California Interscholastic Federation.[2] "Interscholastic athletic programs are considered as an integral part of the total educational program. They supplement rather than serve as substitutes for the basic physical education program and intramural athletic programs. Athletic programs are subject to the same administrative and faculty control as the total education program and must be supervised by certificated teachers. Athletic programs are conducted so that the physical welfare and safety of the participants are protected and fostered and are conducted in accordance with the letter and spirit of the rules and regulations of the appropriate league, section, and national athletic associations"

Adapting Sports to the Interscholastic Athletic Program

Secondary school youths have needs different from athletes at other levels. Therefore, sports activities must be tailored to satisfy these needs if they are to best serve their purposes. This has been done through a scientific study of the relationship of these sports to the high school program and through the establishment of machinery that will enable the nature of the game to be influenced by the people in direct charge of the high school athletic program and by a system of experimentation and observation.

The intrinsic values that accrue from the standards and regulations as controlled by the national, state, and local associations are that they are the same for all schools, they are widely known by the administration and the participants, and they relieve schools from the burden of varying their standards of eligibility from those of other schools the National Federation of State High School Athletic Associations (with which all state assocaitions are affiliated) was founded on the premise that it would concern itself with making uniform eligibility and standards for interscholastic athletics throughout the United States.

Checklist for Minimum Athletic Eligibility Requirements. The provisions for eligibility rules shall apply to all boys and girls who participate in interscholastic athletic competition. Each state association is guided by its own constitution and bylaws, and may interpret a given rule differently. Chapter 28 gives details on the place of the National Federation of State High School Athletics Association in interscholastic athletic programs.

For the purpose of this checklist, major reference should be to the rule rather than to the interpretations. Most schools post the minimum eligibility rules for all participants to read. Form 13-1 represents the basic information that is posted by the Washington Activities Association. Form 13-2 represents the eligibility information that is posted for the students at Stagg High School in Stockton, California.

Schools may vary in their athletic registration procedures. However, the athletic director is ultimately responsible to the principal for determining the eligibility of the participants in his school.

The most common procedure is to have a registration meeting for athletes prior to each sport season. Athletes are instructed as to the exact steps to be taken, and it is made certain that each athlete understands all of the information concerning rules and regulations. A registration form must be completed by each athlete and returned to the coach who checks it for accuracy, making sure that all items have been properly filled out. The coach then files this form with the athletic director. No athlete should be permitted to practice with the team until all items on the registration form have been completed. Some schools require the athletic director to personally look over the eligibility regulation forms and explain all pertinent rules. Condensed versions of eligibility rules are usually posted conspicuously.

Form 13-3 can prove to be a real time saver for the athletic director. This check sheet is for the coach of each team; dates are listed for each item. It also serves another function, especially with the turnover in the coaching ranks, since the athletic director will know he has covered all points of information with the coaching staff.

ATTENTION H.S. ATHLETES!

Guard Your Eligibility

YOU ARE NOT ELIGIBLE:

1. If you are 20 YEARS of age or over at the BEGINNING of the sport season.

2. If you are in a 3-year senior high school after 6 semesters of attendance or in a 4-year high school longer than 6 semesters after you earned your first 6 credits. Attendance for 6 weeks of a semester or participation in an athletic contest shall constitute a semester's attendance under this rule.

3. If you were not in school last semester or if you were in school and failed to pass in at least three regular subjects. (See Principal for exceptions.)

4. If you are not in regular attendance and passing in 3 full-time subjects this semester.

5. If you enrolled later than OCTOBER 1 for fall semester or FEBRUARY 15 for the 2nd semester.

6. If you have participated in the sport for all or PART OF 4 SEASONS (3 for senior high schools).

7. If, during a sport season, you have played on an OUTSIDE team or represented yourself or an organization OTHER than your high school in that branch of athletics.

8. If you have accepted, from any source whatever, awards of intrinsic value except letters awarded by your school or medals or trophies given in high school contests. (Applies to players on school teams.)

9. If you have ever accepted money or a prize of more than $35.00 in value for athletic activity, played on any professional team in any sport, or entered a competition under an assumed name.

10. If you do not have a doctor's certificate of fitness issued within the present school year.

YOUR ELIGIBILITY IS SUBJECT TO SPECIAL RULES:

11. If your parents do not live in this district.

12. If you transfer from a public to a private high school.

NOTE: There are a few exceptions to the above rules. There are also additional requirements. Consult your principal or the W.I.A.A. Handbook.

WASHINGTON INTERSCHOLASTIC ACTIVITIES ASSOCIATION

FORM 13-1 Minimum eligibility rules for all participants to read. (Washington Interscholastic Activities Association. Bellevue, Washington. By permission.)

STAGG HIGH SCHOOL SCHOLASTIC ELIGIBILITY
REQUIREMENTS FOR STUDENT ATHLETES

Adopted January 17, 1973

1. A Stagg High School student athlete is eligible for athletic participation in any current semester if he is passing in 20 semester periods (units).

2. Scholastic checks will be made twice during each sports season. Those checks will be administered by the athletic director once at the beginning and once during the middle of each season.

3. A student reported failing in one (or two) classes, but still passing in 20 semester units shall be encouraged by counseling and administrative action, in concert with the teacher, to improve to a passing grade.

4. In the event that a student is reported as not passing the required 20 semester unit he will be placed on a two week probationary period. During this two week period, an administrative evaluation will take place which will result in one of the following:

   a. The student declared scholastically ineligible for athletic participation during the remainder of the semester.

   b. The student reinstated to regular scholastic eligibility as the result of improving to a passing grade in the required number of units.

   c. Transfer of the student from the course of instruction in which he is failing to a course of instruction more compatible with the student's needs and abilities.

By Permission
C. T. Haan, Principal
Stagg Senior High School
Stockton, Ca 95207

FORM 13-2 Eligibility information for students to read. (Staff High School, Stockton, California. By permission.)

Eligibility Rules. The athletic director should distribute copies of the basic eligibility rules to all coaches. A "Blue Book" Day is held in some states to allow the league commissioner to conduct a workshop for all coaches pertaining to the basic eligibility rules. This seems to be an excellent idea. If this cannot be done, then each athletic director has the responsibility of conducting a workshop for the coaching staff.

A coaches' handbook should be developed that gives eligibility

Due dates relative to the athletic department.

_____ *Insurance* — Claim form to attending physician and athletic director within 24 hours of accident.

_____ *Budget* — To athletic director by last school day of March.

_____ *Parent Permission Cards* — To athletic director at beginning of season prior to first contest.

_____ *Physical Exams* — Prior to each sports season.

_____ *Schedules* — To athletic director for approval prior to last school day in May.

_____ *Team Rosters* — To athletic director at beginning of each season.

_____ *Activity Passes* — Distributed to team members prior to first contest.

_____ Bulletin Notice for Player Release (Notice in faculty bulletin day prior to contest)

_____ Bulletin Notice for Contest Publicity (Notice in student bulletin day of contest)

_____ Bulletin Notice for Contest Results (On all call day following contest)

_____ *Awards and Certificates* — Prior to end of season

_____ Invitation to try out for sport activity in daily bulletin

_____ *Transportation Arrangements* — Prior to season at beginning of school year.

_____ *ELIGIBILITY REQUIREMENTS* —
1. Eligibility cards submitted prior to season
2. Scholastic checks twice each season by the athletic director

_____ *Banquets* — After conclusion of season
1. Separate
2. In conjunction with Boosters' Club

_____ *Films* (Football — arrangements made prior to season)

_____ Athletic Information to Curriculum Office — Two weeks prior to publication date of the last issue of the "Stagg Line."

_____ *Tournaments* — Contact athletic director at least two days prior to tournament.

_____ *Lockers* — Coordinate through instructor in charge of lockers.

_____ G.P.A. and Test Scores — See registrar.

_____ Substitute teachers — At least two days prior to the day needed.

_____ Vacation time coaches pay — Immediately upon completion of vacation time coaching.

FORM 13-3 Check sheet for the coach of each team. (Source: unknown.)

rules as well as the necessary information for departmental use, such as filing an accident report, reporting trip expenses, and on the athletic department administrative organization.

The summation of each rule should be included in a coaches' handbook with (references to the state association bylaws for the number and particulars of each rules). Suggested material in the coaches' handbook concerning basic statewide rules is given below.

Eligibility Requirements: (Reference State Hand Book-Site Numbers). A summation of material or information includes: requirements concerning age, and for entering students; eight semester regulations; attendance; residence eligibility, and continuing scholastic eligibility; waver of the requirements because of serious illness or injury or travel abroad or court order; requirements of the legal guardian, and for continuation school eligibility; transfer students, hardship cases, and intradistrict and interdistrict transfers; requirements for summer school and military service.

Form 13-4, submitted by Ed Long, Phoenix, Arizona, Union High School System, is an excellent example of how the bookkeeping for semester hours, semester hours completed, date of birth, and other basic information can be combined into a simple format.

Form 13-5 Residence Eligibility Approval Request, provided by the Washington Interscholastic Activities Association, is a sample form used for transfer students.

School Regulations (Reference State Handbook-Site Numbers). Basic school regulations should be included in the coaches' handbook. A brief summation of what is included under this section in the state handbook should be provided. If a coach needs a particular rule defined, he could refer to the state handbook. Items under school regulations to be included are: the furnishing of eligibility information to the state association or section; action taken when section boundary lines are crossed for competition; school's responsibility for the amateur standing and eligibility of the team and team members; practice and participation requirements for a single or multiple campus; junior high school students practice or participation requirements in regard to participating on a high school team; the requirement of a physical examination prior to participation; faculty supervision of a visiting team; days that no games or practice may be held, for example, Christmas or Sunday; days that may be missed from school for approved contests or tournaments.

PHOENIX UNION HIGH SCHOOL SYSTEM
ATHLETIC ELIGIBILITY CHECK

Ident No. _____

Last Name	First Name	Middle Initial	Birth Date	Birth Place

Street Address	City	Birth Certificate Recorded by	Date

Transfer From	Date	Birth Certificate Returned To	Date

Enrollment Date		SEMESTER of ATTENDANCE	SCHOLARSHIP		PARENTAL PERMISSION	ATHLETIC PHYSICAL	EMERGENCY MEDICAL REFERRAL	INSURANCE OR WAIVER	ELIGIBILITY STATUS			
MO.	DAY	YR		1st Sem.	2nd Sem.					1	1	2	2

FORM 13-4   Basic eligibility information. (Ed Long, Athletic Director, Phoenix, Arizona, Union High School District. By permission.)

WASHINGTON INTERSCHOLASTIC ACTIVITIES ASSOCIATION
RESIDENCE ELIGIBILITY APPROVAL REQUEST

Current

Name of Student _____ School _____ Date _____

Enrollment

Year in School _____ Date of Birth _____ Date _____

Name of Parent(s) _____

School

Address of Parent(s) _____ District _____

Person(s) with Whom Student Resides _____

School

Address of Person(s) _____ District _____

HAS LEGAL GUARDIAN BEEN APPOINTED   YES   NO   (Encircle one)

Submit certified copy of court order or letter of guardianship and list reasons why neither parent is the legal guardian. _____

_____

Is support from parent(s) continuing to student?   YES   NO   (Encircle one)

IF THERE IS OR WILL BE NO LEGAL GUARDIAN, indicate relationship of student to person(s) with whom he resides: _____

_____

Indicate reasons for living with this particular person(s) _____

_____

List specific and complete reasons why student is not residing with parent(s).
(Give financial condition, health condition, other children at home, etc.) If necessary, use back of page.

_____

_____

_____

_____

_____

The following signatures are required: _____

_____   _____

    Student   Parent(s)

_____

Person(s) with whom student resides   School Principal

Send with this completed form: (1) Transcript of credits (2) Letter from parents describing condition in home (3) Letter from adults in new home (4) Letter from previous principal(s) describing conduct in school and conditions in his home (5) Court orders or letters indicating guardianship (6) Any other information that would be helpful in substantiating hardship, such as medical and/or financial statements, etc.

FORM 13-5 Residence eligibility approval request. (Washington Interscholastic Activities Association. Bellevue, Washington. By permission.)

Each school must develop its own forms for the various school regulations. Form 13-6 is an example of a eligibility exchange sheet as used by North Dakota High School Activities Association.

Form 13-7 is an excellent example of the medical examination report for interscholastic athletic participation as used by the Phoenix,

TO BE USED FOR ALL INTER SCHOLASTIC SPORTS

Form A

ELIGIBILITY EXCHANGE SHEET

North Dakota High School Activities Association

School Colors. . . . .

Color Jersey . . . .

Alternate Colors . . . .

Student eligible to represent the . . . . High School in a . . . . Contest

. . . . Month   Day   Year

with . . . . at . . . . on . . . . Month . . . . . . Day . . . . . . Year

NAME	Jersey Number	DATE OF BIRTH Mo. Day Yr.	Code	Date of Enrollment For This Semester	Enrolled Number of Full Regular Studies Carried Successfully Last Semester	Number of Full Regular Studies Carried Successfully This Semester To Date	*Number of Semesters Previously Enrolled In H. S.	*Number of Seasons in This Form of Inter- H. S. Athletics Previous To This	Other H. S. Attended Previously If Any

The above named pupils of the . . . . High School meet all of the eligibility requirements of the N. D. High School Activities Ass'n.

I affirm that this High School is a member of the Association, having paid our dues on . . . . 19 . . . .

CODE: (a) Bureau of Vital Statistics Record; (b) Infant Baptismal Certificate;
          (c) School Records; (d) Parental Statements; (e) Other.   . . . . Superintendent

*DO NOT Include This Semester or Season.   Principal

175

FORM 13-6 Sample eligibility exchange sheet. (Duane Carlson, Athletic Director, Minot High School, Minot, North Dakota. By permission.)

1. MEDICAL EXAMINATION REPORT FOR INTERSCHOLASTIC ATHLETIC PARTICIPATION.

Name of student: _____ Age: _____ Student number: _____

Address: _____ Phone numbers: Home: _____ Office: _____

Doctor _____ Emergency _____

Family physician: _____ Address: _____

We carry accident insurance with: None _____ Blue Cross _____ Blue Shield _____ Other _____

NOTE TO PARENTS: In order that the best plans may be made for your child, it is necessary that we have your cooperation in filling out this questionnaire accurately before he can participate in interscholastic competitive sports. After conferring with your child, please sign your name after each sport in which you permit him to participate.

Baseball _____ Football _____ Rifle _____ Track _____

Basketball _____ Golf _____ Swimming _____ Wrestling _____

Cross Country _____ Gymnastics _____ Tennis _____ Other _____

Has your child had any of the following: (Each item must be checked either "Yes" or "No")

	Yes	No			Yes	No
1. Rheumatic fever			10. Has had illness lasting more than a week. Date			
2. Tuberculosis			11. Is under a physician's care now			
3. Heart disease			12. Takes medication now			
4. Poliomyelitis			13. Wears glasses.			
5. Fracture			Contact lenses			
6. Back injury			14. Has had a surgical operation. Date			
7. Head injury			15. Has been in a hospital (for other than tonsillectomy). Date			
8. Dental bridge or false teeth						
9. Has had injuries requiring medical attention? Date			16. Do you know of any reason why this child should not participate in all sports?			

Please explain any "Yes" answers to above questions:

17. Has had complete poliomyelitis immunization by inoculation (Salk) or oral vaccine (Sabin).   Date _____

18. Has had tetanus toxoid and booster inoculation within past ten years . . . . _____

PARENTAL CONSENT: I hereby give my consent for_____ to engage in Arizona Interscholastic Association approved athletic activities as a representative of his high school, as approved below by the examining physician, and I also give my consent for him to accompany the team as a member on trips.

Date: _____   _____
                                          SIGNATURE OF PARENT OR GUARDIAN

2. MEDICAL EXAMINATION REPORT (to be filled out by physician only).

Past history pertinent to competitive sports _____

Height: _____ Weight: _____ Blood pressure: _____ Pulse: _____

	Normal	Abnormal	Remarks
EENT			
Respiratory			
Cardiovascular			
Abdomen			
Hernia			
Genitalia			
Musculoskeletal			
Neurological			
Deformities			
Surgical scars			
Skin			
Urinalysis (sugar)			

Weight loss permitted to make lower wrestling weight class: Yes _____ No _____ ; if "Yes", student may lose _____ pounds.

There appears to be no medical reason why this student should not participate in athletics.

Date of examination: _____   _____
                                                          SIGNATURE OF EXAMINING PHYSICIAN

Physician's address: _____ Phone Number: _____

FORM 13-7   Medical examination report. (Ed Long, Athletic Director, Phoenix Union High School District, Phoenix, Arizona. By permission.)

Arizona Union High School District.

Amateur Standing Rule (Reference: State Handbook-Site Numbers).
Information concerning the amateur standing rule should be included
in the coaches' handbook. A summary of the material covered under
this section would inclued: definitiom of an amateur sportsman, the
spirit of amateurism; personal gain; fraudulent misrepresentation;
services as an official; reimbursement for actual expenses; tryout for
a collegiate or professional team; dollar value of an award; duration
of eligibility for violation of amateur or award rules.

General Rulings (Reference: State Handbook-Site Numbers). The
following information should be included: participation of an ineligible student; application of rules to all contests including practice
contests; period of suspension; disciplinary action; approved competition; age requirements for teams in football and wrestling; who
may coach; reimbursement for the coach's service; coaching salary
from other than school funds; recruiting; season of a sport; number
of seasons for participation; appeals procedures; intersectional dis-
putes procedures.

Outside Competition (Reference: State Handbook-Site Numbers).
Information includes: eligibility requirements for a person playing on
an "outside" team in the same sport, during the season of sport; spon-
taneous recreational activity; disqualification during current season;
international amateur competition; unattached competition; special
regulations for track and field, cross-country, swimming, and wrestling;
unattached recognition or certification; school uniforms.

Sanctioned Events (Reference State Handbook Site Numbers). In the
coaches' handbook it should be mentioned that high school students
who represent their high school in approved athletic competition shall
be under the auspices of the state association and that section approval
is required for four teams or more in one league. Sports approved for
interstate competition, the mileage requirement for sanctioned contests or events, outside organizations sponsoring high school events,
information on open meets, and regulations concerning suspension
of schools should be mentioned.

Awards (Reference State Handbook Site Numbers). Governing body for participation in state competition, monetary award for coaches in tournaments, monetary value for athletic awards to the student-athlete, holding awards until after graduation; and commercial advertising should all be discussed.

All-Star Competition (Reference State Handbook Site Numbers). The following topics should be included: participation in all-star competition; participation by member schools, for example, providing school facilities or equipment; officiating, management. organization, supervision, player selection, and coaching or promotion; suspension of the school because of violations; violation of game officials; ineligibility of high school graduated for state competition.

International Competition (Reference: State Handbook Site Numbers). The following information should be included in the coaches' handbook: application for approval of international competition; original contract; qualifications for state consideration and final approval; approval of all international high school competition by the National Federation of State High School Athletic Associations and the sanctions of the appropriate international body involved; sanctioning of qualifying trials for individual or team.

Approved Sports (Reference: State Handbook Site Numbers). Here is a summary of the following information to be included: Approved interscholastic sports without any special rulings generally are baseball, basketball, bowling, crew, fencing, golf, gymnastics, lacrosse, riflery, rugby, skiing, soccer, tennis, volleyball, and water polo. Approved interscholastic sports with special rulings generally are cross-country, football, track, swimming, and wrestling. Sports not listed are not the concern of the state association. In all sports, where National Federation rule books are published, the National Federation State High School Athletic Rule Book shall be official. In sports where the National Federation does not publish rule books, the NCAA rules (scholastic division) shall apply. All interscholastic athletic contests or tournaments in state approved sports are to be arranged so that no student shall take part in more than two athletic contests in any one day in all sports with the exception of badminton, bowling, tennis, volleyball, and wrestling. No student shall take part in more than one tournament in any one day. Concerning sports participation during the school year: state association rules and regulations for approved sports apply. During the summer, state rules do not apply except for preconditioning in football, unless authorized by the state association. Boxing is not an approved sport. School participation in interscholastic boxing shall mean suspension from all state interscholastic competition for a period of one year (California).

Summation

Eligibility determination and certification requires that the school's administration exercise constant vigilance since any misrepresentation or misinterpretation of the facts or rules usually results in adverse publicity. It may make little difference that the errors were unintentional and were honest judgmental mistakes. It would remain fact that student-athletes were erroneously certified by the school administrators as being eligible for athletic competition when indeed they were not. Depending on the circumstances where sanctions may or may not be imposed on the student-athletes and on the school's athletic program, the adverse publicity that accompanies the situation casts a stigma on all parties involved, possibly for years to come. Both the principal and athletic director must know the eligibility rules. It is the latter's responsibility to educate the coaches and students. The athletic director may have to devise and implement or revise a procedural system for eligibility determination and certification. Most certainly it is the athletic director's responsibility to monitor the data collecting-compilation system, affixing definite responsibilities as to who does what and when and how it should be done. All factual data placed on the eligibility form must be validated. In this way the principal , when asked to sign the completed form, feels secure that all factual data is valid and reliable.

Questions

1. Why does eligibility determination and certification require the athletic director's utmost attention and vigilance?
2. Your principal has asked you to propose or devise a procedural system for eligibility determination so that when he receives for his signature the certificate declaring all on the list are eligible, he knows the information is accurate, reliable, and has been vaildated. Set up such a system for your principal's approval that can be

implemented for eligibility determination or certification.

3. Two days before your big basketball game, your opponent's athletic director calls and states that he has been informed by several of the school's players that your school's two star basketball players have been playing basketball downtown in "outside competition," which is a definite violation; the opponent's athletic director asks you to look into it. Discuss how you would handle this situation; justify your decision.

4. Enumerate and discuss ways of educating and informing the coaches, students, and general public of eligibility rules, determination, and certification.

REFERENCES

1. Klumb, John J., Position Paper, Chief Bureau Health, Physical Education, Athletics and Recreation, California State Department of Education, September 1, 1975, Sacramento, California.
2. Russell, William, State Commissioner, California Interscholastic Federation, Santa Barbara, California.

SUGGESTED READINGS

Forsythe, C. E. *Administration of High School Athletics* (4th edition), Prentice-Hall, Englewood Cliffs, N.J., 1972, Ch. 4, Athletic Eligibility Regulations.

Grieve, A. W., *Directing High School Athletics,* Prentice-Hall, Englewood Cliffs, N.J., 1963, Ch.12, Eligibility Regulations.

Purdy, R. L., *The Successful High School Athletic Program,* Parker Publishing, West Nyack, N.Y., 1973, Ch. 8, Developing Relevant Eligibility Procedures for Athletes.

Chapter 14
Disciplinary Responsibilities of the Coach And the Student-Athlete

The role of the coach has been challenged in many quarters during the past decade. Many people consider the coach's authority, responsibilities, ideals, and methods to be outmoded in today's changing society. Coaches cannot take the existence of athletics for granted and can no longer assume that all people concerned with the interscholastic athletics program believe in the values of a well-rounded athletic program.

The coaching profession must constantly emphasize the values of athletics that underlie and influence attitudes and behavior not obtainable in other parts of the school curriculum. In this period of cynicism, the old clichés about character building and sportsmanship are not as readily accepted. Coaches will have to demonstrate or give evidence that definite advantages accrue to those students who participate in the interscholastic athletic programs.

Coaches must convince the community that interscholastic athletics have goals that are unique and not necessarily indentical to those of collegiate or professional sports programs. If one of the goals of the secondary school is to produce well-rounded individuals and to meet the needs and interests of all students, the interscholastic athletic program then must be considered as an integral part of the total school curriculum. Through appropriate experiences in interscholastic athletics, participants can be assisted to develop physically, intellectually, socially, and morally. Self-actualization, self-fulfillment, and self-realization should be the ultimate result.

ADMINISTRATIVE SUPPORT

The athletic director and the coaching staff must have the support of the principal, superintendent, and school board if they are to implement policies and carry out the goals and objectives of a sound athletic program. The lack of administrative support in recent years, as pointed out in Chapter 1, has been a difficult task for the athletic director and coach to overcome. Administrators have become socially or politically oriented and frequently refuse to take a stand on serious issues contrary to the best interest of athletics.

In a competitive situation involving teams, the democratic process, in its purest sense, would not be successful. As each generation moves into its era of responsibility and power, it brings to the culture new ideas and thoughts. Contributions by individuals to the decision making process are important and valuable. New thoughts and ideas are encouraged, but ultimately, one person must make the decision. The coach is that person. Most coaches agree that individuality is a healthy quality until it adversely affects a team and the people on it. Consequently, youngsters learn that a certain amount of individuality is always sacrificed when they become members of a team.

SPORTS REVOLUTIONISTS

Some students, taking their cue from the "sports revolutionists" of the late sixties and seventies tried to use athletics as a political arena to express their beliefs on some issues. William J. Bennett, Chairman of the Committee on Law and Society, Boston University[1] in his article in *Commentary Magazine* writes, "A flurry of books, Jack Scott's *The Athletic Revolution*, Paul Hoch's *Rip off the Big Game*, Joseph Durson's *The Sprots Factory*, George Leonard's *The Ultimate Athlete* present related themes telling us the whole truth about our games. These books, written mostly by non-athletes, have come in the wake of books by the players themselves, *Out of Their League* by Dave Meggysey, *They Call it a Game* by Bernie Barrish, *High for the Game* by Chip Oliver and the early and popular *Ball Four* by Jim Bouton. Mixed in have been some works of fiction which simultaneously apotheosize and make fun of sports and athletics, the sybaritic *Semi-Tough* by Dan Jenkins and the interesting but maudlin *North Dallas Forty* by former Dallas receiver Pete Gent."

Bennett continues,

> The lessons these books teach are that sports and sportsman are exploited by a power elite; that college football players are member of a "frenzied slave market" and victims of torture and drills which resemble concentration camp muster; that drugs and amphetamines are part of the professional athlete's steady diet; that organized athletics systematically emphasizes "cool" over character; and that athletics offer a particularly offensive and dangerous misrepresentation of the sporting life to children.
>
> Sports in America is alleged to be sexist, racist and male-chauvinistic. America's gods of the playing field are made of clay, or lesser stuff. "The politics of sports are reactionary," says Jack Scott, pointing to "the conservative militaristic nature of intercollegiate athletics.

Although most of these comments are directed to professional and intercollegiate athletics, they have filtered down to the secondary school level in forms of "sports literature classes". Jack Scott's *Athletics for Athletes*, which teaches the overthrow of the "militaristic" coach, is frequently required reading in such classes.

In the case of *Neuhaus v. Torry*[2], Scott's book was used as a guideline to overthrow the rules and regulation of a high school athletic department. However, here, the judge upheld the athletic director in establishing that "In these parlous, troubled times when discipline in certain quarters appears to be an ugly word, it should not be considered unreasonable nor regarded as an impingement of constitutional prerogatives, to require plaintiffs to bring themselves within the spirit, purpose and intendments of the questioned rule."

In concluding his article, Bennett says,

> No matter what else it is, sports has always been an arena in which children can grow in light of unambiguous, tangible universal standards and measures. With the proper supervision and coaching the only limits are those of an individual's abilities and the abilities of the best players of the game. Sports is still an activity in which excellence can be seen and reached for and approximated each day; sports has been relatively unaffected by the general erosion of standards in the culture.
>
> Everyone knows where the truth lies in these matter, really. It is not for nothing that the attempts to de-athleticize athletics and to deflate the country's interest in sports have met with uniform failure. Counter-cultural sports programs have dried up. As a nation, Americans have expressed more, not less interest in a growing number of competitive athletics since the "revolution" began, and if anything seem to be resisting the tendencies toward leveling in sports.

ESTABLISHING RULES

The courts established the right of the coach to set reasonable standards and rules for his team. The legal aspect of interscholastic athletics is discussed in Chapter 15, however, it is appropriate to point out here that the courts recognize "without the need of any evidence of actual experience, that discipline, uniformity and a proper atmosphere are all essential ingredients for team spirit and safe, efficient operation of a team."[3]

Once the rules are established and the coach makes a decision, he must know that he has the support of the athletic director, the principal, and the superintendent.

To avoid conflict, the coach must orient his players to the responsibilities they have as athletes. The rules must be published and posted so that everyone concerned is aware of their responsibilities. When rules are imposed as whims of a coach, without explanation or apparent reason, the coach may not receive support. It is best to have a clear understanding before finalizing rules, in order to avoid any misunderstandings.

Athletes should share in the development of team goals and be asked for input regarding player conduct rules. Generally speaking, the fewer rules the better. There should be a player's council through which they can have dialogue with the coaching staff regarding player responsibilities.

Responsibilities of the Coach[4]

When one enters the coaching profession, one assumes many responsibilities. Those directly relating to the athlete include:

1. The coach is responsible to the athletes as individuals. The coach assumes the task of developing the athletic skills of each young person with whom he works, developing the ability of each athlete to cope with the mental or stress aspects of athletic competition, knowing his athletes both on and off the field, being sincerely interested in athletes as total individuals not strictly as athletes, developing lines of communication between the coaching staff and athletes so that the coaches may be better able to evaluate the effectiveness of their program.

2. The coach is responsible to the athlete as an individual, as he relates to his teammates and team situation. The coach assumes the task of developing, in addition to the skills necessary for individual achievement, athletic skills which are necessary for the effective performance of the team, developing the ability of each athlete to emotionally and socially work with others in achieving a common goal.

3. The coach is responsible to his athletes as a team. The coach assumes the task of directing the athletes on the team in a way which will bring the greatest achievement to each of them as individuals and as members of a team. Rules concerning training, conduct, appearance are all within the scope of the coach's responsibility when they relate to the team. When problems arise affecting the group, the coach must deal with them in a fair manner. This responsibility inescapably belongs to the coach and to no one else.

4. The coach must assume the task of keeping abreast of all advances made in his particular sport by continued self-education through current literature, by attendance and participation at sport workshops, clinics and seminars. The coach must be receptive to new ideas and learn about new methods, techniques and training concepts.

Responsibilities of the Student-Athlete

While the coach has responsibilities, so do the athletes. One of the most important is the athlete's responsibility to the team. When a young person joins an athletic team, he becomes involved as a member of a group which has several goals. The most common of these is the opportunity to compete, the opportunity to test one's self. If they are successful, they will win. The athlete shouls strive for this.

When the athlete accepts any of the group's goals, he must make personal sacrifices would include:

1. The devotion of training time to the task of self-improvement in the area of developing athletic skills.

2. The acceptance of rules concerning conduct and appearance, realizing that these rules were established not to suppress individuals, but to enable all individuals to better work together as a team.

3. Being aware that an athlete's talents are evaluated and adapted to the team situation, resulting in greater positive achivement for the individual and the team.

The young person who joins a team realizes that if the goals of the team are to be reached, one person evaluating many factors must make the decisions concerning training, conduct, appearance, game strategy, etc. This person is the coach. The athlete realizes that any other type of team direction will result in individual pockets of opinion tugging at the team, at the expense of the team in terms of loss of effort, energy and time. The athlete realizes that the coach is not infallible, but because of his experience and his broad view of the total picture, is best able to reach certain decisions concerning each individual and the team.

When both coach and athlete fulfill their responsibilities, each of them benefits from the athletic experience. In addition, the team, as a group, benefits and athletics truly becomes an instrument in the total education of youth. The concomitant outcomes of athletics are then better realized.

The Need for Discipline. Payton Jordon,[5] highly successful veteran track coach at Stanford University and head coach for the United States Track and Field team in the 1968 Olympics, said,

> Discipline is the sword of success. Each of us is endowed with God given strength, but all too often there is lack of will. This ingredient must come from within the individual. Often it takes a nudge from an outside influence to establish the right and wrong of things. Individuality is the constant hue and cry of the young as they strive for maturity and independence. This is a wholesome thing as long as a true sense of responsibility goes with the privilege. Certainly athletics serve as one of the cornerstone of discipline. It is here, during the shaping of the individual, that an alert and interested eye must be cast to guide and keep proper perspective. Will power is possibly the most important factor for athletic success and it can be bought only through discipline.

Fred C. Clark and Richard S. Rimanoczy[6] in their article, *Discipline—The Keystone of Civilization and Progress*, state,

> Let us start with a simple train of thought. Man's material welfare is based on civilization. Civilization is based on law and order. Law and order is based on discipline.
>
> Discipline is of two types, that which is imposed on children to form the personal habits that make good character. It must also be imposed on adults who do not impose it on themselves. Discipline must prevail, and people who do not discipline themselves within the framework of the law must be disciplined by others.

Constructing a Reasonable Rule

Although this chapter is not dealing with the legal aspects of interscholastic athletics, we are attempting to point out that the student-athlete wants and needs discipline and the coach has a right to set rules for the betterment of the program. Marshall A. Staunton[7], legal counsel for the California Teachers Association, said in his speech to the California State Athletic Directors Association,

> We, the profession, are now in a position to construct a rule that should withstand an attack that is an unconstitutional regulation of a student's right to free expression. First, the rule should apply solely to athletic teams and not to students generally. Second, the rule should contain a statement that restrictions are necessary to prevent disruption of team morale which would have a prejudicial affect on team spirit and proper team discipline cannot be maintained in absence of such rule. Third, the rule should be supported by a statement that proper habits of discipline

and the development of character, inititative and teamwork, outweight an impairment of students' rights, and fourth, the rule should be supported by a statement that proper habits of discipline and the development of personality cannot be achieved by any other available alternative.

Regardless of the fact that the coach and athletic director have the right to set reasonable rules and regulations for their teams, this will be negated unless they have the support of the principal and super-intendent. In the final analysis, It will actually depend on what the parents and the community accept and what rules and regulations the board of education and the superintendent endorse.

DEVELOPING A CODE OF CONDUCT

The success of any athletic program or team can be directly in-fluenced by the nature and amount of discipline to which it is subjected and the response to this discipline. The athlete must will-ingly assume the obligations connected with being a part of an athletic program. The athlete gives time, energy, and loyalty to the program. He also accepts training rules, regulations, and responsibilities that are unique to an athletic program. The athlete's personal contribu-tion are for the welfare of the group. For success, it is not the activity of the sport itself, but the attitude and discipline that become a part of each athlete.

The coach should communicate with the team and instruct the players on the importance of certain rules and help them see the long range effects of good training habits. Rules and discipline vary from school to school. However, each coach should have the rules on paper and have them read and signed by the players and parents so that there will be no question as to the expected behavior of the team members.

Once the rule is in effect, the enforcement should include every-one. The legendary Vince Lombardi[8] said, "The one thing I insist on is that any rule we make, everybody has to live by, without deviation. But is you don't like the rule, you can speak up. We've changed rules when somebody protested, but I have never changed any rule when the form of protest was breaking the rule."

Paul "Bear" Bryant, University of Alabama[9] suspended Joe Namath for violations of training rules. When Coach Bryant made his decision, he told Namath, "All of the coaches except one think I have made a mistake, but I have made up my mind to suspend you because you've broken the rules and I can't change that decision. If I did, or if the University changed my decision, I'd have to retire at the end of the season because I would be breaking my own rules."

Athletic Codes

Athletic codes serve as guides concerning rules and attitudes toward team membership. Once the rules are decided upon, the board of education assumes that the coaches are enforcing them in spirit and in fact. As mentioned previously in this chapter, there are as many codes for athletics as there are schools. The following are samples of athletic codes that may be incoporated into a form that is now in existence in your school or program.

Kent School District, King County, Washington spells out discipline in a letter to the coaches in the district.

Kent District also uses a "Procedure for Athletes" form.

Ben Jones, well-known authority on interscholastic athletics and athletic director for Susquehanna Township School district, Harrisburg, Pennsylvania, has developed a student pledge.

Summation

Coaches should not include a rule in an athletic code or training rules if they are not going to enforce that rule at a later date, if it is violated. The decision should be made in advance because human behavior being what it is, the coach may be tested to see if he will impose the penalty for violation of the rule. The penalty should be specified when the rules are formulated. In this way the student-athletes know in advance what the sanction is going to be for violation of the rules. Although reasonable rules may be devised for all squad members, often the penalty is not imposed uniformly on all violators. The substitute may receive a more severe penalty than the star performer, which is inconsistent on the part of the coach and actually does more harm to team morale than if the rules were applied indiscriminately to all.

Student input is important both in devising the rules and imposing penalties for violation of the rules. However, a coach must use discretion and offer guidance as, at times, students may want to impose unreasonable rules and harsh punishment. They may lose sight of the purpose and objective of rules and discipline. They are merely a means to the end and in themselves, not the end.

DISCIPLINE

The Athletic Code has been our guide for making it clear what rules and attitudes will be. Our school board recognizes this and is assuming that coaches are enforcing this in spirit as well as in fact. It has been my observation that those coaches that have used the Code have had the best discipline and usually the best teams.

Your position as coach provides one of the greatest opportunities to understand the need for discipline that a boy may encounter in all his educational experiences. Your turnout procedures, attendance regulations and game tactics, as well as how you deal with rule violations will reflect your disciplinary abilities, and greatly determine your effectiveness as a coach. It is the weak coach who is the athletes "buddy," instead of his teacher, and leaves the discipline to others or neglects it entirely.

The head coach is usually the judge of what shall be done where rules are violated, but the Athletic Director and Principal should be kept informed when any serious violation occurs. Some standard guide lines might help us to be more consistant, however, when major infractions do occur:

- □ we want to be firm, but insure that justice prevails.
- □ we are concerned first with what is best for all our kids, and secondly with what is best for the individual.
- □ suspension is usually the best device where major discipline is needed as it is felt most strongly by the boy and makes it clear that you will do without him, if he does not live up to standards set.
  - □ it is here that parents, teachers, ánd community do not always understand your actions (the athlete almost always understands quite clearly.)
  - □ a suspension can be for a definite time (day, week, month, season) or can be an indefinite suspension (until a specific purpose has been realized, in your opinion)

If you want your coaching efforts to be taken seriously by administration, teachers, community and most important, by kids themselves, it is in this area that the difference usually lies. In appointment of coaches, it is much easier to evaluate their technical coaching potential than it is this highly subjective ability to handle athletes in a manner that will insure the realization of aims and objectives set forth. This thinking should be applied to "out-of-season" athletes as much as possible as we are most anxious to eliminate the "3 month athlete."

By permission

Jack Burrell
Athletic Director
Kent School District No. 415
King County, Kent, Washington

FORM 14-1 Discipline letter to coaches. (Kent School District, King County, Washington. By permission.)

PROCEDURE FOR DISCIPLINE OF ATHLETES

Probation: There can be a trial period, during which an athlete remains a part of his squad while he attempts to correct his deficiencies in a time prescribed by the head coach. Probation might be used for certain minor cases.

Probation Procedure:

1. Inform the athlete of his deficiencies and how he is to correct them.
2. Send a letter home to his parents (See Dept. form)
3. Send a copy to the Building Chairman.
4. Upon completion of probationary period:
   a. If the deficiency is corrected, the athlete is removed from probationary status.
   b. If the deficiency is not corrected, the probationary period is extended, or the athlete is restricted.

Restricted: This is a dual action taken by both the head coach and the athletic department, during which an athlete is not to participate in any athletic contests and may be restricted from active turnouts until appropriate corrections have been made. Restriction should be used in cases involving serious code violations.

Restricted Procedure:

1. Inform the athlete of the reason for, and the condition of, his status.
2. Send a letter to his parents. (See Dept. form)
3. Send copies to Building Chairman, Athletic Director, Principal, Letterman's Club advisor.

Steps for Reinstating an Athlete who has been Restricted: (See Dept. Form)

1. Student obtains form from his coach, completes it and returns it to his coach.
2. Coach accepts or rejects it and passes it on to the Building Chairman.
3. The Building Chairman accepts or rejects it. If accepted, he then notifies:

   a. The athlete and his parents.
   b. Athletic Director
   c. Coach
   d. Principal
   e. Letterman's Club advisor.

In the event there is a disagreement within the Athletic Department, a hearing will be held. The Building Chairman, Athletic Director and Principal will conduct the hearing.

By Permission:
Mr. Jack Burrell
Kent School District No. 415
King County, Kent, Washington

FORM 14-2 Procedure for discipline of athletes. (Kent School District 415, King County, Washington. By permission.)

SUSQUEHANNA TOWNSHIP SCHOOL DISTRICT
Harrisburg, Pennsylvania 17109

CODE OF CONDUCT FOR ATHLETES

STUDENT PLEDGE

All participants in athletics have received a copy of the Code of Conduct for Athletes. This should be read carefully by the parents as well as the athletes. The Pledge which follows summarized the major features of the Code and is designed to permit the athlete to indicate his or her willingness to abide by the standards and sanctions of the Code.

STANDARD 1 — *SATISFACTORY SCHOOL CITIZENSHIP*

Adheres to all rules of conduct of the school, shows proper respect for students and family, works for the betterment of the school and sets aside personal interests and gains in favor of those of the school.

STANDARD 2 — *ADHERENCE TO PRESCRIBED TRAINING RULES*

Adheres to specific training rules set forth by the coach, refrains from smoking and drinking and appreciates the importance of rest, diet and exercise. Practices healthful habits of cleanliness and personal hygiene.

STANDARD 3 — *CONDUCT BECOMING AN ATHLETE*

Refrains both from moral conduct not considered acceptable by the community and from violating state statutes and township ordinances. Does not use profanity and refrains from any action of conduct that reflects unfavorably upon athletes and the school.

STANDARD 4 — *ADHERENCE TO STANDARDS OF GOOD SPORTSMANSHIP*

Shows respect in defeat and modesty in victory, is courteous to officials, teammates, opponents and coaches. Employs legal tactics as they apply to the rules.

By permission:
Ben Jones, Athletic Director
Susquehanna Township High School
Harrisburg, Pennsylvania 17109

FORM 14-3 Student pledge. (Ben Jones, Athletic Director, Susquehanna Township School District, Harrisburg, Pennsylvania. By permission.)

After obtaining student input, it is suggested that all rules be written, explained, and distributed to the participants at an early meeting. This gives those individuals who do not wish to adhere to the rules the opportunity to terminate their membership on the squad at an early date. It would be well for the coach to explain the purpose and objective of the rules and to help the student-athletes understand why they are necessary. The objective is to get the student-athletes to be self-regulatory and to adhere to the rules because of their value. Also to impose adherence to the rules on each other rather than forcing the coach to impose the penalty when he learns of a violation. The coach must decide in advance how he will validate information concerning the breaking of rules by his athletes that comes to him from an outside source.

The fewer rules the better. All rules should be reasonable. A coach must keep up with changing times and be careful not to impose outdated training rules. Through the athletic director's guidance, if unanimity can be reached by all of the coaches on the athletic code, training rules, discipline and grievance procedures, many problems will be resolved in advance. Problems can also be alleviated if there is a uniform policy for handling coach and student-athlete grievances.

Questions

1. Discuss what you think the reasons are for the coaches' lament, "There is apathy and lack of discipline in the schools today and the administration won't back us in imposing training rules and discipline on our squad members!"
2. Why is it desirable to have one "Athletic Code" for all student-athletes for all sports, rather than permitting each coach to set up his own athletic code for his particular sport?
3. In this chapter we spoke of the responsibilities of the coach and those of the participant, the student-athlete, in the interscholastic athletic program. Enumerate and discuss the responsibilities of both people in this context.
4. What are methods or techniques that coaches could utilize to "sell" or get student-athletes to accept training rules and discipline, so that they would be self-regulatory or self-policing as an individual or a group?
5. Training rules and sanctions that are imposed should be reasonable. If you were a member of a coaching staff, which training rules would you formulate, along with the sanctions for violating your training? Enumerate and discuss.

REFERENCES

1. Bennet, William J., *"A Defense of Sports"* reprinted from *Commontary* by permission; Copyright (c) 1976 by the American Jewish Committee. Commentary Magazine, 165 E. 56th Street, New York.
2. Harris, Judge George B., United States District Court, Northern California *Neuhaus v. Torrey*, No. c-70304 GBH, March 10, 1970.
3. Ibid.
4. Baeta, Albert, American River College, *"Responsibilities of the Coach and Student Athlete,"* *Cal Coach Magazine*, 445 Crestmont Drive, Oakland, Ca. 94619, 1972, pp. 13-14. By permission.
5. Jordan, Payton, Track Coach, Stanford University, *Discipline is the Sword of Success*. Clinic handout, 1969. By permission.
6. Clark, Fred G. and Rimanoczy, Richard S., *"Discipline—The Keystone of Civilization and Progress,"* *The Economic Facts of Life*, Vol. 22, No. 9, September 1969.
7. Staunton, Marshall A., Legal Counsel, California Teachers Association, *Cal Coach Magazine*, 1970, pp. 5-7. By permission.
8. Kramer, Jerry, *Instant Replay*, The World Publishing Company, New York, 1972.
9. Bryant, Paul, *Football Coaches' Dilemma*, Associated Press, NCAA News, October 1973.

SUGGESTED READINGS

George, J.R. and Lehmann, H.A., *School Athletic Administration*, Harper and Row, New York, 1966, Chs 2 and 12.

Grieve, A.W., *Directing High School Athletics*, Prentice-Hall, Englewood Cliffs, N.J., 1963. Ch. 12.

Hixson, C.G., *The Administration of Interscholastic Athletics*, J. Lowell Pratt, New York, 1967, Ch. 5.

Purdy, R.L., *The Successful High School Athletic Program* Parker Publishing, West Nyack, N.Y., 1973, Ch. 2.

Chapter 15
The Courts and Interscholastic Athletics

The State Athletic Associations have always been the sole judge in the enforcement of rules and regulations and legal action taken against interscholastic athletics. Today the trend has changed and the courts are asserting more and more jurisdiction over the high school athletic program. Rules initiated by the state associations or boards of education have come under attack in most every state. The attack usually stems from a student who claims that he is being denied the right to an education because of a rule or regulation that makes him or her ineligible to participare in interscholastic athletics. John C. Hogan,[1] writing in the *Phi Delta Kappan* said, "The relief sought is an injunction. Professional educators should know that the granting or denying of a temporary injunction neither establishes the law of the case nor constitutes an adjudication on the merits of the issue raised in the complaint. Time, however, is often all the student really wants, since in some cases it will render the controversy moot." Mr. Hogan sites the case of Behagen v. Intercollegiate Conference of Faculty Representatives[2] to explain the criteria for determining the propriety of granting a request for a preliminary injunction. The court said that there are four criteria:

1. Has the plaintiff shown substantial probability of success at trial on the merits?
2. Has the plaintiff shown irreparable injury, one that is going to substantially affect the student's educational process?
3. Will the interest of the other party be substantially impaired by issuance of such an order?
4. How will the public interest be affected?

The athletic director has an obligation to keep himself informed on the current state of the law as it relates to his profession. He should be well informed on the laws in order to foresee problem areas in his own school and take appropriate action.

Dr. Herb Appenzeller, Athletic Director at Guilford College, North Carolina[3], author of *From the Gym to Jury*, and numerous well-received articles on the legal aspects of interscholastic athletics indicates that "the mood of the courts may be changing." Dr. Appenzeller says, "after studying the diversity of regulations among the 50 state associations that have contributed to the numerous suits involving all areas of student life, that the court's decisions are not reassuring for the profession. Athletes continue to challenge the rules by questioning the constitutionality and validity of the regulations in state handbooks." He concludes that state high school associations are no longer immune from law suits.

THE RIGHT OF THE COACH TO ENFORCE REASONABLE REGULATIONS

A landmark decision was handed down by federal court Judge George B. Harris in the *Newhaus v. Torrey* case.[4] This case was mentioned briefly in Chapter 14. We believe the opinion that this important decision for profession should be restated at this point. The plaintiffs, five track athletes, were seeking relief respecting a regulation of the school district, which provided in part:

Grooming Regulations:
(a) Each athlete will be well groomed and neat in appearance at all times.
(b) Each athlete will be clean shaven.
(c) The hair will be out of the eyes, trimmed above the ears and above the collar in the back.
Willful violation of the rules by any athlete will lead to his suspension from all athletic competition during the season in which the rules-infraction occurred.

Plaintiffs concede that they are in violation of the said rule and exceed the standards therein set forth. They further allege that they will be unable to compete in field, track and other athletic competition unless the rule is enjoined.

The court considered the testimony of a number of witnesses, including team coaches.

Judge Harris in his summary stated,

In these parlous, troubled times when discipline in certain quarters appears to be an ugly word, it should not be considered unreasonable nor regarded as an impingement of constitutional perrogatives, to require plaintiffs to bring themselves within the spirit, purpose and intendments of the questioned rule.

This Court does not believe that the application of the questioned rule, under all of the circumstances and in the setting of this case, approximates constitutional proportions, and the Court so holds.

Further, there is a reasonable probability in the present posture that the case, if tried on the merits, would be decided adversely to the plaintiffs.

Accordingly, the motion for preliminary injunction is DENIED, and the temporary restraining order vacated, annuled and set aside.

The foregoing memorandum of decision embraces and contains the Court's findings of fact and conclusions of law in conformity with F.R.C.P. Section 52 (a)

Dated: March 10, 1970 George B. Harris, United States District Judge

The decision was a breakthrough for the profession, but was unheeded in most quarters by coaches and athletic directors. The length of hair became the main issue but this was not the point. The case in point was the right of the coach to set reasonable rules, which the Judge and the Court upheld.

Dr. Herb Appenzeller,[5] authority on school law, stated,

The courts historically have deferred policymaking management of athletics to those who conduct the programs. As long as policies are fair and reasonable, there is nothing to fear from the courts. When programs include rules that are arbitrary and unreasonable, then and only then, will the courts take over. Outdated regulations and a reluctance to change cause problems for coaches and athletic directors.

LEGAL TERMS AND DEFINITIONS[6]

The athletic director must become more knowledgeable concerning the legal aspects of athletics. People are more suit conscious. This is the day of the tort. Generally, people do not feel they are suing the coach; they are suing the insurance company for the money involved. In the end the total athletic program suffers.

The athletic director, while knowledgable in his own field, is often at a loss when discussing jurisprudence or any type of legislation regarding the legalities in interscholastic athletics.

State associations should engage legal counsel to render advice to local districts when coaches and administrators are exposed to legal action in the area of discipline or to other threatened or potential legal action.

A few of the more common legal terms are included. These will afford the athletic director an opportunity to become more familiar with the legal aspects of athletics.

Theories of Governmental Immunity [7]

1. The sovereign theory: The school district acts as an instrument of the state in carrying out the governmental function of education under the concept of "the king can do no wrong."
2. The trust fund theory: The school district is not liable since it is an involuntary corporation, organized not for the purpose of profit or gain, but solely for the public benefit; it has no monies out of whieh such damages could be paid, and it does not have the power to raise monies for such purpose. Since the property they posses is held in trust, the payment of judgment in tort would amount to a diversion or distruction of the trust.
3. The agency theory: This seeks to absolve the boards of public schools from liability because they are agents of the state.

Governmental Function.
This refers mainly to activities of a sovereign nature. Functions such as education, police protection, and public health would fall into this category. Since public education is a governmental function, it is thereby entitled to the state's immunity from liability for its own negligence.

Propriety Function.
This function refers to government's functions which are similar to those of a business enterprise. An example of this function would be the manufacture, distribution, and sale of some product to the public such as a cafeteria conducted for profit or an athletics program charging admission for varsity games. Fees charged have a bearing upon whether recreation is a governmental or a proprietary function.

Negligent Conduct.
This may involve action or a lack of action with foreseeability as the test to determine proper or negligent conduct. In situations where a reasonably prudent person could have forseen or anticipated the harmful consequences of his action, or lack of action, an individual who disregards the foreseeable consequences may be liable if his conduct results in injury to anothers. Failure to act as a reasonably, prudent person would act under the circumstances is the generally accepted rule of thumb for negligent determination.

Defenses of Negligence.
1. An act of God: Circumstances surrounding the injury are beyond the coach's control or that of the school district.
2. Assumptions of risk: If the plaintiff has been well informed as to the risk that exists through his participation in a particular activity, then an injury that might occur would not be entirely unknown to the participant. In a case of this kind, the physical education teacher or coach would be able to use the doctrine, "assumption of risk," in defense of his position.
3. Contributory negligence: In a case of this kind, even though the teacher or coach should be negligent, if the injured participant is also negligent, such negligence could provide some defense in respect to the liability on the part of the teacher or coach.
4. Proximate cause: The negligence of the defendant may not have been the proximate cause of the plaintiff's injury.
5. Sudden emergency: Where the situation requires immediate action on the part of a teacher and, as a result, an accident occurs.

Most Common Legal Terms
1. Abrogate: To annul or repeal a former law by the passage of a new one. Abrogation may be by express words or by necessary implication.
2. Accrue: To grow to, to be added to, as interest to principal. To arise, to happen, to come to pass, as a cause of action.
3. Advocate: One who conducts or pleads a cause for another, a lawyer.
4. Foreseeability: Event anticipated and could have been prevented.
5. In loco parentis: In the place of a parent, usually refers to school of teacher.
6. Liability: A debt or responsibility of the state or one who is bound in law and justice to do something which may be enforced by action. To make a person accountable for his actions.
7. Plaintiff: One who brings an action.
8. Statute: A law encated by the legislative power in a county or state. This covers most of the laws we live under.
9. Third party: One who is a stranger to a contract, or proceeding, not being plaintiff or defendant.
10. Tort: Injury or wrong inflicted upon another involuntarily.
11. Waive: To forego, to decline to take advantage of a legal right or an omission or irregularity of another person.

How to Avoid Liability Suits

The Coaches' Handbook[7] discusses how the reasonable and prudent coach can avoid a law suit. The handbook, published by the American Association of Health, Physical Education and Recreation points out

The relationship of the coach to athletes requires, generally, that the coach act as a reasonable, prudent person, carrying out the duties of the coaching profession. If the circumstances existing at a given moment would cause the fictitious reasonable prudent person to take some action or refrain from conducting himself in some manner, and the coach fails to act or fails to refrain, then he has been negligent. If, however, no reasonably prudent coach would have anticipated the occurrence of the event, or no reasonable precaution could have prevented the particular event, then there is not liability.

A Reasonable, Prudent, and Careful Coach

1. Knows the health status of his players.
2. Requires medical approval for participation following serious injury or illness.
3. Performs services only in those areas in which he is fully qualified.
4. Performs the proper act in case of injury.
5. Has medical personnel available at all contests and readily available during practice sessions..
6. Conducts activities in safe areas.
7. Does not diagnose or treat injuries.
8. Makes certain that the protective equipment worn by his players is adequate in quality and fits properly.
9. Analyzed his coaching methods and procedures for the safety of his players.
10. Assigns only qualified personnel to conduct or supervise activities.
11. Instructs adequately before permitting performance.
12. Keeps an accurate record of serious injuries and his ensuing acts.
13. In all his actions or inactions, he asks himself, "What would the reasonable prudent, careful and discerning coach do under these circumstances?"

Who May be Held Liable[8]

Principals, supervisors, coaches and other teachers are subject to the usual rule covering tort liability. This means that individuals are liable for injuries resulting from their negligence and are not liable, regardless of the kind of injury, if not negligent. The following elements are necessary if a suit based upon negligence is to be successful:

1. Duty to conform to a standard of behavior that will not subject others to an unreasonable risk or injury.

2. Breach of duty.
3. A sufficiently close casual connection between the conduct or behavior and the resulting injury.
4. Damage or injury resulting to the right of interests of another.

In view of these elements, it can be seen that negligence is based not only upon carelessness but also upon conduct or behavior that should be recognized as involving risks to others. A coach who fails to avoid a dangerous situation through carlessness, ignorance, forgetfulness, or poor judgment may be found negligent and held liable for damages. One of the best ways to avoid negligence is to apply the rules of safety at all times.

Because the states differ with respect to legal responsibilities it is suggested that each coach:

1. Be thoroughly acquainted with the statutes and court decisions relative to school district liability in the state.
2. In those cases where the meaning of these statutes is not clear, secure rulings from state legal authorities.
3. When necessary, seek advice of legal counsel; it is unwise for anyone to attempt to be his own attorney.
4. If your school agrees to buy insurance, be sure it is legally permissable to use school money for that purpose.

Elimination of Sex Discrimination in Interscholastic Athletics Programs.

Title IX, Education Amendments of 1972[9] became effective on July 21, 1975 and cannot be changed without the introduction of new legislation. Here are some of the details as they affect programs in interscholastic athletics:

1. The regulation applies to every recipient of federal funds and to each program of activity operated by such recipient which receives or benefits from such assistance.
2. The regulation requires that no person shall, on the basis or sex, be denied admission or subject to discrimination in admission by any recipient subject to the admission provision of Title IX.
3. No person shall, on the basis of sex, be excluded from participation in, be denied the benefits of, or be subjected to discrimination under any academic, extracurricular, research, occupational training or any other education program or activity operated by a recipient.
4. A recipient may provide separate toilet, locker room and shower facilities on the basis of sex, provided that those for one sex are comparable to those for the other.

5. Students may be grouped by ability in physical education classes and activities as long as ability is assessed by objective standards developed and applied without regard to sex. Students may be separated by sex within physical education classes during participation in contact sports.
6. Institutions may not discriminate against any person on the basis of sex in the counseling or guidance of students or applicants.
7. If a recipient awards athletic scholarships it must provide such awards for member of each sex in proportion to the number of students of each sex participating in interscholastic athletics.
8. No person shall, on the basis of sex, be excluded from participation in, be denied the benefits of, be treated differently from another person or otherwise be discriminated against in any interscholastic, club or intramural athletics offered by a recipient, and no recipient shall provide athletics separately on such basis.
9. Separate teams may, however, be operated for members of each sex where: selection for such teams is based upon competitive skill; or the activity involved is a contact sport.
10. Where a recipient operates or sponsors a team in a particular sport for members of one sex but operates no such team for members of the other, and athletic opportunities for members of that sex have previously been limited, members of the excluded sex must be allowed to try out for the team unless the sport involved is a contact sport (boxing, wrestling, rugby, ice hockey, football, basketball, and other sports the major activity of which involves bodily contact.)
11. Equal opportunity for members of both sexes must be provided in interscholastic, club or intramural athletics operated or sponsored by a recipient. In assessing the availability of equal opportunity, HEW will consider among other factors: whether the selection of sports and levels of competition effectively accommodate the interests and abilities of members of both sexes; provision of equipment and supplies scheduling of games and practice time; travel and per diem allowance; opportunity to receive coaching and academic tutoring; assignment and compensation of coaches; provision of locker rooms, practice and competitive facilities; provision of housing and dining facilities and services, publicity.
12. Unequal aggregate expenditures for members of each sex or for male and female teams will not constitute noncompliance, but HEW may consider the failure to provide necessary funds for teams for one sex in assessing equality of opportunity.

All recipient institutions must comply as expeditiously as possible. Secondary schools must be in full compliance with this section within three years from the effective date of July 21, 1975.

Student Communication Rights

George Triezenberg, Principal of D. D. Eisenhower High School, Blue Island, Illinois[10] writing in the National Association of Secondary School Principals Bulletin has this to say about student communication rights.

> We owe it to ourselves to leave to future generations of educators not only vestiges of the problems of our times, origins and developments, but also any insight we may have gained in meeting our daily tasks; insights that might serve as guidelines for current and future administrative behavior over and above legal opinion.
>
> Most of us were reared on the the theory that in loco parentis (acting as the parents) was as American as apple pie and mother love. Due process for students did not somehow meet the needs of a society in which the motto of "children should be seen and not heard" prevailed, and school definitely was not an exception.
>
> In the American system of education, states generally allocated the responsibility for governing and managing public schools to elected or appointed school boards. Regulations of student conduct and appearance stemmed from traditional reasoning community standards (accepted and confirmed by the courts) that school boards were unique in their competence to judge student conduct. Their decisions were not to be questioned except in cases of a flagrant violation of the rules of decency and justice. Then too, it was believed that education was a privilege, not a right, and most importantly, school boards could act in place of the student's parents in enforcing behavioral codes. The rule of "in loco parentis" has been most difficult to dislodge from the minds of administrators.

Defining Student Rights

Triezenberg continues,

> In attempting to survey the scope of student rights American Civil Liberties Union publications probably best describe the broad dimensions involved. They define freedom of expression and communication as the primary liberties in a student's life, those having to do with the process of acquiring learning, acquiring and imparting knowledge, and exchanging of ideas. Paramount among the priorities is the access to varied points of view, and the right to confront and to study controversial issues.

In summary, George Trizenberg states,

> It would appear that the following points are of major and practical

import to me as a secondary school principal:

1. Case after case clearly indicates that schools must establish proof of disruption to invoke disciplinary action in regard to rights of free speech and distribution of printed matter.
2. While schools have been directed by the courts to recognize the fact that the Bill of Rights is also the possession of juveniles, school disciplinary hearings are not required to be a criminal adversary hearing to measure up to due process demands.
3. Recent court decisions involving students, when courts have ruled against schools, have not abolished the authority of schools to regulate students. Rather they have spelled out the boundaries within which rules are permissible. Within these boundaries schools can and must continue to make regulations which enhance educational opportunities for students or young people.
4. School personnel would be well advised not to conclude that the courts and the public they serve, are not concerned with proper discipline in the schools. While recent court decisions may appear to allow a greater degree of permissiveness for students, the public has consistently regarded discipline problems in the schools as the major problem facing its educational institutions. It was only this year that discipline has yielded its top ranking to finance and integration.
5. From 1964-1968 assaults on school personnel increased 70%. This period of time parallels an era of court decisions which diminished disciplinary prerogatives of school authorities. Is there a cause and effect relationship here or must we look to other factors in operation in our society?
6. Acts of truancy, violence, disruption, libel, obscenity and disorder often accompany free speech and protest. School personnel would do well to focus on these illegal acts rather than zero in on freedom of expression and criticism in meeting the challenge of orderly, effective schools. They stand to be more successful in meeting the challenges of the day and the scrutiny of the state and federal courts.
7. As the school administrator seeks to measure up to his responsibilities as an educator in the decade of the '70's, he welcomes the contributions and assistance from his colleagues in the legal community. At times they are a welcome ally and a resource of considerable magnitude. On many occasions, however, they fall short in providing a dependable beacon light as we seek to chart our course to meet the challenges of our day.
8. We need and we welcome more clearly and more consistently the assistance of the legal community in making education more accountable and more effective for our youth, our nation and our world. Schools are more than legal aid societies.

Dr. Herb Appenzeller[11], writing in the *Kendall Sports Trail Magazine* concurs with Mr. Triezenberg in regard to courts and school administration.

> Not only do courts tend to back school administrators, but they expect action when violence is imminent and the safety of people is threatened. Students are not given immunity just because they attend school, nor do they have the right to violate the constitutional guarantees of others. The court has said specifically that administrators have the duty to create a climate that is conducive to learning and that a student does not have the right to hinder the educational process of others through disruptive behavior.

Dr. Appenzeller offers several recommendations: "(1) adopt policies that are applicable to your school; (2) involve all factions of your school in policymaking; (3) adopt regualtions that are specific and not too vague or too broad, keeping fairness and reasonableness as the guiding features; (4) publish and announce the rules and regulations in advance; and (5) have a plan ready to go into action before disruption occurs."

Summation

It is impossible in a single chapter dealing with the legality and liability in athletics to give more than a cursory treatment to the subject. Athletic coaches and administrators of interscholastic athletic programs would do well to pursue the subject further. Since every individual is responsible for his own acts including those of negligence, one would do well to check in advance with school administrators (including boards of education and state athletic associations) as to their rights as teachers, coaches, and athletic directors who may be exposed to legal action.

Any teacher, including a coach or athletic director, would do well to take out a "professional person liability" insurance policy, It could be a rider on an existing policy covering "business pursuits" or "professional person." The typical homeowner's policy does not cover a professional person such as a teacher, coach, of athletic director in liability cases.

At one time many professional people were practically immune to lawsuits. It was almost unheard of to sue a teacher or coach. As we pointed out in this chapter, the concept has changed. Although a student or his parents may bring a lawsuit against a faculty member or athletic coach, they delude themsleves into thinking their suit is actually against the insurance company from whom they expect to receive financial compensation. The faculty member or coach may be merely a means utilized in order to attain an end. Unfortunately, the individual teacher or coach's reputation as a competent, professional person may be ruined or greatly damaged as a result of the lawsuit, even though he may be covered by professional liability insurance.

Many times the teacher or coach's sole defense is that he acted as a reasonable prudent person. Should a jury prove otherwise, it is reasonably certain the courts will find for the plaintiff bringing the suit and likely damages will be awarded. Therefore, anyone in the teaching profession, including the athletic coach and administrator of the interscholastic athletics program should know the court's definition of a "reasonable and prudent person" and not act to the contrary.

Questions

1. What is your interpretation of a "reasonable prudent person"?
2. What is a tort and tort liability? Can you think of some specific instances where, if a coach does not act as a "reasonable prudent person," the coach would be subjected to tort liability?
3. Define and discuss "student rights." Does this mean if a student-athlete does not agree with the training rules, it is within his rights not to adhere to them and is free from any impunity imposed by the coach?
4. Define and discuss "coach and teacher rights." Does this mean because one is a teacher or coach this individual can impose any rule on students, including punishment for the violation of such a rule?
5. Enumerate three or more sources of information, where one could locate specific information relevant to liability in athletics, that is likely to provide enlightening and beneficial information to the reader.

REFERENCES

1. Hogan, John C., *Sports in the Courts, Phi Delta Kappan*, October 1974, pp. 132-135, Bloomington, Indiana. By permission.
2. Ibid.

3. Appenzeller, Herb, *From the Gym to the Jury*, The Michie Co. Law Publishers, Charlottesville, Va., 1970. By permission.
4. *Neuhaus v. Torrey*. United States District Court, Northern District, Judge George B. Harris, March 10, 1970, No. G70-304-GBH. By permission.
5. Appenzeller, Herb, *"Bench and Bar,"* *Kendall Sports Trail Magazine*, November to December 1974, p. 13. The Kendall Company, Sports Division, 20 Walnut Street, Wellesley Hills, Mass. 02181. By permission.
6. Leibee, Howard C., *Liability for Accidents in Physical Education, Athletics, Recreation*, Ann Arbor Publishers, Ann Arbor, Michigan 1952, p. 23.
7. *Coaches Handbook*, American Alliance for Health Physical Education and Recreation, 1201 Sixteenth St., N.W., Washington, D. C. 20036. By permission.
8. *Coaches Manual*, National Association for Sport and Physical Education, American Alliance for Health, Physical Education and Recreation, 1201 Sixteenth St., N.W., Washington D. C. By permission.
9. Title IX of the Education Amendments of 1972, obtained from Director, Office of Civil Rights, HEW, Washington D. C. 20024. By permission.
10. Triezenberg, George, Principal, Eisenhower High School, Illinois, *"Student Communication Rights,"* *National Association of Secondary School Principals Bulletin*, April 1973, Reston, Va. 22091. By permission.
11. Appenzeller, Herb, *"Bench and Bar,"* *Kendall Sports Trail Magazine*, November to December 1974, p. 13, The Kendall Company. Sports Division, 20 Walnut Street, Wellesley Hills, Mass. 02181. By permission.

SUGGESTED READINGS

Appenzeller, Herb, *From the Gym to the Jury*, Michie Company, Charlottesville, Va., 1970.

Grieve, Andrew, *Legal Aspects of Athletics*, A. S. Barnes & Co., South Brunswick, N.J. 1969.

Hogan, John C., *The Schools, the Courts and the Public Interest*, D. C. Heath, Lexington, Mass., 1974.

Leibee, Howard C., *Liability for Accidents in Physical Education, Athletics, Recreation*, Ann Arbor Publishers, Ann Arbor, Mich., 1952.

Lacy, Dan E., *Teacher Liability in Physical Education in California*, Ed. D. (doctoral dissertation) Stanford University, 1970.

Moskowitz, Joel S., State Department of Justice, Deputy Attorney, *Law in the School: A Guide for California Teachers and Students*, P. Smith, Monclair, N.J., 1974.

Chapter 16
Medical Aspects of
Interscholastic Athletics

In the previous chapter we touched briefly on the medical phase of interscholastic athletics relevant to its legal ramifications. In this chapter we discuss current studies on the medical aspects of interscholastic athletics; problems and solutions; the role of the team physician and athletic trainer; the athletic director's role and responsibility for accident reports and insurance coverage. Safety and sanitation in interscholastic athletics are discussed in Chapter 22.

The American Alliance for Health, Physical Education and Recreation has taken an active role in combating sports injuries and initiated a National Sports Safety Congress under the direction of Dr. Donald Cooper, team physician for Oklahoma State University. Dr. Cooper, speaking at a NCAA meeting, called for the government to set up a federally funded sports injury institute.

Numerous bills have been introduced in Congress[1] for federal studies to determine the exact extent of injuries in the nation's interscholastic athletic programs and to decide the "why" of injuries and define solutions to the problems.

The National Federation of State High School Associations Rules Committee has always been concerned with safety. Periodically, the rules are reviewed and changed when needed. When unsafe conditions of play have been identified, rules have been established to reduce the hazardous conditions as much as possible. The rules committee is also concerned with intelligent coaching and competent officiating of contests for the full protection of the participants.

There have been many studies on safety in athletics. One such study that merits inclusion in this chapter is the North Carolina study on the causes of football injuries to high school football players.

AN EPIDEMIOLOGIC STUDY OF HIGH SCHOOL FOOTBALL ININJURIES IN NORTH CAROLINA[2]

This investigation was supported by a United States Public Health Service Grant from the Environmental Control Administration, under the direction of Dr. Carl S. Blyth, Ph.D. and Dr. Frederick O. Mueller, Ph.D., Department of Physical Education, University of North Carolina. The following organizations contributed to the project: North Carolina State Department of Education, North Carolina State High School Athletic Association, University of North Carolina Department of Epidemiology, and the University of North Carolina Department of Biostatistics.

Introduction to the Problem

In support of interscholastic athletics the Educational Policies Commission stated: "We believe in athletics as an important part of the school physical education program. We believe that the experience of playing athletic games should be a part of the education of all children and youth who attend school in the United States."

With this growing interest in sports and their inclusion in the programs of more and more schools it becomes increasingly apparent that additional consideration must be given to the inherent danger to participants in these activities. Athletics are hazardous. In sports requiring vigorous activity injuries are bound to occur. However, the organization, administration, and supervision of all extracurricular activities, including interscholastic athletics, are the direct responsibility of the school system in which they operate and in exercising this responsibility educators should exert every effort to assure that the potential for injury is kept to the absolute minimum commensurate with the values and the benefits of participation.

One of the primary responsibilities that school administrators, physical educators, recreators, coaches, and others involved in school athletic programs must face is that of providing adequate protection and care against injuries that occur in these activities. Injuries in football occur much more frequently and receive much more publicity than do injuries resulting from participation in other activities. To meet their growing responsibility to protect the athlete, educators must take a greater leadership position in evaluating the risk of involvement in sports participation, developing preventive measures where applicable, and enforcing greater adherence to accepted safe practices with regard to participation.

Statement of the Problem

The investigation studied the extent of football injuries in North Carolina high schools. A scientific methodology, that is, a descriptive epidemiology was used. It is intended to arrive at the *causes of the injuries*, not just who was injuried, the diagnosis of the injury, and how soon the injured would be able to return to participation.

The purpose of the study is as follows:

1. To demonstrate the effectiveness of applying a standard health research method to measuring the distribution of football injuries, and to apply the determinants of the noted distribution, to the problem of risk in athletics, specifically high school football.
2. To determine the epidemiology of high school football injuries in North Carolina high schools.
3. To provide a descriptive epidemiologic baseline of data on football injuries upon which to evaluate further analytic and experimental efforts in solving the problem of prevention or mitigation of injuries incurred by football participants.
4. To determine the relationship of certain predictor variables associated with the occurrence of high school football injuries.
5. To study the relationships between the injuries to high school boys participating in football and the certification, teaching, coaching, and playing experience of their coaches. The intention is to reduce the severity and frequency of these injuries through a better understanding of the coaches' role in injury prevention.
6. To determine if there is a relationship between types, condition, and fit of selected types of football personal protective equipment and the incidence of injury to high school football participants.

Significance of the Problem

The significance of this problem is its uniqueness. It is unique in that it is the first attempt to apply accepted, proven research design techniques to an increasing health problem in our nation's schools. It is significant because it will, for the first time in athletic medicine research, direct attention to the differences between the injured and the noninjured participant in an athletic activity. Without such differential data, the potential for planning for prevention remains in the realm of speculation rather than scientific hypotheses testing.

Limitation of the Problem

This study was concerned generally with the demonstration of the effectiveness of the application of a research methodology, little used in educational research, to an educational and health problem in the public schools. Specifically, it was an attempt to determine the extent of the problem of football injuries in the state, to provide leads to possible prevention or intervention techniques, and to form a baseline for the analysis of future preventive research applications more experimental in nature.

The Term "Epidemiology" Defined

This term was defined by a group of epidemiologists as the study of all the factors (and their interdependence) that effect the occurrence and course of health and disease in a population. The general definition of the word is a return to the original Greek *epi*, upon, and *demos*, people. Thus, epidemiology is the study of the health of human groups in relation to a total environment: the study of human ecology. For the purpose of this study epidemiology is interpreted as the study of the distribution and determinants of disease prevalence in man.

PRINCIPAL FINDINGS OF THE NORTH CAROLINA STUDY

Distribution of Injuries

1. The most common types of injury to high school players are sprains, contusions, fractures, pulled muscles, strains, lacerations, and concussions.
2. A greater frequency of fractures, concussions, and lacerations

were found than ever reported in the past.

3. The most frequently injured part of the body was the knee (19.3 percent) and the ankle (15.3 percent).
4. The knee received the greatest number of contusions.
5. Almost 35 percent of the student-athletes injured were disabled for seven days or more.

Environmental Variables

1. Injuries were most frequent in schools with 500 or fewer students.
2. September was the month in which the most injuries occurred (36.0 percent).
3. Fifty-one percent of all injuries occurred in practice.
4. The second quarter of the game accounted for the highest percentage of game injuries (27.2 percent).
5. Of the total number of youths injured, who received treatment, 4.4 percent did not receive it until at least four days after the injury occurred.

Host Variables

1. Players eighteen years of age had the highest injury rate.
2. There is a distinct correlation between age and injury, in that injury risk increases with increased age.
3. No differences were found between the black and white youth's injury experience at football.
4. Varsity level players risk a significantly greater chance of injury than do junior varsity players.
5. Players with greater experience at football risk a significantly greater chance of injury than do players with less experience.
6. Student-athletes with a history of football injury sustain injury at a significantly higher rate than their associates with no history of prior football trauma.

Activity at Time of Injury

1. During practice activities, exclusive of scrimmage, the various tackling drills were the most hazardous activities, accounting for 33.8 percent of the injuries.
2. The one-on-one tackling drills were the type where youths were injured most frequently.
3. Defensive play was responsible for the greatest proportion of

game and scrimmage injuries (44.4 percent).
4. Athletes sustained more serious injuries when blocking, tackling, and receiving blocks and tackles in the open field.

The Agent of the Injury

1. Injuries caused by a blow from an object accounted for 31.2 percent of all injuries sustained.
2. The helmet was the object causing the most injuries to players (12.1 percent).
3. Almost 5 percent of the injuries sustained were of a type related to torsion or twisting and involved no contact at all.
4. Only 20.1 percent of the injuries sustained in the study were caused by a collision between players that could be classified to no other injurious agent.

Coaches' Background and Experience

1. The age of the head coach was important when considering injury prevention. As the age of the coach increased, the injury rate of his team steadily decreased.
2. The number of years a coach had played football did not seem to affect his team's injury rate, but a coach who had college playing experience in his background was associated with teams that had lower injury rates.
3. Football coaches with the least amount of coaching experience were associated with teams that had the highest injury rate when compared to teams whose coaches had more experience.
4. Advanced degrees were an asset to football coaches when reduction of injury rates was considered.
5. A large percentage of football coaches in this study were not aware of the proper methods of administering liquids and salt during preseason practice.
6. The full-speed tackling drills were the most hazardous in producing injuries.
7. More than half of the total concussions was associated with players who were using improper blocking or tackling techniques.

Injury Data Related to Type, Condition, and Fit of Protective Equipment

1. The condition and fit of the football helmet did not seem to affect the risk of injury.

2. There was no significant difference in injury rates because of different-type helmet mounts.
3. It is evident that there is a reduction in the rate of knee and ankle injuries to players wearing soccer shoes when performing on well-maintained fields.
4. Schools following a limited contact practice program were associated with lower injury rates.

Countermeasures to protect the student-athlete from harm would include, but are not limited to:

1. Physicians limiting drastically the number of boys who are participating at "marginal" levels of physical well-being.
2. Physicians, coaches, and other responsible for athletic programs and as consumers of athletic protective equipment, must take a firm stand in demanding safer equipment. This would require manufacturers to provide soft external padding on all helmets and shoulder pads to limit the injuries from blows delivered by these items.
3. Those responsible for the conduct of interscholastic football must initiate action to insure that the game is played only on well-maintained turf surfaces in quality soccer shoes.
4. Game officials must give appropriate emphasis to and accept their responsibility for the protection of the student-athlete. No new rules are needed. What *is* needed is more stringent enforcement of those rules currently "on the books."
5. Limiting "live contact," particularly tackling and blocking drills, to the extent consistent with the instruction of youths in fundamental game skills.

The greatest need to be fulfilled before the prospects for football injury prevention are to be realized to the fullest without detrimental effects on a great many athletic activities is the establishment of a "Sports Trauma Institute" through which efforts could be made to coordinate research ventures, provide adequate medical specialist consultation, and disseminate research findings to the athletic community.

This "Institute" with adequate support could provide opportunities to stimulate research on the extent, character, and nature of injuries resulting from participation in many sports activities other than football alone.

QUALIFIED PERSONNEL

As stated in Chapter 9, "Certification of Coaches and Athletic Administrators," it is becoming more difficult to employ certified physical educators for every coaching assignment. As a result, faculty members, other than physical educators, are frequently given the responsibility of coaching athletic teams.

It is essential that anyone connected with the coaching of athletic teams on the interscholastic level have an understanding of the proper methods and techniques relating to the prevention and care of athletic injuries. More than half of all athletic injuries occurs in practice sessions, and it is the responsibility of the coach to immediately determine the seriousness of the injury.

Program Implementation

Unqualified personnel, stagnation of the coaches, and apathy in relationship to the prevention, care, and treatment of athletic injuries have caused great alarm among members of the medical profession. Efforts are being made by the medical profession to inform team physicians, coaches, and all persons associated with athletics of new techniques in the area of care and treatment of athletic injuries. Workshops, seminars, and sports medicine conferences have been designed to help update athletic directors, coaches, and trainers. Various materials in the form of books, pamphlets, tape-recordings, and cassettes are now available in the field of sports medicine. Penn State University has programs that will be available on both film and video cassettes, a continuing education program in health supervision, conditioning, environmental problems and nutrition, head and neck injuries, upper extremity injuries, lower extremity injuries, and other phases of athletic injuries.

Sports Medicine Workshops

Throughout the country, workshops on sports medicine are being conducted to reeducate the coaching profession on new methods and safety in the treatment of athletic injuries. It is the responsibility of every athletic director to allocate funds and to encourage staff members to attend these workshops.

The Berkshire Sports Medicine Institue, Massachusetts,[3] designed a plan for the Central Berkshire Regional School District to present new concepts in the field of athletic medicine. This course served as a refresher course for people who had some background in athletic training, as a basic introductory course for those with little or no background, and as an advanced seminar for those with extensive athletic training experience. James T. O'Connor, Athletic Director at Wahconah Regional High School in Dalton Massachusetts organized a workship following the Berkshire plan, which was conducted at Wahconah Regional High School. The course outline included: First Aid Athletic Training; Respiratory Emergencies, Artificial Respiration and C.P.R.; Wounds—First Aid Management; Specific Injuries; Drugs and Their Abuse; Bone and Joint Injuries; First Aid, Taping; Bone and Joint Injuries—Ankle; Bone and Joint Injuries—Knee; Bone and Joint Injuries—Hip and Lower Extremities; Bone and Joint Injuries—Trunk Upper Extremities; Rescue and Short Distance Transfer; Athletic Training Administration; Student Athletic Trainer Program; Recordkeeping.

One of its projects of the North Carolina State Department of Public Instruction Sports Medicine Division, under the direction of Al Proctor,[4] is "developing a system of teacher-athletic trainers to serve the high schools of the state in regard to prevention, emergency treatment, and rehabilitation of sports injuries to student sports participants in the public schools."

Corona Del Mar High School in Newport Beach, California[5] solved the problem of hiring a trainer by combining the duties of adapted physical education teacher with the additional duties as athletic trainer. "It is our belief," said Ron Davis, Athletic Director, "that an individual trained in adapted physical education would also be trained in the treatment of athletic injuries."

NATIONAL ATHLETIC TRAINERS ASSOCIATION[6]

The following proposed solution is not in any opposition to the concept that N.A.T.A. certified athletic trainers represent the ideal answer to the health care problems in interscholastic sport programs. It simply represents one additional method to provide N.A.T.A. certified personnel on all levels of athletic competition.

The high school faculty members constitute the best recruitment pool of manpower. Young men and women currently on a high school faculty, possessing a degree and teaching certificate as well as a strong interest in athletics could be motivated to embark upon an additional career as an athletic trainer. The faculty member provides greater stability and should be at home in the educational processes that should lead this individual, hopefully, to ultimate success in obtaining N.A.T.A. certification.

The Program

1. Selection of faculty member
   A. Must be interested in the health care of athletes and able to devote the necessary time
   B. Faculty member(s) with academic preparation in physical and biological sciences and/or health related field are most desirable.
   C. Must have time available during the summer for study
2. Faculty training program
   A. This program could be offered by universities and colleges that have N.A.T.A. approved athletic training educational programs. Continuing and graduate education programs or any institution of higher education that meets the following N.A.T.A. guidelines:
      (1) Program director must be a Certified Athletic Trainer
      (2) N.A.T.A. approved instructional staff
      (3) Course work follows the N.A.T.A. program outline
      (4) Program must be structured to give course credit

Organization and Administration of the Faculty Training Program

At the present time the N.A.T.A. is the only organization that has taken positive steps to provide interscholastic sports programs with a qualified athletic trainer. The N.A.T.A. has established certification procedures that assure school administrators and the public of quality personnel for the role of teacher-trainer. In addition, it has developed and is still developing education programs in colleges and universities across the nation for the professional preparation of teacher trainers. These athletic training educational programs have been established and approved by the membership of the N.A.T.A.

The Team Physician

Dr. Herb Appenseller, in his article, "Bench and Bar,"[7] points out that team physicians are often put in a delicate position that warrants unusual discretion. Athletic administration tests frequently recommend that schools utilize their presence at all practices. This is the ideal, but is hardly practical since most schools feel extremely fortunate to secure the services of a doctor just to conduct pre-season examinations and attend home games. The answer seems to be in hiring a teacher who can serve also as a certified athletic trainer. The trainer should be prepared to handle first aid emergencies, not to treat injuries. He refers such injuries to the team physician or the athlete's family physician for treatment.

Dr. Appenzeller is in accord with the National Athletic Trainers Association in the teacher-trainer concept. Other people have suggested that the student-trainer work in conjunction with the coach and team physician. Several schools have suggested a qualified male nurse be hired who could act as a trainer for the school athletic program after normal school hours. The school nurse is the liaison between the physician, parents, and coach and, in addition, usually handles all of the paper work in regard to accident reports and other matters such as insurance and followup on physical examinations.

According to Dr. James C. H. Russell, M.D., team physician for Fort Atkinson High School, Wisconsin for twenty eight years,[8] "The title 'team physician' denotes a physician who is vested by the school with authority to make medical judgments relating to the participation and supervision of students in school sports." Dr. Russell summarizes the duties of the team physician as follows, "Although the functions of a team physician can be handled by alternating physicians, it is better to designate a single physician to function regularly in this capacity.

"His duties are related to decisions of medical eligibility of student participants in athletics. This involves preparticipation evaluation, competent management of injuries, including necessary referrals and follow-up, counseling, being available and working as part of a team consisting of the athlete, his parents, the coach and the administration."

Relationship Between the Team Physician and the Coach[9]. The coach, athletic trainer, and the school physician should function as a team. In order to help the athlete participating in the program, they must work together. They should understand the existing problems and realize that there are many overlapping conditions that require close cooperation.

In caring for the athlete, a team physician should primarily keep in mind is that it is more important to prevent an injury than to treat one. Injured athletes are different from the general run of patients. An athlete is, or should be, strong and in excellent physical condition. Because he is young, his healing and recuperative powers are above average. Since he has an incentive to get well, he will cooperate and tolerate early rehabilitation. For this reason, an athlete is often able to return to competitive sports much sooner than the average man is able to go back to his work.

Most school physicians become acquainted with the athletes and follow them for four years in high school. They learn the background of the boys and know their medical history. In many cases, the school physician knows the parents of the athletes and is aware of any abnormalities a student may have.

The team physician through the preseason physical examinations often advises certain students not to participate in athletics because of some physical abnormality and will closely observe any questionable cases.

The team physician, the athletic director, and coach should work together to see that proper equipment is furnished. In some areas a Sports Injury Conference is held each year to which sporting goods dealers are invited and the team physician has a chance to check all the equipment and ask questions about the safety of a particular item. The team physician should also give advice on the type of equipment that should be purchased for the training room and the staff should be instructed on how and when to use the equipment, such as the heat lamp, whirlpool, and on general first aid methods relevant to athletic injuries.

Proper diet and nutrition for the athletes is another phase of the program in which the team physician should be involved. We believe that one of the most serious matters facing the high school coach is the dietary habits of the athletes. Working with the team physician on this matter could solve many of the problems.

The psychological or mental injury is a very important part of the high school program. The team physician, being associated with the athletes for a long period of time, will be able to recognize when this occurs. This perhaps happens to the athlete who is participating for other reasons rather than because he wants to play. He uses the injury as an out and would rather spend most of his time in the whirlpool instead of on the field.

The team physician should be with the players from the time they are dressing until they shower at the end of the contest. He should be as much a part of the team as the coach. He should advise whether a student should play or not and be the ultimate judge as to whether a player should go back into the contest after an injury. A coach would do well to adhere to the physician's decision and not try to override it.

The team physician should be available after the game to check any injuries and take the proper steps in treating such injuries rather than wait until the next day to see an injured player. The team physician should also treat the visiting team.

There must be confidence and an understanding between the physician and the coach. They must develop a close and personal as well as a professional relationship.

Responsibilities of the Team Physician on the Playing Field[10]
1. To disallow further participation when an injury has been sustained that could be detrimental to the athlete's future well-being.
2. To allow further participation when an injury has been sustained that is not potentially serious and does not interfere significantly with the effectiveness of a player's performance.

Adequate Preparations for Carrying out the Responsibilities of the Team Physician on the Field
1. Be prepared to perform a complete and competent examination as soon as possible after the injury.
2. Make prior arrangements for emergency first aid on the playing field.
3. Make prior arrangements to obtain expert consultation when required.
4. Have a prior knowledge of the participants if possible.
5. Make his presence known to the coaches and officials.
6. Be available in the dressing room after the game.

Sound General Principles to be Utilized as Guide Posts in the Examination of the Injured Athlete
1. Listen (to a description of):
   A. Mechanism of injury, complaints, and area of localization pain.
2. Look (and feel) for:
   A. Deformity, swelling defects, loss of function, loss of motion, instability, areas of tenderness, and crepitus.
3. Stop (and):
   A. Rule out the most serious injury first.
   B. Use a stretcher if needed.
   C. Reconsider before unnecessarily moving a player with a possible neck injury.
   D. Complete your examination before allowing a player to return to the game.
   E. Reconsider before telling an injured player that he has a potentially serious injury.

Additional Duties for the Team Physician

The team physician should make a periodic evaluation in relation to the safe and healthful factors of each and every athlete. Here are some of the areas of which the team physician should be cognizant:
1. The relationship between proper conditioning and the prevention of injuries.
2. Sound coaching lowers the incidence of injuries. Safe teaching methods in blocking and tackling, planned practice sessions, proper substitution during games, and the attitude of the coach toward his players. .
3. Officials should enforce rules for safe play; the coach and the players should attend to the rules.
4. Safe equipment and facilities are necessary for the protection of athletes.

Moving the Injured Athlete. The American Medical Association lists six guidelines to follow when moving an injured athlete:
1. Avoid being hurried into moving an athlete who has been hurt.
2. Obtain medical supervision before moving an athlete with a suspected neck or spinal injury.
3. Have near at hand for ready use at the site of participation (1) stretcher, (2) telephone, and (3) safe means of transportation to the nearest hospital.
4. If the player can be moved, support the injured joint or limb.
5. If the player is to be moved, move him away from the proximity of the crowd.
6. Post conspicuously and have understood by all supervisory personnel the step-by-step directions for emergency first aid procedures.

Medical Care and Insurance

In Chapter 13 and 15 we discussed briefly medical care and insurance coverage regulations stipulated by the state or district boards of education.

Athletic participation in relationship to medical care and insurance coverage varies from state to state. All state associations, however, require some type of health insurance coverage for athletes. Whether the state-approved plan or commercial coverage is used is left to the discretion of the boards of education. Education Code

No. 11709, State of California[11] specifies in regard to medical and hospital service for athletic programs,

> The governing board of any school district or districts may provide, or make available, medical or hospital service, or both, through non-profit membership corporations defraying the cost of medical service or hospital service, or both, or through group, blanket or individual policies or accident insurance from authorized insurer, for pupils of the district or districts injured while participating in athletic activities under the jurisdiction of, or sponsored or controlled by, the district or districts or the authorities of any school of the district or districts. The cost of the insurance or membership may be paid from the funds of the district or districts, or by the insured pupil, his parent or guardian.

According to Lawrence W. Grimes, Executive Secretary of the New York State High School Athletic Protection Plan, Inc.,[12] "Some state associations terminated their benefit plans (in deference to commercial plans) for a variety of reasons: (1) their prime function being athletics and not insurance, in that it was now available to schools through the insurance industry; (2) volume of underwriting was not sufficient to withstand any competition; and (3) insurance companies contracted with state associations to write policies for its member schools. Competition is good for any community. As a consequence, the basic philosophy of school athletic insurance was made more comprehensive in that most of the benefit plans included 'pupil' coverage for all school activities, from kindergarten through twelfth grade. This change in style broadened the scope of coverage both in activities and in insurance."

California is the only state in which the school is required by statute to furnish accident insurance for the pupils (Education Code section 31751-55).[13] It requires every member of an athletic team to have accidental bodily injury insurance providing at least $1500 of scheduled medical and hospital benefits, and at least $1500 accidental death benefit. This requirement can be satisfied by membership in the California Interscholastic Federation Protection Fund or by any bona fide commercial insurance agency. As stated above, (Ed. Code section 11709) this insurance may be purchased either by the school district or by the individual pupil.

Specific Responsibilities. It is the obligation of the athletic director to have a definite "policy and procedure" routine pertaining to

athletic accident insurance. Some school districts require all participants in athletics to be covered by school insurance or sign a waiver
relieving the school district of any financial responsibility in the case
of accident or injury. A form, such as the one used by the Easton
Area School District (Form 16-1) is sent to parents to sign and return
to the athletics director.

It is imperative that the parent know the type of coverage and the
legal responsibilities in case of accident or death. An elaborate explanation of medical, hospital, and first aid care and payment for
such care is sent to all parents or guardians in the Houston Independent School District (Form 16-2). This form also includes catastrophic insurance coverage for all students.

The athletic director must keep an accurate filing system available
in case of accident. Form 16-3 as used by the Houston Independent
School District is a simple but accurate method of listing insurance
coverage for each sport. A copy of this should by in the athletic
director's office and a copy in the coach's file.

It is the responsibility of the athletic director to inform the
parents regarding the limitations and benefits of the school coverage.
In the case of another agency supplying the insurance, it would be up
to that agency to supply the needed information. Some of the basic
information included in most school policies concerns pupil coverage.

Pupil Coverage[14]

Pupils are covered only under the following circumstances and
conditions.
1. While practicing under the supervision of the coach of the school
   athletic team that is under the sponsorship of the school in which
   the pupil is enrolled.
2. While participating in games as a member of the school athletic
   team, during the season of sport as defined by the state or section
   rules for the particular sport.
3. While traveling in school-provided or school-sponsored transportation to or from school and the place of the school team's athletic
   event.
4. That coverage begins with the first authorized team practice as
   permitted by the state or section rules for the particular sport and
   that coverage ends with the last school team contest permitted by
   the state or section rules for that particular sport.

5. That most school insurance does not guarantee full payment of claims submitted in connection with athletic injuries but does provide scheduled benefits for medical, hospital, and dental services rendered within 365 days from the date of first medical care. Benefits are available only if the first medical care is rendered within 120 days from the date of injury.

6. School insurance coverage varies; however, an average payment of $750 for medical benefits and up to $750 for hospital benefits seems to be the most common practice.

The information should also include explanation of catastrophic injury insurance, services included such as ambulance, orthopedic appliance, medicines and drugs, physical therapy, X rays, and hospital benefits.

Insurance companies have made student accident insurance policies available at a low cost. These policies usually cover all injuries sustained in practice sessions, games, and travel to and from games for all sports other than contact football or rugby. Insurance for contact football and rugby may be purchased for a nominal fee ranging from $20.00 to $25.00 per season.

Summation

Several of the ideas expressed in Chapter 13 relevant to publicizing and adhering to well-established policies and procedures for eligibility certification may also be utilized here.

Informing students, coaches, and others of clearly defined policies and procedures for handling athletic injuries, filing accident reports, handling insurance claims, insurance coverage, and related areas dealing with medical aspects of the athletic program is strongly recommended. The authority, responsibility, and legal status of the physician caring for and treating the student-athletes must be made knowledgeable to all.

The extent of insurance coverage and whether it is provided by the district or the parents or guardian of the student-athlete is a most important issue that must be understood and agreed upon before the student participates in the program. Frequently misunderstanding occurs as to who pays for the medical treatments when the student-athlete goes to a physician of his own volition or upon the insistence of his parents, other than the team or school physician. This may occur *after* a student-athlete goes home from

EASTON AREA SCHOOL DISTRICT
Athletic Department
PARENTAL CONSENT AND PHYSICAL HISTORY FORM

PART I

_____, _____ _____ _____
Last Name(Print)   First Name(No Nicknames) Initial School Attending

_____ _____ _____
Address   Telephone   Grade

_____ _____
Date of Birth   Place of Birth (City, State)

I give my consent and approval for the above named student to compete on the

_____ _____team during the _____
School   Sport   Year

school year. I also give my consent and approval for the above-named student
to be treated and cared for by the team physician and/or whomever he may
designate as his agent.
I understand that participation may include, when necessary, early dismissal
and travel for interscholastic competition and I hereby relieve the Easton
Area School District, and the Easton Area High School Athletic Fund and/or
their agents of responsibility in case of accident or injury resulting from
such participation.

Date:_____Signed:_____(Parent or Guardian)

PART II

Do you have: Blue Cross _____ _____   Blue Shield _____ _____
                         Yes   No   Yes   No

If Yes _____ _____ _____
        Subscribers Name   Group Number   Certificate Number

Other insurance:_____
                              Please Name

The Board of Education has rules that all participants in athletics must
purchase school insurance. Such insurance covers injuries only to the limits
of the policy as stated therein but it does cover those injuries even though
they may be covered by some other insurance which you may have. However, if
it be your desire to forego the student insurance you must sign a waiver relieving the Easton Area School District of any financial responsibility in case
of accident or injury. Such a waiver is available in Cottingham Field House.

- -

PART III

                                   _____ _____
                                   Sport   Family Physician

_____ _____ _____
Student's Name   Grade Level   Phone Number
                                                  YES   NO

A. This is to state that the above-named student:
   1. has had injuries requiring medical or surgical attention in
      the past year.
   2. has had illnesses lasting more than one week in the past
      three years.   _____ _____
   3. is under a physician's care now or has been in the past
      three years (other than routine case).   _____ _____
   4. takes medication now.   _____ _____
   5. wears glasses or contact lens.   _____ _____
   6. has had a surgical operation (explain below).   _____ _____
   7. is allergic to any medication: aspirin, sulfa, penicillin,
      or other substances (bee stings, food, etc.).   _____ _____
B. Do you know of any reason why this person should not compete in
   sports?   _____ _____
C. Has she/he had a tetanus booster within the past three years? _____ _____
   (If not, it is advisable to have one prior to the start of practice).
D. If you answered "yes" to any of the above or you wish to explain further
   please write below or on reverse hereof.

_____

_____

Date:_____ Signed:_____(Parent or Guardian)

224

By Permission

EASTON AREA SCHOOL DISTRICT
Department of Health
Physical Education and Athletics

Cottingham Field House
11th and Church Streets
Easton, Pennsylvania 18042

Telephone 252-3202 — 258-2361   John B. Maitland, *Director*

STATEMENT OF RELEASE

The undersigned releases the Board of Education, the coach, and the school from any liability for hospital charges, doctors fees, or any other costs resulting from any injury suffered by:

Name:_____ Sport _____

It is understood that private insurance will cover any charges incurred.

Signature of Parent
or Guardian   _____

Address   _____

Telephone Number   _____

Date   _____

Since you have other insurance, it is necessary that the Athletic Department know the name of the Insurance Carrier, the name of the Insurer, the Policy Number, and type and limit of liability of the Insurance Policy.

Name of Insurance
Carrier _____

Name of the Insurer _____

Policy Number   _____

Type of Insurance _____

Limit of Liability _____

(*b*)

FORM 16-1 Financial responsibility waiver form. (Easton Area School District, Easton, Pennsylvania. By permission.)

HOUSTON INDEPENDENT SCHOOL DISTRICT
MEDICAL, HOSPITAL, AND FIRST-AID CARE FOR ATHLETES AND
PAYMENT FOR SUCH CARE

1. One or more team physicians shall be assigned to each Senior High School participating in interscholastic athletics. Interns will be used for Junior High School games when available.

2. If a vacancy should occur for a team physician, the Director of School Health Services and the Director of Athletics shall select a medical doctor who is acceptable to the principal and the head football coach of the school involved.

3. All injuries of a minor nature, requiring first-aid only, will be treated by the coach or the athletic trainer at either Delmar, Jeppesen or Butler Stadium.

4. In case there is a doubt in the minds of the coach or the stadium trainer regarding the need of a physician, the regular team physician shall be called.

5. At any time the regular team physician cannot be reached, an injured boy will be sent to another team physician who is available, and the regular team physician will be notified.

6. In case there is conflict with the parents regarding the medical care of the athlete, the parent may be given a list of team physicians from which one may be chosen.

7. If the parents refuse to accept any of the team physicians and insist on using their family physician, the Houston Independent School District will be responsible for only the amount normally charged by team physicians.

8. The Houston Independent School District Athletic Department will only be responsible for prescriptions when administered in a hospital or clinic.

9. The team physicians and stadium trainers may call in specialists if necessary.

10. The team physician who is on duty during a football game *must check all of the players (both teams) in the dressing room after the game for injuries* that were not brought to his attention during the game.

11. Team physicians may admit injured athletes to an emergency room or to a hospital when deemed necessary. The athlete should be dismissed from the hospital as soon as he is able to leave. *When an athlete is hospitalized, semi-private rooms will be used.*

12. Team physicians will send all boys to a stadium trainer with instructions for simple X-ray work and for physiotherapy, under the direction of a physician, if in their opinion they feel that the stadium trainer can perform such duties. Simple X-rays may be made at the stadium, but diagnosis of the X-rays must be made by the physician.

13. Dental Treatment — for injury to sound, natural, teeth only. Players using Shield mouthpieces will be covered by insurance furnished by this company.

14. *Catastrophic Insurance Coverage.* Effective August, 1971 all athletic participants will be required to purchase a Catastrophic Insurance Policy that will cover injuries over $5,000.00 and up to $50,000.00 limit. The cost for this insurance is $1.80 per boy and will insure him for all sports conducted by his school for a one year period.

(Adopted by Board of Education, Houston Independent School District, August 9, 1971)

- -

Our son _____ brought this information on the care of athletes to us and we have read the above information.

Our family carries some form of health and accident insurance.   ( ) Yes   ( ) No

We would be willing to use this policy to defray expenses of medical and hospital bills for our son if he is injured while participating in interscholastic athletics and if he requires medical and/or hospital care.
(Parents are to keep one copy and return one signed copy to the head coach)

Date _____   19_____

                                        Signature of Parent

If the policy does not make full payment, the Department of Athletics will pay the balance, according to the rules and regulations of the Houston Independent School District.

JCT mb   Joe C. Tusa
                                        Assistant Superintendent for Athletics,
                                        Health and Physical Education

By permission — Joe Tusa

FORM 16-2 Explanation of medical, hospital, and first-aid care and payment. (Houston Independent School District, Houston, Texas. By permission.)

By Permission: Houston Independent School District.

PARENT APPROVAL MASTERSHEET

	ATHLETE	INSURANCE COMPANY	POLICY NO.	GROUP NO.	PARENTS' PHONE NO.
1					
2					
3					
4					
5					
6					
7					
8					
9					
10					
11					
12					
13					
14					
15					
16					
17					
18					
19					
20					

SCHOOL   SPORT

FORM 16-3 Method of listing insurance coverage for each sport. (Houston Independent School District, Houston, Texas. By permission.)

practice or an athletic contest and later indicates to his parents or guardian that he was injured earlier and needs treatment.

It is the athletic director's responsibility to set up clearly defined policies and procedures to be followed by all, then to "educate" coaches, student-athletes, and their parents to cover all situations, including the one cited above.

As in Chapters 13, 14, and 15, the athletic director should move the administration of the athletic program out of gray areas into black or white areas, that is, in problems that are easy to resolve by "yes" or "no" answers understood by all. Problems frequently surface when the director operates in gray areas and administers a program from his "hip pocket." Although one may do this in other fields and get by with harmless errors, the chance of costly errors are greater in the medical area because of the ever present problem of liability that is becoming more prevalent in athletics (Chapter 15).

Questions

1. Of what value to coaches, athletic directors, physicians, and others is the North Carolina Study by Drs. Blyth and Mueller that deals with the causes of football injuries in high school football players?

2. Enumerate factors contributing to injuries that were examined and studied by Drs. Blyth and Mueller, and were included in the final report.

3. As the athletic director, what course of action would you follow if, during the course of a football game, you observed the following events: one of your student-athletes is injured; the trainer, after administering first aid, informs the coach that the player should not compete further until cleared by the team physician who is on call; the coach ignores his trainer's admonition and advice and sends the player back into the game? As the athletic director, would you take any action immediately, or wait until the coach "cools off"? Would there be any difference if the team physician instead of the athletic trainer told the football coach not to play the injured player but did so because "I'm the head football coach and this is my team!" Your course of action? Any legal ramifications in this case?

4. Enumerate the individual duties and responsibilities of the following, relevant to the prevention and care of athletic injuries, in-

cluding first aid and possible treatment:
(a) Coach
(b) Athletic trainer
(c) Team physician
5. Which procedures should be followed by a head coach, traveling without an athletic trainer, when one of his student-athletes is injured at an away contest, must remain overnight in the hospital for observation, and the team must return after the game to the high school campus? Which procedures should be followed by the head coach when a player is injured at an away contest but returns with the team to the high school campus after a Saturday night athletic contest?

REFERENCES

1. Forsythe Amendment, passed and signed August 1974, PL 93-380.
2. Blyth, Carl S. and Mueller, Frederick O., *An Epidemiologic Study of High School Football Injuries in North Carolina* 1968-1972, U.S. Consumer Product Safety Commission under Contract CPSC-C-74-18. By permission of the authors.
3. O'Connor, James T., Athletic Director, Wahconah Regional High School, Dalton, Massachusetts, "An In-Service Course of Care and Prevention of Athletic Injuries," *Interscholastic Athletic Administration Magazine*, Summer 1975, Vol. 1, No. 3. National Federation of State High School Associations. Published by Spencer Marketing Services, New York, New York 10017. By permission.
4. Proctor, Al, North Carolina State Department of Public Instruction Sports Medicine Division, *Interscholastic Athletic Administration Magazine*, Summer 1975, Vol. 1, No. 3. National Federation of State High School Associations. Published by Spencer Marketing Services, New York, New York 10017. By permission.
5. Davis, Ron, Athletic Director, Corona del Mar High School, California, "The Teacher-Trainer at Corona del Mar," *Interscholastic Athletic Administration Magazine*, Summer 1975, Vol. 1, No. 3, National Federation of State High School Associations. Published by Spencer Marketing Services, New York, New York. By permission.
6. *NATA Approved High School Faculty Athletic Training Instructional Program*, Safety in Interscholastic Athletics Conference, Los Angeles, May 1975, Dr. Frank B. Jones, Ed.D, chairman and recorder. By permission.
7. Appenzeller, Herb, "Bench and Bar," *Kendall Sports Trail Magazine*, 1974, p. 14., The Kendall Company, Sports Division, 20 Walnut Street, Wellesley Hills, Massachusetts 02181. By permission.
8. Russell, James C., M.D., "Duties of the Team Physician," *Interscholastic Administration Magazine*, Summer 1975, Vol. 1, No. 3, pp. 16-17. National

Federation of State High School Associations. Published by Spencer Marketing Services, New York, New York 10017. By permission.

9. Troppmann, Robert J., *Relationship Between the Team Physician and the Coach, Athletic Journal,* Vol. XLIV, No. 5, January 1964, p. 54. By permission of the author.

10. Blazina, Martin E., M.D. "A Guide for a Team Physician's Responsibilities and Techniques of Field Examination in Football." By permission. Dr. Martin E. Blazina, M.D. Inglewood, Ca. 90301.

11. Education Code (State of California) 11709 Medical and Hospital Services for the Athletic Program.

12. Grimes, Lawrence A., *Trends in Athletic Insurance, Secondary School Athletic Administration—A New Look,* 1969, p. 70, American Alliance for Health, Physical Education and Recreation, Washington D.C. By permission.

13. Education Code (State of California) 31751-55 Athletic Insurance.

14. California Interscholastic Federation Protection Fund, *General Information Bulletin—Athletic Insurance,* Santa Barbara, California.

SELECTED READINGS

Forsythe, C. E., *Administration of High School Athletics,* 4th edition, Prentice-Hall, Englewood Cliffs, N.J. 1962, Ch. 11, Safety and Sanitation in Athletics—Accident Benefits and Protection Plans.

George, J. F. and Lehmann, H. A., *School Athletic Administration,* Harper and Row, New York, 1966, Ch. 7, Insurance.

Grieve, A. W., *Directing High School Athletics,* Prentice-Hall, Englewood Cliffs, N.J., Ch. 15, Medical and Insurance Questions.

Hixon, C. G., *The Administration of Interscholastic Athletics,* J. Lowell Pratt, New York, 1967 Ch. 8, The Safety and Welfare of Participants.

Purdy, R. S., *The Successful High School Athletic Program,* Parker Publishing, West Nyack, N.Y., 1973, Ch. 13, Implementing Advantageous Insurance and Medical Assistance for the Athletic Program.

Yost, Charles Peter, Ed., *Sports Safety,* Division of Safety Education of the American Alliance for Health, Physical Education and Recreation, 1971, Washington D.C.

Chapter 17
The Administration of Interscholastic Athletic Events

The athletic director has the main responsibility for administering the athletic program, which includes overseeing any athletic contest that his school. The athletic director is the manager of all home contests. When the director's presence is required elsewhere or when two or more home contests are being simultaneously conducted, there should be an officially appointed designee who will have full authority.

Since interscholastic athletics are an integral part of the total educational program, the administration of the athletic contest should conform to the philosophy of the school and to the rules and regulations of the local and state athletic associations. Once this philosophy is established and policies understood by everyone involved in the athletic programs, a checklist should be made covering the management of all athletic contests.

The athletic director is responsible for the conduct of the program, but must have the aid of subordinate personnel to take care of the many details involved in staging an athletic event. The athletic director, as mentioned in Chapter 3, is to oversee the program yet not be expected to personally perform each of the many details.

Many of the items covered in the checklist are discussed in detail in appropriate chapters, such as Chapter 24, Transportation for Athletes and Athletic Teams, and in Chapter 16, Legal Aspects of Interscholastic Athletics.

The checklist is designed as a ready reference for the athletic director to make certain that all details have been attended to. The checklists cover games and contests played away from home, pre-home game, home contests, and postgame activities.

CHECKLIST FOR CONTESTS PLAYED AWAY FROM HOME

Personnel. The coach should submit a list of names of the athletes who are making the trip to the athletic director, who will check for the following:

1. _____ Player's name appears on the eligibility list.
2. _____ Player has taken a physical examination.
3. _____ Player has adequate insurance coverage.
4. _____ Player has turned in his parental permission form.

The coach should post a list of those players making the trip and indicate the time the players should report to the point of departure, the time the transportation departs, and the time the transportation will return from the road trip. At a designated time prior to boarding the transportation, the coach should check the following:

1. _____ Player's equipment
2. _____ Player's appearance
3. _____ Game equipment

Transportation. Arrangements for transportation must be made well in advance. The coach should have a copy of the transportation contract indicating the name of company, phone, time of arrival, driver's name, and any speical arrangements. The coach will be in charge of the conduct of his squad to and from the game. See Chapter 23 for detailed information concerning liability of private transportation and contractual forms. Players should receive printed information about leaving and returning with the team and how and why they may be released to parents following the game.

Finances. The financial arrangements should be made well in advance if the trip is an out of town trip, overnight trip, or a trip in which a meal is provided. The coach will be the custodian of the funds and will be responsible for a strict accounting, such as for meal or lodging receipts.

Game Contracts. The athletic director should provide the coach or the person in charge of the trip with a game contract. This contract should indicate the time for the game, the site it will be played, the location of the dressing rooms, the names of the officials, price of admission, and regulations concerning complimentary tirckets. Band, manager, and cheerleader arrangements must also be included as well as any activities such as a homecoming, half time or any ceremony prior to the game.

CHECKLIST USED PRIOR TO A CONTEST
HELD AT THE HOME SCHOOL

Contest Officials. In the selection of officials, contracts should be made stipulating date, time of contest, fee, location of contest, and location of official's dressing facilities. Form 17-1 is a confirmation form for officials as used by Ron Davis, Athletic Director, Corona del Mar High School, Newport Beach, California.

Facilities. Unusual locations or temporary circumstances may make special arrangements necessary concerning field, courts, or pools where contests are to be played. The home school athletic director should confirm all such arrangments in writing in order to avoid confusion. The visiting school's athletic director should be fully informed of any change in plans. The home school's principal should also be notified of any change in facilities so that there will be no conflicts in assignment of supervisory personnel.

Preliminary Game. If a preliminary game is to be played, the athletic director must make complete arrangements, especially in regard to dressing facilities and ticket arrangements.

Visiting School Courtesies. Informational material should be sent to the athletic director of the visiting school indicating color of uniforms, locations of visitors' dressing facilities and bench, routes to field, parking instructions, and a printed form with time and arrangements of pregame and half time activities. The visiting team should also be advised of the admission prices, student admission, number of complimentary tickets, league passes, and press information. A sample of this type of information is indicated of Forms 17-2a, b, and c as utilized at Corona del Mar High School, Newport Beach, California.

Complimentary Tickets. If special season or complimentary tickets are to be prepared and distributed, this should be accomplished early in the school year. The Houston Independent School District, Houston, Texas sends out a form annually to the junior high school principals, offering each school general passes.
The Easton Area School District, Pennsylvania uses a unique student identification card for all students who participate in the athletic programs.

Corona del Mar High School
Boys' Physical Education Department

TO: _____

You have accepted an officiating assignment at Corona del Mar High School. My records indicate that you have accepted the following assignment:

_____   _____   _____
Date   Day   Time

_____   _____   _____
Sport   Classification   Opponent

Others assigned to help you officiate this contest.

_____   _____   _____

Dressing facilities and lockers are available to you in the coaches' dressing room in the boys' gym. If there is anything you need, please contact me as I will be in attendance. We hope your assignment at Corona del Mar High School will be a pleasant one and please feel free to ask our cooperation at any time.

Respectfully,

By Permission of
Ron Davis
Director of Athletics
Corona del Mar High School,
Newport Beach, Ca
714-644-1000

FORM 17-1 Confirmation form for officials. (Ron Davis, Athletic Director, Corona del Mar High School, Newport Beach, California. By permission.)

Programs. Contest programs contribute to the informational and interest aspects of an athletic contest as well as being an excellent fund raiser. The programs should be informative, inexpensive, and easily accessible. This can be an excellent booster club operation, but must be organized with an efficient sales force under strong leadership. Booster organizations are discussed in Chapter 30. The programs should be accurate and in good taste. Contents should not violate school policy and should support the educational aspects of athletics.

Concessions. Food concessions should be properly managed with reasonable and fair prices. The quality of items sold must conform to the best health standards. Complete financial reports of all sales and transactions must be required. Most concessions are handled by the booster organization as a fund-raising project for the interscholastic athletic program.

Condition of Facilities. Upkeep of the facilities should be performed by maintenance personnel. Coaching and athletic administrative personnel should not be expected nor required to line fields or perform janitorial functions. All items needed should be forwarded to the head of the maintenance department well in advance of the event. Form 17-5 is a sample of a request for work to be performed by the maintenance department.

It behooves the athletic director to have a close working relationship with maintenance personnel. The athletic director can assist by using students to aid in setting up the area. There is a legal problem in connection with volunteer help, and this help should be closely supervised by the faculty person in charge.

Some of the more important items that should be checked for example, stadium bleachers should be clean and in good repair; existing bleachers should be approved for use prior to the first contest. If temporary bleachers are to used, they should be properly inspected and approved. Rest rooms should be inspected and fully equipped, sanitary and available. It is wise to have all of the facilities checked by the local fire department before the season and again at intervals during the season. The fire department is not accountable for any injury that may occur; however, it can report its findings to the administration of the school.

II. *GENERAL INFORMATION*

    A. SCHOOL COLORS: Light blue, dark blue and silver.

    B. SCHOOL NICKNAME: "Sea Kings."

    C. UNIFORM COLORS: Blue Jersey, white pants at home
                                    White Jerseys, white pants away.

    D. ADMISSION: Adults $1.50 Home ASB card holders FREE.
                           Visitor ASB card holders .50 pre-sale.
                           Under high school age accompanied by parent .75, not accompanied by parent $1.50.
                           Children under six FREE.

    E. PARKING FACILITIES: Davidson Field, Harbor High School. Enter 16th St. entrance for visiting parking.

    F. BUS PARKING: 16th St. Entrance

    G. PRESS BOX: Located on top of the west side of the stadium. Reserved specifically for press, hometeam spotters and team stataticians.

    H. SCOUTING: There is no specific area for scouts. The press box is not large enough for scouts. Most scouts frequent the top rows of the stadium.

    I. FILM CAMERAMEN: All filming must be done from the top of the press box. Electrical outlets are available.

    J. PHOTOGRAPHERS: Contact Mr. Ron Davis, Director of Athletics for Field Passes to be admitted to the field.

    K. CONCESSIONS: There are two concession stands located on the East and West sides of the stadium.

    L. P.A. FOR VISITING YELL LEADERS: A public address system is provided for home and visiting yell leaders. Yell leaders are to be located on the concrete aisleway directly in front of the rooting section.

III. *SEATING ARRANGEMENTS*

    A. HOME STUDENT: West side — center section

    B. HOME GENERAL: West side — end sections

    C. VISITING STUDENT: East side — center section

    D. VISITING GENERAL: East side — end sections

IV. *DRESSING FACILITIES*

Visiting team will dress in the girl's gym. There is very limited locker space. In the event of an emergency please see Mr. Louis' GliesenKamp, Stadium Manager.

V. *STARTING LINE-UP AND ROSTERS*

These should be delivered to Mr. Art Janess, Game Announcer by 7:45 P.M.

VI. *SONG LEADERS RESPONSIBILITIES*

It will be expected that song leaders from home and visiting schools will use their good judgment in types of songs and activities involving rooting sections. Song and yell leaders will be expected to refrain from raids and other actions against opposing rooting sections.

VII. *CdM PEP SQUAD*

A. DRUM-MAJOR: Bill Hedge   ASSISTANT: Jeff Goggel
B. CHEER LEADERS: HEAD: Shelley Savage, Pam Allen, Gretchen Fry, Pat Michaels, Stacy DeNaut and Michelle Weaver
C. SONG LEADERS: HEAD: Nancy Smith, Holly Anderson, Laurie Bayless, Jan Birnie, Dennie Newcomb and Thea Nibblett
D. DRILL TEAM: MAJOR: Astrid Store   CO-CAPTAINS: Linda Jacobus and Mari Jo Rodheim

VIII. *FOOTBALL TIME SCHEDULE*

PREGAME:

Band and drill team form at the end of the field	7:40
Both football teams leave field	7:45
Band and drill teams move on to field	7:46
National anthem and flag raising	7:50
Bands leave field	7:53
Football teams return to field	7:55
Band seated	7:58
Kick-off	8:00
Half-time (15 minutes)	

Performance groups to leave the field after 12 minutes, and football teams return to field. Kick-off at end of 15 minutes.

POSTGAME:

Teams meet in center of field
Teams face visiting school for alma mater
Teams face home school for alma mater.

FORM 17-2 Informational material for visiting schools. (Corona del Mar High School, Newport Beach, California. By permission.)

HOUSTON INDEPENDENT SCHOOL DISTRICT
GEORGE G. GARVER, GENERAL SUPERINTENDENT
3830 Richmond Avenue
Houston, Texas 77027

(713) 623-5491

C. Pat Riley
Director of Athletic Business

July 19, 1973

MEMORANDUM

TO: JUNIOR HIGH SCHOOL PRINCIPALS

SUBJECT: ATHLETIC PASSES

We wish to remind you that we are again offering each Junior High School 5 General Passes for teachers who offer to help with your games this year.

If you list the names below and return to us we will send you the passes in the school mail. (Please type names.)

SCHOOL_____

1. _____

2. _____

3. _____

4. _____

5. _____

CPRvw   _____
                                       C. Pat Riley

FORM 17-3 Complimentary passes. (Houston Independent School District, Houston, Texas. By permission.)

August 27, 1973

To: Mr. Phillip J. Spaziani, Principal
From: John D. Maitland, Director of Health, Physical Education
           and Athletics
Subject: Player's I.D. Cards

In order to facilitate the handling of player I.D.'s for varsity and junior varsity football, band twirlers, drill team, and varsity and junior varsity cheerleaders, we are sending the *coaches* of those students the player I.D. cards to distribute to their players.

We are sending to you a sufficient quantity of the regular *student I.D.* cards (red) for every student in the school (including the above students). Please distribute these cards to each student as in the past, but ask the home room teachers when they distribute the I.D.'s to their students, to announce to them that those students who are members of the teams listed above *must exchange* their red student I.D. card for the player I.D. This will be done by the head coaches.

Thank you.

EASTON AREA SCHOOL DISTRICT

2450

STUDENT IDENTIFICATION CARD

This is to certify that

. . . . *is a*
student in the Easton Area Schools for the year

1973 - 1974

This card entitles above-named student to student prices at all Easton Area School Athletic Contests

SCHOOL. . . . . SEASON TICKET . . . . .

NOTICE—This card is to be used for purchasing tickets for each contest. It is valid only when presented by the student to whom issued. Abuse of this privilege will result in forfeiture of the membership card.

NC   CC   D   R   L

FORM 17-4 Student identification card. (John Maitland, Easton Area School District, Easton, Pennsylvania. By permission.)

MAINTENANCE REQUEST

Date _____ NO. _____

Request by_____ Room_____ Approved _____

Description: _____

_____

_____

_____

For Maintenance Departmental Use

Received_____ Assigned to_____ Date _____

Completed by_____ Date_____ Time _____

Check by_____ Supervisor_____

(Make rough drawing on reverse side if needed to explain request)

Approved:_____

Division Chairman of Office Head

Please note: Approval of your request is not necessarily indicated by the investigation of your project by Maintenance personnel. Approval or disapproval will be indicated on "Report of Work Request" form.

Emergency requests should be telephoned to Ext. 241

_ _

MAINTENANCE STAFF USE ONLY

_____

_____

_____

CSU 10-07
1971

FORM 17-5 Maintenance department request form. (California State University, Sacramento, California. By permission.)

Scoreboard: Scoreboards are essential pieces of equipment in almost all athletic events. The school electrician should check the scoreboard well in advance of the contest. There should be an electrician on call during the contest in the event an emergency arises. There have been too many experiences where the scoreboard did not function or the stadium lights malfunctioned during a game. To have an electrician on duty is an added expense, but should receive high priority. At the very least, one should be on call.

Dressing Rooms for Visiting Teams: The dressing or locker room facilities for the visiting teams should be adequate, clean, and open for their use upon arrival. A manager or faculty representative should be assigned to meet the visiting team and assist it in any way possible.

Accommodations for Spectators. The safety and comfort of spectators are the responsibility of the athletic director. Arrangements should be made to appeal to spectators through efficient and courteous treatment to encourage their enjoyment of the contest. Faculty, student, or booster club members can be useful in assisting in seating and traffic control for spectators. The ushers should be identified by arm bands, jackets, blazers or hats. The athletic director must attempt to anticipate all problems that may arise in handling spectators.

Athletic Director's Notebook. The athletic director should use a master organizational chart that covers all items that need to be taken care of prior to any athletic contest. He should also carry a notebook and jot down items that need attention. With all of the last minute details the athletic director must attend to before a contest, the chart and notebook helps him remember items of importance he may overlook.

Supplies and Equipment. All supplies and equipment to be used in the contest should be checked and ready well in advance. Extra supplies should be anticipated in the case of an emergency.

Police Protection and Parking. Arrangements with the law enforcement agencies should all be arranged at the beginning of the school year. A meeting with all concerned prior to the season will enhance the operation. All emergencies should be discusses; the security force should meet with a faculty representative, who will cover all the details and assign stations. A police time card as used by the Phoenix

PHOENIX UNION HIGH SCHOOL SYSTEM
POLICE TIME CARD

_____

Date

_____   _____
NAME (Print)   Serial No.

OFFICER ☐   REGULAR ☐

SERGEANT ☐   RESERVE ☐

                                         NUMBER OF
EVENTS WORKED   HOURS WORKED

First: _____   _____

Second:_____   _____

A-36 Dist. Dup.70

By Permission

FORM 17-6 Police time card. (Ed Long, Phoenix, Arizona, Union High School District. By permission.)

Union High School System (Form 17-6) should be filled out by all persons assigned to the contest for this purpose. This card will clear up any problems and will assure the faculty person in charge that all details have been covered.

Cheerleaders and Songleaders. Cheerleaders and songleaders can do much in regard to crowd control. This does not just happen. They must be trained by a faculty representative in proper sideline conduct. Their main task is to secure recognition for outstanding plays and examples of good sportsmanship on the part of both teams and to aid the school and game officials as the contest progresses.

The cheerleaders and songleaders aid in promoting school spirit prior to the contest by posting signs around the campus and putting

DEADLINE: 3:15 P.M.

DAILY ANNOUNCEMENT FOR _____
(Date or inclusive dates)

( ) Student

( ) Faculty   (Please print or type)

_____
(Name of Club or Activity)   (Location)   (Time)   (Days or Day)

_____
(Program — other information)

_____

_____

_____

☐   Check here if more information
     appears on the reverse side

_____
(Full signature of sponsoring teacher)

FORM 17-7   Daily bulletin announcement form. (Corona del Mar High School, Newport Beach, California. By permission.)

notices in the daily bulletin to inform the students of game time and various spirit activities taking place prior to the game. A sample form for announcements in the daily bulletin in Form 17-7.

Arrangements for Scouts, Announcer, and Statisticians. Special arrangements should be made for visiting scouts, the announcer, and statisticians in order to avoid a conflict at an already crowded gate. Press passes should be sent to all concerned, and a special gate should be arranged with a faculty person in charge to meet and assist the passholders in any way possible. Arrangements should be made for refreshments at half time as a means of establishing good public relations.

The athletic director should make it a policy to telephone the visiting athletic director prior to the game to check on any last minute details. At game time, the home athletic director should make it a point to meet with the officials, visiting scouts, and the visiting coach. He should inform them that all details have been taken care of and that he is ready to be of assistance if needed.

Checklist for Game Day. All arrangements for the home contest have been made and it is time to put the operation into action. Assuming all details have been taken care of, this is a day for the athletic director to check that all assignments are covered. A check-list as used by Elmer Carpenter of Wichita High Form 17-8 School could prove to a valuable aid to the athletic director.

Tickets. Tickets should be at each booth with sellers and ticket stations previously assigned. The ticket sellers should be on duty sufficiently early before the game with change, tickets, forms, and instructions. Form 17-9 is an example of information that should be supplied on forms to all people involved.

Ushers. The ushers should report to the faculty person in charge at least one hour prior to the start of the contest. They should be at their assigned stations at least 30 minutes prior to the start of the contest. A simple form can be devised to those assigned to a contest. Ron Davis, Athletic Director, Corona del Mar High School, Newport Beach, California uses Form 17-10 as a reminder to the faculty.

Programs. Supplies of programs and change should be in the hands of the distributors who have been assigned to stations. They should report to the person in charge of selling programs at least one hour prior to game time.

Officials' Dressing Room. Officials should have a private dressing room, away from both teams, coaches, spectators, and visitors. A student manager should be assigned to host the officials. Towels and half time refreshments should be provided. A check for payment of officials should be written before the game and delivered to them prior to the game or at half time.

Bands and Halftime Arrangements. If bands are to be present at a game, make certain reserved seats are provided for them in the bleachers, stadium, or on the field. The band director of the home team should be advised of the amount of time he will have for maneuvers between halves. If a ceremony is to precede the game, make all arrangements with the home band director. Allow time for each team to warm up and make sure the teams do not interfere with the ceremony. Joe Tusa, Assistant Superintendent for Athletics, uses Form 17-11 for the Houston Independent School District.

Decorations. If the field or gymnasium is to be decorated for a contest, include color schemes of both schools. Rule books contain various regulations for decorations. Be sure the decorations do not interefere with the playing facilities.

Public Address System. Public address systems can be a most valuable aid to any athletic contest. Announcers should be trained in their job before the contest. Only pertinent information such as information regarding completed plays, substitution, and explanations of penalties should be announced. The announcer should recognize that the spectators are seeing the game in person. He should also refrain from political endorsements, comments on injuries, or any type comment that would agitate the visiting team or spectators. He should be aware of good sportsmanship and aid in crowd control. He should be ready for any emergency that may occur. Key informational announcements should be prepared in advance. The announcer, coaches, and other key personnel should have a printed time schedule of events immediately preceding, during, and following the contest.

Visiting Team Quarters and Courtesies. The athletic director, coach or student manager should greet the visiting team, show them their dressing facilities and the way to reach the field or gymnasium. The student manager should assist the visiting team in any way possible.

Players' Bench. Reserved areas for substitutes, coaches of the home and visiting teams should be provided. They should be roped off and the area should be protected by faculty or security guards. Bench discipline is discussed in Chapter 30; however, it is the responsibility of the coach to see that bench discipline is maintained.

Physician. Check to see if the physician expected for the contest is present. Have a standby physician in case the scheduled physician has an emergency and cannot attend. Have the phone number of the physician with you at all times. A call to the physician's office the day before the game can save embarrassment, prevent possible liability charges, and may help avoid the more serious consequences of some kinds of injuries.

_____ — _____ FOOTBALL GAME

_____ — _____ _____ , 197 __

1. *Game Time* — 7:45 p.m.
2. *Place of Play* —_____Stadium
3. *Gates Open* — 6:30 (Ticket takers are to stay on gates until game is completed.)
4. *Information for Ticket Sellers and Ticket Takers* —
   a. _____ student activity tickets (_____) will be honored and punched at the gate. (Punch #_____)
   b. _____ and adults will be admitted on presentation of $1.00 tickets (_____). Pre-game sale at_____.
   c. Wichita Board of Education employees who have purchased a ticket for 50¢ (_____) must present their ticket and identification card to be punched at the pass gate. (Punch # _____)
   d. Admit holders of Greater Wichita Athletic League tickets which have stamp of school on front of the ticket. Collect this (_____) one game ticket.
   e. Admission price at the gate:
      (1) General admission ticket (_____) $1.50. (Adults and students)
      (2) Children under 12 — 75¢ (_____) ticket.
      (3) Children under 6 — no ticket required.
   f. The following tickets and/or passes will be admitted through the pass gate *only:*
      (1) All faculty (_____ and _____) passes. *Do not collect.*
      (2) Cannady's ticket (_____). *Do not collect.*
      (3) Special athletic tickets signed by_____ or (*collect*)
      (4) News media who have been given tickets by Cannady's office.
      (5) Cheerleaders in uniform.
      (6) Band members in uniform.
      (7) Scouts properly identified who play one of these schools.
      (8) WSU Turf Club members. (at WSU only)
      (9) Wichita BCE members who have purchased a 50¢ ticket. (_____) *Punch #_____ and collect ticket.*
      (10) Admit all Golden Age (over 65) who can present credentials certifying their age. (Medicare card I.D.)
   g. Players are to be admitted at southwest entrance by coach's verification.
   h. WSU and Friends players pay the $1.50 admittance charge.
   i. _____ will make arrangements to admit junior league football teams.
   j. There is *one* ticket that may enter either the pass gate or the regular ticket gate. That ticket is a gold ticket and the holder will be one of the eight league principles, the superintendent, deputy superintendent, or Dr. McElhiney.
5. *Spectator Seating Arrangements:* All spectators will be seated in the stadium as per following instructions:
   a. _____ pep club will sit in lower center section _____ side.

FORM 17-8 Checklist for home contests. (Elmer Carpenter, Athletic Director, Wichita High School, Kansas. By permission.)

b. _____ band will sit in section immediately south of the pep club.

c. _____ students sit south of the band and back of the band and pep club.

d. _____ student body and pep club will sit in the lower section, north of the_____ pep club, which is north of the north 40 yd. line.

e. _____ students will sit north of the _____ pep club or back of the pep club.

f. Seating in the Turf Club (3 rows of bright gold seats under the press box) is prohibited at high school games except for members of the Turf Club. (WSU only)

6. *Dressing Room Assignments* — (will be open at 5:30)
   a. _____ — _____
   b. _____ — _____

7. *Bench Assignments:*
   a. _____ — _____ side of field.
   b. _____ — _____ side of field.

8. *Color of Jerseys:*
   a. _____ — _____
   b. _____ — _____

9. *Doctor on bench* — _____ .

10. *Towels* — _____ will furnish towels for officials.

11. *Field Phones* — _____ will use the VISITOR'S telephone and _____ will use the HOME telephone.

12. *Filming Games* — Facilities are available in the press box.

13. *Ambulance Service* — Red Cross

14. *Press Box Occupants:*
    a. Timer, scorer, announcer, school officials, scouts, news media.
    b. No women or children are allowed in press box.

15. *Star Spangled Banner* — Played by _____ band at 7:35 while teams are in dressing rooms.

16. *Car Parking* — Available to students at 25¢ per car; adults at 50¢ per car at Cessna Stadium.

17. *Half-Time Entertainment* — _____ marching band.

18. *Programs* — _____ .

19. *Police Protection* — _____ .

20. *Goal Posts* may not be decorated.

21. *Player's Buses* — May be parked in any parking lot.

22. *Remind* students that confetti is not allowed in the stadium. Also remind students that they are not allowed to stand on the seats.

23. *Game Officials:* (Meet at 7:00 in official's dressing room.)
    a. *Referee* — _____
    b. *Umpire* — _____
    c. *Head Linesman* — _____
    d. *Field Judge* — _____
    e. *Timer* — _____
    f. *Scorer* — _____
    g. *P.A. Announcer* — _____
    h. *Down Box* — _____

247

Easton Area School District

Department of H. P. E. and Athletics

November 15, 1973

Memorandum

To: Workers at *Wrestling* and *Basketball* Contests
From: Thomas Sweeney, Ticket Manager
Subject: Reminders for 1973-74 Season

The Following information should be kept in mind for the coming season:

1. *Doors open at 6:00 p.m.* — Workers report by 5:55 p.m.

2. *ALL SALES* will be on the night of the games:

    A.   Wrestling — General Admission: $1.00
                      Reserved: $1.25
        (approximately one half of the gym will be
        reserved seats)
                      Student: (with I. D.) $ .75

    B.   Basketball — Reserved Seats: $1.25
                      (one section only)
                      General Admission: $1.00
                      Student: (with I. D.) $ .75

3. Sportswriters, photographers, etc. will be admitted by Mr. Sweeney or Mr. Maitland, or, if these men are not nearby, at the discretion of the ticket takers.

4. For wrestling, all scouts from opponent schools must have scouting passes that are issued from Mr. Maitland's office. For basketball an official East Penn League Scouting Pass must be shown.

5. Board of Education members will have complimentary season tickets issued from Mr. Maitland's office.

6. No teachers, off-duty janitors, off-duty referees, off-duty police, etc., will be admitted without tickets.

    TS/ah

ccs: Mr. Spaziani   Mr. Debellis
      Dr. Beers   Mr. DiMarcantonio
      Mr. Bubba   Mr. Martocci
      Mr. Kearn   Mr. Fisher
      Chief DiVietro   Visiting Schools

All Principals: Please note first two items on above notice.

FORM 17-9 Ticket sellers form. (Easton Area School District, Easton, Pennsylvania. By permission.)

248

TO:_____   ROOM_____

REMINDER OF ATHLETIC EVENT

_____
(DUTIES)

_____   _____
(ACTIVITY)   (DATE)

PLEASE REPORT TO YOUR ACTIVITY BY: _____
                                                          (TIME)

THANK YOU FOR YOUR HELP!

RON D. DAVIS

DIRECTOR OF ATHLETICS
CORONA DEL MAR, CA.
NEWPORT BEACH, CA.

By Permission

FORM 17-10 A faculty reminder for those assigned to a contest. (Corona del Mar High School, Newport Beach, California. By permission.)

Contracts. The athletic director should have a copy of the game contract available for possible reference.

Guarantees and Payments. The athletic director should have the checks for the guarantee to the visiting team and for the officials unless they have been mailed by prior arrangements. The checks should be given to the person concerned during the intermission period or immediately following the game.

Eligibility List. Have the eligibility list for both competing schools accessible at the time of the contest. Usually these are exchanged prior to the contest.

Scoreboard Arrangements. The scoreboard has been checked by the electrician and people have been assigned to operate it. Take one last check to make sure everything is in working order. There should be a faculty person responsible for this phase of the operation.

HOUSTON INDEPENDENT SCHOOL DISTRICT
DEPARTMENT OF ATHLETICS

PRE-GAME and HALF-TIME SCHEDULE

FOOTBALL — 1973

August 1973

Normal starting time at the various stadiums:

Joe Kelly Butler Stadium	7:30 p.m.	*Band Directors* and *Drill Squad*
Jeppesen Stadium	7:30 p.m.	*Sponsors* will please synchronize
Delmar Stadium	7:30 p.m.	their watches with the *Head*
Dyer Stadium	8:00 p.m.	*Coaches'*.

Schedule for games which start at 7:30 p.m.:
(Teams will leave the field not later than 7:15)

7:15 — Good Sportsmanship talk, etc. (home team)
7:18 — School song — visiting school
7:20 — School song — home school
7:22 — Invocation (home team)
7:23 — National Anthem (home team)
7:25 — Coin toss and announcement of starting lineups
7:30 — Kickoff

Schedule for games which start at 8:00 p.m.:
(Teams will leave the field not later than 7:45)

7:45 — Good Sportsmanship talk, etc. (home team)
7:48 — School song — visiting school
7:50 — School song — home school
7:52 — Invocation (home team)
7:53 — National Anthem (home team)
7:55 — Coin toss and announcement of starting lineups
8:00 — Kickoff

(NOTE: There will be no pre-game on-the-field performance. The R.O.T.C. Color Guard representing the home school will have the option of presenting the colors in conjunction with the home school band's playing of the National Anthem, *from the stands.* The above time allotment must be observed.

Half-time activities will last 20 minutes as follows:

Ten minutes for visiting school
Ten minutes for home school

ADOPTED BY THE DISTRICT EXECUTIVE COMMITTEE

Bands and drill squads will be ready to go on the field at the proper time and must finish drills and be off the field within the time allotted.

The invocation will be given from the press box by a student representing the home school.

The *home team* will *wear dark jerseys.*

The team using the West dressing room will work out on the South end of the field.
The team using the East dressing room will work out on the North end of the field.

Each coach will be responsible for providing the announcer a qualified spotter and an up-to-date starting lineup before 7:15 p.m. (or 7:45 p.m., if an 8:00 p.m. game).

We solicit your cooperation in planning schedule herein outlined.

APPROVED:

Joe C. Tusa
Assistant Superintendent for Athletics,
Health, Physical Education and Recreation

Dr. Sylvester Rains
Coordinator, Regular Education Division

FORM 17-11 Bands and halftime arrangements. (Houston Independent School District, Houston, Texas. By permission.)

Concessions. Check to see that the concessions are being properly handled. Prices should be posted and the athletic director should make sure they are fair and justified.

Public Address System. Check the public address system prior to the start of the game.

Rest Rooms. Make certain rest rooms are properly equipped and designated and available when the gates are opened.

Press and Radio. Spotters should be assigned to the press box, and all facilities must be in order and available when the people involved arrive.

Pregame Activities. Provide all concerned with a time schedule of pregame activities, location of players' bench, and assigned area for pregame warmup. In baseball, have a batting practice schedule.

POSTGAME DUTIES

Storage of Equipment. Student managers should be assigned the responsibility of collecting and storing all field, court, or game equipment after each contest.

Ticket Sale Report. The receipts for tickets should be indicated on the ticket sale report form and turned into the athletic director following the game (Form 17-12).

General Financial Statement. A complete financial statement should be ready within three days following the close of the contest. Form 17-13 is used by Minot High School, North Dakota.

Concession Report. If the concessions are handled by school authorities, a financial report and an inventory of goods left are made out after each game. If school clubs or booster organizations handle the concessions, a financial report should be submitted to the athletic director after the conclusion of the season.

Rating of Officials. The coaches are usually asked by the official's association to rate the officials. The coach should keep this record and rate each official the day after the game. At the conclusion of the season, he should turn his ratings in to the commissioner unless required earler by conference of official's association. Such records will be of value when the officials are assigned in the future.

EASTON AREA SCHOOL DISTRICT

TICKET SALE REPORT

EAHS vs. _____ SPORT_____ DATE _____

Reserved Tickets

No. Received   _____

No. Left   _____

No. Sold_____ @_____ $ _____ .

General Admission
Next no. on roll
after sale or
no. received   _____

No. of first
ticket sold or
number left   _____

No. of tickets
sold   _____ @ _____ $ _____ .

Student Tickets
Next no. on roll
after sale or
no. left   _____

No. of tickets
sold   _____ @ _____ $ _____ .

Amount of cash due from sale $ _____ .

Change at start of sale $ _____ .

Total amount of cash due $ _____ .

Cash turned in $ _____ .

Amount Short $ _____ Over $ _____

Signature of Seller _____ .

Signature of Collector _____

JBM/8 - 73

By permission

FORM 17-12 Ticket sale report form. (Easton Area School District, Easton, Pennsylvania. By permission.)

By Permission

MINUT — NORTH DAKOTA

FINANCIAL REPORT

ACTIVITY_____ DATE _____

MINOT HIGH SCHOOL -VS-

SALES:

Season	_____@_____	= $ _____ . _____
Adult	_____@_____	= $ _____ . _____
H.S. Student	_____@_____	= $ _____ . _____
Elem. Student	_____@_____	= $ _____ . _____
H.S. Activity	_____@_____	= $ _____ . _____
H.S. Programs	_____@_____	= $ _____ . _____

TOTAL SALES: $_____ . _____

EXPENSES:

Referees	_____@_____	= $ _____ . _____
Police	_____@_____	= $ _____ . _____
Bench	_____@_____	= $ _____ . _____
Supv. & Gate	_____@_____	= $ _____ . _____
Other	_____@_____	= $ _____ . _____

TOTAL EXPENSES: $_____ . _____
TOTAL EXPENSES:
PROFIT OR (LOSS) $_____ . _____

CASH SETTLEMENT

Adults	$_____ . _____
H.S. Students	$_____ . _____
Elem. Students	$_____ . _____
Programs	$_____ . _____
Other	$_____ . _____

TOTAL DUE $_____ . _____

CASH TO BANK $_____ . _____

LONG OR (SHORT) $_____ . _____

_____
SUPERVISOR OF ACTIVITIES

Copies to: Superintendent
            Principal
            Activities
            Finance Office

ACT: 8/20/71 — 500

FORM 17-13 Postgame financial statement. (Minot Public Schools, Minot, North Dakota. By permission.)

253

STAGG HIGH SCHOOL
ATHLETIC CONTEST RESULTS

. . . .
Sport

. . . .
Date

TEAMS INVOLVED

Stagg

. . . . vs. . . . .

Team   Team

SCORE

. . . . to . . . .

. . . .
Coach

FORM 17-14 Contest data. (Stagg High School, Stockton, California. By permission.)

Participation Records. A student manager should be assigned to check the participation of all players, total quarters, total innings, etc. This record may be used for award purposes, final season reports, and permanent information.

Athletic Awards. Awards are discussed in Chapter 19; however, it should be mentioned now that the requirements for earning athletic awards should be determined as a matter of policy and published for the information of athletes, and should not deviate with team success or the whim of a coach.

Contest Data. Form 17-14 is a card used by Stagg High School, Stockton, California; it is a simple yet efficient method of keeping contest data.

PROSPECT HIGH SCHOOL

SUMMARY OF ————————————————————
(Sport)

COACHES: SEASON RECORD: WON   LOST

SEASON SCHEDULE AND SCORES: WE   THEY

MOST VALUABLE PLAYER: TEAM CAPTAIN:

AWARD WINNERS:

INDIVIDUAL OUTSTANDING PERFORMANCES:

BRIEF STATEMENT:

——————————————————————————————————————

——————————————————————————————————————

——————————————————————————————————————

GG:ez
6/68

FORM 17-15   Season data. (Prospect High School, Mt. Prospect, Illinois, George Gattas, Athletic Director. By permission.)

Season Data. A summary form submitted by Prospect High School, Illinois should be completed at the end of the season (Form 17-15). The athletic director should have a file for all sports.

Report of Injuries. Be sure all injuries are given immediate attention and reported as required by the board of education, the insurance company or accident benefit plan. Insurance companies usually require that an injury be reported by a certain time at the end of the season. The athletic director should file all reports of injuries related to the sport and keep a log book on every injury. Careful records must be kept for liability purposes.

Closing Correspondence. Send letters of thanks and commendation to deserving people. This public relations is a very important part of the athletic director's job. Write letters of thanks to faculty members who helped make the season a success.

Awards and Banquets. Make all arrangements for awards assemblies and team banquets.

Evaluation. Make a list of things that should have been done and things that should be done for next year. Receive input from everyone in this regard and write down all suggestions.

Forms 17-16*a*, *b*, and *c* include suggested procedures to be used for administering home basketball games.

Form 17-17*a* and *b* is a sample checklist for review prior to a game.

Questions

1. Even though the electrician has checked out the electric scoreboard on Friday afternoon, the board has malfunctioned during last Saturday night's football game. Discuss your "backup" plan to resolve this dilemma should the scoreboard malfunction again during this Saturday night's football contest, even though the electrician has informed you the scoreboard is operable.

2. Operating on the basis of the 5 P's of Success, "Prior Planning Prevents Poor Performance," what is your game plan in the event all of the lights go out during a night athletic contest in the stadium? In the gymnasium?

3. During a contested and closely fought basketball game, the game's announcer, one of your school's students, is critical of the officiating and his comments are "firing up" the players and spectators. As athletic director, how would you handle this situation? What should you have done prior to the contest to insure that this situation would not have occurred?

4. The pep band, made up of your school's students, has brought noisemakers to the basketball game. Everytime the opposition attempts a four shot, the pep band members raise a ruckus with the noisemakers. The home crowd thinks this is great strategy and it has been a disruptive factor so far. As athletic director, how would you handle this situation? What should you have done prior to the contest to insure this situation would not have occurred?

HOME BASKETBALL PROCEDURES

The following are only suggested procedures to be used for home basketball games, but they are not necessarily applicable to all situations. Any of these duties may be performed by an assistant or student manager.

PREPARATIONS PRIOR TO DAY OF GAME:

1. Check with teachers and students who will assist with game. (ticket sellers, ticket takers, scorers, timers, greeter of visiting team, etc.)

2. Confirm game preparations with service help. (janitor, bus driver, police-men)

3. Confirm time and place game is to be played with referees.

4. Meet with band director (time, space available, etc.)

5. Printing of programs and posters for publicity.

6. Confirm time and place of game with opposing team's coach.

7. Make provisions for early meal.

8. Make provisions for visiting team's dressing room.

9. Check equipment for cleanliness and repair (spotted uniforms, dirty shoes, rips and tears in whites, etc.)

DAY OF GAME:

1. Arrange uniforms and warm-ups by size and number for players.

2. Post schedule. (taping, dressing, warm-up, game time, early meal, etc.)

3. Check to make sure there is sufficient laundry.

4. Check and replenish first aid kit for missing articles and supplies.

5. Check training room supplies and replenish if necessary.

6. Have gym floor cleaned. (just before warm-up if possible)

7. Check to see that there will be hot water and soap in both dressing rooms.

8. Remind people who are to help with the game of their duties. (Use text.)

9. If game is played at night, remember outside lights.

BEFORE GAME PREPARATION:

1. Check to see that all help are at or are doing their jobs.

2. Issue equipment. (uniforms, warm-ups, whites, etc.)

FORM 17-16 Procedures to be used for administering home basketball games. (Source: unknown.)

3. Tape and treat injuries.

4. Take towels to visiting team's dressing room.

5. Take towels to referees dressing room.

6. Clean basketballs and fill with air.

7. Prepare scorebook. (Fill in names and positions of potential players.)

8. Pass out basketballs to players. (Two players per ball, centers each have one.)

9. Collect valuables if necessary. (Don't forget visiting team's.)

PRE-GAME WARM-UP

Take to playing floor.
1. Ball bag. (easier to keep practice balls together)

2. Scorebook. (give to official scorer)

3. First aid kit. (don't forget gum)

4. Shot charts. (Important item for record of players' participation in game.)

PRE-GAME CRITIQUE:

1. Collect basketballs and bring to dressing room.

2. Pass out wet and dry towels.

3. Have chalk and blackboard for last minute strategy.

4. Adjust last minute repairs.

5. Assign starting five and collect their warm-ups.

6. Give starters one ball for practice.

____MINUTES BEFORE GAME:

Take to playing floor:
1. Wet and dry towels.

2. Give starters warm-ups.

3. Lock dressing room if necessary.

PRE-GAME HUDDLE:

1. Pass towels around huddle.

2. Pass "firm-grip" and sprinkle area with "rosin powder."

3. Pep talk.

Requested Copy

TIME OUTS:

Same procedure as Pre-game huddle.

FIRST HALF OF GAME:

1. Keep warm-ups ready for players coming out of the game.

2. Collect warm-ups from players going into the game. (Keep warm-ups in safe place.)

3. Pass towels to players.

HALF TIME:

1. Have floor dry mopped.

2. Take all towels, all disguarded warm-ups, all towels, practice ball, first aid kit, scorebook, shot cards, to the dressing room.

3. Pass out towels to players in dressing room.

4. Keep all people out of dressing room.

5. Return warm-ups to players.

6. Distribute refreshments.

7. Check scorebook and shot charts.

8. Half time critique of game and new strategy.

9. Make repairs and check taping.

10. Assign second half starters and give them ball.

11. Pass out balls to bench team.

12. Take ball bag, first aid kit, scorebook, shot charts, wet and dry towels to the floor)

PRE-SECOND HALF HUDDLE:

1. Proceed the same as the first half.

SECOND HALF OF GAME:

1. Proceed same as the first half.

GAME END:

1. Congratulate or accept congratulations.

2. Take all equipment to dressing room. (Balls, towels, first aid kit, etc.)

3. Pay officials and visiting coach. (Latter pertains to guarantee.)

Requested Copy

ADMINISTRATION OF ATHLETIC CONTESTS

One of the most important responsibilities of many athletic directors is the management of home athletic contests. This task must be done well because the public, students, and visiting team will resent and be critical of inefficient management. Poor administration of any athletic contests will eventually result in reduced income from gate receipts.

This check list, if properly used, will assure the completion of various arrangements prior to each contest. Such details as the engagement of the officials, procurement of equipment, preparation of publicity materials such as posters, schedules, and programs, arrangement for a physician, ordering of tickets and other necessary supplies, and repair and improvement of facilities must be taken care of far in advance of a particular contest. The following is a check list to be followed prior to a game.

CHECK LIST FOR FOOTBALL OR BASKETBALL CONTEST

I. Week of game.

    A. Personnel
        ( ) 1. Secure student help and arrange to meet them at definite time and place on day of game.
            ( ) Ticket sellers; ( ) ticket takers; ( ) program sellers; ( ) concession salesmen; ( ) ushers; ( ) guards; ( ) parking attendants; ( ) score board operation.
        ( ) 2. Complete arrangements for police.
        ( ) 3. Assign managerial duties (visiting team, officials, home team).
        ( ) 4. Arrange for physician.
        ( ) 5. Write officials and indicate when and where to report.
        ( ) 6. Arrange for scorer and timer.
    B. Publicity
        ( ) 1. Advertising posters distributed.
        ( ) 2. Daily press releases.
        ( ) 3. Program material submitted to printer by Tuesday.
        ( ) 4. Press box arrangements completed.
        ( ) 5. Complete complimentary ticket distribution to press and radio.
        ( ) 6. Arrangements completed for band.
        ( ) 7. Arrangements completed for half-time entertainment (if any).
    C. Equipment
        ( ) 1. Laundry and dry cleaning sent out (Monday)
        ( ) 2. Laundry and dry cleaning returned and ready.
        ( ) 3. Game uniforms ready.
        ( ) 4. Game balls ready (2).
        ( ) 5. Officials accessories ready.
        ( ) 6. Medical supplies and stretcher ready.

FORM 17-17 Administration of athletic interests with check list.

D. Facilities
   ( ) 1. Facilities inspected. ( ) game field; ( ) goal posts;
        ( ) bleachers; ( ) fences and gates; ( ) scoreboard;
        ( ) ticket booths; ( ) press box; ( ) canvas fence covers;
        ( ) toilets; ( ) concession booths; ( ) dressing rooms;
        ( ) water fountains; ( ) benches.
   ( ) 2. Facilities cleaned and repaired.
   ( ) 3. Field lined day prior to game.
   ( ) 4. Decorations arranged.
   ( ) 5. Bleachers erected (if necessary).

E. Administration
   ( ) 1. Write visiting team to determine time of arrival and
        requirements.
   ( ) 2. Make arrangements to accommodate visiting team.
   ( ) 3. Get tickets and forms ready for ticket sellers.
   ( ) 4. Place tickets on sale (Monday) at appropriate places.
   ( ) 5. Request cash needs for ticket sellers, concessions, and
        program sellers.
   ( ) 6. Make arrangements for meals for home team.

II. Day of Game
A. Personnel
   ( ) 1. Pick up change and tickets and meet ticket sellers.
   ( ) 2. Distribute change to program sellers and concession sellers.
   ( ) 3. Meet and assign duties to other student help.
   ( ) 4. Check with physician.
   ( ) 5. Meet and assign duties to police.

B. Publicity
   ( ) 1. Public address equipment set-up.
   ( ) 2. Public address announcer information ready.
   ( ) 3. Programs and starting line-ups for press available.
   ( ) 4. Check half-time entertainment (if any).

C. Equipment
   ( ) 1. Game uniforms issued.
   ( ) 2. Towels and soap provided for visiting team.
   ( ) 3. First aid kit prepared.
   ( ) 4. Officials' accessories available. ( ) gun and blanks
        ( ) watches; ( ) scorebook.

D. Facilities
   ( ) 1. Check to see that scoreboard and time are functioning
        properly.
   ( ) 2. Check facilities.
   ( ) 3. Check public address system.

E. Administration
   ( ) 1. Make out checks for ( ) visiting team; ( ) officials;
        ( ) police; ( ) student help.
   ( ) 2. Check in receipts from ( ) ticket sellers; ( ) concessions;
        ( ) program sellers.
   ( ) 3. Deposit funds.
   ( ) 4. Check on weather early on day of game, and make any
        adjustments which are indicated.

5. Without a doubt the officials are not on top of the situation and are inconsistent in their calls in a basketball contest. Players and coaches on both benches are criticizing the officials. At half time, your basketball coach follows the officials into their dressing room. How would you handle this situation? As athletic director, would you take corrective action? Would it be prior to the second half or after the game? How would you rectify the situation so that it did not occur again?

SUGGESTED READINGS

Albers, Henry H., *Principles of Management: A Modern Approach*, 4th edition, Wiley, New York, 1974, The Dynamics of Delegation, pp. 245-247.

Forsythe, Charles E. and Keller, I. A., *Administration of High School Athletics*, 5th edition Prentice Hall, Englewood Cliffs, N.J., 1972.

George, J.F. and Lehmann, H.A., *School Athletic Administration* Harper and Row, New York, 1966.

Hodge, Billy J. and Johnson, Herbert J., *Management and Organizational Behavior—A Multidimensional Approach*, Wiley, New York, 1970, Delegation, pp. 404-412.

Scanlan, Burt K., *Principles of Management and Organizational Behavior*, New York, Wiley, 1973, Ch. 11, Delegation—A Positive Approach to Management, pp. 233-250.

Williams, Jesse F. et al., *The Administration of Health Education and Physical Education*, Saunders, Philadelphia, 1964.

Chapter 18
Game Officials: Selection, Assignment, and Evaluation

In recent years the state, section, or league officials' associations have emphasized as their main goal, providing professional, trained, and competent officials for the interscholastic athletic program. Official associations usually have frequent meetings during the sports season to aid the schools in the selection of reliable, competent, and experienced officials. Clinics, tests and on the court evaluation as part of these meetings are the most effective means of grading the officials.

Form 18-1 is an example of clinics for officials by the North Dakota High School Activities Association. It is noted on the form that these clinics are mandatory for all prospective officials in the area.

Form 18-2 describes a follow-up meeting where officiating tests are given for the various sports.

ASSIGNMENT OF OFFICIALS

Once the clinics have been given and the tests administered, a list of officials is sent to participating schools in each league. The coach or athletic director indicate the choice of officials he prefers for the contests. The coach or athletic director will rate all officials listed to make it easier for the official's commissioner to assign officials for each school. The commissioner will try to assign the officials requested where possible. The commissioner usually assigns younger or less experienced officials with a veteran official to assure proper coverage of the contest. The veteran official is assigned, for example in football, as the referee and the less experienced official will be the umpire or head linesman. The commissioner will also try to assign the new officials to the less demanding games, such as freshman or

From: Dick Schindler, Assistant Secretary
North Dakota High School Activities Association
Box 1007, Valley City, North Dakota 58072

_____June 20_____ 1973__

To   _Duane Carlson, Ath Dir_____

_Board of Education Building_____

_Minot_____, N. D. 58 701_

The North Dakota High School Activities Association has scheduled the following rules clinic (s) in _New Sr High School._

1.	Girls Basketball	clinic at 7:00 P.M. on	September 4	19 73
2.	Wrestling	clinic at 7:00 P.M. on	October 16	19 73
3.	Boys Basketball	clinic at 7:00 P.M. on	November 6	19 73
4.		clinic at ____ P.M. on		19
5.		clinic at ____ P.M. on		19
6.		clinic at ____ P.M. on		19

I would like you to confirm these dates as soon as possible and let me know the building and room in which it is scheduled. I will need the usual equipment such as blackboard and chalk, 16 mm projector and screen, desk or podium from which to talk. FOR FOOTBALL AND BASKETBALL CLINICS, I WILL ALSO NEED AN OVERHEAD PROJECTOR.

I would appreciate it if you would notify the press, radio and TV about the clinic (s), where and when it will be held, and the starting time. The press release should stress that it is a mandatory requirement for OFFICIALS AND HEAD COACHES TO ATTEND IN FOOTBALL, BASKETBALL (BOYS), WRES— TLING, HOCKEY AND GYMNASTICS. It is also required that head coaches in both boys and girls track attend. The release should make it clear that other interested people and fans, ets., are welcome to attend any of the meetings.

Thank you very much for your trouble and I will be looking for confirmation from you.

Duane: I could use the gymnasium for all meetings as the crowds will be large. I'm anxious to see your new building. The football and track meetings are scheduled at MSC and I have contacted Elgie on those. The only meetings you will have to line-up are those listed above.

By permission, Dick

FORM 18-1 Clinics for officials. (North Dakota High School Activities Association. By permission.)

North Dakota High School Activities Association
Valley City, North Dakota

_____June 20_____ 197**3**

Duane Carlson, Ath Dir_____

Board of Education Bldg_____

Minot_____, N.D. 58 701

Dear Sir:

I am again asking for your cooperation in administering a very important part of our officiating program in North Dakota. Would you please administer the following officials tests scheduled in your city:

Sport Football_____, Date September 17_____, Time 7:30 P.M.

Sport Wrestling_____, Date November 12_____, Time 7:30 P.M.

Sport Gymnastics_____, Date November 26_____, Time 7:30 P.M.

Sport Boys Basketball____, Date December 3_____, Time 7:30 P.M.

Sport Hockey_____, Date December 3_____, Time 7:30 P.M.

Sport_____, Date _____, Time _____ P.M.

Either you or some very responsible staff member should supervise the test under the same conditions you would use for any closed book test given in your school. YOU MUST BE FIRM IN THIS MATTER. DO NOT ALLOW OFFICIALS TO HELP EACH OTHER.

We will allow the supervisor $4.00 for the administration of a test in any of the sports listed above. The allowance will be mailed following the basketball test in December.

When the tests are completed, the answer sheet should be mailed to this office _together with any unused tests._

It would be helpful if you would make an announcement of the time and place of the test in your local media. The announcement should include the information that the tests are mandatory for all officials.

The tests will be mailed under separate cover and will be marked _OFFICIALS TESTS._ If an official has a definite conflict at the scheduled time of the test, you might make an exception and allow him to take the test after the scheduled time. DO NOT MAKE A PRACTICE OF THIS——THIS IS WHY WE HAVE SO MANY PROBLEMS IN SOME OF THE TEST CENTERS. Only an extreme emergency should qualify under this provision. Again, thank you for your continued cooperation in our testing program.

Sincerely,

DS:lv

Dick Schindler, Assistant Secretary

FORM 18-2 Clinics for officials. (North Dakota High School Activities Association. By permission.)

sophomore contests, although he will usually have one veteran with the officiating crew.

The league commissioner will send a complete list of officials to each participating school. This list should include officials' fees, rate of travel pay, and position assignment. Form 18-3, North Section Sacramento, California, is an example of football officiating assignments. This type of form is used for all sports.

Form 18-4a shows an elaborate "contract for officials" form as used by the Pennsylvania Interscholastic Athletic Association.

Form 18-4b is a simple but efficient "contract for officials."

The athletic director should follow up on the assignments of officials once he receives the list from the commissioner's office. Ron Davis, Athletic Director at Corona del Mar High School, California sends a letter to each official (Form 18-5) as a doublecheck on the assignment. The letter indicates who will be assigned to the official's crew, where to park, and where the officials will dress for the game.

Payment of Officials

The efficient athletic director will have the paychecks for the officials ready by the time of the contest. This means preplanning by the athletic director, but it is good public relations. Form 18-6 is a request for payment voucher as used by the San Juan Unified School District in California. This form is filled out as soon as the officials list is sent to the school and the check for the officials is ready on the day of the contest.

The reimbursing of officials for their services was discussed in Chapter 17. The official should not have to look for the athletic director to get paid. It should be presented in a professional, business-like manner. If it is presented after the game, a word of thanks for a job well done should go along with the check, regardless of the personal feelings of the athletic director.

Evaluation of Officials and School

All officials are evaluated on their performance, mainly for the purpose of helping them become better officials. The commissioner will send out forms during a season and the coach or athletic director rates the officials after each contest. Kansas State High School Activities Association has a unique way of evaluating officials. The evaluation of an official is done by a computer. IBM cards are sent to each school by the official, one week prior to officiating at that school. If he fails to send the IBM card, his pay is held up until the card is received. The coach sends the evaluation card to the commissioner's office and the results are tabulated on an official rating sheet. This is sent to each official at the end of the season and published in the association's publication.

The officials also rate the schools. Form 18-7 is an example of the North Dakota High School Activities Association school rating form. The survey indicates to the school where improvement is needed in the area of equipment, court or field, player attitude, administrator attitude, coach attitude, or crowd attitude.

Responsibilities of the Officials to the Schools

Witcher Beverly, Director of Athletics, Yorktown High School, Arlington, Virginia[1] lists the responsibilities of the officials to the schools as follows:

1. To be on time
2. To be neat in appearance
3. To approach the job in a businesslike manner
4. To be prepared physically and mentally
5. To be competent, have a working knowledge of the rules and the mechanics of officiating
6. To be aware of the safety of our athletes
7. To recognize that the captains of our teams are the official representative of our teams and school and that they extend to them all the courtesies due them during the game
8. To recognize a need to use psychology in working with the players
9. To treat the game as a contest
10. To work scrimmages as a service to the school, this also provides an excellent opportunity for training new or inexperienced officials as well as a chance for the older officials to work out and get in shape for the season.

FOOTBALL OFFICIATING ASSIGNMENTS
September 12-14

Richard A. Schromm, Commissioner, 2901 Marco Way, Carmichael (95608) Phone 482-7682
Ron Heberer, Administrative Asst. 4301 Glen Vista St., Carmichael 489-9062

Officials Fees 1974-76

Travel Time:

Each official paid at rate of 10¢ per mile.

Travel time will be paid from home town of official to the town assigned.

Minimum travel time $2.00 up to maximum travel time $10.00.

Football Fees:

$30.00 per official, two consecutive games, four officials.

22.00 per official, one game, four officials.

13.50 per official, games other than varsity, two or more officials.

27.50 per official, one game championship or playoff, all leagues, four officials.

HOME TEAM	OPPONENT	GAMES	TIME	REFEREE	UMPIRE	H.L.	F.J.
Thursday, September 12							
McClatchy	Modesto	2	6:00	Misquez	Kozlowski	Hayward	Brown*
Highlands	San Juan	2	5:30	Higgins	Kays	Perry	Willett*
Washington	Oakmont	2	6:00	Johnson	Rogers	Chappin*	Zahniser
Encina	Foothill	2	6:00	Gilmour	Swartz	Vogt	Hill*
Casa Roble @ S.J.	Bella Vista	2	6:00	Kerns	Marquardsen	Hardy*	Lazark
Folsom	Kerr - Fr.	1	4:00	Olmstead	Caruso		
Mills	Casa Roble - Fr.	1	4:00	Hutchinson	Vaughn		
Nevada Un.	Wheatland - Fr.	1	6:00	Soden	Marsh		
Friday, September 13							
Del Campo	Jesuit @ S.J.	2	6:00	Gilmour	Pelletier	Willett	Hill*
La Sierra	Davis @ E.C.	2	6:00	Crabb	Tipton	Frias	Chappin*
Fairfield	Kennedy	2	5:45	Johnson	Lord	McBride	Zahniser*

Johnson	Lodi	6:00	2	Higgins	Ruggles	Garcia	Smith*
Elk Grove	Edison	6:00	2	Lease	Rogers	Molden	Frates*
Rio Linda	Galt	6:00	2	Langer	Kays	Emery	Gilchrist*
Yuba City	Red Bluff	6:00	2	Marquardsen	Hetzel	Lovelady	Williams*
Nevada Un.	Grant	6:00	2	Keys	Martin*	Beagle	Burch, J.
Roseville @ Oakmont	El Dorado	6:00	2	Moore	Cooley	Carlson	Cannon*
John Swett	Esparto	6:00	2	Brown	Swartz*	Linck	Reidt
Dixon	Winters	6:00	2	Belke	Koster	Kammerer	Hardy*
Amador	Linden	6:00	2	Hanlon	Thompson	Borgen	Lazark*
Jackson	Rio Vista	6:00	2	McKenzie	Helms	Takuma	Olmstead*
Marysville	Oroville	6:00	2	DeLotty	Davies*	Stewart	Najarian
Marshall	Folsom	6:00	2	Perry	Kozlowski	Muehlbauer*	Elliott
Ponderosa	Del Oro	6:00	2	Dibben	Spencer	Augusta	Vogt*
Vacaville	Norte	6:00	2	McAllister	Jones	Allen	Matthews*
Woodland	Tokay	6:00	2	Vukovich	Kinyon	Skipworth	DiRe*
A.R.C.	Sierra	7:30	1	Gilbert	Piacentini	Rodness	McFayden

Saturday, September 14

El Camino	C.B.S.	6:00	2	Crabb	Piacentini, N.	Huntley	McFadven*
Mira Loma	Burbank @ ARC	6:00	2	Gilbert	Davies	Williams	Hanlon*
Cordova	Rio Americano	11:30	2	DeLotty	Cooley	Cannon	McKenzie*
S. Tahoe	Carson City	11:30	2	Moore	Hayward	Kinyon	Keys*
Sacramento	Oakland	11:00	2	McAllister	Garcia	Smith	Vukovich*
Benicia	Albany	11:00	2	Lease	Spencer	Matthews	Jorgensen*
Justin	St. Helena	11:00	2	Rodness	Krieger	Abramson	Frates*
Ione	Ripon	12:00	2	Belke	Haskell	Langer*	Reidt
Hazel Chris. (8 men)	Mercy @ B.V.	1:00	2	Dibben	DiRe*	Miller, J.	Piacentini, A.

FORM 18-3 Example of football officiating assignments. (Richard A. Schromm, Commissioner, Carmichael, California. By permission.)

NORTH HUNTERDON REGIONAL HIGH SCHOOL
ANNANDALE, NEW JERSEY 08801

ATHLETIC DEPARTMENT

ATHLETIC OFFICIALS CONTRACT

MR. . . . .   DATE . . . .

. . . .

. . . .

You are invited to officiate as . . . .

in a . . . . game at NORTH HUNTERDON REGIONAL H. S.

NORTH HUNTERDON REGIONAL H. S. vs. . . . .

DATE . . . .   TIME . . . . FEE $ . . . .

If you can accept, please sign the duplicate and return as soon as possible. The original is for your file.

ACCEPTED: Sincerely yours,

. . . .
           Name   DIRECTOR OF ATHLETICS

. . . .
           Date

FORM 18-4*b* Contract for officials. (Bob Hopek, Athletic Director. North Hunterdon Regional High School, Annadale, New Jersey. By permission.)

TO:_____

You have accepted an officiating assignment at Corona del Mar High School. As you know, our home games are played at Newport Harbor. My records indicate that you have accepted the following assignment:

_____   _____   _____

DATE   DAY   TIME

_____   _____   _____

SPORT   CLASSIFICATION   OPPONENT

Others assigned to help you officiate this contest:

_____   _____   _____

Upon your arrival you may park in the lot adjacent to the gymnasium off 16th Street. You may dress in the faculty room located in the most southern part of the gymnasium. A custodian will be on hand to help you with anything you may need. I hope that your assignment here will be a pleasant one. Please feel free to ask our co-operation at any time.

Respectfully,

By Permission
Ron Davis,
Director of Athletics
Corona del Mar High School
Newport, California

FORM 18-5   Letters to officials prior to contest. (Corona del Mar High School, Newport Beach, California. Ron Davis Athletic Director. By permission.)

```
            SAN JUAN UNIFIED SCHOOL DISTRICT
                 Request for Payment Voucher          Voucher #_____
                                                      Date_____
                 STUDENT BODY FUNDS

  Pay to_____
  Address_____
  Amount_____ $_____
  Purpose or Event_____ Date_____
  Description_____
  _____

  Charge to:_____ Account #_____
                    Name of Account
  MAKE VOUCHER IN TRIPLICATE               ATTACH ALL RECEIPTS TO VOUCHER
  Purchase Order #_____ Check #_____ Date of Check_____
  The materials and/or services covered by this voucher have been received in good order and
  prices charged are O.K.
  School_____ Signed_____Advisor
  Code #_____Approved_____Principal

  B.sb.3
  6/1/65
```

FORM 18-6   Payment of officials. (San Juan Unified School District, California. By permission.)

The Responsibilities of the School Personnel to the Officials

Beverly also lists the school's responsibilities to the official as follows:

1. To provide a student manager to greet the officials and show them to their dressing rooms. He also has the responsibility to provide towels and refreshments at half time
2. To sign and return contracts on time
3. To provide accurate schedules in advance of the first game
4. To provide adequate dressing facilities away from the coaches' office or spectators
5. To provide proper crowd control
6. To provide adequate police protection
7. To have proper court and field markings
8. To provide adults as official scorers and timers
9. To provide a qualified person for the public address system, preferably a member of the faculty
10. To require coaches to attend rules clinics
11. To require coaches to approach game in a mature, business-like manner
12. To require the coach to recognize that he and the officials play an equal role in influencing crowd control

13. To provide an assembly program and invite officials to explain rule changes and to explain the rules that are commonly misunderstood
14. To see that players and coaches play the game with respect for officials
15. To see that our student body respects the officials
16. To provide for evaluation of the officials, rating cards for immediate feedback to the officials' association, a summary to the state office at the end of the season
17. To notify the commissioner in advance of cancellation or any change in game times or sites

Women Officials[2]

Most associations are using both men and women officials for girls' athletics especially with the rapid increase in the number of contest in girls' athletics which has drained the supply of women officials. The National Association for Girls and Women in Sports, formerly Division of Girls and Women in Sport (DGWS), has supplied officials for girls' sports in the past; however, it has not kept pace with the insurgence of women and girls sports. In the past, women physical education teachers have been assigned many outside activities such as the pep club, cheerleading group, drill team, pom pom girls along with their coaching duties; hence there has been little time for them to also officiate. However, the women coaches will have to spend more time officiating until the women's physical education departments of our colleges and universities and the National Association for Girls and Women in Sport has a chance to catch up with the rapid growth of girls' interscholastic athletics.

The women coaches are busy with rules interpretation and testing meetings in volleyball, basketball, gymnastics and track and field in an attempt to fill the void. The national federation has come to the aid of the girls' program with films and audio visual aids and the national rules interpretation meetings as a service to state associations as a step in enhancing the quality of state officiating programs for girls' athletics. Part of the problem with the lack of supply of well trained coaches and officials would have to be attributed to the men and women who are involved in the training of these people.

Challenge Areas for Basketball Officials[3]

While officiating is an integral part of the interscholastic athletic program, it is not a position that all people are qualified or suited for. It takes a person with a certain temperment; a person who can work and function in pressure type situations. Officiating in any sport is tedious at best. However, we have cited basketball to indicate the stress and challenge areas related to officiating. These challenges could be related to any sport. We are using basketball as an illustration.

NORTH DAKOTA HIGH SCHOOL ACTIVITIES ASSOCIATION
Valley City, North Dakota

SCHOOL RATINGS IN BB & FB BY OFFICIALS
FOR THE_____SCHOOL YEAR

SCHOOL_____

The following are results of a survey of football and basketball officials which were registered with our Association last year, rating the schools for which they officiated, and the average rating of your school for the past year.

We have taken the totals of the ratings by the officials in each sport and divided it by the number of officials which rated your school in each sport to determine the average rating.

RATING KEY:

1 point for excellent
2 points for good
3 points for fair
4 points for unsatisfactory

BASKETBALL		FOOTBALL RATING	
Rated by	officials	Rated by	officials
Average rating		Average rating	

The survey showed your school needed improvement in the items marked after the key and under basketball and/or football. The number indicates how many officials checked that item of the key.

Improvement Key:	*Basketball*	*Football*
1. Equipment.	_____	_____
2. Court or field	_____	_____
3. Player attitude	_____	_____
4. Administrator attitude	_____	_____
5. Coach attitude	_____	_____
6. Crowd attitude	_____	_____

F. U. SMITH, EXECUTIVE SECRETARY
NO. DAK. HIGH SCHOOL ACT. ASSN.

FORM 18-7 School rating form. (North Dakota High School Activities Association. By permission.)

School_____

REQUIRED REPORT---RATING BASKETBALL OFFICIALS

MAIL TO

IOWA GIRLS' HIGH SCHOOL ATHLETIC UNION

615 Securities Building

DES MOINES, IOWA 50309

Please rate all major officials who have been used in your games either at home or away this season. These ratings will be transferred to cards in the Union Office and will have a bearing on the classification of the official.

SUGGESTED RATING SCALE: **SUPERIOR:**—Good enough for State Basketball Tournament. **ABOVE AVERAGE:**—Qualified for District Tournament. **AVERAGE:**—Acceptable for a game of average importance. **BELOW AVERAGE:**—Acceptable for a game of minor importance only. **VERY POOR:**—Not acceptable for any game.

CONDUCT OF THE GAME

1. Knowledge of the rules.
2. Care in supervising and signaling officials and bench personnel.
3. Quickness and sureness of decision.
4. Impartiality and fairness.
5. Extent to which his decisions are affected by comments of spectators, players or coaches.
6. Agility in following the ball or the play.
7. Extent to which he maintains complete control of game.
8. Consistency in his decisions and interpretations.

9. Extent to which his officiating promotes good sportsmanship, a clean, fast game and a festive feeling.
10. Self control and poise on the floor or field.

PERSONAL

11. Neatness of appearance at contests.
12. Degree in which his ideals are such as you would require in a high school teacher.
13. Promptness and business-like attitude in matters pertaining to his contract.
14. Tactfulness and modesty (as opposed to being overbearing and boastful).

NAME	ADDRESS (TOWN)	No. of Dates Worked	Superior	Above Average	Average	Below Average	Very Poor	Needs Improvement in Items Number
		YOUR ESTIMATES AS TO ABILITY						
(Sample—John Doe)	Oquawka							6-10-13

MARCH

_____, 19____   Signed:_____ Supt., Principal or Ath. Director

(SEND ONE COPY TO UNION OFFICE—RETAIN ONE COPY IN YOUR FILE)

(List Tournament Officials on Back)

(Over)

1. Jealousies with other officials: Think they are better than other officials that are working more games. Unhappy with the assigning secretary because he/she has not give official a fair chance.
2. Pressure cooker situations: Comes from coach, crowd and players as well as a particular game being played.
3. Stress/tension: Cannot relax and watch what is important to have smooth game; too many inconsistencies.
4. Attitude: Oral and body language tells coach, players and fans that official is a dictator. Official controls game by this method, antagonizes all parties involved. Coaches are against officials in general and will not accept them as individuals. If the official has had a fight with his wife, boss, or tough day on the job, he/she is not up to calling a ball game and carries this attitude onto the court.
5. Locks out important aspects of the game. Listens to crowd, watches good player perform and does not cover his/her assigned area. Newspaper articles sometimes influence the official's attitude on the court.
6. Officiates from a conscious level rather than free flow. Reaction time slowed down in making decisions. Not able to accept partner as to what he/she is and his/her outlook and philosophy of the game's importance. One official cannot work a good game if both officials cannot.
7. Fear of making a mistake: In awe of partner working with. Black team vs. white team situation. Fear of coach yelling from bench. If official does not do a good job, he/she will not make coach's list for future assignments.
8. Prejudge/prejudice/preconceived thoughts: Knows something is going to happen before it happens. Prejudges coaches, players and fans; thinks that fellow official is weak and marginal official.
9. All officials' calls in basketball are negative for at least 50 percent of the coaches, players and fans. How do you make a positive out of a negative?
10. How do you appear fresh and feel energetic when you have worked an afternoon game and have a night game, plus a schedule that has you assigned four to five nights in succession, with two to three games per day/night?
11. Many officials do not know or study the rules. Other officials predetermine a partner by looking at his/her test scores.

Relationship with Game Officials

Officials should be treated with the courtesy due any guest. As indicated in Chapter 16, officials must be notified well in advance as to the time and place of the contest, parking facilities available, separate dressing facilities and should be greeted by the athletic director or a representative of the school upon arrival.

The coach has a definite responsibility to know the rules of the sport being coached. The entire coaching staff should attend rules clinics and, if possible, have an official speak to the team prior to the opening game and officiate an intrasquad game. The official at such a meeting could go over the pertinent rules of the game and conduct a discussion period for the athletes. Excellent films are available on all aspects of officiating, and it is the responsibility of the coach to show these films to the team.

A coach can present a positive public image by maintaining a good relationship with game officials. The coach must keep his composure during the contest. Any disagreements may be handled through proper channels such as the post game evaluation form and the rating of officials. The coach must realize that the official is the "expert" because of his training as an official and bases his judgments on his experience as a member of the officials' association. Any public display of anger toward an official is poor public relations.

Questions

1. Discuss the pros and cons of paying the officials by check (a) *before* they officiate the contest; (b) *immediately after* the contest; (c) reimbursements are mailed from the board of education or athletic office and the athletic director doesn't give the checks to the officials personally. Why is a policy necessary?

2. Should the game officials have a separate room for conferences and changing clothes that should be off limits to coaches, players, and spectators? After implementing such a policy, as athletic director, how would you enforce this off limits policy to protect the officials?

3. You have a good head football coach, but he is a "fireball." He was a losing coach as the result of an incompetent official's call. He not only went on the field and told the official off immediately after the blown call, he charged into the official's locker room after the game and rehashed with the official the mistake. When he saw the films and the official's error, he was incensed further, so he showed the films to the sportswriters and the downtown booster's club. The fans and players love him because he's a winner, "tells it like it is" and "fights for the kids"! What course of action should you, as athletic director, take? Is a policy necessary? Has the coach violated his profession's code of ethics?

4. What course of action would you as the athletic director take if two officials show up to officiate one of your school's athletic contests and they request complimentary tickets for their wives, children, and friends accompanying them? Is a policy necessary?

REFERENCES

1. Beverly, Witcher, Director of Athletics, Yorktown High School, Arlington, Virginia, *"Relationships between School Personnel and Official's Associations,"* *National Conference of High School Athletic Directors Proceedings*, December 8, 1974, Hershey Pa., p. 42. National Federation of State High School Associations. By permission of the author.
2. Ecker, Wanda, Supervisor of Girl's Athletics, Wichita South High School, Wichita, Kansas, *"Training Women Coaches and Officials,"* *National Conference of High School Athletic Directors Proceedings*, December 10-13, 1972, p. 47. National Federation of State High School Athletic Associations. By permission of the author.
3. Goforth, Jeff, *Challenge Areas for Basketball Officials*, The Pacific Institute, 10647 Culpeper Court, Seattle, Washington 98177. By permission.

SUGGESTED READINGS

Coaches Manual, A Guide to Athletic Coaching in Florida Schools, Bulletin 741, State of Florida Department of Education. Reprinted by AAHPER, 1201 16th St., N.W., Washington, D.C. 20036, pp. 50-60.

Gallon, Arthur J., *Coaching Ideas and Ideals*, Houghton Mifflin, Boston, 1974, pp. 238-239.

Grieve, A. W., *Directing High School Athletics*, Prentice-Hall, Englewood Cliffs, N.J., 1963, Ch. 7. Securing and Paying Officials.

Purdy, R. L. *The Successful High School Athletic Program*, Parker Publishing, West Nyack, N.Y., 1970, Ch. 9, Building Schedules, Hiring Officials, and Dealing with Transportation.

Chapter 19
Interscholastic Athletic Awards

An athletic award is a symbol of athletic accomplishment. Its value lies in its implication rather than in its monetary worth. The purpose of an award is to give recognition to interscholastic athletes who exemplify the highest standards and who have met the criteria for such an award.

It is important that criteria be determined and published to remove any question about the requirements for receiving an award. The student-athlete must meet the requirements and receive the coaches' recommendation. Awards should not be given on the whim of the coach, nor should team success be a determining factor.

Awards are not a motivating factor. The value of athletics lies in participation itself. The award, being a symbol of accomplishment, establishes that an athlete has fulfilled participation requirements in a particular sport, has met other criteria, and has received the recommendation of the coaching staff for a job well done.

The coach must think of the total program and not just a particular team. The criteria and standards should be the same for all athletes, regardless of the sport. Special awards, such as awarding game balls or retiring jerseys, are generally not recommended. Special awards should be kept to a minimum or discontinued altogether as they become rather common, with one coach trying to outdo the other. Policies, standards, and criteria must be established at the outset and all coaches must abide by these regulations. For a baseball coach to give an award for the "300" club or a basketball coach to give an award for the best left-handed shooter or the football coach to give an award for the fastest tackle, contributes to a situation that can create animosity among teams and coaches while rendering the entire awards program meaningless.

In the late sixties, many schools were moving away from the trend
of wearing a school letter and participating in letterman clubs. In
many instances, students and even athletes themselves would not be
in attendance when awards were presented, indicating perhaps,
in our changing society, that there was no longer a need for this type
of recognition. However, there seems to be a return in popularity of
block letters, wearing of a letter jacket, especially in the Midwest.

Many state associations have established monetary and other limits
relative to permissible awards. Frequently the type of award permitted is spelled out—for example, no jewelry or anything of value.
Awards that have become popular are the wall plaque or lacquered
certificates. Girls in some states are receiving medallions that can be
worn as a necklace or bracelet with a charm symbolic of the sport.

Financing Athletic Awards

One of the most important aspects of the award system is financial,
especially today when most schools are feeling the financial pinch.
In the past, awards were budgeted as any other item in the interscholastic athletic program. Today many schools can no longer
sustain this practice, and awards are purchased through other means
such as candy sales, vending machine sales, or financed by the
booster or parents' club. The latter is undesirable in that the community becomes overly concerned with the presentation of awards.
Awards should be financed by school funds and monitored by school
personnel: namely, the athletic director. If a booster organization
becomes involved in the financing of awards, a friction may develop
between the coaches, especially during a championship season. The
coach of the championship team, obviously, would like to have many
special awards for that team. This causes a hardship on the rest of
the coaching staff if they have not won a championship. This is not
the intent of interscholastic athletics. All participants should be
honored, not just those on championship teams.

General Policies. There are many different athletic awards systems
in vogue today and it is not practical to recommend one as more
worthy than another. There has, however, been a trend to standardize awards as much as possible, both in type and requirements.

It is common practice to treat all sports in the same way. The
recipient of a water polo award deserves as much recognition as a
member of the basketball team.

1. The size of the letter award, plaque, or certificate for all sports should be the same.
2. High standards of achievement should be required for awards in all sports.
3. Awards generally are made on the basis of a combination of factors included recommendation of the coach, student-faculty committee action, and a required amount of competition, with exception for extenuating circumstances. (See below)
4. The requirements for the award should be clearly understood by all concerned, including the general public.
5. In schools where a point system is used, the points earned in each sport are usually cumulative. That is, they apply in successive seasons toward the award requirement.
6. Where a specified amount of participation is required for the award, the coach is responsible for keeping accurate records of the playing time of each athlete.
7. In some schools, awards are limited to one letter in a sport during a student's athletic career; subsequent recognition usually is in the form of a certificate.
8. Schools generally make awards to students for other activities as well as athletics. They usually include dramatics and music.
9. Two types of awards systems are generally recognized:
   (a) an award system based largely on participation in an individual sport and (b) general recommendations award system relates to a team sport.
10. Most schools present the awards at the end of each sport season.
11. Most schools seem to be moving away from the traditional award system.
12. Generally, there are two methods of awards presentation:
    (a) Awards' assembly with the entire student body present.
    (b) An awards banquet.

State Association Awards Policy. State Athletic Associations vary in their award policies; however, all states agree on the purpose of awards. The Iowa High School Athletic Association[1] cites the current awards policy in that state.

   9.15 (9) *Awards*
   a. No member of an athletic team shall receive any compensation in any form for services rendered as a member of the student's team. No

student shall be eligible to participate in contests sponsored by a governing organization if the student, or any member of the student's family, is receiving any remuneration, either directly or indirectly, to influence the student to attend, or the student's family to reside in a given school district in order to establish eligibility on a team of said school.

b. A student will be permitted to receive only the customary ribbon or medal for participation in an interscholastic athletic contest. A student will be allowed to receive from the student's school, for participation in the interscholastic athletic program, only a trophy, plaque, cup, medal, unattached letter, monogram, or other insignia of the student's school. The value of any school award cannot exceed $10.00.

No student shall receive any award from an individual or outside organization for high school participation while enrolled in high school.

No student shall accept any trip or excursion of any kind by an individual, organization, or group outside the student's own school or the governing organization.

The superintendent or the superintendent's designee shall be held responsible for compliance with the above rules. Questions or interpretation regarding medals or awards shall be referred to the executive board.

Nothing in the above rules shall preclude giving a complimentary dinner by local individuals, organizations or groups with the approval of the superintendent to members of the local high school squad.

Nothing in the above rules shall preclude or prevent the awarding and the acceptance of an inexpensive, unmounted, unframed paper certificate of recognition as an award or an inexpensive table favor which is given to everyone attending a banquet.

If a student participates in an outside school activity during the school year, the student may accept a statuette trophy, plaque or cup for participation in a particular event as long as the award is not in violation of the amateur sanctioning body for that sport. The student may not receive any other award of money or in the form thereof. The student may not receive any other award the value of which exceeds $10.00.

During the summer months a student may enter an event in any sport as an individual or as a member of a team not representing the student's school. If such student wins an award, the student may accept the award provided it does not violate the amateur award rule of the amateur sanctioning body.

Authority to Make Awards. The coach shall recommend the members of his squad who have met the requirements for an award. These recommendations are to be approved by the director of athletics and, in some cases, the athletic council and submitted to the principal of the school for his authorization. In an extenuating circumstance when a problem arises regarding the awarding of letters, a committee consisting of the coach of the team, athletic director, and a member of the student council shall recommend the final decision to the principal.

Special awards are usually given to student-athletes who compete on teams that win the championship or state or sectional titles. The type of award should be established in this category prior to the beginning of the school year. An example of establishing criteria for championship or state championship teams is used by Susquehanna Township School District, Harrisburg, Pennsylvania (Form 19-1).

Easton Area High School, Pennsylvania is very explicit on the types of awards to be given (Form 19-2) and distributes this form to all athletes at the school orientation meeting so there will be no mistake on the qualifications for the "all school award" as well as the individual requirements for their individual award.

Sacramento Senior High School, Sacramento, California uses Form 19-3 to authorize the distribution of letters. Each coach is responsible for the completion of the form and must turn it in to the athletic director upon completion of the sport season.

Questions

1. What are the purposes of athletic awards to deserving student-athletes?
2. Why should the awards be the same for all student-athletes regardless of the sport?
3. Discuss the pros and cons of "retiring" game jerseys, awarding game balls and special awards to outstanding athletes.
4. What is the value of giving the awards to student-athletes at a special assembly program in the school auditorium?
5. Why is it important to have a written criteria, approved by the athletic director and athletic council after input by the coaching staff, so that everyone can to see the basis on which awards are given?

By permission
Ben Jones-Athletic Director

SUSQUEHANNA TOWNSHIP SCHOOL DISTRICT
Harrisburg, Pennsylvania 17109

PERM-AWARDS PLAQUES OR TROPHIES WILL BE AWARDED ON THE BASIS OF THE SEASON RECORD AS INDICATED:

BOYS	SEASON RECORD	AWARD	RECIPIENTS
Football	Undefeated or League Champion	Perm-Award	Varsity Squad Managers, Coaches
Cross Country	Undefeated	Perm-Award	Varsity Squad, Coach,
	District State Champion	Perm-Award	Letter Winners
	Individual State Champion	Trophy	Individual
Basketball	Undefeated or League Champion (District-Regional)	Perm-Award	Varsity Squad, Managers, Coaches
	State Championship	Trophy	Varsity Squad, Coaches, Managers
Wrestling	Team Undefeated	Perm-Award	Varsity Squad, Coaches, Managers
	Individual District Champion	Trophy	Individual
	Individual State Champion	Trophy	Individual
Tennis-Boys	Undefeated Team	Perm-Award	Squad, Coach
	Individual State Champion	Trophy	Individual
Golf	Undefeated including Playoff (division)	Perm-Award	Squad, Coach
Baseball	Undefeated or League Champion	Perm-Award	Squad, Coaches Manager
Track	Undefeated or League Champion	Perm-Award	Varsity Squad, Coaches, Manager
	District Champion	Trophy	Individual
	State Champion	Trophy	Individual
GIRLS			
Hockey	Undefeated League Champion	Perm-Award	Varsity Squad, Coach, Manager
Basketball	Undefeated or League Champions	Perm-Award	Varsity Squad, Coach, Manager
Softball	Undefeated or League Champions	Perm-Award	Varsity Squad, Coach, Manager
Tennis	Undefeated or League Champions	Perm-Award	Varsity Squad, Coach, Manager

FORM 19-1 Criteria for special awards. (Susquehanna Township High School District, Harrisburg, Pennsylvania. Ben Jones, Athletic Director. By permission.)

284

REFERENCES

1. Harty, David
   Association, *9.15 (9) Awards, p. 12, 1976,* Boone, Iowa 50036. By permission.

SUGGESTED READINGS

Forsythe, C.E., *Administration of High School Athletics* 4th edition, 1962, Ch. 9, Athletic Awards.

George, J.F. and Lehmann, H.A., *School Athletic Administration* Harper and Row, New York, 1966, Ch. 17, Awards.

Grieve, A.W., *Directing High School Athletics,* Prentice-Hall, Englewood Cliffs, N.J., 1963, Ch. 14, Awards Systems.

Purdy, R.L., *The Successful High School Athletic Program,* Parker Publishing, West Nyack, 1973 Ch. 12, Designing a Balanced System for Honoring Athletes

Easton Area School District

EASTON AREA HIGH SCHOOL

Athletic qualifications for the ALL SCHOOL AWARD, also known as the Uniform School Award, will be similar to the awards policy heretofore used and listed below. This new award, presented at the end of the senior year at a school-sponsored banquet, shall consist of a wooden wall plaque with a bulldog mounted in front and a plate upon which shall be engraved all of the activities in which the student "won" an award through his three year career. Along with varsity athletes, student trainers and cheerleaders, other activities which qualify for the award are: band, orchestra, chorus, twirlers and majorettes including drill team, National Honor Society, chess team, and synchronettes. (This award supersedes all other school awards, banquets, etc.).

Statistics for award winners in athletics, cheerleaders, student trainers and synchronettes will be kept in the office of the director of athletics. Coaches will submit the names of all "letter winners" at the completion of each season.

QUALIFICATIONS:

BASEBALL — A baseball player must participate in one-half the number of innings of the varsity games scheduled. The exception to this is a pitcher, who must participate in a total of 14 innings or more.

BASKETBALL (Boys & Girls) — A basketball player must compete in one-half the number of quarters of the scheduled varsity games.

CROSS COUNTRY — A runner must compete in 75% of the scheduled varsity matches.

FIELD HOCKEY — A player must compete in 75% of the scheduled varsity games, and in one-half the number of halves of scheduled varsity games.

FOOTBALL — Football players must compete in the following number of varsity quarters in one season: Seniors 8 quarters; Juniors 10 quarters; Sophomores 12 quarters.

GOLF — An athlete must compete in 75% of the scheduled varsity matches.

SOCCER — An athlete must compete in 75% of the scheduled varsity matches.

SOFTBALL — An athlete must compete in 75% of the scheduled varsity games.

SWIMMING (Boys & Girls) — An athlete must compete in 50% of the scheduled varsity meets and score total points at least equal to the number of dual meets and tournaments in the season.

SYNCHRONETTES — Synchronettes must be recommended by the synchronettes coach each year at the conclusion of the annual synchronettes show.

TENNIS (Boys & Girls) — Each scheduled varsity match shall be assigned a value of two points. Participation in a singles match shall win a player two points toward his award; participation in a doubles match, one point. Awards shall be given to all players whose season point total is equal to, or more than, one-half the number of scheduled, varsity matches.

FORM 19-2 Distribution of letters. (Sacramento Senior High School. Sacramento, California. By permission.)

Awards - continued

TRACK & FIELD   A player must score 10 points in varsity competition.

TRACK-WINTER   An athlete must place in 75% of the meets in which he is entered by his coach.

TRAINER-STUDENT   Trainers must be recommended by the director of athletics following each year of satisfactory duty.

VOLLEYBALL   An athlete must compete in 75% of the scheduled varsity matches.

WRESTLING   A wrestler must participate in 60% of the varsity meets or earn twelve varsity points in competition including tournaments.

MANAGERS, SCOREKEEPERS   Must be recommended by the coach following each season of satisfactory duty.

John B. Maitland

Director of H.P.E. and Athletics

JBM dm
8/73

Sacramento Senior High School - California
AUTHORIZATION TO DISTRIBUTE LETTERS AND EMBLEMS (SPORTS)

Sports and Division _____

Coach _____

(Signature)

Names (Alphabetical)	Letter or Emblem to be Awarded							
	Varsity Letter	J. V. Letter	B Letter	C or D Letter	Soph. Numeral	Emblems Footballs Basketballs Etc.	Gold Award Champs	Silver Award Champs	3 Year Gold Varsity

FORM 19-3 Authorization to distribute letters and emblems (sports). (Sacramento Senior High School. Sacramento, California. By permission.)

288

PART V
MANAGEMENT FUNCTIONS: CONTROLLING AND REPORTING

Chapter 20
Purchase of Athletic Equipment

In purchasing equipment for the interscholastic athletic program, five major factors must be considered: safety, comfort, appearance, usage, and the budget.

Safety

The athletic director is not usually in a position to research or to test for specifications on various items of equipment. An expert should be consulted as to the best possible protective equipment available. Sporting goods dealers, college certified trainers, and reconditioners of athletic equipment can assist the athletic director in selecting quality equipment.

Comfort

Comfort is a consideration that can be closely related to safety. Improperly fitted uniforms can easily result in a loss of mobility and decreased efficiency on the part of the player.

Appearance

Appearance is a consideration that does not affect the comfort or safety of the player. It may, however, play a major role in determining team pride.

Usage

Practice equipment should conform to the same specifications as game equipment. In the selection of practice uniforms, the coach should be just as conscious of comfort as he is with game uniforms. Although color is important is practice uniforms, the primary consideration should be durability, maintenance, and comfort.

Budget

A budget proposal should be prepared and submitted by the head coach to the athletic director. (See Chapter 6, "Budgeting and Financing.") Basic considerations in devising a list of needed equipment includes the number of athletes involved in the program and the existing inventory. The athletic director should approve an itemized budget before any money is spent.[1]

THE IMPORTANCE OF ORDERING EQUIPMENT EARLY

The ideal time to order equipment is soon after the close of the sports season. The athletic director and the coach are able to review their needs for the coming season without the pressures that are involved during the season or in preparing for the season. The equipment can be delivered, checked, marked, and stored well in advance of the next season. This gives the equipment manager or the coach the chance to assign equipment to players and be ready for the first day of practice. When equipment needs are filled well in advance of the season, it limits the last minute problems that interfere with the coach's demanding practice schedule.

By ordering equipment early, it affords the dealer a chance to give better service. It also assures the coach and the athletic director of the opportunity to select and receive the quality and quantity of equipment desired. The earlier the manufacturer receives the order, the better the service rendered.

PURCHASING PROCEDURES

There are basically two methods of purchasing athletic equpiment: the direct purchasing approach and the bid specification method. Both systems of purchasing equipment have their pros and cons.

Direct Purchasing

In many schools, once the budget has been approved, the athletic director gives the coach authority to purchase athletic equipment for

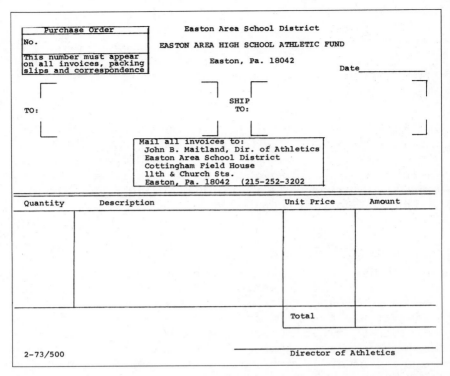

FORM 20-1 Purchase order form. (Easton Area School District, Easton Pennsylvania. By permission.)

his sport. The advantage to this method is that the coach becomes a comparison shopper, visiting various sporting goods outlets and examining equipment at clinics and dealer exhibits. The experienced coach, knowing the extent of his budget, will be able to extend his purchasing power to the fullest. Most coaches have one or two local sporting goods dealers who call on the school regularly and who know the basic equipment needs of the coach. The coach tends to use the dealer as his equipment advisor and builds up an extensive inventory over the years. A purchase order such as used by Easton Area School District, Easton, Pennsylvania may be used in the direct purchasing method Form 20-1.

Bid Purchasing

In some districts, purchase of equipment and supplies requires a competitive bidding system. Specifications must be drawn up to describe the exact nature of the equipment and supplies desired. These specifications must give the brand name or equivalent, a description, the design, the size, color, quality and other pertinent information. Specifications must be sent to all local and area sporting goods dealers at a designated time.

Bidding Information. A detailed bidding procedure as submitted by the Houston Independent School System is as follows: (This packet of material is sent to all firms interested in bidding on athletic equipment.)

NOTICE TO BIDDERS (Form 20-2). This information sheet includes the date and time that bids will be publicly opened and where this event will take place.

SPECIFICATIONS (Form 20-3). The specification form gives detailed information on prices, right to rejection, submission of samples, delivery date, firm bidding price, billing, and delivery date of the specification.

SPECIAL NOTICE REGARDING PRICE PROTECTION Form 20-4 is used in the event the item or items bid upon have any special clauses or information about price control.

BID PROPOSAL AND SPECIFICATION Form 20-5 includes the item number, description, quantity, unit, brand name, unit price, and total price.

BID PROPOSAL AND SPECIFICATION SUMMARY Form 20-6 must be filled out by the firm official with information on days required for delivery after receipt of purchase order, terms, and address of firm.

BID BOND Form 20-7 is used for "faithful performance and proper fulfillment of said contract or contracts." It serves as protection for both the school and the bidding party.

REQUEST FOR PURCHASE ORDER (Form 20-8). The request for purchase order form as used by the Minot Public Schools, Minot, North Dakota must be submitted to the district business office prior to the issuance of a purchase order.

Sealed bid proposals, bound in duplicate, addressed to the Board of Education, Houston Independent School District, c/o Mrs. Ruby Clifton, 3830 Richmond Ave., Houston, Texas 77027, will be received at the Board of Education, on Level 1 West of the Administration Building at the above address until 2:00 P.M. on the 15th day of May 1973 at which time they will be publicly opened and read. Envelops should be plainly marked, "Sealed Bid Proposals for

<u>ATHLETIC MEDICAL AND TRAINER SUPPLIES</u>

Do not open until 2:00 P.M., May 15, 1973." Any bid received later than the specified time, whether delivered in person or mailed, shall be disqualified.

All bids are to be on the basis of F.O.B.
Delmar Stadium
2020 Mangum Rd., Houston, TX.

Bids may be submitted on any and/or all items. Item and/or items not meeting specifications must be so indicated and submitted as an alternate to the specified item.

A cashier's or certified check, payable without recourse to the order of the Board of Education, Houston Independent School District, or an acceptable bidder's bond, in an amount in either event not less than ten per cent (10%) of the greatest aggregate amount bid in all proposals submitted, shall accompany each bidder's proposal or proposals if the aggregate amount bid by the bidder is in excess of $1,000.00.

A performance bond, in an amount not less than one hundred per cent (100%) of the contract and/or purchase order sum, conditioned upon the faithful performance of the contract and/or purchase order and upon the payment of all persons supplying labor or furnishing materials, will be required with each contract of $5,000.00 or more.

Forms of proposed documents, including specifications and bid forms, are on file at the office of the Administrative Assistant for Procurement, Purchasing Department, Level 3 North, School Administration Offices, 3830 Richmond Avenue, Houston, Texas, and are available to bidders. The School District assumes no responsibility for mailing bid forms and specifications.

No bids shall be withdrawn for a period of thirty (30) days subsequent to the opening of bids without the consent of the Owner.

All suppliers of goods or services must be in compliance with the requirements of Title VII of the Civil Rights Act of 1964, as amended March 24, 1972, and the Rules and Regulations of the Equal Employment Opportunity Commission issued pursuant thereto. An affidavit to this effect is enclosed and shall be signed by each company at the time of submission of bids to the Houston Independent School District. It is understood that this Affidavit is not an admission by any party that he has been in violation of Title VII of the Civil Rights Act of 1964, as amended.

The Owner reserves the right to reject any and/or all bids and to accept any bid deemed most advantageous to the Houston Independent School District, and to waive any informalities in bidding.

HOUSTON INDEPENDENT SCHOOL DISTRICT
ARTHUR D. PETERSON
ADMINISTRATIVE ASSISTANT FOR PROCUREMENT

By Permission: Joe Tusa

FORM 20-2 Notice to bidders. (Houston Independent School District. Houston, Texas. By permission.)

HOUSTON INDEPENDENT SCHOOL DISTRICT
Bid Opening March 2, 1976 10:00 AM
General Conditions
ANNUAL ATHLETIC MEDICAL AND TRAINER SUPPLIES
Project 76-3-17

SPECIFICATIONS FOR ATHLETIC MEDICAL & TRAINER SUPPLIES - 1976 - 77

All prices are to be FOB Delmar Stadium, 2020 Mangum Road, Houston, Texas 77092

The Houston Independent School District reserves the right to reject any and/or all bids or to accept any part of any bid deemed most advantageous.

Submit sample of Medical Supplies, if other than brand specified, to Delmar Stadium.

All articles will be delivered not later than July 16, 1976, or within a guaranteed delivery date specified, which must be satisfactory to the Houston Independent School District.

All articles will be bid at a guaranteed firm price.

All articles which have been delivered will be billed as of August 5, 1976.

C. Pat Riley
Director of Athletic Business
and Athletic Activities

Joe C. Tusa
Assistant Superintendent for Athletics,
Health Education, Physical Education, and Recreation

NOTE: Both copies of the bid must be signed by authorized representative of the firm.

FORM 20-3 Specifications. (Houston Independent School District. Houston, Texas. By permission.)

295

HOUSTON INDEPENDENT SCHOOL DISTRICT

ANNUAL BIDS 1973 - 1974

SPECIAL NOTICE REGARDING PRICE PROTECTION

In the event the item or items bid upon have a 50% additional clause at the same price, or a firm price is required for 12 months and you are unable to quote a firm price for that period, fill in the information as follows:

Vendor agrees to furnish 50% additional quantity at the same price for _____ days.

AND/OR

Vendor agrees to a firm price for _____ days.

Products or items:

TELEPHONE _____

SIGNATURE OF FIRM OFFICIAL _____

DATE _____

FORM 20-4 Special notice regarding price protection. (Houston Independent School District, Houston, Texas.)

HOUSTON INDEPENDENT SCHOOL DISTRICT
Bid Opening March 2, 1976 10:00 AM
Specifications and Bid Proposal
ANNUAL ATHLETIC MEDICAL AND TRAINER SUPPLIES
Project 76-3-17

FIRM NAME _____

Page 1

ITEM NO.	DESCRIPTION	QUANTITY	UNIT	BRAND NAME	UNIT PRICE (Specify)	TOTAL PRICE
1	Elastic Wraps, Parke-Davis or equal 24 dozen 3″ and 12 dozen 4″	40	dozen		$	$
2	Bandage rolls — bulk, redi-cut — 2″ mesh, 28 x 30, gauze 90/box	60	box			
3	Gauze, non-sterile, 3 x 3 (over sponges) 100 to a bag, 4000/case	8	per case			
4	Isopropyl alcohol pints	40 dozen	dozen			
5	Curity Telfa Sterile 3 x 4 gauze pads, or equal	3	dozen			
6	Parke-Davis, J & J, or Bike Bandaid Plastic Strips, 1 x 3, plain pad, or equal 100's	20	dozen			
7	Bike Pro Wrap, 3″ rolls, 40/roll/case or approved equal	3	cases			

FORM 20-5 Bid proposal and specification. (Houston Independent School District, Houston, Texas. By permission.)

```
                    HOUSTON INDEPENDENT SCHOOL DISTRICT
                      Bid Opening May 15, 1973  2:00 P.M.
                        Bid Proposal and Specifications
                    ATHLETIC MEDICAL AND TRAINER SUPPLIES




Days required for delivery after receipt of purchase order _____


Terms _____


FIRM NAME _____


FIRM ADDRESS _____

             _____

TELEPHONE _____


SIGNATURE OF FIRM OFFICIAL _____


DATE _____
```

FORM 20-6 Bid proposal and specification summary. (Houston Independent School District, Houston, Texas. By permission.)

KNOW ALL MEN BY THESE PRESENTS, That we,_____

as _____ as PRINCIPAL, and

as SURETY, are held and firmly bound unto the Board of Education, Houston Independent school District, Houston, Harris County, Texas hereinafter called Owner, in the penal sum of _____ ($ _____)
Dollars lawful money of the United States, for the payment of which sum well and truly to be made, we bind ourselves, our heirs, executors, administrators, and successors, jointly and severally, firmly by these presents.

THE CONDITION OF THIS OBLIGATION IS SUCH, that whereas the Principal has submitted the accompanying bid or bids, dated _____
19___, being for the furnishing and placement of certain equipment in certain schools in Houston Independent School District.

NOW THEREFORE, if the Principal shall not withdraw the accompanying bid or bids within sixty (60) days after the date set for opening thereof, and shall within ten (10) days after the prescribed forms are presented to him for signature, enter into a written contract or contracts with the Owner in accordance with the bid or bids as accepted; and give bond with good and sufficient surety for the faithful performance and proper fulfillment of such contract or contracts including the payment of all persons supplying labor or materials therefor, and including correction of any defects in materials or workmanship which appear within one year after completion of the contract, or in the failure to enter into such contract or contracts and give such bond within the specified time, if the Principal shall pay to the Owner the difference between the aggregate amount specified in said bid or bids and the aggregate amount for which the Owner may enter into a contract or contracts for the same kind and quantities of equipment with another bidder; if the latter amount be in excess of the former; then the above obligation shall be void and of no effect, otherwise to remain in full force and virtue.

IN WITNESS WHEREOF, the above-bounded parties have executed this instrument under their several seals this   day of   ,
19   , the name and corporate seal of each corporate party being hereto affixed and these presents duly signed by its undersigned representatives, pursuant to authority of its governing body.

_____   _____
(Business Address)   (Individual Principal)

_____   _____
(Business Address)   (Corporate Principal)

ATTEST: By _____
                                    (Its President)

_____
(Secretary)

                                 (Corporate Surety)

                                 By _____

By permission

FORM 20-7   Bid bond. (Houston Independent School District, Houston, Texas. By permission.)

299

FORM 20-8 Request for purchase order. (Minot Public Schools, Minot, North Dakota. By permission.)

ADVANTAGES OF THE BIDDING SYSTEM

Many school systems favor the bid method of purchasing athletic equipment. Dr. Griffith C. O'Dell, recently retired Director of Physical Education and Interscholastic Athletics for the Minneapolis school system, lists the benefits of bid purchasing.[2]

1. It saves the school board substantial amounts of money because of discount prices and lower transportation charges through quantity bidding.
2. It tends to bring about greater uniformity of quality equipment.
3. It reduces the possibility of local school officials' haphazard buying from unknown sources.
4. It insures that supplies and equipment will be on hand when school opens or before the sport season starts.
5. It saves the local school administrators and clerks the trouble and inconvenience of purchasing and delivering supplies and equipment.
6. It relieves the coach of the responsibility of purchasing supplies and equipment and gives him time for the instruction needed on the athletic field.
7. It omits the possibility of salesmen disrupting school routine by calling upon coaches during the day.

CENTRAL PURCHASING

Many school districts that purchase supplies and equipment for several schools, stock central warehouses with large quantities of standardized materials. Some large districts standardize all sports equipment and supplies, the only difference among the different schools' uniforms is color.

The advantage of centralized purchasing is that materials can be bought well in advance and thus are available when needed. Competitive bidding for large quantities usually results in greater economy. Also, use of a central warehouse ensures that all orders, specifications, contracts, and records are kept in one location and are always accessible.

The disadvantages of the system are that it permits the coach little if any freedom in choosing material, it tends to foster waste, thinking that the central supply well can never run dry, coaches and athletes may become careless about caring for equipment and supplies.

FACTORS IN THE PURCHASE OF ATHLETIC EQUIPMENT

As mentioned earlier in the chapter, the basic factors in purchasing athletic equipment are safety or protection, comfort, appearance, usage, and budget considerations. Each sport is unique in the type of equipment needed. The most talked about piece of protective equipment is the football helmet. We have chosen the helmet to demonstrate the procedure that should be used in purchasing athletic equipment.

How to Buy Football Helmets

The *Rawlings Athletic Handbook*[4] outlines the procedure to be used in the purchase of football helmets.

Protection.   There are several factors to consider when buying football helmets, but one is more important than all other combined: protection. (Note: the *1975 National Federation Rule Book*[5] p. 9, has the following statement: "It is recommended that only those head protectors carrying the NOCSAE stamp of approval be purchased. Beginning in 1980 each player shall be equipped with a head protector which carries the NOCSAE stamp of approval.")

Protection fundamentally depends on the rigidity of the shell in distributing impact while being flexible enough to keep from cracking. The shell itself should be designed to provide maximum protection to the lower jaw, temple, base of the skull, and other vital areas. Many coaches prefer the head cushion-style helmet with its optimum combination of padding and suspension that has proven effective in holding the shell away from the head and absorbing impact. The padding in a helmet should be made of a resilient material that can better absorb the force of a blow.

EMERGING TRENDS IN ATHLETIC UNIFORMS

Hank Derieth, President, Medalist Sand Knit[6] states,

In reviewing the trends that have emerged in the last five years, the fabric, style or design and new garments are significant. The fabric used today is a stretch fabric of some type. The stretch is provided by cloth construction (knit) or the yarn used in the knitting process. In many cases a combination of both. By definition, knit fabric is a series of closed loops interlocked horizontally and vertically. Woven fabric is an interlacing of two or more different yarns. Due to this basic difference, knit fabric inherits more potential stretch. Whenever stretch and comfort are used as criteria for fabric, knitted construction is considered first.

The most significant changes that have occurred in the past few years are:
1. The use of ventilated mesh fabric in all types of uniforms, shirts and jerseys.
2. Coaches and athletic staffs have become part of the team by dressing uniformly and in school colors.
3. New basketball uniforms conform to our more casual life-style. Shirts made to be worn outside the pants have appeared.
4. Screen printed lettering using various types of vinyl paints and inks have become very popular. Today's screen printed lettering will stretch, is lighter weight, durable and less expensive, than previous sewn on lettering.
5. Some specific team uniform trends have developed. In wrestling, one piece suits have replaced the shirt and trunks previously worn. Pullover style tops have replaced button or zipper front garments in baseball and some warm-ups.

The selection of new uniforms should be dependent on a number of factors. The price has to be considered because we all have to live within our means and budgets. Quality is important because it means you are getting a garment of consistent size, properly sewn and fabric that will withstand many seasons. Service is a very important consideration in selection. Next to quality, the service you receive from a salesman should be the most important criteria in selection of your uniforms. Buy from a salesman who knows his fabric, can help you size the garment and select a style best suited for your needs. He will probably be the one who will deliver a shoestring or a supporter in an emergency. Close rapport with a salesman is important. Value for price paid is most important.

Forms 20-9 and 20-10 are the various material comparisons from the *Rawlings Athletic Handbook.*

Form 20-11 shows how to measure the head, chest, waist, hips, inseam, outseam, sleeve, and back for proper fit of athletic equipment.

RECOMMENDATIONS FOR PURCHASING ATHLETIC EQUIPMENT

Generally speaking, the athletic director, after a period of time, will become a quasi expert in the ordering and purchasing of athletic equipment. Here are some basic recommendations.

1. Formulate a policy for purchasing equipment and supplies.
2. Use the inventory system for anticipating future needs of sizes, quantity, and replacement of standard items.

MATERIALS COMPARISON

FABRIC / KNIT

FABRICS	General Characteristics	Color Characteristics	Cleaning Qualities	Uses in Uniform
Nylon Contact Cloth	Specially constructed twill weave of all Nylon. Great strength. Drapes well. Smooth slick surface. Very tightly woven. High sheen.	True athletic colors. Rather translucent in light colors.	A satisfactory fabric to clean. Bleaching may change colors. Repeated cleaning tends to subdue colors.	Excellent for football and basketball pants. White basketball pants should be lined.
Nyl-Twill	Lighter than Contact Cloth. Great strength. Drapes well. Smooth slick surface. Tightly woven. High sheen.	True athletic colors. Rather translucent in light colors.	A satisfactory fabric to clean. Bleaching may change colors. Repeated cleaning tends to subdue color.	Excellent for football and basketball pants. White basketball pants should be lined. Good for warm-up jackets.
Royal Label Twill	Woven of high tenacity rayon yarn. Great strength for an all rayon fabric. Drapes neatly.	Colors excellent. All shades true and good.	An excellent fabric to clean. Excessive brushing will subdue the original sheen.	Excellent for basketball warm-up clothing and hockey pants.
Royal Label Satin	Rayon faced, cotton reinforced fabric. High lustre. Good strength. Drapes well.	Colors brilliant and true. Most beautiful colors of any athletic fabric.	Excellent care should be taken to retain original high sheen.	Excellent for basketball pants.
Hi-Glo Acetate Satin	A lustrous acetate, high sheen. Satisfactory strength and draping qualities.	Colors brilliant and true.	Colors commercially fast. Must be cleaned with care.	Good for basketball pants and warm-up clothing.
Gabro-Cloth	Medium quality. Sanforized all cotton twill weave.	Colors true.	Washable.	Recommended for softball uniforms, lacrosse, soccer, ice hockey pants, and boys' football pants.
Flannel OOO (HOF)	4 oz. weight. Fine weave. Strong and durable.	Colors are true. White is bleached.	A good fabric to clean.	An excellent professional grade flannel for baseball uniforms. Choice of the major leagues.
Flannel AA-A	5 oz. weight. Medium coarse weave. Strong and durable.	Colors are true. White is bleached.	A good fabric to clean.	Excellent for baseball uniforms.
Flannel BB-B	6 oz. weight. Medium coarse weave. Strong and durable.	Colors are true. White is bleached.	A good fabric to clean.	Excellent for baseball uniforms.
Flannel HH-H	6½ oz. weight coarse weave. Good strength.	Colors are true. White is bleached.	A good fabric to clean.	Good for baseball uniforms.
Flannel P	8 oz. weight. Tightly woven and durable. Soft, smooth feel.	White is unbleached.	A good fabric to clean.	Very popular in baseball uniforms.
Nylon Pedro Cloth	Oxford type weave. Tightly woven. Great strength. High abrasive resistance.	Colors bright and true.	A satisfactory fabric to clean. Bleaching may change colors.	Excellent for ice hockey pants.
Nyl-Taf Nyl-Weave	Light in weight. Great strength. Smooth slick surface. Tightly woven and wind resistant.	True athletic colors. Rather translucent in light colors.	A satisfactory fabric to clean. Bleaching may change colors.	Excellent for baseball warm-up jackets and casual wear jackets.
Nylox	Oxford type weave. Heavier than Nyl-Weave. Great strength. Tightly woven and wind resistant.	Colors bright and true. Rather translucent in light colors.	A satisfactory fabric to clean. Bleaching may change colors.	Excellent for casual wear jackets.

FORM 20-9 Material comparisons. (Rawlings Sporting Goods Company, St. Louis, Missouri. By permission.)

3. Encourage the staff to keep an up-to-date inventory.
4. Purchase only quality equipment and supplies. Quality, rather than cost, should be the deciding factor.
5. Adopt a standardized uniform for replacement purposes.
6. Plan a long range purchase program. Use a revolving plan to assure the same amount of equipment for each activity.
7. Seek advice from reputable sporting goods dealers, equipment managers, and college trainers.

MATERIALS COMPARISON

FABRIC / KNIT

KNITS	General Characteristics	Color Characteristics	Cleaning Qualities	Uses in Uniforms
Stretch Nylon-Spandex	A knit fabric with extreme stretch characteristics, even when wet. Provides better fit and longer wear.	Colors bright and true.	Take great care in cleaning. Do not dry clean any garment containing this material. Wet clean only in warm (100° Fahrenheit) water, using a mild no-bleach detergent. Drip dry at room temperature.	Excellent for football pants and jersey inserts.
Durene Nylon-Spandex	A knit fabric with extreme stretch characteristics, even when wet. Provides better fit and longer wear.	High lustre colors.		Football pants and wrestling clothing.
Stretch Nylon-and Durene	A stretch yarn. Excellent fit, strength and elasticity. Wears well.	Colors bright and true. Subdued sheen.	Launders well. High temperatures should be avoided.	An excellent material for football jerseys, basketball shirts, and athletic stockings.
Nylon and Durene	A balanced combination of Nylon and Durene. Lightweight, yet has great strength. Excellent elasticity. Good fit.	Colors bright and true.	Launders well. High temperatures should be avoided.	Very popular for both football jerseys and basketball shirts.
Cotton and Rayon	A well balanced combination of cotton and rayon. Fits well. Good sheen.	Colors in all shades are bright and true.	A good material to launder. Tends to lose sheen after repeated laundering.	Popular in football jerseys, basketball shirts and warm-up clothing.
All Durene Cotton	A medium weight knit material. Wears well.	Colors bright and true. Subdued lustre.	Launders well. High temperatures should be avoided.	Fine for football jerseys. Particularly suited for use in hot water.
Nyl-Knit	A specially knitted Nylon fabric. Extremely lightweight.	Colors bright and true.	Launders well. High temperatures should be avoided.	Used on front of Half and Half and knit football pants.
Nylon Fleece	Good quality fabric. Excellent wearing qualities. A lightweight material.	True athletic colors. Bright shades.	A satisfactory fabric to wash.	All types of warm-up clothing.
Orlon Fleece	Good quality fabric. A medium weight material.	True athletic colors. Bright shades.	A satisfactory fabric to wash.	All types of warm-up clothing.
Nylon and Cotton Double Knit	A double knit fabric with good stretch characteristics. Lightweight, yet has great strength. Good fit and comfort.	Colors are true.	Launders well. High temperatures should be avoided.	An excellent knit material for baseball uniforms. Choice of the major leagues.
Cotton and Nylon	A medium weight, moderately priced knit material with good elasticity. Fits well.	Colors are true.	Launders well. High temperatures should be avoided.	Popular for baseball and softball uniforms.
Cotton and Stretch Nylon	A stretch knit with good fit, strength and elasticity.	Colors are true.	Use care in laundering. Cold water is recommended.	Popular for baseball uniforms, softball uniforms, football jerseys, ice hockey jerseys and knit jackets.
Stretch Nylon and Nylon	A stretch knit. Excellent fit, strength and elasticity. Wears well.	Colors bright and true.	Launders well. High temperatures should be avoided.	An excellent material for football and soccer jerseys, warmup shirts, wrestling clothing and hockey stockings.
Nylon Double Knit	A double knit with good stretch characteristics. Excellent fit and strength. Drapes well.	Colors bright and true.	Launders well. High temperatures should be avoided.	Excellent for football pants, basketball pants and warm-up clothing.
Nylon Mesh	A lightweight knit fabric with good stretch characteristics. Mesh provides breathing feature for cooler wear.	Colors bright and true.	Launders well. High temperatures should be avoided.	Popular in football jerseys. Particularly well suited for thigh and knee pad pockets in half and half pants used on synthetic turf.
Nylon Tricot	A medium weight knit fabric. Has good strength and stretch characteristics. Wears well.	Colors bright and true.	Launders well. High temperatures should be avoided.	Popular in football jerseys.
Acrilan Fleece	Good quality fabric. A medium weight material.	True athletic colors. Bright shades.	A satisfactory fabric to wash.	All types of warm-up clothing.

FORM 20-10 Material comparisons. (Rawlings Sporting Goods Company, St. Louis, Missouri. By permission.)

8. Protection and safety should be the first prerequisite when purchasing equipment.
9. Do not neglect the lower level teams. Each athlete, regardless of classification, should be afforded the highest quality equipment.

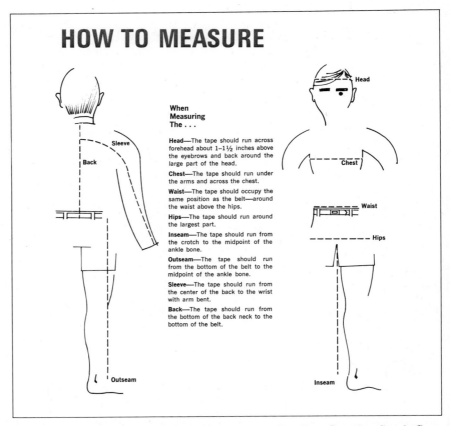

FORM 20-11 Proper fit of athletic equipment. Rawlings Sporting Goods Company. St. Louis, Missouri. By permission.

10. Give preference to local sporting goods dealers if prices are equitable.
11. Order well in advance to assure a good selection and delivery in time for the first practice date.
12. Take time to fit each athlete individually, especially in the area of protective equipment.
13. Avoid gifts and favors from sporting goods salesmen or manufacturers. This limits the athletic director's freedom of choice for the best interests of the program.
14. Adhere to rules and recommendations concerning equipment; for example, numbering of jerseys, home and away jersey, etc.

REPLACEMENT OF EQUIPMENT

In uniforms and practice apparel, select an attractive, distinctive design in standard colors so that over a period of several years, jerseys, sweat pants, and other cloth goods can be replaced if necessary and desirable, but without requiring the purchase of a complete set if several are lost or destroyed.

In general, buying equipment is the same as any other business practice; it involves certain skills and techniques. The athletic director and coach should keep in mind that the purchase of equipment is for the improvement of service to the athletes and this should be done with the most economical use of funds.

Most districts have a rather carefully drawn policy regarding coaches relationships with sales people and the preserving of the "open market" in purchasing school athletic equipment and supplies.

Questions

1. What is the importance of getting sturdy, durable, safe equipment and game uniforms, as compared to frills, flashy, and even gaudy game uniforms, which may be durable and safe too?

2. A board of education policy is, " No athletic equipment may be purchased/secured without an approved purchase order." As athletic director, it is your job to implement or enforce the board's policy. By accident, you learn that your track coach has been picking up athletic equipment in advance and getting purchase order approval later. He has not exceeded his budgetary allocation for track, but he is not following the prescribed policies and precedures. As long as he stays within his allocation, should you mention it to him? What, if any, corrective action is necessary? How would you handle it? Is enforcement of the policy necessary?

3. As athletic director, you discover that your football coach is exchanging approved equipment for unapproved equipment. As an illustration, after having gone through the proper and prescribed channels to purchase and receive equipment and supplies for the football season, your coach traded back to the sporting goods dealer sufficient equipment and supplies of monetary value to receive several extra blocking dummies. You confront him and he states, "I needed the blocking dummies more than the other equipment and supplies and I didn't exceed my equipment allocation." What, if any, corrective action is necessary? How would you handle it? Is enforcement of the policy necessary here?

REFERENCES

1. *Coaches' Manual, "The Coach Looks at Equipment and Facilities,* p. 63, National Association of Sport and Physical Education, American Alliance for Health, Physical Education and Recreation, Washington D. C. By permission.
2. O'Dell, Griffith C., Director of Health, Physical Education and Athletics, *"Advantages of the Bidding System," Department of Interscholastic Athletics Manual, 1973-74,* Minneapolis Public Schools, Minneapolis, Minnesota. By permission.
3. Gallon, Arthur, J., *Purchasing and Caring for Equipment—Central Purchasing, Coaching: Ideas and Ideals,* p. 123, Houghton Mifflin, Boston, Massachusetts 02100, 1974. By permission.
4. *"How to Buy Football Helmets," Rawlings Athletic Handbook,* 1st ed., Rawlings Sporting Goods Company, St. Louis, Missouri, 1971. By permission.
5. *National Federation Football Rule Book, 1975,* p. 9, National Federation of State High School Associations, 400 Leslie Street, P.O. Box 98, Elgin, Illinois 60102. By permission.
6. Derleth, H., President, Medalist Sand Knit, *"How Important is the Appearance of your Team," Medalist Sports News,* Vol. 1, No. 4, March 1976, p. 5, Medalist Sports Education, 737 North 5th Street, Milwaukee, Wisconsin, 53202. By permission.

SUGGESTED READINGS

Bucher, Charles A., *Administration of Health and Physical Education Program Including Athletics,* C. V. Mosby, St. Louis, Mo., 1971, Ch. 10.

Forsythe, C. E. *Administration of High School Athletics,* Prentice-Hall, Englewood Cliffs, N.J. 1972, Ch. 10.

Grieve, A. W., *Directoring High School Athletics,* Prentice-Hall, Englewood Cliffs, N.J., 1963, Ch. 9, Equipment: Purchase, Care and Storage.

Purdy, R. L., *The Successful High School Athletic Program,* Parker Publishing Co., West Nyack, N.Y., 1970, Ch. 7, Procurement and Maintenance of Athletic Equipment and Facilities.

Resick, M. C., Seidel, B. L., and Mason, J. B., *Modern Administration Practices in Physical Education and Athletics,* Addison-Wesley, Reading, Mass. 1970, Ch. 10.

Chapter 21
Inventory, Care, and Storage of Athletic Equipment

The value of an efficient system of purchasing equipment can be lost through lack of judgment, poor discipline, and the failure of the coach to educate the student-athletes on the proper care of the equipment issued to them. One can build pride and morale through having well-dressed teams and safe equipment. The coach should utilize this approach in educating his players.

Most schools have the finest equipment money can buy; however, it will not serve their purpose if the equipment is lost, stolen, or in need of repair.

The care of equipment, other than teaching the proper use of such equipment, may be categorized as cleaning, repairing, and storage. Policies and procedures should be established to prolong the life of equipment and supplies, to insure the safety of all participants using the equipment and supplies, to inspect equipment to keep it in a safe and sanitary condition, and to discard any equipment that is deemed unsafe for use.

CARE OF GARMENTS

Most sporting goods manufacturers sponsor a publication on "how to care for athletic equipment," which is available upon request. On such publication is the *Rawlings Athletic Handbook*,[1] which provides basic information of the care of garments. The following information is reprinted, as one source of professional advice.

The care of garments can be covered in four phases: prior to their being used; during the season; the care of garments on a trip; and the care of garments after the season is over and between seasons.

New Garments

The care of new garments should begin as soon as they are received. If they are ordered early and arrive in advance of the season, they should be kept in the boxes in which they are received.

To prevent mildew, garments should be stored in a cool, dry area, away from the humidity of a swimming pool or shower room.

Another important item on the pre-season checklist is to familiarize your cleaner with the materials in your garments. Needless to say, it is important to work with a cleaner who has had experience in cleaning athletic garments and who is willing to take the time and effort necessary to do a good job for you.

During the Season

The period immediately following a game is most important to the care of the garments used in the game. Before turning the garments over to the cleaner, each garment should be inspected for possible tears, rips or pulled seams. Garments needing repair should be separated so the cleaner can make necessary repairs as quickly as possible. Lettering and numbering should be checked to see if any have pulled loose.

On a Trip

Trips always present a problem because it is impossible to follow the prescribed rules for garment care. Pack the garments after the away game and then hang them up in your equipment room as soon as you arrive home.

If a team is going to another game, the time schedule will dictate just when and where it will be possible to dry the garments. If the team spends the night in the town in which the game was played, it may be possible to make arrangements with the hotel to hang the garments somewhere overnight and then pack them in the morning for the next phase of the trip. While the proper caring for garments is extremely difficult on a trip, it is very important to the life of the garments to give them as much care as possible.

Between Seasons

After the last game has been played, a very important phase of equipment care begins, the final cleaning, repair and storage of garments. Careful attention to this important task immediately after the close of the season will result in savings of both time and money when you prepare for the start of the following season.

The Wilson Sporting Goods Co. publication, *Care of Athletic Equipment.*[2] offers some "Don'ts" for the care of knit and cloth athletic wear:

Don't—pile up wet soiled garments as all cotton will mildew quickly (in 48 hours) causing loss of strength and causing garment colors to run.

Don't—use cleaning fluid on material made of elastic two way stretch, as the fluid will injure or dissolve the rubber yarn.

Don't—wring out knit goods by hand, as it distorts the fabric and the shape of grament.

Don't—tumble dry at high temperature, as this frequently causes excessive shrinkage.

Don't—purchase any athletic clothing that is not colorfast. Make sure of this by securing and washing a sample.

Don't—pack athletic wear in closed lockers unless thoroughly dry.

BASIC CLEANING PRINCIPLES[3]

1. Removal of dirt, stains, and perspiration, color retention, and sustained legibility of number and other distinguishing marks are the ultimate goals of proper laundering and cleaning of athletic garments.
2. There are many advantages to the use of specialized all-automatic athletic laundry in your school that gives insured protection against shrinkage, fading, bleeding, fabric, and yarn snags.
3. Prior to the first cleaning of a set of garments, emphasize to your cleaner the need for special care and handling of the garments.
4. Dry cleaning will generally remove dirt and stains from athletic garments but it will not remove perspiration.
   A Note: Many people today are stressing in the strongest possible terms that dry cleaning is damaging to fabrics and simply does not get the garment clean, particularly with regard to perspiration, which is the biggest problem. Other things being equal, select items that can be cleaned with soap and water.)
5. After a game, garments should be inspected for snags, tears, stains, and cleaned immediately.
6. Garments of different colors should not be laundered together.
7. Use of strong chemicals and/or alkalis will fade colors and

weaken materials.

8. Do not use a chlorine bleach.
9. The water level in your washing equipment should be kept high to hold down mechanical action. If uniforms are badly soiled, water level should be lowered to increase mechanical action. Avoid overloading because this causes shrinkage and impedes the cleaning process.
10. All knit materials have a tendency to shrink slightly.
11. Stretching (back to original size) and steam pressing garments are recommended when a commercial steam press is used.
12. Garments should be completely dry before being stored.
13. Do not wash in water temperatures above 120° F. Extreme hot water temperature will fade color and cause excessive shrinkage.

In a recent publication, *Cleaning Athletic Garments*,[4] published by Wilson Sporting Goods Company, a detailed description of how to care for athletic equipment is present. For example:

Method D, Sideline Capes and Jackets
Cleaning agent: Soap or detergent
Wash: Clean outer surface with sponge of cloth dipped in soap solution.
Rinse: Remove soap solution with sponge or cloth moistened with clear water.
Dry: Air dry on rustproof hangers. NOTE: Never use cleaning fluids.

The Wilson publication gives a step-by-step cleaning description on each and every item in the athletic department's inventory.

STATE LEGAL PROVISIONS REGARDING ANNUAL CLEANING AND STERILIZING OF EQUIPMENT

Most states have legal provisions for the cleaning and sterilizing of athletic equipment, especially football equipment. The legal provisions in California are as follows:

Annual Cleaning, Sterilizing, and Repair of Football Equipment

Education Code 15812:[5]

The governing board of each district maintaining a high school or community college and the president of each state college shall provide for the annual cleaning, sterilizing, and necessary repair of football equipment of their respective schools, community colleges, or state colleges pursuant to Section 15812 to 15814, inclusive.

Frequency of Football Equipment Cleaning and Sterilizing

Education Code 15813:[5]

All football equipment actually worn by pupils shall be cleaned and sterilized at least once a year. Football equipment used in spring training shall be cleaned and sterilized before it is used in the succeeding fall term.

Contracts for Repair of Football Equipment

Education Code 15814:[5]

Any contract with a dealer or craftsman for the repair of football equipment belonging to the district or the state college shall specifically state or describe the materials to be used by the dealer or craftsman in repairing such equipment.

THE EQUIPMENT MANAGER

The equipment manager, whether a student or a paid employee, plays an important role in the interscholastic athletic program. With the economic pinch becoming a big factor in the program, the equipment manager can save money without sacrificing the athletes' safety.

The equipment manager is able to get more mileage out of old equipment by having adequate, well-ventilated storage space for uniforms, repairing equipment promptly, and supervising the cleaning of equipment.

Money can also be saved by keeping an up-to-date athletic equipment record that makes each athlete accountable for all equipment issued to him. By reducing the loss of equipment, the equipment manager is able to build up the inventory and only has to replace equipment that is no longer safe for use in the program.

The Phoenix Union High School System has a unique check out and check in system (Form 21-1). Each athlete is required to sign an Athletic Equipment Record Card, which is filed with the equipment manager. A brief statement explains the purpose of the card to the athlete. "I received the above described articles. I agree to be responsible for the condition of these articles and to return them immediately at the end of the sport season or for the purpose for which checked out, or upon request of the Equipment Manager. I further agree to be financially responsible for loss or damage due to my negligence. I understand that if I am held financially liable for any of the above because of failure to return them the amount

Student's Name_____No._____School_____

WRESTLING　　　Phoenix Union High School System
ATHLETIC EQUIPMENT RECORD

Locker No._____

Date Issued	Date Returned	No. on Article	Article and Description	Condition of Equip.	Amount Charged
			Pr. Practice Tights		
			Pr. Sweat Pants		
			Sweat Shirt		
			Head Guard		
			Traveling Bag		
			Knee Pads		
			Pr. Match Tights		
			Pr. Match Trunks		
			Match Warm-up Jacket		

I received the above described articles. I agree to be responsible for the condition of these articles and to return them immediately at the end of the sport season, or for purpose for which checked out, or upon request of the Equipment Manager. I further agree to be financially responsible for loss or damage due to my negligence. I understand that if I am held financially liable for any of the above because of failure to return them the amount may be checked against my registration card now in the Registrar's Office.

_____　　_____　　_____

A-13　　　Student's Signature　　　　Address　　　　　Phone No.
Dist. Dup. 63　　(in ink)

FORM 21-1 Inventory record of equipment. (Phoenix Union High School District, Phoenix, Arizona. By permission.)

may be checked against my registration card now in the registrar's office."

By keeping accurate records such as the above, the equipment manager makes sure that either the equipment is returned or that lost equipment is paid for and replaced, The Phoenix Union High School System uses different card for each sport.

ATHLETIC INVENTORY

The first consideration in any system of accountability is the inventory. Inventories are detailed records of equipment and supplies. Form 21-2, as used by the Phoenix Union High School System,

PHOENIX UNION HIGH SCHOOL SYSTEM

ATHLETIC INVENTORY

UNIT _____ _____ (SPORT)

DATE _____

Items Used In This Sport	Previous Inventory	Total To Be Accounted For	Present Inventory (1st Class Condition)	Present Inventory (2nd Class Condition)	Present Inventory (Need Repair)	Item to Be Discarded (Beyond Repair)	Total Usable Equipment	Estimated Number New Items Needed Next Season

FORM 21-2 Athletic Inventory. (Phoenix Union High School District, Phoenix, Arizona. By permission.)

315

Phoenix, Arizona contains the following information: Items Used in the Sport; Previous Inventory; Total to Be Accounted for: Present Inventory (1st Class Condition); Present Inventory (2nd Class Condition); Present Inventory (Need Repair); Item to be Discarded (Beyond Repair); Total Usable Equipment; Estimated Number New Items Needed Next Season.

Inventories are basic instruments used in making determinations regarding management and control of supplies and equipment. They serve as a guide for the selection and replacement for the coming year.

Before any equipment is issued, it should be marked, identified, and inventoried. The identification of athletic equipment alleviates the problem of the campus store selling jerseys that resemble those issued by the athletic department. The identification mark should include the year in which the item was first issued, such as 75-1 and 76-1. This will help the coach or equipment manager in identifying when the item was first purchased and how well the item has worn.

When equipment is lost, stolen, or destroyed, the student-athlete involved should pay for the replacement of the article. The coach or equipment manager should devise a system of reimbursement so that the money is placed in the athletic account and earmarked for the purchase of equipment.

The coach must enforce this phase of the inventory program and must have the backing of the administration by withholding the student's grade until the equipment is paid for.

STORAGE OF ATHLETIC EQUIPMENT

Most secondary schools face the problem of inadequate storage space. The ideal situation would be to have an equipment manager, large accessible storeroom, bins, racks, and storage space for each sport, which can be locked when the season is not in progress with the equipment manager having full control of the equipment room.

Most athletic directors and coaches have had to become creative and innovative in planning for the storage of athletic equipment. With the help of the school woodshop teacher, maintenance department, booster or parents club, the athletic director and coach can utilize all facilities available by building bins, cabinets, hangers, and drying rooms. As new facilities are built or old facilities remodeled, priority should be given to a storage area for athletic equipment during the offseason and to adequate space for the issuing of equipment during a season.

Questions

1. What are your state's legal provisions regarding the annual cleaning and sterilizing of athletic equipment, particularly football equipment? Discuss.
2. "Brainstorm" ways of storing athletic equipment, specifically 100 pairs of shoulder pads and 100 football helmets, in the smallest space possible.
3. Discuss the advantages and ways of marking, identifying, and inventorying all new athletic equipment upon its receipt and before it is issued.
4. In an effort to "educate" participants in the sport of which you are the head coach, which convincing arguments are you going to use in your orientation talk relevant to why they should take care of their equipment?
5. As a control factor, you as athletic director should implement a policy that all athletic equipment issued to participants must be returned or paid for at the conclusion of the sports season. You have discovered your head football coach is not requiring some of his players to pay for equipment that they have not returned at the end of the football season, and that the coach has accounted for the missing equipment as "worn out," "beyond repair,"or "unsafe to repair." How do you handle this situation? How would you correct it?

REFERENCES

1. *Athletic Handbook* 1st edition, Rawlings Sporting Goods Company, 2300 Delmar Boulevard, Saint Louis, Missouri 63166. Used by permission.
2. *Care of Athletic Equipment*, Wilson Sporting Goods Co., 2233 West Street, River Grove, Illinois 60171. Used by permission.
3. *Athletic Handbook*, Rawlings Sporting Goods Company.
4. *Cleaning Athletic Garments*, Wilson Sporting Goods Co. Used by permission.
5. California State Department of Education, Education Code, Sacramento, California, 1973.

SUGGESTED READINGS

Bucher, Charles A., *Administration of Health and Physical Education Programs, Including Athletics* 5th revised edition, C.V. Mosby, St. Louis, Mo., 1971.

Forsythe, C.E. and Keller, I.A., *Administration of High School Athletics*, 5th Edition Prentice-Hall, Englewood Cliffs, N.J., 1972, Ch. 8, Athletic Equipment.

George, J.F. and Lehmann, H.A., *School Athletic Administration*, Harper and

Row, New York, Ch. 9. Equipment. 1966.

Grieve, A.W., *Directing High School Athletics,* Prentice-Hall, Englewood Cliffs, N.J., 1963. Ch. 9, Equipment; Purchase, Care and Storage

Hixson, G.C., *The Administration of Interscholastic Athletics*, J. Lowell Pratt, New York, 1967. Ch. 7, Facilities and Equipment.

Purdy, R.L., *The Successful High School Athletic Program,* Parker Publishing, West Nyack, N.Y., 1970. Ch. 7, The Procurement and Maintenance of Athletic Equipment and Facilities.

Resick, Matthew C. and Erickson, Carl E., *Intercollegiate and Interscholastic Athletics for Men and Women,* Addison-Wesley, Reading, Massachusetts, 1975 Ch. 6.

Resick, Matthew C., Seidel, Beverly L., and Mason, James G., *Modern Administrative Practices in Physical Education and Athletics,* 2nd edition, Addison-Wesley, Reading, Massachusetts, 1975, p. 234.

Chapter 22
Safety Considerations In Interscholastic Athletics

Safety in athletics has never been more pertinent than it is today. A recent nationally televised program[1] offered a challenge to the coaching profession, especially on the secondary school level. It cited the danger involved in interscholastic athletics, that is, football, and asked, "What are you going to do about it?"

The safety and welfare of the athletes should always be the number one priority of any coach or athletic department. Not only does the coach have a moral and personal obligation to each student-athlete regarding his safety, but there are state-mandated laws relevant to certain aspects of athletics that insure a proper and safe working relationship between the coach and athlete.

Dr. Kenneth S. Clarke, Chairman of Health Education, Pennsylvania State University[2] sheds a slightly different perspective on safeguarding the health of the athlete.

> With all due respect to a coach's natural sympathetic feelings for an injured human being, he knows that his game plans and strategies hinge directly on the availability of his athletes and of the opponents as well. Moreover, the winning-losing factor in athletics creates a potent temptation to flirt with the health and safety aspects of sportsmanship and regulations governing play. This may appear to produce a conflict of interest between health and winning but is this truly the case? The healthy athlete is the available athlete. Unhealthful practices can cause disability, thus removing the athlete from competition. Premature exposure to reinjury and other inappropriate activity can retard healing, add to the seriousness of the disability, and delay the return of the athlete to a competitive level of performance.

319

Dr. Clarke discusses the nature of competitive athletes "Calling for sacrifice to the cause and imposing arbitrary boundaries, removes some of the natural self limiting safeguards found in informal sports. For example, the varsity athlete who becomes fatigued or disinterested usually cannot just quit and rest at will. The responsibility falls on the perception of the team's leadership, the coach, trainer and team physician who, while encouraging maximal effort, also must educate and protect the athletes in their charge regarding the risks involved."

Although, as Dr. Clarke states,[3] "The responsibility falls on the perception of the tean's leadership, the coach, trainer and team physician," state departments of education, national and state athletic associations exercise general control over all athletic activities and have as their main purpose to promulgate and provide for implementation of rules and regulations for the safety and protection of all concerned.

STATE AND NATIONAL ASSOCIATIONS FUNCTIONS

Some of the more important functions of the national and state organizations, in regard to the safety and health aspects of interscholastic athletics, are to regulate the playing rules and safety in interscholastic athletics; to institute rules and regulations relevant to insurance for athletes; to legislate that medical and hospital services are available in regard to physical examinations for athletes and physicians performing services at athletic events and to take every precaution for the care and treatment of athletic injuries.

Although there are general administrative policies based on national and statewide supervision of athletic safety, the athletic director must place safety procedures as the major concern on his management list. The athletic director should provide for adequate sports accident reporting and an analysis of these reports. He must take positive action to eliminate causes of frequently occurring accidents and to take other indicated precautionary measures to see that they will not happen again.

Inherent Risks of Athletics

Dr. Kenneth Clarke, in his article *Sports Medicine in Perspective,*[4] writes, "While sports medicine may be defined as the supervision and study of man in activity, sports medicine is better discussed than defined. The contradictions and paradoxes found by a practitioner as he becomes a sports medicine practitioner makes definition irrelevant. What does one call an accidental injury in football when there are millions of premeditated collisions between football athletes every fall weekend? What does one call disability when a simple blister can mean several weeks on the bench for a pitcher? What does one call supervision when a young boy is medically certified for participation is sports that expose him to risks so considerable that few scientists would subject others to the same forces in a laboratory setting? What does one call competence when the practitioner must deal with the complexities of human behavior and the complexities of sports, often with but seconds for reflection?"

Dr. J. Duke Elkow, Professor of Health and Physical Education, Brooklyn College[5], writing in *Sports Safety*, stated, "When the hazards of an activity are known, coped with, reduced in intensity, or eliminated, the probability of injury is curtailed. Therefore, players must understand the nature of hazard controls. This responsibility rests fully on the sports administrators."

Dr. D. C. Seaton[6], in *Administration and Supervision of Safety Education* submits, "An athlete runs a 50-50 chance of receiving an injury. About 90 percent of all sports related injuries are contusions and minor muscle pulls. The majority of these injuries may not be of accidental origin but an inherent part of the sport. The remaining 10 percent are more serious. They require appropriate therapeutic measures and should be assessed as to their accidental or nonaccidental nature and measures for prevention or control must be initiated when feasible."

NATIONAL ATHLETIC INJURY/ILLNESS REPORTING SYSTEM (NAIRS)[7]

The National Athletic Injury/Illness Reporting System is a new mechanism for collecting meaningful athletic injury/illness data continuously in a nationally uniform manner. On a developmental basis, NAIRS began collecting data in Fall, 1974. An abridged version of NAIRS is being developed for schools who are without the assistance of an athletic trainer or for sports that have little product safety relatedness.

NAIRS records descriptive detail on illnesses and injuries that keep an athlete from participating in sports. All forms. codes, and statistical analyses are designed for and orientated toward both the decision tasks of sports personnel and the constraints of scientific inquiry.

NAIRS represents the combined thinking of an advisory committee representing groups sharing responsibility in the conduct of sports.

Endorsement of NAIRS has never been sought. However, official endorsement has already been received from the American College Health Association, American Society for Testing and Materials' F-8 Committee, NCAA's committee on Competitive Safeguards and Medical Aspects of Sports and the Research Committee of the National Athletic Trainers Association.

PLAYING RULES AND SAFETY IN INTERSCHOLASTIC ATHLETICS

Dr. Frank B. Jones, Professor of Physical Education, California State University, Sacramento, California in his information paper, *Playing Rules and Safety in Interscholastic Athletics*[8] points out, "Over the years, the rules committees have been concerned with safety. Periodically the rules are reviewed and changed when needed. When unsafe conditions of play have been identified, rules are established to reduce hazardous conditions as much as possible. Intelligent coaching and competent officiating of contests are indicated as well, if players are to be afforded full protection." Dr. Jones diccusses the rules pertaining to safety for each sport.

Football

The most popular sport (in terms of participation) in the secondary schools in the United States. The rules committee of the National Federation annually surveys coaches, officials and school administrators to determine where rules need to be changed to meet current playing styles and conditions. A large portion of the Federation Football Rule Book is devoted to the safety of players. Following is an explanation of the 1975 Federation rules as they pertain to safety.

Burns

(Section 2, Article 3), Fields are to be marked with a material which is not injurious to eyes of skin. No lime or caustic material of any knid may be used.

Pylons

(Section 2, Article 6), A soft, flexible pylon is to be used to mark the intersection of the sidelines with the goal lines and end lines. Any player hitting these approved pylons should never be injured.

Mandatory Equipment

(Section 5, Article 1), Details the equipment each player must wear during participation in any contest. These include:
1. A head protector secured by a properly fastened chinstrap
2. A face protector (multiple bar type recommended)
3. A intraoral mouth and tooth protector which includes an occlusal (protecting and separating the biting surfaces)
4. Soft knee pads
5. Shoes

In the past few years the federation has been an active member of the National Operating Commission for Safety in Athletic Equipment (NOCSAE). This body worked for several years to establish standards for football helmets. In the 1975 Rule Book (p. 9) is the following statement: It is recommended that only those head protectors carrying the NOCSAE stamp of approval be purchased. Beginning in 1980 each player shall be equipped with a head protector which carries the NOCSAE stamp of approval.

Prohibited Equipment

(Section 5, Article 3) Illegal equipment shall not be worn by any player. This applies to any equipment which, in the opinion of the Umpire, is dangerous or confusing. This section of the rule book is designed to prevent any player from being cut or hit a damaging blow by a hard, unyielding surface.

Injury studies have shown that the most frequently injured area of the body is the lower leg (knee, ankle, foot). Players now must wear a cleat that is: (1) not more than ½ inch in length, (2) have a tip that is parallel to the base, (3) have an effective locking device, and (4) is made of material that does not chip or develop a cutting edge. In a longitudinal study of injuries conducted in North Carolina,[4] it was established that the short cleat was one factor in the reduction of lower leg injuries.

MAJOR SAFETY RULES FOR THE 1976 SEASON

1-5-1 e and f.   Specifies plastic materials covering protective pads to be rounded with a radius equal to one half the thickness of the material.

2-2-2.   Defines butt-blocking as to technique involving an initial blow with the face mask. frontal area, or top of the helmet driven directly into an opponent as the primary point of contact, either in close line play or in the open field.

2-2-4.   Identifies face-tackling as driving the face mask, frontal area, or top of the helmet directly into the runner.

9-3-21.   Categorizes butt-blocking and face tackling as personal fouls.

Spearing

The rules committee has done two things to discourage spearing. First, the penalty for spearing has been changed to 15 yards and disqualification. Second, the points of special emphasis in the rule book state that not only is spearing dangerous, but that coaches should not teach or permit players to use this tactic.

9-1-3.   Prevents any player from being blocked below the waist by any opponent who lined up more than four yards away from the ball and who blocks back toward the ball. This is called a "crackback" block.

9-1-4.   There shall be no blocking below the waist after a free kick (kickoff) has been made or a scrimmage kick (punt) has crossed the neutral zone. This rule also will help reduce knee and ankle injuries.

Track and Field

To safeguard the highly skilled competitor, the rules limit him to competition in four (4) events during a track and field meet. This becomes a safety mechanism to protect the athlete against his own enthusiasm or the coach who would overwork the athlete.

Pole Vault.   The advent of the fiberglass vaulting pole has revolutionized pole vaulting and the 1975 rules are concerned with the pole vault landing pit. The pole vault pit shall be at least 16 ft wide by 12 ft long. It shall be filled with a material other than sand or sawdust, or such composition and construction with a depth or thickness sufficient to provide a safe landing for the vaulter.

High Jump.   To protect jumpers who use the "flop" method (landing on the back, neck, and shoulder) the rules specify that the same type of resilient material as used in the pole vault pit must be used in the high jump pit.

Shot Put and Discus. To protect competitors and spectators, both events use a throwing sector. The shot or discus must land within the boundary lines of the throwing sector to be a "fair throw."

Basketball

The Playing Court (Rule 2, Section 2). The referee shall inspect and approve all equipment including the court and baskets. The referee shall not permit any player to wear equipment that in his judgment is dangerous to other players.

Backboards (Rule 1, Section 8). The bottom and sides of the backboards are to be padded.

Dunking Prohibited (Rule 4, Section 9). This shot is prohibited in high school basketball. Players have had injuries to fingers and arms as a result of "dunking" the ball. In some cases, the basket has been bent or torn loose from the board. Dunking has caused the fracture of glass backboards also. It is dangerous to the players, particularly to the rapidly growing high school player who does not have the ability to completely control his body.

As the game becomes faster, the players bigger, the techniques more advanced, the amount of player contact has increased. As a result, basketball has become a contact sport. To make certain the players are protected, the rules committee has established some basic principles to guide officials, coaches and players. The Comments of the Rules 1974-75 Rule Book, pages 36-37, discuss the following: incidental contact, responsibility for contact, that is, guarding and screening, hazardous situations, when moving into the path of an airborne player such as a player taking a jump shot.

Baseball

One of the more dangerous elements of baseball is the pitcher-batter relationship. To make this part of the game as safe as possible for the batter, the rules provide the following:

1. The pitcher may not use gray or white undershirt.
2. The sleeves of the undershirt may not be ragged, frayed, or slit.
3. The pitcher's glove may not be gray or white and must be one color.
4. The pitcher may not wear anything on his shoes other than the standard toe piece.

5. No dangerous reflective buttons or ornaments may be worn on the uniform.

These rulings are to prevent the pitcher from using any means, other than pitching the ball, from distracting the batter.

Each batter, catcher, and base runner must wear a helmet with extended ear flaps that cover both ears and temples. In addition to the head protector, the catcher must wear a mask, protective cup, or body protector.

Rule 6, Section 2, Article 1 states in boldface type:[8]

A PITCHER SHALL NOT:
DEFACE A BALL nor deliver a defaced ball
Rule 6, Section 2, Article 3 states:
A PITCHER SHALL NOT—INTENTIONALLY THROW CLOSE TO A BATTER'S HEAD

The Code of Ethics for baseball players and coaches precedes Rule 1. The code stresses that the highest standards of ethics and sportsmanship must be maintained. The following rules, because they refer to safety, are quoted:[8]

1. Coaches and players should comply with the meaning and spirit of the playing rules. Purposely ignoring or willfully violating rules is intolerable.
2. Coaches with ethical approach will not tolerate actions by players which are physically dangerous to opponents, such as a pitcher purposely throwing at a batter or a base runner deliberately trying to injure an opponent during a double play.

Wrestling

The National Federation Rules Committee has been conscious of safety for many years. Rules concerning illegal holds are illustrated by photographs in the 1974-1975 Rule Book. In addition to the photographs, the Points of Special Emphasis (pp. 37-38) stress that: (1) legal headlocks are dangerous and (2) gives potentially dangerous holds. Both of these statements note that even legal holds may become dangerous to opponents, particularly when a body part is forced to the limit of its normal range of motion.

For the safety of competitors, the rules specify the following:

1. No wrestler may represent his school in more than one weight

class or compete in more than four full length matches in any one day.

2. The wrestling mat shall be of uniform thickness, a minimum of 24 ft. square or 28 ft. circular and surrounded by at least 10 ft. of the same type of material.

3. The referee is responsible for:
   (a) Legality of all equipment; mats, markings, uniforms, pads, and taping
   (b) Wrestler's appearance, no oily or greasy substance, rosin, objectional pads, improper clothing, finger rings, long fingernails, or improper grooming. The latter ruling complies with specified health, sanitary, and safety measures.

4. Each wrestler must wear a properly fitted and designed uniform, wear heelless shoes that reach above the ankle and be laced, be clean shaven, free of mustaches, with sideburns trimmed no lower than the earlobes, and have hair trimmed and well groomed.

Rule 7 is entitled "Infractions." Section 1 is concerned with illegal holds, that is, slam, hammerlock, headlock, full nelson, strangle holds, keylock, and any hold used for punishment alone.

Article 7.[8]

No hold over the mouth, nose, eyes, or front of the throat shall be permitted.

STATE OF CALIFORNIA SAFETY CONFERENCE[9]

The state of California, in order to meet the challenge of safety in sports, instituted a working Conference of Safety in Interscholastic Athletics. The conference, under the direction of the State Department of Education, had representatives from the following organizations:

The California Association for Health, Physical Education and Recreation
The California Coaches Association
The Association of California School Administrators
The California Women's Coaches Academy
The California Teachers Association
The California Interscholastic Federation
The National Trainers Association
The California Medical Association

The California State Athletic Directors Association
Southern California Football Officials Association
The conference also invited members of other institutions, members of the California School Boards Association, college health and physical education faculty members, members of the Athletic Institute, and members of the National Athletic Health Institute.

The primary purpose of the conference was to determine short-range and long-range priorities for action by the Department of Education. The entire body agreed that the State Department of Education appoint an advisory commission on safety in interscholastic athletics.

DISCUSSION AREAS

Standardizing Physical Examination Forms for Student-Athletes

Recommendations: The department should develop a certification program for men and women who wish to coach or continue to coach in the public schools of California (See Chapter 9, "Professional Preparation and Certification of Coaches" for a discussion of a suggested level of competency.)

Preseason and Season Conditioning Programs

Recommendations: The department should establish a committee of qualified medical and athletic personnel to develop criteria for preseason condition programs. That the department publish a position paper concerning the importance of preseason conditioning programs. The school districts in California should be informed of the necessity of student-athletes being physiologically conditioned for the rigors of practice and competition.

Certification of Trainers

Recommendations: The department of education should recommend very strongly that school districts encourage men and women faculty members to attend inservice or continuing education programs in athletic training. The department should develop and issue a strong position paper concerning the need for such services that would provide legislation enabling each county to employ an athletic trainer to provide the following services to school districts.

1. Implementation of athletic training programs.
2. Inservice or continuing educational programs for men and women serving as trainers.
3. Overall supervision of training room facilities and supplies at practice and contest sites.

The key impetus for having certified trainers available to all schools will be a statewide requirement (certification). Some flexibility will be required so that trainers will have an auxillary teaching area and an opportunity to full faculty employment.

The department should encourage counties, school districts, and individual schools to obtain the services of certified trainers.

CERTIFICATION AND ENDORSEMENT
OF ATHLETIC TRAINERS

The National Athletic Trainers Association faculty instructional training program was discussed in Chapter 16, "Medical Aspects of Interscholastic Athletics."

Certification and endorsement of faculty trainers will be discussed briefly in this chapter. The National Athletic Trainers Association states, "If secondary school administrators find it impossible to create the position of athletic trainer and hire a graduate from one of the N.A.T.A. approved curricula, then the high school faculty members constitute the best recruitment pool of manpower.

The certification and endorsement for faculty approved trainers would have three levels of competencies with each level offered during the summer.

1. First level: 120 clock hours, taught by three certified athletic trainers.
   A. Course content
      a. First aid
      b. Anatomy
      c. Physical signs
      d. Symptoms
      e. Proper care and transportation
      f. Taping
      g. Proficiency post test
2. Second level: 90 clock hours, taught by three certified athletic

trainers.

    A. Qualifying pretest, must pass to take second level study or repeat first level work.

    B. Course content

        a. Injury management (treatment)

        b. Evaluation of disability

        c. Rehabilitation

        d. Proficiency post test

3. Third level: 90 clock hours, taught by three certified athletic trainers.

    A. Qualifying pretest, must pass to take third level study or repeat second level work.

    B. Course content:

        a. Diet and nutrition

        b. Athletic hygiene and safety

        c. Equipment: fit, selection, and care

        d. Conditioning

        e. Injury reporting and recordkeeping

        f. Administration

        g. Student trainer programs

        h. Medical ethics

        i. Medical team concepts

        j. Cumulative proficiency test

N.A.T.A. Endorsenent and Certification

1. At the start of this training program each program participant is required to become a member of the NATA and apply for NATA endorsement.

2. NATA endorsement is good for four years and certification requirements must be completed by the end of this four year period or endorsement will be terminated.

3. The program participant would have four years to complete the 3 level training program and pass the N.A.T.A. certification examination to become a certified athletic trainer.

EQUIPMENT AND FACILITIES: ATHLETIC DIRECTORS' RESPONSIBILITY

The athletic director must assume the responsibility for purchasing high quality protective equipment. (See Chapter 20, "Purchase of

Athletic Equipment.") Safety should be the first consideration when purchasing equipment rather than the cost. It is better to wait until next year to purchase proper equipment or to drop a sport rather than subject the athlete to unsafe equipment. The athletic director should be concerned with the freshmen or lower level teams who sometimes get the leftover or hand-me-down equipment. Unless suitable equipment can be purchased for the lower level teams, especially football helmets, the school should not field a team in that sport.

The athletic director must be conscious of the overzealous coach who will put his boys in anything as long as he can suit them up. As mentioned earier in this chapter, it is recommended in the football rules book that only those head protectors carrying the NOCSAE stamp of approval be purchased. The National Operating Committee for Standards of Athletic Equipment are working on a method of testing and restoring helmets in an effort to maintain the present supply the schools have on hand. If they cannot work out a method of certification for the old helmets, schools will have to purchase helmets that carry the seal of the NOCSAE by 1980. Although this seems to be a tremendous financial burden on the secondary schools of the nation, the NOCSAE is thinking of the safety of the student-athlete first. The cost factor is not involved.

Proper fitting equipment is extremely important to the safe play of the athlete. The athletic director must require that the coaching staff fit each athlete personally and that the coach does not let a student practice or play if the equipment is not prpoerly fitted.

The NOCSAE also has been instrumental in specifying types of cleats that may be worn on football shoes. This has not only helped to protect possible injury, but recent surveys have shown that the shorter, soccer-style cleats have helped in reducing knee injuries, the number one injury in football.

Reconditioners of athletic equipment have contributed to the safety and sanitation of athletic participants. They have helped to make sure not only that sterilized athletic equipment is but that all equipment used is in proper repair. Most schools have the athletic equipment sterilized and repaired at the end of each season. (In some states, this is a state law.) In addition, old or unsafe equipment must be replaced. Most equipment is marked so that the coach can readily see the year in which the equipment was purchased; this enables him to know when it should be replaced. The markings would display the year the equipment was purchased such as 74-1 or 75-2.

Field and Gymnasium Safety

The use of synthetic grass is not too common at the secondary school level. The athletic director can make certain the playing field for practice and games is in good condition. All obstructions, such as chuck holes, should be replaced; goal posts should be padded; and the sideline benches should be placed in such a way to remove the risk of injury. In baseball, there should be screens along the first and third base line to protect spectators. In basketball, the athletic director should check to see if the bleachers are too close to the side and end lines for the protection of participants and spectators. All obstacles such as buck and horses should be stored prior to practice or a contest and placed in a safe place after the physical education classes have been completed. For safety reasons, they should not be rolled against exit doors. Trampolines should be locked and placed in a storage area away from spectators and participants.

The Locker Room

The locker room, shower room, and equipment areas are potential areas of accident. Provisions should be made to eliminate or minimize features that may contribute to accidental injury. The type of floor surface, placement of lockers and benches, or any protruding objects should be carefully planned for the safety of the participants. First aid equipment to be used for emergency care should be placed in areas where it is readily available for use. A telephone should be placed in a strategic area for use in case of emergency. Emergency numbers and procedures should be prominently posted near the telephone.

Officials

Officials can play a big part in the safety of any contest by enforcing the rules of the game and perhaps by being a little overprotective if the game seems to be getting out of hand or if the teams are mismatched. In this regard, it is also the responsibility of the athletic director and coach to provide competition that is as closely matched as possible. In some instances, the lure of the gate receipts might induce the athletic director or coach to schedule a "big" game or a large school for a practice game in order to bolster the budget, with the end result being a high risk decision for the safety of the players.

The rules committee makes it mandatory for the officials in a football game to check each player prior to the beginning of the game to see that each is wearing a mouth protector and will penalize a team if the mouth protector is not worn porperly during the contest. Officials are also obligated to check on arm pads, cover or padded casts, and other items or player equipment that might injure another player. The officials also check the playing field prior to the contest and deem it safe or unsafe for the contest to be played. The officials actually play a big role in the safety of the participants in any athletic event.

Treatment and Handling of Injuries

The medical aspects of interscholastic athletics have been discussed in Chapter 16; however, it must be stated at this time that the treatment and transportation of an injured athlete is of the utmost importance in the safety of athletic contests.

Physicians are a required part of the athletic contest, for example, football, and are professional in their care for the athlete. However, injuries also occur during practice sessions and the coach must, in lieu of a physician or trainer, take utmost caution in the treatment and transporting of an injured player. The safety of the player must come first, regardless of the tempo of the practice. The coach must also be concerned with the conditioning of the players and must not be adverse to using reserves if a player is obviously tired late in a game or practice session.

In extreme weather areas, water breaks must be given the players. The coach should try to schedule his practices in the early morning or early evening hours to avoid the hot humid weather. The type of equipment worn on extremely hot or humid days is important. Jerseys of a knit mesh seem to be the most popular and safe because of the "breathing" quality of the fabric.

Common sense is perhaps the best factor in the safety of the athlete. Safe and sane judgment should be the byword of every coach and athletic director.

School Board Responsibility for Care and Maintenance

To provide the most consideration for the health and safety of participants, each facility needs daily supervision and maintenance. It is impossible for the athletic director to perform the many duties related to supervision and maintenance of the athletic facilities. There is a growing trend for district school boards to accept major responsibility for proper care and maintenance of the athletic and physical education facilities through improved custodial and plant services. There should be an extensive list of daily, weekly, monthly and seasonal maintenance needs prepared and assigned to appropriate custodial personnel and student managers.

Maintenance matters should not be left to chance or the memory of one or a few persons. For health and safety reasons they should be specifically designated and routinely accomplished. It should be remembered that the coach is a professional teacher and administrator whose time should not be consumed by the lining of fields, picking up broken glass on the playing and practice fields or by performance of maintenance tasks that relate to the safety of the participants.

INJURY RATE VARIES WITH COACHING[11]

This survey of safety in athletics was touched on briefly in Chapter 16, "Medical Aspects of Interscholastic Athletics." Dr. Carl S. Blyth, Ph.D., Chairman of the Department of Physical Education at the University of North Carolina and Dr. Frederick O. Mueller, Ph. D., Director of Football Injury Studies and Associate Professor in the Department of Physical Education at the University of North Carolina, conducted a football injury survey that investigated the training and experiences of coaches. The study was mainly concerned with the head coaches. Here are some of the interesting findings.

Age

The age of the head coach is clearly a factor in the injury rates. Injury rates were highest in those schools with coaches under the age of thirty and lowest in the schools with coaches age forty five and over. In fact, as the age of the coach increased, the injury rate of their teams steadily decreased.

Playing Experience

It was sited that playing experience of the coach did not significantly affect injury rate. It was noted, however, that coaches who had a background of only high school playing experiences were associated with teams with high injury rates. Coaches who had a background of both high school and college playing experience had teams with low injury rates. The data also showed that teams coached by men with only college playing experience had the lowest injury rate.

Coaching Experience

Not surprisingly, football coaches with the least amount of coaching experience (one to four years) were associated with teams with the highest injury rates. Coaches with the most experience (twenty or more years) were associated with teams with the lowest rates. It is clear that coaching experience is an important factor in injury rates.

Education

It was found in the survey that teams with coaches who had a major in physical education had injury rates similar to those teams whose coaches majored in other academic areas. The interesting finding here was that the coaches with a minor in physical education coached teams with the lowest injury rate. The data failed to establish a significant relationship between a coach's possession of a degree in physical education and a lower injury rate among his players. It was also found that football teams coached by men who had master's degrees had lower injury rates than those coached by men who do not have master's degrees. Surprisingly, however, teams whose coaches had master's degrees in physical education had higher injury rates than those teams whose coaches had MA's in other areas. This finding is difficult to explain and the authors of the survey believe that more research is needed.

Assistant Coaches

The survey clearly showed that the more assistant coaches a school hires, the lower the injury rate. In fact, the injury rate of schools with only one assistant coach was almost double that of those with seven assistant coaches. It seems logical that a greater number of assistant coaches would do a better job in the total football program, which includes injury prevention.

Contact Work

Since football is a contact sport, it would seem that teams who have the most days of live contact practice would have the most injuries. The survey indicated that teams who had live contact work on Monday and Tuesday had the highest injury rate. Teams who had contact on Tuesday and Wednesday had the lowest injury rate. One reason for this difference may be that the coaches whose teams had contact on Monday did not give their players an opportunity to recover from the games that had been played on Friday or Saturday. Many of the coaches in this study did say that the outcome of the Friday game determined the contact work on Monday. It is evident that more research is needed in this area.

Administering Liquids

High school football practice in North Carolina begins in the second week of August. The first week is limited to acclimatizing the players to the intense heat. During this time, players are prohibited by the North Carolina High School Athletic Association from wearing protective equipment. These precautions are designed to prevent heatstroke and possible death. The surveyors wanted to know whether coaches gave their players water during practice and, if so, when. Also if and when the coaches gave a salt additive or a commercial drink. Most reports recommended giving water during both practice and games at intervals of thirty to forty five minutes. The survey findings indicated that 50% of the coaches gave water to their squads as recommended. It is interesting that 34.1% of the coaches gave water only once during practice and that was when practice was half over.

Of the coaches who gave salt additives, a major portion did not give them at the right time. The best time for salt intake during preseason football practice is after practice and during meals. Salt taken right before going on the field does not get into the system fast enough to take effect. If salt is taken two hours before practice, it is of much greater value. The salt taken after practice can replace what was lost in practice. This type of information should be fundamental knowledge for a high school football coach. Eighteen of the forty-one coaches bought commercial drinks to give their squads. There is nothing wrong with this practice if the school has enough money. The school can make a drink that will serve the same purpose for a fraction of the cost.

Limited Contact

Practice activity accounted for 51.1% of all injuries and live contact, tackling, and blocking drills accounted for 10%. There is no doubt that live contact during football practice is a necessity, but it is also true that field equipment can be used to teach the fundamentals of football and the amount of live contact during practice can be reduced without affecting the won and lost record of the participating teams. In fact, the school that had limited contact had a better winning percentage than the school in the normal contact program. Of course a limited contact program does not ensure a winning record, but it does refute the theory that hard contact in practice is a prerequisite for a successful football team.

Summary and Conclusions of the Survey

The date clearly suggests that coaches with a specific type of background and training are associated with a low injury rate. The variables in a coach's background and training which have shown to be important when related to injury data are age, college playing experience, coaching experience, and advanced degrees. The number of assistant coaches is also an important factor in the injury rate. The data also indicates that a limited contact program in practice will reduce the number of high school football injuries and will not affect the won-lost record.

Questions

1. Your port-a-pit for pole vaulting has seen better days as it does not have sufficient filling, so you know it is unsafe. Your track coach has informed you in writing that since it is unsafe, he will

not be held legally accountable for any accidents or injuries. There are no funds available to purchase a new pole vaulting port-a-pit and the present one is beyond repair. With the track season opening in less than three days, as athletic director, what is your course of action to resolve this dilemma?

2. Prior to the football season, enumerate all items which you would check in your school's stadium to make certain all unsafe conditions are corrected and no safety hazards exist in, for example, the bleachers, playing field, control fences, locker rooms, etc.

3. Although you either have personally checked out or had checked out the gymnasium where your basketball games will be played, as athletic director, enumerate items or areas which should be spot-checked prior to the actual contest, since physical education classes have been held in the facility for most of the day.

4. Despite insufficient funds and a small budget, your basketball coach develops a good team that is contending for the championship in your school's small 1573-seat gymnasium against the crosstown rival. Three hours before the varsity game, every seat is filled. You estimate there are at least another 1500 paying customers who want to get in to see the game. As athletic director, do you authorize "standing room only" tickets and pack 'em in to pick up the much needed revenue; or do you adhere to the fire marshall's regulations of 1573-seat capacity? If you did the former, enumerate safety hazards you have created by "packing 'em in." From a legal standpoint if there was a fire, accident, or riot, would you, as athletic director, be liable?

5. Your head football coach produces good, physically strong, aggressive football teams that reflect his personality and manner of coaching. He doesn't believe in taking time or fooling around pairing off players for drills by matching them up by age, size, height, weight, or class. He admonishes his player to grab any partner and "knock," whether it is blocking, tackling, or whatever. You have observed the older, bigger, and stronger eleventh and twelfth graders frequently pair off with the younger, smaller ninth and tenth graders. Only the biggest and strongest survive and the injury rate is high among the younger, smaller football aspirants. Enumerate the safety hazards the coach is creating by following his philosophy and practice of "grab any partner and knock." From the legal standpoint, could the coach be held personally liable for serious injuries.

REFERENCES

1. ABC-TV Documentary, *"Danger in Sports,"* 1974.
2. Clarke, Dr. Kenneth S., Professor and Chairman, Health Education, Pennsylvania State Univeristy, University Park, Pennsylvania. *Safeguarding the Health of the Athlete.* Presented before the 5th Annual Clinic of the West Virginia High School Coaches Association. By permission.
3. Ibid.
4. Clarke, Dr. Kenneth S., Professor and Chairman, Health Education Pennsylvania State University, University Park, Pennsylvania. *Sports Medicine in Perspective,* presented at the West Virginia University Sports Medicine Seminar, Morgantown, September, 1969. By permission.
5. Elkow, J. Duke, Ph.D., *Philosophy of Sports Accident Prevention and Injury Control, Safety in Sports,* p. 12-13, American Alliance for Health, Physical Education and Recreation, Washington, D.C. By permission.
6. Seaton, Dr. D. C., *Administration and Supervision of Safety Education,* Macmillan, New York, 1968, p. 228.
7. National Athletic Injury/Illness Reporting System (NAIRS) *Information Brochure.* Director, Dr. Kenneth S. Clarke, Ph.D., Pennsylvania State University; Coordinator, Sayers J. Miller, Jr. R.P.T., A.T.C. Sports Research Building, Pennsylvania State University, University Park, Pa. 168-2.
8. Jones, Dr. Frank B., Ed.D., Professor of Physical Education, *Playing Rules and Safety in Interscholastic Athletics,* information paper, California State University, Sacremento, California. By permission.
9. *Safety in Interscholastic Athletics.* A working conference sponsored by the State Department of Education, California, edited by Dr. Frank B. Jones, Ed.D., Chairman, May 1975, State University, Sacremento, California.
10. *Coaches Manual,* National Association For Sport and Physical Education, American Alliance for Health, Physical Education and Recreation, Washington, D.C., p. 69.
11. Blyth, Carl S. and Mueller, Fredrick O., *An Epidemiologic Study of High School Football Injuries in North Carolina* 1968-1972, U.S. Consumer Product Safety Commssion under contract CPSC-C-74-8. By permission of the authors.

SUGGESTED READINGS

Forsyth, C. E., *Administration of High School Athletics* 5th edition, Prentice-Hall, Englewood Cliffs, N.J., 1972, Ch. 11, Safety and Sanitation in Athletics.

Hixson, C. G., *The Administration of Interscholastic Athletics*, J. Lowell Pratt, New York, 1967, Ch. 8, The Safety and Welfare of Participants.

Chapter 23

Transportation of Athletes and Athletic Teams

The education code in most states allows the school boards to provide transportation for supervisors, participants, and student spectators to and from athletic events. All transportation should be in either school-owned or certified public bonded carriers. However, with schools facing financial problems, more and more athletes and athletic teams are being transported in private carriers such as player's, coaches, or parents cars. The legal ramifications of this practice seem overwhelming. In our opinion, because athletics are an integral part of the total school program, funds should be provided for the transportation of athletes and athletic teams.

A common practice today is for the coach to announce the site of the game and have the players meet at that site. Another common practice is for the coach to tell his players to go home first and then report to the site of the game. The coach obviously feels this relieves him of legal responsibility. Although at this time the practice has not been tested legally, it appears from similar lawsuits that the school may be liable in case of accident to one of the participants.

It seems logical that the school must provide transportation for all athletic teams or if funds are not available, the contest should not be scheduled.

TRANSPORTING STUDENT-ATHLETES
IN PRIVATELY OWNED VEHICLES

If the student-athletes travel to athletic contests in privately owned vehicles, all parties concerned must know and understand the public utility and public liability laws of their state. When private vehicles, belonging to coaches, students, or anyone else are used, the administration should determine whether such use conforms with the state statues regarding liability. These private vehicles should not be permitted unless their use is recognized and authorized by the state statues.

Liability Factors

Most teacher's organizations have a professional liability coverage policy as it relates to school-sponsored field trips. The policy (which every member automatically has) applies to teachers while "performing duties within their professional capacity." This is a very broad definition and does not limit coverage to specific situations.

It is important to remember that the professional liability coverage does not include vehicle liability. For example, suppose the student-athletes, while being transported to an athletic contest, are injured in a vehicle accident. There is no coverage under the professional liability. There is coverage under the liability carried by the owner of the vehicle. All individuals who transport students should be very sure that their vehicle liability coverage is adequate.

To protect one's self from legal action, the athletic director and the coach should have a parent's permission form filled out prior to any athletic trip that involving privately owned vehicles. Form 23-1 used by the Tamalpais Union High School District, Larkspur, California, gives permission for a son or daughter to be transported in a privately owned vehicle driven by either a student, parent, or faculty member. In the case of a son or daughter driving a parent's car, there is provision for the parent to sign a "permissions" form for the use of the car for school activities. Other information to be provided include registered owner of the vehicle, capacity of the vehicle, amount of public liability and property damage insurance, whether or not the person driving the car has a valid driver's license, and whether or not the vehicle shows evidence of a recent inspection by the California Highway Patrol.

Whether this form will relieve the legal responsibilities remains to be tested in a court of law. Even though we run the risk of being redundant, we must repeat that the use of privately owned vehicles for athletic transportation should be avoided and is definitely not recommended.

TAMALPAIS UNION HIGH SCHOOL DISTRICT
Larkspur, California

PARENT PERMISSION SLIP
TO
TRANSPORT STUDENTS IN PRIVATELY OWNED VEHICLES

I. I give my son/daughter permission to participate in the following school activity:

_____

YES / NO

(circle one)   _____
                         (Parent's Signature)

II. I give my son/daughter permission to be transported in a privately owned vehicle driven by either a student, parent, or faculty member.

YES / NO

(circle one)   _____
                         (Parent's Signature)

III. I give my son/daughter permission to use my car for school activities

YES / NO

(circle one)   _____
                         (Parent's Signature)

Registered Owner _____ Capacity of Car _____

Amount of Insurance:

Public Liability _____ (100,000 - 75,000)

Property Damage _____ (10,000 - 5,000)

Does your son/daughter possess a valid California Driver's License?

YES / NO (circle one)

Does the vehicle show evidence of a recent inspection by the California Highway Patrol?

YES / NO (circle one)

FORM 23-1 Parent permission form. (Tamalpais Union High School District, Larkspur, California. By permission.)

If privately owned vehicles are to be used for team travel, the coach may find it prudent to publish an itinerary, require all cars to go together in "convoy" style, assign riders, prearrange rest stops, and take any other appropriate precautionary measures he sees fit.

Travel Information

Most school districts have detailed information concerning transportation for student-athletes. The Houston Independent School District (Form 23-2) issues explicit information on transportation for all teams for playoffs and for tournaments.

Bus Request

Arrangements for transportation (Form 23-3) must be made well in advance. The coach should receive a copy of the transportation contract indicating the driver's name, telephone number, and any special arrangements. An example of this form is used by Minot Public Schools, Minot, North Dakota.

Policy Pertaining to Transportation Regulations

A policy must be developed by each school or school district pertaining to transportation. Information in the policy should include dismissal times as authorized by the principal, the designated faculty representative will be who must accompany each bus, for example, coach, assistant coach, etc, financial arrangements for the transportation; whether the teams will dress at home or at the visiting school, out-of-town trips, use of common carrier or private cars that are adequately covered in insurance, reimbursement per mile, permission of the principal to use private cars, estimated time schedule to various schools in the league or conference, estimated time for travel, to be subtracted from dressing time and pregame warm-up.

Athletics Department Transportation Schedule. Form 23-4 indicates the type of form that should be posted after all transportation arrangements have been made. The form includes the date, team that is to travel, destination, departure time, number of student-athletes that will make the trip, and estimated time of return.

Travel Permission Form. Form 23-5 is a sample of the parent permission form that should be used prior to any trip away from school. It includes destination, area from which the team will leave, time the

HOUSTON INDEPENDENT SCHOOL DISTRICT
DEPARTMENT OF ATHLETICS

TRAVEL INFORMATION

FOOTBALL - Out of County - Varsity
1. The Athletic Department will furnish bus transportation for 39 people.
2. The Athletic Department will allow $2.00 for pre-game meal and $3.50 for post-game meal.
3. No expenses will be allowed for hotel or motel trips as all teams are expected to return to Houston after the game.

FOOTBALL - Out of Town - In County - Varsity
Houston Independent School District School Bus will be furnished and a $3.50 meal will be allowed if this is the only trip made by a school.

PLAY-OFF GAMES
All reasonable and necessary expenses will be allowed. Contact the Athletic Business Manager as to amount of money that will be reimbursed.

FOOTBALL - Junior Varsity
One bus will be furnished to transport teams for each J V football game.

FOOTBALL - 9th and 8th
One bus per traveling school will be furnished.

BASKETBALL - Varsity
$125.00 per year is allowed to teams for tournament games. No other expenses are allowed.

PLAY-OFF GAMES
All necessary and reasonable expenses will be paid. Contact the Athletic Business Manager as to the amount of money that will be reimbursed.

BASKETBALL - 9th and 8th
One bus furnished. No expenses paid for Junior Varsity.

BASEBALL
No expenses paid except for play-off games.

TRACK
$100.00 per high school and expenses to State Meet.

SWIMMING
$40.00 per high school and expenses to State Meet.

TENNIS
State Tournament expenses only.

GOLF
State Tournament expenses only.

The Physical Education budget pays for (1) $125.00 Basketball, (2) $100.00 Track, (3) $40.00 Swimming, (4) Expenses to State Meet for Swimming, Golf, Tennis and Track.

The Athletic Budget pays all others.

FORM 23-2 Information concerning transportation for student-athletes. (Houston Independent School District, Houston, Texas. By permission.)

343

MINOT PUBLIC SCHOOLS
Minot, North Dakota
BUS REQUEST

School	Department		Requested By	Date of Application
Date(s) of Use	No. of Pass.	No. of Bus(es)	Time Leaving School	Scheduled Arrival Time

Estimated Time of Return to School	Destination	Purpose of Trip	

Check One	Field Trip	Athletic	Pep Club	Other, Identify

Signature of Principal: _____   Signature of Supervisor: _____

TO BE FILLED IN ONLY FOR SPECIALLY FUNDED TRIPS

INCOME   **EXPENSE**

    No. of Passengers _____   **Drivers' hrs.** _____ **X Rate** _____
            X Rate _____   **Gas & Oil** _____
                            Others _____
                            Check to Business Office _____

        GROSS INCOME _____   **TOTAL** _____

                                Signature _____

TO BE FILLED IN BY DIRECTOR OF TRANSPORTATION

Ending Miles_____   Driver_____

Beginning Miles_____   Vehicles(s) Assigned_____

Total Miles_____   Driver's Hours_____

Cost per Mile_____   Comments_____

APPROVAL

DATE _____   **BUS SUPERVISOR** _____

NOTE: ALL THREE COPIES TO BE SENT TO THE BUSINESS OFFICE FOR APPROVAL

PS3-2/17/72
1000/ 2-17-72

FORM 23-3 Bus request. (Minot Public Schools, Minot, North Dakota. By permission.)

344

Kent Public Schools   ATHLETIC DEPARTMENT
School District No. 415   TRANSPORTATION
King County   SCHEDULE
Kent, Washington

DATE	TEAM	DESTINATION	DEPARTMENT TIME	NUMBER OF STUDENTS	ESTIMATED RETURN

FORM 23-4   Athletic department-transportation schedule. (Kent Public Schools, King County, Kent, Washington. By permission.)

4/18/72 Revised

TRAVEL PERMISSION FORM
ATHLETIC DEPARTMENT
KENT PUBLIC SCHOOLS
School District No. 415, King County
Kent, Washington

Date _____

Dear Parents:
The team of which your child is a member is planning a school trip to

_____ as a part of their regular schedule. This

group will leave from _____ , about _____ , on
                                  (Place)   (Time)

_____ and will be back at the school
   (Day)   (Date)

about _____ , riding with _____ .

This trip is a part of the regular activities and will be under the same careful
supervision which your child has while at school. In order for your child to make
the trip it will be necessary for us to have your approval. You can express your
approval by signing the slip below and returning it to us.

_____
                                   Coach

— —

I give permission for my child _____ to make

the _____ trip on _____
               (Team)   (date)

to _____ , knowing that every precaution will be

taken for his safety and well-being. I understand my youngster will be riding

with _____ .

Date _____   _____
                                          Parent or Guardian

FORM 23-5 Travel permission form, Kent School District No. 415, King
County, Kent, Washington.

346

team will leave, and estimated time of return. If the team is using school-provided transportation, this should be mentioned. If private vehicles are to be used, the form should indicate with whom the student-athlete will be riding. This part of the form is signed by the coach. The parent or guardian will sign the remaining portion of the form, giving permission for their son or daughter to make the trip.

Conduct of Student-Athletes

Members of athletic teams should be cautioned regarding adherence to a code of conduct and safety while representing their school on trips away from home. They should be neat in appearance, be on time for the bus or transportation departure, be responsible for the personal game equipment, and show common courtesies while on the bus and in the visiting team area.

The coach is responsible for the discipline of the team members and must enforce the rules and regulations.

Most school travel policies stress that all players must travel to and from all contests as a team member via school-arranged transportation and that all official team trips originate and terminate at a designated area. Conditions under which players may be released to parents for return travel should be specified. The parental permission form should stress that players are required to return with the team via team conveyance and that the only exception is when a player is released to the parents.

The coach can solve many travel problems by having the team dress at home, especially if the contest is nearby, board the bus, play the game, return on the bus, and shower and dress at the home school. We have briefly discussed the liability factor involved in transporting teams; however, another important factor is team morale. The ideal situation is for the team to travel to and from the contest as a unit.

Financial Arrangements. The athletic director or coach should be the custodian of the funds that will be used on a trip. A form, such as Form 23-6, used by the Easton Area School District, must be completed well in advance of the contest so that funds may be drawn and be in the hands of the coach prior to the departure time for the trip. A common practice, especially today when funds for transportation are not available, is for the home team to pay the cost of transporting the visiting team.

```
                    EASTON AREA SCHOOL DISTRICT

                      Athletic Department

                         EXPENSE FORM
                                              _____
                                                        Date
                                          SCOUTING _____  vs. _____
    SPORT _____           (Contestants)
                                          TOURNAMENT(S)_____
    NAME(S)_____
                                          LEAGUE MEETING_____
    DATE_____
                                          OTHER_____
    PLACE_____



    MILEAGE:    Reimbursable at rate of $.10 per mile
                Total Mileage_____@$.10          = $_____
    MEALS:      Breakfast $2.00, Lunch $3.00, Dinner $4.00
                (Receipt required)

                Number _____  @_____   = $_____

                Other  _____  @_____   = $_____

    LODGING:    (Receipt required)

                Number _____  @_____   = $_____

    OTHER EXPENSES:    _____   $_____
    (Parking,programs,
    tickets, etc.      _____   $_____
    Receipts where
    possible.          _____   $_____

                       _____   $_____

                       _____   $_____

                       _____   $_____

                       _____   $_____

    General Information:            TOTAL =    $_____

    1.  All scouting trips that require overnight lodging and/or meals are
        limited to two (2) persons.

    2.  Meals are reimbursable at a rate no higher than the above mentioned.

    3.  For reimbursement, return this form to the Athletic Office.

    ┌──────────────────────┐
    │ For office use only  │   Check to be made payable to:
    │ Date Paid_____  │
    │ Check No._____  │   _____
    │ Chg'd.To _____  │
    ├──────────────────────┤   Dir. of Athletics:_____
    │ Advance check desired│
    │ Yes_____  No_____  │   Treasurer EAHS Ath.Fund_____
    └──────────────────────┘
```

(a)

FORM 23-6   Expense form. (Easton Area School District. Easton, Pennsylvania. By permission.)

TRAVEL PARTY: _____ DATE: _____
_____
SPORT   Opponent and Location

Alphabetical,
PLAYERS (LAST NAME FIRST)   PLAYERS (LAST NAME FIRST) - (cont'd.)

1. _____   26. _____
2. _____   27. _____
3. _____   28. _____
4. _____   29. _____
5. _____   30. _____
6. _____   31. _____
7. _____   32. _____
8. _____   33. _____
9. _____   34. _____
10. _____   35. _____
11. _____
12. _____   COACHES/MANAGERS/TRAINERS
13. _____
14. _____   1. _____
15. _____   2. _____
16. _____   3. _____
17. _____   4. _____
18. _____   5. _____
19. _____
20. _____   ADMINISTRATION
21. _____
22. _____   1. _____
23. _____   2. _____
24. _____   3. _____
25. _____   4. _____
                                        5. _____

(b)

INSURANCE COVERAGE

The athletic director or the district employee involved in hiring of the carriers would find it advisable to check on the type of insurance and the limits of such insurance carried by the transportation company. In the event of an accident, proper coverage could save either the school district or individuals involved from large financial losses.

RESPONSIBILITIES OF THE SCHOOL BUS DRIVER

Most states have regulations and laws concerning operation of school buses. This is briefly mentioned because many coaches, especially in rural areas, are required to drive the bus on athletic trips. A few of the more common regulations are given below.[1]

Bus Inspection by Driver.
Each school bus shall be inspected by the driver daily, before use, to ascertain that it is in safe condition, equipped as required by all provisions of law, and that all equipment is in good working order.

Safe and Lawful Operation Required.
A driver of a school bus shall at all times operate in a safe, prudent, and careful manner with due regard to the traffic and the use of the highway by others.

Authority of Driver.
Pupils transported in a school bus shall be under the authority of, and responsible directly to, the driver of the bus, and the driver shall be held responsible for the orderly conduct of the pupils while they are on the bus or being escorted across a street, highway, or road.

Use of Seat Belt.
The school bus shall not be driven unless the driver has properly restrained himself in a seat belt assembly.

Leaving Bus.
The driver shall not leave the driver's compartment of a school bus that is stopped, standing, or parked on any street, highway, or road without first stopping the engine and effectively setting the parking brake.

Operation in Motion.
The driver shall not permit a school bus when traveling to coast with the transmission in neutral or the clutch disengaged.

Repairs.
A driver of a school bus, unless he is the mechanic charged with the care and maintenance of the bus, shall not make any repairs to the bus

or its equipment except necessary emergency repairs while on the road.
Vision of Driver.

The driver shall not allow any person to occupy any a position in a
school bus that will interfere with the vision of the driver to the front,
sides, or by means of the mirror, to the rear, or interfere with the operation of the bus.
Unnecessary Conversation by Driver.

A driver of a school bus shall not carry on unnecessary conversation
while the vehicle is in motion.
Hours of Labor of Driver.

Except as otherwise expressly provided by law, no person shall drive
any school bus for more than 10 consecutive hours nor for more than 10
hours spread over a total of 15 consecutive hours.

Summation

It is the responsibility of the boards of education to provide transportation for athletes and athletic teams. The use of private vehicles
for athletic trips should be discouraged by the athletic director and
the coach.

No amount of liability coverage, no contest, no trip is worth the
lives of young students. The administration, which approves all
athletic schedules, must also provide finances for travel. If they
cannot provide the necessary funds to furnish adequate transportation then they, the administrators, should not approve the schedule.

School administrators must come to grips with the very serious
problem of additional teams and participants.

Questions

1. Your policy is that all players travel together with the team unless
   personally released to their parents or guardian. *Situation:* After
   an away contest, a player's aunt, whom you do not know, indicates that her nephew will not be returning with the team but
   she will see that he returns home safely. How do you handle
   this situation?

   Situation: A young lady indicates she is a player's sister sent by
   her parents to get her brother so that the family can drive back
   home together. How do you handle this situation? Are the
   situations the same or different? Discuss.

2. At the conclusion of practice on Friday afternoon, you inform your squad members that, "All of you will be making the trip on the school bus tomorrow for the football game at (site). You should have your gear on the bus and be ready to leave at 11:00 a.m. As soon as the game is over, get to the locker room quickly, shower, dress, put your gear on the bus. We want to depart not later than 45 minutes after the game."
Situation: On Saturday at the announced hour of departure for the away contest, two of the players are not present. How do you handle this situation?

Situation: The game is now over and 45 minutes after the game, all players are on the bus with the exception of one squad member. How do you handle this situation?
3. Would you permit to play in the game two players who missed the bus but who showed up at the game ready to play? Discuss.
4. At 3:00 a.m. the phone rings. It is a parent wanting to know where his son is. The game was over at 11:00 p.m. What do you do?

REFERENCES

1. California State Department of Education, *Regulations and Laws Concerning Operation of School Buses in California*, Sacramento, 1970.

SUGGESTED READINGS

Appenzeller, Herb, *From the Gym to the Jury*, The Michie Co., Charlottesville, Va., 1970, Ch. 5 to 7.

Bucher, Charles A., *Administration of Health and Physical Education Programs Including Athletics*, 6th edition, C.V. Mosby, St. Louis, Missouri, 1971.

Forsythe, Charles E. and Keller, I.A., *Administration of High School Athletics*, 5th edition, Prentice-Hall, Englewood Cliffs, N.J., 1972, Ch. 11.

Gallon, Arthur J. *Coaching: Ideas and Ideals*, Houghton Mifflin, Boston, Ch. 9, 1974.

Hixson, G.C., *The Administration of Interscholastic Athletics*, J. Lowell Pratt & Co., N.Y. 1967, Chs. 8.

Purdy, Robert L., *The Successful High School Athletic Program*, Parker Publishing, West Nyack, N.Y. 1973, Ch. 9.

Resick, Matthew C. and Erickson, Carl E., *Intercollegiate and Interscholastic Athletics for Men and Women*, Addison-Wesley, Reading, Mass., Ch. 7.

Resick, Matthew C., Seidel, Beverly L., and Mason, James, *Modern Administrative Practices in Physical Education and Athletics*, Addison-Wesley, Reading, Mass., 1970, Ch. 10.

Chapter 24

Effective Office Management and Recordkeeping

The success and prestige that characterize the interscholastic athletic program is closely related to the spirit and efficiency with which the athletic director conducts departmental business.

The athletic director's office is usually the coordinating center for various functions, services, and programs carried out by the department. The office also serves as an information center, negotiating-conference-reception room and a space for recordkeeping.

The trend in athletic administration is moving toward a full-time administrator with office space and secretarial services, who handles routine matters in a manner similar to other school administrators.

During the present transitional period, many athletic directors function on a part-time basis with teaching and perhaps coaching assignments. Under such circumstances, the athletic director has little time available to spend in the office. Many of the tasks that are required of him are handled while he is on the move or at any time during the school day when the opportunity to do the task presents itself. Obviously necessary paper work and myriad administrative details are likely to receive cursory attention during school hours if one has multiple teaching-coaching duties and little free time for athletic director duties. The only other time available to accomplish these details, if one is desirous of doing a good job, is before and after school hours.

The athletic director, to be effective must learn how to organize and control his efforts in relation to time by applying basic scheduling controls to his own activities.

OFFICE MANAGEMENT

Regardless of the time allotted for athletic director's functions or the office space available, the athletic director must set up a routine and schedule his time to carry out the basic functions in a business-like manner. There is no one "right" system. However, the athletic director should set up some system of doing business and try to manage it as a business operation.

In larger school systems, funds may be allocated for full-time or part-time secretarial help. The person selected for this position will become the "right arm" of the athletic director and be able to carry out many of the routine functions expected of the director. In the smaller schools, where no professionally trained secretary is provided, the athletic director must seek help from the business classes, typing classes, and try to secure student help for certain hours of the day. In schools that have a "work experience" program, the teacher in charge would be most happy to assign a student or students for certain periods of the day to the athletic director. This is good on-the-job training for students and can prove to be of valuable assistance to the athletic department.

In many larger districts, schools are adding a coordinator of athletics to aid the athletic director in taking care of the physical examination reports, insurance coverage of the student-athletes, or the eligibility lists, for example. The pattern is to have a coordinator for the boys' program and a coordinator for the girls' program in addition to the athletic director, who may be male or female.

Office Hours

The athletic director should set aside a specific time each day of the week for conferences, committee work, telephone calls, and correspondence. If the situation calls for the athletic director to teach classes and to coach a sport, a secretary or student assistant should be employed to handle the phone and to attend to routine office chores during the athletic director's absence.

The secretary's time must be well organized to enable the athletic director to carry on his other daily responsibilities. Correspondence, recordkeeping, filing, and daily notices to the coaching staff or administration will occupy most of the secretary's time.

An important duty of the secretary is to answer the telephone and relay messages to the staff and to the athletic director. The telephone, while vital for conducting business, is also potentially detrimental to any school's physical education or athletic department. This is because some of the staff lack professional judgment on when to use the phone. Teachers called away from class to discuss athletic business cause friction between the physical education department chairperson, the coaching staff, and the athletic director.

The athletic director should not conduct personal business during business hours because the staff will follow the same practice. The athletic director should make it clear that his is a business office and that the business phone should not be used for personal calls when business activities have priority.

This situation can be avoided if the secretary takes telephone messages and channels them to the proper source. Many coaches, who are also physical education teachers, have a conference period during which all calls should be answered. Where a secretary or student is not available to answer the telephone in the athletic director's office, the school operator should have a schedule of all classes and have calls returned during the coaches' conference period or during the athletic director's office hours. An answering device on which the caller's number and message can be recorded and the director's whereabouts noted may provide a short-term solution to a vexing problem.

THE ATHLETIC DEPARTMENT HANDBOOK

The *Athletic Department Handbook*, discussed in Chapter 3, can be of great assistance in efficient office management. Once established, the handbook can be used as a reference by the coaching staff. All policies, forms, purchase orders, requisition blanks, schedules, and contracts are accessible and, in lieu of the athletic director, the secretary or student assistant will be able to assist the coaches and anyone else in providing information or in the performance of their duties.

The handbook should be a looseleaf-type notebook, catagorized by numbers for easy reference. A file cabinet in the athletic director's office should mirror the athletic handbook. Any form that is needed is filed under the corresponding section of the handbook. For example, a coach needs a copy of the eligibility form, which is number 642 in the handbook. The coach or the secretary would find a copy of the form 642 in the file cabinet that had been indexed in the same manner as the handbook. This simple but effective method of filing not only helps the coach, but means that the athletic director must concern himself with one less minute detail.

Below is an example of what should be included in the handbook and file cabinet; it is taken from the *Athletic Handbook Guide for* Directors of Interscholastic Athletics,[1] Michigan Association of Directors of Physical Education and Athletics. Contents of the *Athletic Directors Handbook* were previously discussed in Chapter 3; however, to emphasize keeping up-to-date files, we are listing the pertinent information that should be included:

1. *The Administration of Interscholastic Athletics*
    A. Statement of philosophy
    B. Objectives of participation
    C. Administrative organization
    D. Affiliations
2. *Staff Responsibilities*
    A. Faculty manager
    B. Athletic director
    C. Coaches
3. *Business Policies Pursuant to Athletics*
    A. Annual budget
    B. Purchasing
    C. Financial statements
    D. Medical policy
    E. Injury insurance protection
    F. Transportation of player personnel
    G. Transportation of spectators
    H. Liability assumed by board of education
    I. Maintenance of facilities and grounds
    J. Tournament play
    K. Gate revenues
    L. Banquets
    M. Ticket information
4. *General Information*
    A. Eligibility requirements for interscholastic athletics
    B. Scheduling of events
    C. Invitational considerations
    D. Official hiring practices
    E. Use of athletic equipment and facilities
    F. Girls' Athletic Association

    G. Behavioral expectation of athletes
    H. Suspension procedure
    I. The School letter
    J. Special awards
    K. Practice sessions
    L. Publicity and promotion
    M. Cheerleaders
5. *Directory of Activities and Personnel*
    A. Administration
    B. The Athletic Board of Control
    C. Coaching staff personnel
    D. Auxillary staff personnel

COACHES' ACCOUNTABILITY

By their nature, coaches do not seem to be the best "paper" men in the school. There are many forms to be completed during a sport season and the athletic director seems to be constantly seeking a coach to fill out an eligibility form, purchase order, or purchase requisition, list of award winners, or take care of a multitude of paperwork that never seems to make the designated deadline. The coach is accountable for his office work and if a form is to be in on a certain day, he should make sure that it is turned in on time. In many cases, the athletic director ends up filling out the form for the coach. This is a mistake; it is not the athletic director's function. "Athletic Director Leadership" is discussed in Chapter 27 and the daily tasks specifies what is eficient and effective leadership.

FACILITIES

In most high schools, space is at a premium. The athletic director must find space to set up an office. The size of the office is not the most important factor, but it must be private and well organized and accessible to staff members. Ideally, it is located to afford supervisory possibilities for a major departmental area for example, a locker room or a gymnasium.

    The type of equipment needed depends on the ingenuity of the athletic director. Obviously, a desk, telephone, typewriter, and file cabinets are necessary. If the office is large enough, it may be set up as a conference room where staff meetings can be held. The athletic director is responsible for making the office effective.

A recent trend, with the advent of Title IX, is to have one office for use by the combined men and women physical education and athletic staffs. This provides for better communication, especially in implementing the new legislation.

REFERENCES

An Athletic Handbook Guide for Directors of Interscholastic Athletics, Michigan Association of Directors of Physical Education and Athletics, 1969. By permission of Harry Kraft, President.

SUGGESTED READINGS

Campbell, James H. and Hepler, Hal W. (eds.), *Dimensions in Communication,* Wadsworth, Belmont, California 1956.

Ewing, David, W., *Writing for Results in Business, Government and the Professions,* Wiley-Interscience, Wiley New York, 1973.

Lakein, Alan, *How to Get Control of Your Time and Your Life,* Peter H. Wyden, New York, 1973.

Miller, Besse May, *Private Secretary's Encyclopedia Dictionary,* Prentice-Hall, Englewood Cliffs, N.J., 1958.

Purdy, Robert, *The Successful High School Athletic Program,* Parker Publishing, West Nyack, N.Y., 1973.

Schindall, Henry, *How to Add Hours to Your Day Without Working Extra Hours,* Henry Schindall Associates, Management Consultants, New York, 1965.

Chapter 25

Evaluation of the Interscholastic Athletic Program

The primary purpose of evaluating an interscholastic athletic program is to provide the basis for program improvement. The result should be better communication and exchange of ideas between the coach, athletic director, and the administration. A well-conducted appraisal of individuals and of the total program creates an environment that will bring about self-improvement and accountability within the athletic department.

Traditionally at the interscholastic level, the evaluation of coaches has been on an informal basis with the exception of the state-mandated tenure appraisal given to all teachers. The athletic department is unique in that the community constantly evaluates it based on how active it is and on results of contests. There are also many one-on-one evaluations between the athletic director and the coaching staff.

Never before in the history of our profession has the athletic program been so thoroughly scrutinized by administrators and the public, especially since there have been many changes in the law and state codes relevant to the interscholastic athletic program. The advent of Title IX is certain to have a tremendous effect on the total athletic program, particularly in the evaluation of the current program being conducted in the secondary schools. In fact, the provisions of Title IX require a self-evaluation.

Participation for the many rather than a few is the theme of the seventies. Great change in program content and methods will take place in the administration of interscholastic athletics. Balance and emphasis of purpose are key points in the evaluation of the athletic department. The way in which the total program is viewed by the faculty, student body, parents, and community should guide the standards in setting up an evaluation procedure.

ANNUAL EVALUATION

The interscholastic athletic program should be evaluated annually at the conclusion of the school year by a committee consisting of a member of the board of education, representative from the superintendent's office, principal, athletic director, coaches, and students. The results of the evaluation, with appropriate recommendations, should be made available to all concerned. The evaluation should deal with questions on the administration, facilities, equipment, finances, relationship of the athletic program to the total education program, students, and the relationship of the athletic program to the community.

The sample questions that may be used to evaluate the interscholastic athletic program appeared in *Evaluating the High School Athletic Program*,[1] as developed by the National Council of State High School Coaches Association in conjunction with the National Council of Secondary School Athletic Directors and various knowledgeable athletic administrators.

Evaluation of Objectives and Goals of the Interscholastic Athletic Program

1. The statement of purposes and objectives is sufficiently comprehensive to describe what the athletic program is attempting to accomplish.
2. The statement was developed and designed for this school's athletic program.
3. The statement was developed by consultation with the entire athletic staff.
4. The entire school community shared in the development of the statement.
5. Efforts have been made to acquaint the student body and the entire school community with the statement.
6. The statement preceives and meets the needs of the students

attending the school and of the larger school community.

7. The statement involves objectives that can be evaluated in appraising the program's progress toward their fulfillment.
8. The objectives are concerned with participant outcome, rather than with the coaches' won and lost record.
9. The program in effect is in accord with the statement of purposes and objectives.
10. There are specific plans for the ongoing revision of the statement as changing conditions warrant.

Evaluation of Administration of the Athletic Program

1. The school board has a written policy governing athletics that includes philosophy, selection and retention of personnel, methods of financing program, and receptivity to new programs.
2. The board is responsive to requests for additional needs of students.
3. The board has a written policy regarding line-and-staff and grievance procedures.
4. The board provides for insurance needs of participants.
5. The board provides for insurance needs of the athletic staff.
6. The superintendent implements the school board's athletic policy including selection and retention of personnel, methods of financing, responsiveness to request for additional needs of students, line-and-staff procedures, and philosophy.
7. The principal implements the school board's athletic policy including philosophy, program, selection and retention of personnel, and line-and-staff procedures.
8. The principal is responsible for following rules established by the state and conference association; they relate to active participation in state and conference association and establishment of a moral and ethical climate essential for maintaining leadership standards.
9. The athletic director recognizes the principal as the leader of the individual school program.
10. The athletic director establishes a moral and ethical climate essential for maintaining leadership standards.
11. The athletic director has a comprehensive position descriptive of the duties and responsibilities.
12. The coaching staff establishes a moral and ethical climate essential for maintaining leadership standards.

13. The coaching staff shows leadership capacity through the establishment of clear and well-defined line of communication with administration, staff, athletes, student, news media, and community.

14. The coaching staff has respect for the letter and intent of rules and regulations.

15. The coaching staff shows respect for authority.

16. The coaching staff understands and follows line-and-staff procedures.

17. The coaching staff demonstrates self-control during contests and with faculty, students, parents, news media, staff and administration.

18. The coaching staff demonstrates humanistic attitudes in the following areas: respect for athletes, welfare of athletes, athletic department personnel, respect for parents, and respect for guests.

19. The coaching staff shows professional competency by meeting the established criteria of the educational profession, maintaining coaching proficiency through in-service training programs, and professional clinics.

20. The athletic department has the support of faculty, team doctor, custodian and maintenance personnel, clerical personnel, school treasurer, band director, cheerleaders and sponsor, booster club, and pep clubs.

21. The athletic department maintains a checklist for game management including adequate police protection, an adequate number of parking attendants, ticket takers, ticket sellers, trained concession workers, ushers and service personnel, adequate assistance for game management, and a ticket manager.

Evaluation of Facilities for the Athletic Program

1. The existing facilities for the entire athletic program have been designed, constructed, and maintained to meet the standards established under the philosophy of the board of education.

2. The athletic facilities are the result of careful planning and are in a constant state of being reevaluated to determine present effectiveness and future needs.

3. Goals have been established to anticipate future needs, foster orderly growth, and provide renovation of existing facilities.

4. Scheduling of events takes place to obtain maximum utilization of existing facilities.

5. Community and school officials cooperate in long range planning and in the use of each party's facilities.
6. Facilities are designed to meet the needs of the total athletic program.
7. Facilities are available to both boys and girls on an equitable basis whether separate or shared.
8. There is provision for proper space or area for both indoor and outdoor sports programs.
9. Permanent equipment adequately meets minumum standards for dealing with the peak requirements of each athletic activity.
10. Facilities meet the minimum standards for sanitary and safety code requirements.
11. There is adequate provision for spectator seating for each sports activity.
12. Facilities are made available through a central scheduling agency to all schools in the system to school groups, and to the community.
13. Functional and well-equipped offices are available for each sports activity.
14. There are convenient ticket distribution booths or centers centrally located for all sports.
15. There are adequate parking areas, well-illuminated for night contests, and with adequate means of egress after contests.
16. There is a hospitality room for coaches, school officials, and visiting school personnel.
17. Adequate concession facilities are located for maximum use at peak requirement periods.
18. There is an adequate training room and first-aid station to provide services for both athletes and spectators.
19. There are rest room and drinking water accommodations for peak periods of use; these meet minimum standards of equipment and cleanliness.
20. Where needed, facilities are equipped with sound amplification systems for music and voice.
21. Adequate maintenance and custodial personnel is available to keep facilities safe and sanitary.
22. There is adequate lighting to meet minimum requirements in all facilities.
23. Athletic facilities are aesthetically designed.
24. All facilities meet fire and safety code requirements.

25. Facilities are located on the school campus or in the immediate vicinity.
26. Facilities are provided with adequately prepared and equipped areas for playing and practice.
27. There is adequate and readily accessible storage space or area for equipment and materials.
28. There is a laundry for use on a regular basis with adequate facilities for cleaning equipment and uniforms.
29. There are shower and drying room facilities to meet peak demands.
30. There are sufficient lockers of the proper type to meet the needs of the program.

Evaluation of Equipment for Athletic Program

1. Adequate equipment and supplies are provided for participants in each sport.
2. The coaches, or the athletic director should make an inventory of supplies and equipment at the end of each sport.
3. Coaching staff participates in determining type, amount, and quality of supplies and equipment.
4. Long range planning is done to replace and purchase major equipment items.
5. Adequate consideration is given, when purchasing, to the aesthetic quality of uniforms and equipment.
6. The athletic department provides specific procedures for the issue and return of equipment and supplies.
7. Adequate individual locker storage is provided for the security and care of the participants' personal and school property.
8. Adequate off-season storage is provided for equipment and supplies.
9. Adequate precautions are taken to insure the proper fit and use of uniforms and equipment for maximum comfort and safety.
10. Adequate arrangments are made for the daily laundry of practice equipment.
11. Adequate arrangements are made for the laundry of game equipment.
12. Adequate arrangements are made for the repair and reconditioning of supplies and equipment.
13. Written policies are following for the purchase of all supplies

and equipment.
14. Where practical, competitive bidding procedures are followed in purchasing supplies and equipment.

Evaluation of Athletic Program Finances

1. Written policies govern the derivation and expenditure of funds for athletics.
2. Policies governing finances are known to all staff members.
3. As needed, the complete budget is available for the use of all coaches.
4. Adequate consideration of participant cost is given to the equitable distribution among the sports in the program.
5. All income for athletics goes into a common or general fund.
6. Unless prevented by law, the athletic program is supported by the educational tax fund or a comparable source.
7. Money raised by a booster club or similar type of supporting group is used to support the entire athletic program.
8. Any special fund-raising projects are approved by the athletic administration in advance.
9. The athletic director prepares a yearly itemized written athletic budget.
10. The principal knows all parts of the athletic budget.
11. Each head coach works with the athletic director to draft the final budget for the sport involved.
12. Adequate finance records are kept by the athletic director during the year to faciliate the proper use of the budget by coaching staff.
13. Necessary financial records of past years are maintained to provide information for evaluation and future planning.

Evaluation of the Relationship of Athletic Program to the Total Educational Program

1. The sports are an outgrowth of the physical education program.
2. A variety of sports is available for all students.
3. The educational values of sport are the foremost parts of the philosophy.
4. All students have an opportunity to participate in a sport.
5. Athletics are used appropriately as a school's unifying force.
6. Athletes are not excused from courses, including physical

education, because of athletic participation.

7. Coaches have an adequate opportunity to exercise the rights and privileges of other faculty members in determining school and curricular matters.

8. Coaches attend, and they are scheduled so they can attend, faculty meetings.

9. Coaches are not expected to assume more duties of a general nature than are other faculty members.

10. Teaching tenure and other faculty privileges are available to athletic personnel.

11. Assignments for extra duties are made for coaches on the same basis as for other teachers.

12. Athletes are held accountable scholastically at the same level as other students.

13. Game trips should not cause the students to miss an excessive number of classes.

14. Counseling services emphasize the importance of academic records.in regard to career education.

15. Athletes are required to attned classes on days of contests.

16. New coaches are made aware of the board policies, and informed that they will be expected to follow them in spirit as well as letter.

17. All coaches are regularly informed by the principal and athletic director that they must practice within the framework of board policy.

18. A procedure is available for the athletic director and coaches to make recommendations regarding policy change.

19. Noncoaching faculty members are made aware of board policy regarding athletics, so that they may discuss it from a base of fact.

20. The philosophy of the board is written and made available to all personnel.

21. Only those intrinsic awards authorized by local conferences and state athletic associations are given.

22. Diligence is exercised to insure that outside groups do not cause violations of the award regulations.

23. Care is taken to assure that athletes are not granted privileges not available to the general student body.

24. It is emphasized that participation in athletics is a privilege.

25. Development of critical thinking as well as athletic performance

is planned into the program.

26. Development of self-direction and individual motivation is a real part of the athletic experience.
27. Athletes are allowed to develop at their own cognitive, psychomotor, and effective readiness level.
28. Accepted social values are assumed to be standards of behavior both on and off the playing area.
29. The student in athletic performance is not used to provide an activity that has as its main purpose entertainment of the community.
30. The student's academic program is in no way altered to allow him to maintain eligibility with less than normal effort on his part.
31. The student is not given a false impression of his athletic ability through the device of suggesting the possibility of a college scholarship.
32. Athletes are not given a false image of the value of their athletic prowess to the material and cultural success of the school and community.

Evaluation of Athletic Department Personnel

1. All personnel meet the standards of state and local certification requirements.
2. An attempt is made for all coaches to have at least physical education or coaching minors.
3. No nonteaching personnel are allowed to coach.
4. Additional staff is hired if the popularity of a sport, indicated by the number of prospects, shows demand for additional schedules and coaches.
5. Where numbers indicate, assistant coaches are provided in all sports.
6. Adequate supportive personnel is provided to insure that coaches have time for coaching.
7. Properly qualified personnel is provided to take care of the health service of the athletic program.
8. Properly qualified and certified athletic officials are obtained for all contests.
9. All facets of credentials (not only winning records) are pursued when personnel are selected.
10. No fringe benefits, not available to all faculty, are offered to

secure athletic personnel.

11. Athletic personnel to be assigned teaching in any area must be qualified and well motivated in that area.
12. Athletic personnel carry the same teaching load as other faculty, unless release from same is part of computed compensation.
13. Athletic personnel are members of general educational organizations.
14. Athletic personnel are members of the professional organizations appropriate to their teaching and coaching areas.
15. Some athletic personnel are leaders in their areas as indicated by research, publications use of new techniques, and service to professional organizations.
16. Athletic personnel operate under a code of ethics that at least is as lofty as that of National Educational Association.
17. Athletic personnel have moral standards that at their minimum would, if emulated by their athletes when they become adults, provide a social image felt to be desirable in the community.
18. Athletic personnel make positive efforts to teach the spirit as well as the letter of playing rules, sportsmanship codes, and other valuable areas in sports.
19. Salary standards are commensurate and equitable with established professional schedules.
20. Compensation for coaching is based on length of season, number of participants, and scope of responsibility.
21. Percentage scales or comparable scales are used to provide fair increments for experience.
22. Extreme differences in salary among coaches of different sports are avoided.
23. Coaching increments are not used to lure outstanding teachers in academic areas who are not qualified to coach.

Evaluation of Students in the Athletic Program

1. Every student is given an equitable opportunity to try out and participate in an athletic activity.
2. The program of athletic activities is designed to offer a wide variety of opportunities to meet the individual differences of the student body.
3. The student participates in a decision-making role in regard to athletic policies, rules, and regulations.
4. Regular channels of communication are established to impart

program values and standards to all students.

5. Each student is given a complete physical examination before trying out for an athletic activity.

6. The student is provided with an adequate insurance program to defray the cost of medical attention in case in injury.

7. Services are available to aid the participating student in finding the college of his choice or in selecting a career upon graduation.

8. The student is provided with the best equipment, facilities, and evnironment possible in view of existing minimum standards and the financial ability of the school.

9. The participant is able to appeal to a higher authority for a redress of an arbitrary decision on the part of a coach or administrator.

10. The participant is protected from a loss of class time by proper scheduling of athletic events.

11. The participant is given consideration in regard to scheduling of competition commensurate with school size and program interest.

12. The student is encouraged to participate in a variety of sports, and, if unable to participate on the varsity level, he is encouraged to continue competition on the extramural or intramural level.

13. Students are permitted to participate only in one given sport at a time.

14. The nonparticipating student is made to feel a part of the athletic program by serving in a decision-making role in regard to athletic policies affecting the entire student body.

15. Nonparticipating students are given preferential opportunities to attend athletic contests before the adults in the community.

16. Nonparticipating students are encouraged to join supportive groups of the athletic program.

17. Student leaders are given the opportunity to serve on committees for awards recognition and pep assemblies.

18. Every effort is exerted toward directing the nonparticipant into a school-sponsored event of a physical nature to promote interest and appreciation of the values of physical activity.

19. How well does the athletic program enrich the total school experience for both participating and nonparticipating students.

20. To what extent does the student body view the athletic program as a valuable extracurricular experience?
21. To what extent have policies been established to insure maximum student interest and participation in the athletic program?

Evaluation of the Overall Athletic Porgram

1. The school is a member of the state activities of athletic association.
2. All sports seasons meet state activities association regulations.
3. Appropriate practice schedules are established for all sports.
4. Appropriate competitive schedules are established for all sports.
5. Appropriate facility schedules are established for all sports.
6. Seasons are in harmony with coaches' and administrators' desires.
7. The sports seasons are in harmony with community resources and desires.
8. The established sports seasons permit the participant maximum conditioning and development.
9. Sports seasons are established to take advantage of the best weather situations.
10. The number of contests established is consistent with state association regulations.
11. The number of contests permitted is consistent with sound educational philosophy.
12. The number of contests is consistent with the financial capabilities of the school and the community.
13. The number of contests permitted is consistent with good physical, mental, and emotional health practices.
14. The number of contests is established by school authorities, not by outside interests.
15. Athletics are an integral part and an outgrowth of the physical education program.
16. The competitive program does not displace the instructional physical education program.
17. Facilities and equipment are appropriately scheduled for physical education and athletics.
18. An adequate intramural program is maintained for students whose skills and needs are not met by the interscholastic pro-

gram.

19. The sports program is flexible and scheduled to permit students to participate in both sports and other extracurricular activities.
20. Emphasis of the extracurricular program is placed on the development of a well-rounded student experience.
21. Sponsors of various extracurricular activities respect the student's desire and welfare during the student's participation in the activity.
22. Competitive schedules are developed on the basis of fair competition.
23. Competition at the state level is based on equitable school enrollment.
24. Coaches participate in the development of their schedules.
25. The community is kept informed of the competitive schedules.
26. Proper balance is maintained in scheduling home and away contests.
27. Out of season sports activities, where permitted, are agreed upon by coaches and administrators.
28. The entire athletic staff has an interest and appreciation for each member's program.
29. The department has regularly scheduled meetings to develop policy and resolve problems.
30. The athletic department is governed by a written policy.
31. Head coaches of each sport have a written policy governing the procedures for their sports.
32. Head coaches prepare daily practice schedules and brief assistant coaches concerning the schedule.
33. Ethical and professional behavior are practiced by all coaches in the department.
34. To maintain good staff relationships there is an equitable salary scale for all staff members.
35. Head coaches have an opportunity to participate in the selection and retention of personnel for their particular sport.
36. Excellence in coaching is recognized by the administration and is based on criteria other than winning; recognition is in the form of a yearly written evaluation.
37. A written evaluation of assistant coaches if provided for the athletic director by each head coach.
38. Coaches and administrators are consulted by state and local agencies controlling athletic activities.

Evaluation of the Relationship of the Athletic Program to the Community

1. The program meets the needs of the community, including its ethnic, religious, and financial, needs.
2. The community supports all phases of the athletic program.
3. School facilities are made available for community activities.
4. Community facilities are made available for school activities.
5. Athletic schedules do not conflict with community activities, such as religious services.
6. Community groups are given advance notice of all athletic schedules.
7. Community leaders make an effort to inform school officials of the community programs and activities.
8. Coaches have regularly scheduled meetings with parents to inform them of the desired goals of the athletic program, as well as other information.
9. Efforts are made through news media to inform the community of the goals of the athletic programs.
10. School officials maintain constant contact with interested groups, such as booster clubs and civic groups, so that club activities are in accord with the goals of the athletic program.
11. Members of the community and especially parents are informed in writing of school athletic policies.

Questions

1. What is the purpose of formally evaluating the interscholastic athletic program? Why isn't a cursory evaluation suffice?
2. Which criteria should be utilized in the evaluation of the interscholastic athletic program?
3. Which methods should be utilized in the valid evaluation of coaches and the athletic director?
4. From the educational standpoint of the administrator and the athletic director, how much weight should by put on the win-lost record of the coach in evaluating his performance.
5. What is the criteria utilized when evaluating the relationship of the athletic program to the total educational program?

REFERENCES

1. *Evaluating the High School Athletic Program*, National Council of Secondary School Athletic Directors—Division of Men's Athletics. American Alliance for Health, Physical Education and Recreation, 1973, Washington D.C. (Task force for evaluating the athletic program included Elmer Carpenter, Wichita Kansas; James Czanko, Kentwood, Michigan; Charles Hilton, Richmond, Indiana; Mark Dean, Dekalb, Illinois; and Robert Metcalf, Normal, Illinois.

SUGGESTED READINGS

Gallon, Arthur J. *Coaching: Ideas and Ideals.* Houghton Mifflin, Boston, 1974.

Palmieri, Joseph, "Solving the Problem of Evaluating Coaches," *Athletic Administration*, Vol 8, No. 1, Fall 1973, pp. 16-18.

Resnick, Matthew and Erickson, Carl E., *Intercollegiate and Interscholastic Athletics for Men and Women*, Addison-Wesley, Reading, Mass. 1975.

Sabock, Ralph, J. *The Coach*, W. B. Saunders, Philadelphia, 1973.

PART VI
MANAGEMENT FUNCTION: INNOVATING

The Changing Role for Girls' Athletic Competition: The Effect of Title IX Legislation

The most frequently discussed issue in recent years concerning athletic programs, particularly at the secondary and college levels, is the Title IX regulation that prohibits sex discrimination in education. The Title IX regulation, implementing education amendments of 1972, became effective on July 21, 1975. Succinctly, Title IX legislation requires that schools must provide equal opportunity for both sexes to participate in intramural, interscholastic, and intercollegiate athletics.

Title IX enhances opportunities for women in athletics, but it will also allow schools the flexibility they need to keep competitive sports alive. Probably the basic scope of Title IX and the heart of the regulation is nondiscrimination in admissions to educational institutions and sex discrimination in employment at the elementary and secondary school levels.

Basic Explanation of Title IX[1]

The regulations require each district to carry out a self-evaluation of all aspects of its policies, practices, and programs, and to take steps to make any changes that are needed during the present year, and implement the total program in a period of three years from the date the regulation became effective.

The regulations specify three steps to be taken as part of the self-evaluation:

1. An evaluation to identify any discrimination on the basis of sex.
2. Modification of policies and practices needed.
3. Appropriate steps to eliminate the effects of past discrimination.

Regulations Concerning the Requirements for Athletics

1. The regulations require equal opportunities for both men and women. However, the concern is with the totality of the program rather than with specific portions of it.
   A. Separate or coed teams in every sport are not required.
   B. Equal expenditures are not required.
   C. Additional opportunities are to be provided when opportunities for members of one sex have been limited in the past.
2. The regulation provides a checklist of eight areas to consider in evaluating the athletic programs:
   A. Whether the selection of sports and levels of competition effectively accommodate the interests and abilities of members of both sexes.
   B. The provision of equipment and supplies.
   C. Scheduling of games and practice time.
   D. Opportunity to receive coaching.
   E. Assignment and compensation of coaches.
   F. Provision of locker rooms, practice and competitive facilities.
   G. Provision of medical and training facilities and services.
   H. Publicity.
3. In respect to athletics and physical education, secondary schools are permitted three years for implementation.

Interpretation of Title IX

Notwithstanding the requirements of paragraph (a) of Section 86.41 of the amendment, a recipient may operate or sponsor separate teams for members of each sex where selection for such teams is based upon competitive skill or where the activity involved is a contact sport. However, where a recipient operates or sponsors a team in a particular sport for members of one sex but operates or sponsors no such team for members of the other sex, and athletic opportunities for members of that sex have previously been limited, members of the excluded sex must be allowed to try out for the team offered unless the sport involved is a contact sport. For the purposes of this part, contact sports included boxing, wrestling, rugby, ice hockey, football, basketball, and other sports the purpose of major activity of which involves bodily contact.

Equal Expenditures

Unequal aggregate expenditures for members of each sex or unequal expenditures for male and female teams if a recipient operates or sponsors separate teams will not constitute noncompliance with this section, but the director may consider the failure to provide necessary funds for teams for one sex in assessing equality of opportunity for members of each sex.

Adjustment Period

A recipient that operates or sponsors interscholastic or intramural athletics at the secondary school level shall comply fully with this section as expeditiously as possible but in no event later than three years from the effective date of this regulation.

COMPLYING WITH TITLE IX

Claudia Dodson, Girls' Sports Programs Supervisor, Virginia,[2] in her speech to the National Conference of High School Athletic Directors, suggested that in complying with Title IX, "First and foremost, support change or deletion of state association rules which discriminate on the basis of sex. Rules that need change may include: eligibility, training rules, curfews, and marital status of athletes; also administrative rules such as the number of games allowed per season, length of sport season, types of awards provided, travel reimbursement schedules, levels of competition provided, official's fees and stipends, and the requirements for coaches of teams may need revision. Regulations must be established without regard to sex."

Dodson also suggested, "To review the policies and practices of your school board or district council regarding: (1) Hiring policies of men and women coaches; (2) Payment of coaching salaries; (3) Benefits of coaches that is, office space, telephone, secretary; (4) Insurance for men and women teachers; (5) Provisions for team transportation; (6) Number of team uniforms provided; (7) Number of and levels of sports to be offered; and (8) Buying athletes' insurance coverage."

Virginia Whitaker, Assistant to the Athletic Director, Cherry Hill, New Jersey[3] states,

> Guidelines that will equalize athletic opportunities and eligibility for all participants must come from the very top, you state athletic associations. When state associations become involved, you will then be able to direct interscholastics for student athletes, not a girls' program and a boys' program, and this is as it should be. After all, our purposes are the same. I shall list a few:
> 1. To foster and develop amateur athletics among the high schools of our states.
> 2. To equalize athletic opportunities by standardizing rules of eligibility of individuals and classifying the high schools for competitive purposes.
> 3. To promote uniformity in the arrangement and control of contests.
> 4. To cultivate ideals of clean sport in their relation to the development of character and good citizenship.

Whitaker concluded: "We are faced with rapidly changing times. The athletics director of the '70's must be ready to meet this change just as he has met changes and challenges in the past."

GIRLS' ATHLETIC SPECIALIST[4]

The Beaverton School District in Beaverton, Oregon, which is a suburb of Portland, comprises 28 elementary schools, six junior high schools, three high schools, and approximately 20,000 students.

In order to keep pace with the growth and development of girls' athletics on the various levels mentioned above, it was decided that a specialist should be added to the district's administrative staff. The following rationale for this decision is instructive to those facing similar problems.

Development of the Program

The development of the athletic program in the Beaverton School District, particularly the girls' program, has increased tremendously in the past few years.

Planning, monitoring, and developing the rapid increase of the girls' program has placed additional demands on the Central Athletic Office.

To run an outstanding program it is important that coaches be given every opportunity to make their program succeed. This is accomplished when outstanding coaches are hired, and continued evaluation of the program and coaching staff takes place.

As a result of this overwhelming growth and development the position of Physical Education—Girls' Athletic Specialist became necessary. It will be the responsibility of the specialist to assist in the general administration of the program with particular emphasis on elementary physical education and girls' athletics.

Job Description—Womens' Athletic Specialist

Title
Physical Education—Girls' Athletics Specialist.

Function
The Physical Education—Girls' Athletics Specialist works under the direction of the Coordinator of Physical Education and Athletics and, at the request of the building principals, to provide necessary services to the staffs in the area of program development, revision, and coordination. The specialist is a resource person to building staffs and to central office personnel in matters pertaining to physical education and girls' athletics.

Responsibilities and Duties
The responsibilities and duties of the Physical Education—Girls' Athletic Specialist fall primarily in the instructional areas as described below.
The Specialist will:

1. Assist in identifying physical education curricular needs.
2. Provide advice and consultation in regard to district policy formation and priorities as they affect physical education and girls' athletics.
3. Provide structure and leadership to facilitate physical education curriculum change.
4. Help principals, department chairmen, building level inservice needs.
5. Identify district-wide physical education and girls' athletics inservice needs and recommend appropriate inservice programs to the Coordinator of Physical Education and Athletics.
6. Assist in planning, developing, and monitoring girls' athletics.
7. Assist in the evaluation and purchasing of physical education and athletic equipment and supplies.
8. Assist in the total promotion of the physical education and interscholastic athletics program, but only as they are educationally sound and in harmony with other phases of the total educational program of the district.
9. Assume other responsibilities and complete other duties as assigned by the Coordinator of Physical Education and Athletics.

Authority
The Physical Education—Girls' Athletics Specialist has authority as delegated by the Coordinator of Physical Education and Athletics.

Relationships

The Physical Education—Girls' Athletics Specialist is directly responsible to the Coordinator of Physical Education and Athletics and works closely in providing services to all principals and building staff members. In addition, the specialist works cooperatively with all persons who provide district-wide program services.

Skills and Abilities

The effectiveness of the Physical Education—Girls' Athletics Specialist is dependent upon the specialist's skills in all areas of the instructional program, i.e. group leadership, organization, communication, interpersonal relations and program evaluation.

THE TOTAL ATHLETIC PROGRAM

In discussing interscholastic athletics, today, the focus is on the student-athelte, not the boys' program or the girls' program. It is one program for all students, regardless of sex. This is obviously a change in direction from the established pattern of communication in the athletic program. The challenge that is now before the profession is a healthy challenge that can be wisely dealt with once the skeletons are out of the closet. As stated before in this chapter, the total program must begin with the state associations and the school administration and must be implemented by the athletic director and the combined athletic staff.

Dorothy E. McIntyre, Assistant to the Executive Secretary of the Minnesota High School League[5] suggests "that a plan should be developed by a school district for the purpose of implementing a total program for all students, which would include an implementation schedule for all sports, girls and boys, the budget for new and existing programs, a rationale for scheduling facilities, staff needs and resources, in-service training program for students, officials and coaches and public relations activities." McIntyre continues by stating that the plan could be implemented by the formation of an athletic council to include coaches of girls and boys teams, administrators, students, and appropriate community personnel.

The Athletic Council

1. The council should develop the athletic philosophy, the long-range blueprint of activities and the budget.
2. The council can establish mutual priorities and democratic decisions for all activities.

3. The council can develop the criteria used to determine salaries of coaches for girls and boys teams. The index may be based on ratios such as number of participants, length of season and number of games.
4. The council should develop a job description for the coach which delineates his or her responsibilities and assignments.
5. Individuals can learn about and develop an appreciation for the program of other coaches. It can help to enlarge the "tunnel vision" which is an affliction generally attributed to leaders of a specialized program.

FUTURE PLANNING

In the light of the rules and regulations stated in Title IX and the recent rulings by state associations concerning girls' eligibility for teams that were traditionally composed of males, there are several areas of concern to be considered.

In Chapter 1, "Problems and Forces Shaping Interscholastic Athletics Today and for the Future," we discussed interscholastic athletic problems affecting current girls' programs: the problem of inadequate coaching salaries for women; the problem of inadequate transportation for girls' athletic teams; and the problem of lack of qualified officials for girls' contest. Although these problems are not insurmountable, they are no longer just problems of the girls' athletic program, they are now problems of the total athletic program.

Other areas of concern in present and future planning are as follows: state athletic associations must increase the number of women coaches in their membership and encourage women to take an active part in the administration of these associations. The Division of Women and Girls Sports, The Academy of Women Coaches, and all other women's coaches associations should now combine into one organization. We do not infer that women should join men's athletic association, but that there should be one state athletic association for coaches, regardless of sex.

Colleges and universities must prepare more women for the coaching ranks. School administrators should encourage the women who are now physical education teachers in the high schools who, in some cases may not be too anxious to coach, to enroll in specialized classes and to attend clinics, seminars, and workshops in the areas of coaching, training, and treatment of injuries, which will prepare them for the interscholastic athletic program.

Administrators must consider the athletic program when hiring women teachers. At this time there are not enough qualified women coaches and it is difficult for the administration in charge of hiring to find applicants who have had athletic training. Professional preparation and certification were discussed in Chapter 9. Not uncommon questions asked by administrators today to job applicants are, "Will you be willing to coach a sport? What is your background in athletic training?"

The officials' associations will have to take leadership in training and encouraging women to officiate athletic contests. Most women would like to see girls' teams coached and officiated by women. However, with the rapid growth of girls' sports, this is not always possible. Other factors being equal, a woman should coach girls' teams and a man boys' teams. However, the most qualified person should be given preference. It is preferable to have a qualified man coach the girls than to assign a poorly qualified woman or vice versa.

Equality also means duties and responsibilities should be shared by all. Women should be cognizant of the slow growth of boys' athletics and the fact that its present status was not instantly achieved. Many accomplishments in boys' athletics are the result of the sincere dedication and hard work of the professionals in the field over a long span of time.

Administrators will have to find teachers outside of the girls' physical education department to supervise the pep clubs, song leaders, and drill teams so that the physical education teachers are free to coach. Some schools have delegated these clubs to the home economics and the business departments.

Women coaches should be prepared in the psychology of coaching. Many women physical education teachers have a basic knowledge of the team skills and the techniques of coaching, but need additional help in the field of the psychological problems involved with winning and losing, crowd pressures, and the many facets that are involved in competitive interscholastic athletics.

When Gwendlyn Armitage, President of the Pennsylvania State Athletic Directors Association[6]was asked why there weren't more women involved in athletic administration, she replied, "I find this area to be most deficient due to the passiveness displayed towards women's athletics over the past several decades. Suddenly, we find a great surge in women's athletics and lack of qualified personnel to coach and administer them. I feel that this can be alleviated by motivating girls interested in high school athletics to strive for a career in this field, which has been a common practice for boys for many years. Colleges have begun to make the move to prepare qualified young women to accept the responsibilities for coaching at the competitive level of today's high school athletics. However, it will take several years before the supply of qualified coaches catches up with the sudden demand."

SCHEDULING OF FACILITIES

Scheduling of facilities was discussed in Chapter 8, "Planning and Management of Athletic Facilities." Mutual cooperation has developed between the joint departments in this regard. As stated in Chapter 8, schedules have been drawn up so there will be no conflict with either girls' or boys' sports. Teams are practicing and using facilities at the same time in sports such as track and swimming. Much encouragement has been given to the girls' athletic teams and their coaches. Athletic directors have met the challenge by the increased cooperation of the coaching staffs of both departments, not only in scheduling and the use of facilities, but in meet management and organization of athletic contests.

As the initial aspects of the rules and regulations involving girls in interscholastic athletics settle down, it will develop that, by turning our efforts toward the girls, it will not restrict the activities of the boys' program. It will be a healthy innovation for all students. We, as professional educators, will truly reach our lifetime goal of education of the individual student rather than of a gifted few.

In the development of interscholastic athletic programs that are designed primarily for women and girls, many of the women professionals in the field are taking a careful look at the men's and boys' athletic programs. Many of them want to develop programs that are not mere imitations of the boys' and men's program. And they are making their opinions known to those in leadership positions; they are making clear how women feel about such issues as scouting, recruiting, scheduling contests during vacation periods and on weekends, and other practices that are commonplace in the men and boys' athletic programs. At this time, specific, noticeable trends have not surfaced pertaining to these issues in the girls' and women's athletic programs.

Questions

1. It has been said that Title IX legislation (July 21, 1975) has had (and will continue to have) the most profound effect on women's and girls' athletics than anything else that has occurred to this point in time. Succinctly explain Title IX legislation. Discuss the profound effects this legislation has had and will continue to have on women's and girls' athletics.

2. Does Title IX mean that girls must be given the opportunity to try out for the boys' football team? Must girls be given the opportunity to try out for the basketball team if there is only one team?

3. Does Title IX mean that boys must be given the opportunity to try out for a field hockey team, traditionally a sport for girls and women, if there is only one team at the high school? Explain each of your answers as you interpret Title IX legislation.

4. Since most boys' and men's athletic programs are well established as the result of being operable over a relatively long period of time, would the girls and women be better off to fashion their athletic programs after the boys' and men's programs or develop their own programs? Explain the rationale for your answer.

REFERENCES

1. Final Title IX Regulations Implementing Education Admendments of 1972. Office of Civil Rights, Health Education and Welfare, North Building, Washington, D.C. 20201.

2. Dodson, Claudia, *How to Comply with Title IX* Fifth Annual National Conference of High School Athletic Director's Proceedings, Hershey, Pa., 1974, p. 14. National Federation of State High School Associations, Elgin, Illinois. By permission.

3. Whitaker, Virginia, *Let's Take a Look at You, Mr. Athletic Director*, National Conference of High School Athletic Directors, Hershey, Pa., 1974, p. 18. National Federation of State High School Associations, Elgin, Illinois. By permission.

4. Pflug, Jerry, Coordinator of Physical Education and Athletics, Beaverton School District #48, Beaverton, Oregon 97005. *Physical Education—Girls Athletics Specialist.* By permission.

5. McIntyre, Dorothy E., *Girls Interscholastic Round Table*, p. 54-55, Fourth Annual National Conference of High School Athletic Directors Proceedings,

Chicago, Illinois, 1973.

6. Armitage, Gwendlyn, President, Pennsylvania State Athletic Directors Association, *Interview with Gwen Armitage*, Interscholastic Athletic Administration, Vol. 1, No. 3, 1975, p. 25. National Federation of State High School Associations, published by Spencer Marketing Services, New York, N.Y. 10017. By permission of the author.

SUGGESTED READINGS

Association for Intercollegiate Athletics for Women. *AIAW Handbook of Policies and Operating Procedures.* Published yearly. AAHPER. Washington, D.C., 1976.

Division of Girls and Women Sports. *Philosophy and Standards for Girls and Women's Sports.* AAHPER. Washington, D.C., 1973.

Flath, Arnold (ed.), *Athletics in America,* Oregon State University Press, Corvallis, Oregon, 1972.

Harris, Dorothy V. (ed.), *DGWS Research Reports: Women in Sports.* American Association of Health, Physical Education and Recreation, Washington, D.C., 1971.

Klafs, Carl E. and Lyon, Joan M., *The Female Athletic-Conditioning, Competition and Culture,* C. V. Mosby, St. Louis, 1973.

Poindexter, Hally B. W. and Mushier, Carole, *Coaching Guides for Women's Sports,* W.B. Saunders, Phildelphia, 1973.

Wakefield, Frances, Harkins, Dorothy, and Cooper, John M., *Track and Field Fundamentals for Girls and Women,* 3rd edition, C. V. Mosby, St. Louis, 1973.

Chapter 27

Athletic Director Leadership: Creativity, Innovativeness, and Motivation

ORGANIZATION—THE KEY TO SUCCESSFUL LEADERSHIP

The importance of sound organization can never be underestimated. If there is a secret to leadership, it lies in perfect organization. Therefore it is well to examine several dictionary definitions of the word *organization*.

> The act of process of grouping and arranging into one whole a set of parts dependent on one another.
>
> To cause to unite and work together in orderly fashion.
>
> A body made up of parts mutually dependent on one another.

Probably few athletics directors would ever acknowledge that they are poorly organized and fewer still that they are disorganized. Probably most athletic directors feel they are well organized, especially if they put in long hours at their job. Unfortunately, long hours on the job do not guarantee a well-organized department.

Time

Kurby Lyle, Supervisor of Athletics, Cherry Creek School, Englewood, Colorado, in his article *Staff Management*,[1] discusses the issue of time. "How you, the Athletic Director, control the destiny of your time to effectively manage your staff, will control your success or failure." Lyle breaks time down into three catagories: "Superior's imposed time, to accomplish those activities the boss requires;

387

System imposed time, to accommodate those requests to you for active support from your peers; self-imposed time, to do those things which you originate or agree to do yourself."

Every individual has the same amount of time available, 24 hours a day! How each individual utilizes his time is different, and obviously so is the difference in what one accomplishes. Time priorities must be made. The duties of the athletic director are never ending. Most high school athletic directors have multiple teaching-coaching duties, yet they must perform the middle management functions of their position. This takes planning on their part. Planning tasks usually suffer most when the day-to-day detail functions consume more time than there are hours to do them.

The duties and functions of the athletic director have been discussed in Chapter 3. However, it is imperative that we again refer to several key points in this chapter on leadership because the athletic director who cannot organize his time will not be an effective leader. Nor will he accomplish the many duties that he must perform on a daily basis.

As discussed by Lyles'[2],

There are things that must be done, there are some things that come up unexpectedly and there are many items that you have on the agenda that you want to get done. Perhaps the key to this dilemma is being organized to handle the unexpected. How often do you begin your day with the thought of what you will accomplish, those things you wish to make happen, only to be met by a staff member who greets you and proceeds to say, "By the way, we've got a problem"? This is not uncommon and you recognize in this problem the same two characteristics common to all the problems your staff members gratuitously bring to your attention. Namely, you know (a) enough to get involved, but (b) not enough to make the on-the-spot decision expected of you. Eventually you agree you are glad the problem was brought up, you have something else on your mind, so you suggest you give it some thought and will let the staff member know later.

   Your subordinate-imposed time began the moment you agreed to get back to the staff member. It was a "we" problem to begin with, but was expertly transferred to the singular by you, the AD. You accepted a responsibility for your subordinate, and promised a progress report.

   When you let this happen three to four times a day, you eventually have a backlog of subordinate-imposed problems that probably should not have been shifted from the staff member to the A.D.'s back in the first place.

The athletic director cannot spend all of his time solving the problems of others. He cannot be all things to all people. A choice must be made. The old axiom of "first things first" must take high priority if the job is to be accomplished.

One of the main qualities of leadership is organization, and organization begins with self-organization. The athletic director should have a plan for everything. There should be a reason for everything that an athletic director does in connection with the program. Otherwise, the program will lack purpose and direction and will not be geared to achieving optimal results. A good philosophy is to plan for all emergencies and you will not have too many of them.

There has to be time during the day to deal with the unexpected as well as to take care of the expected. One approach is to arrange office hours for the unexpected. "I will be available from 12:00-2:00, why don't you drop by and we can discuss the problem." In general, take care of all the action items, clear the desk, don't handle the same piece of paper twice, get the paper work taken care of, then perhaps you will be able to become a leader of the staff.

Attitude

The athletic director should pursue his work with enthusiasm, have loyalty to the school and staff members, and be creative and innovative in the approach to the tasks that lie ahead. The athletic director should dwell on the positive rather than the negative and should spend little time finding fault with the program or staff members.

One of the keys to leadership is the ability to motivate other people, the ability to direct people toward goals without antagonizing them. If the athletic staff respects the athletic director, he can lead them. How the athletic director handles the role of the leader will do much to determine the effectiveness of the interscholastic athletic program and the department.

The athletic director should be a self-motivated person who has set personal and professional goals and objectives for himself and the program.

Good performance in whatever job the athletic director undertakes is important. In order to accomplish this, the athletic director must know what is expected and how he will be judged. A good attitude may be described as a reflection of desirable characteristics, personal motivation, willingness to work hard, and initiative.

Initiative. The successful athletic director has initative, thinks, plans, and gives himself the best possible chance of completing a task. People with initiative are self-starters who jump into a task without prompting and who come up with new alternative ways of accomplishing tasks and getting the job done.

If a person moves into the position of athletic director without having made initiative a personal goal, he will limit his chances for success. Many people do not seek or desire the added responsibilities that belong to the athletic director's position. They are content in what they are doing and do not have the desire to direct or lead other people. They receive personal satisfaction in a nonmanagement role.

Being an athletic director requires more than just showing good leadership, although leadership is an important factor in the motivation of the staff. Basically, people want to be treated as human beings and, in some cases, athletic directors have not treated members of their staff as they expect themselves to be treated. The athletic director will soon realize he cannot be all things to all people.

Sound Personal Philosophy

A person's philosophy expresses the way in which he perceives things, events, relationships, and the values he places upon them. It is his point of view and his attitude toward people, places, and things.

The starting point for all achievement is desire and definiteness of purpose. Therefore, to become a successful athletic director, one must have a strong desire to be and to do.

If the athletic director is going to provide the necessary leadership to his staff and to the program, it is imperative that he develop a sound personal philosophy. The athletic director's thoughts must be well formulated and organized well enough to provide the direction necessary for a successful program. Knowledge is power only when it is organized into definite plans of action and directed to a definite end.

In developing a personal philosophy, it is important for an athletic director to establish a self-image. He should understand himself, his strengths, weaknesses, motives, desires, and drives and learn to live with them. This will facilitate handling success and failure, trials and tribulations, frustrations, and anxieties in striving to meet personal and professional goals and aspirations. As the late, great coach, Vince Lombardi said, "The quality of any man's life has got to be the full measure of that man's commitment to excellence and to victory regardless of what field he may be in."

Possible guidelines for an athletic director are as follows: (1) Be yourself, not only in what you do, but in who you are; (2) believe in the best of others; (3) choose your own style; (4) meet the needs of the staff; (5) use what is available; (6) employ an interaction approach, create support, facilitate interaction, and emphasize goals.

CREATIVITY IN LEADERSHIP

The successful leader will develop creativity in his staff. The leader will welcome productive and prolific ideas and will seek people who are imaginative, original, and innovative. Although we feel it is difficult to be original in today's world, in Biblical times what would have occurred if Noah had waited until after the flood to build the ark? What if Thomas Edison had not had the original thought about the light bulb? One of the great deterrents to creative thinking is one who retorts, "We tried that before and it won't work." Only athletic staffs with imagination will survive. Others just go through the motions. Many of us have been in areas where there are schools that never win any championships or win once every ten years. This is a result of the athletic administration and the feeling of its staff members. It has been said that athletics are neither good nor bad just because they are athletics. They are good or bad depending on the leadership they are given. This is true in the case of an athletic department or athletic director who is not creative and one that will not permit his staff to be creative. "Try it, you'll like it" might well be the slogan for this type of a department.

CREATIVITY IN MANAGEMENT

Drs. Sherman Tingey and Van R. Vibber, both Associate Professors of Management, Arizona State University in their article, "Creativity in Management",[3] pointed out managerial guideposts to increase creativity. Although they are talking mainly about creativity in business organizations, there seems to be a parallel for the athletic director and the athletic department. Drs. Tingey and Vibber set up the following four broad goals for fostering creativity:

The Organization must allow people to act more freely: Allow freedom for individuals to guide their own work. Provide them with specified and formally agreed upon areas of freedom and self-direction, gradually increasing these areas if evidence of growth in maturity and self-reliance warrants it.

Managers must welcome disagreement: Lead and motivate by suggestion rather than by command. Provide opportunity for a variety of experience, change, and learning. Allow people to try occasional pet ideas without premature prejudicial criticism.

Subordinates must be made responsible for change: Personal recognition should be provided for accomplishment. Excellence and extra effort should be rewarded, and special incentives should be established for achievers. Competence should be the primary consideration for advancement. A high value should be placed on creative effort.

Communication must be improved: Individuals should be allowed to participate in decision making and long range planning, particularly in areas which affect them. Personnel should be kept informed about important aspects of company operations, policies and goals. Interchange of information and opinion among groups and departments should be encouraged.

Tingey and Vibber recommend that "these suggested goals be used as a starting point in developing creativity."

GETTING THINGS DONE THROUGH OTHER PEOPLE

Dr. Ralph J. Sabock in his book *The Coach*[4] suggests some guidelines for competent leadership characteristics. The athletic director might well use the following list as a checkpoint in his relationship with members of the athletic staff.

1. Make people on your staff want to do things
2. Delegate responsibility for details to assistants
3. Be a good listener
4. Criticize constructively
5. Criticize in private
6. Praise in public
7. Be considerate
8. Give credit where it is due
9. Avoid domination

10. Show interest in and appreciation of the other fellow
11. Make your wishes known by suggestions or requests
12. Be sure to tell the reason for your requests
13. Let your staff know what your plans and programs are even when they are in the early stages
14. Never forget that the leader sets the style for his people
15. Play up the positive
16. Be consistent
17. Show your people that you have confidence in them and that you expect them to do their best
18. Ask your assistants for their counsel and help
19. When you are wrong or make a mistake, admit it
20. Give courteous hearing to ideas from your staff
21. If an idea is adopted, tell the originator why
22. Give weight to the fact that people carry out their own ideas best
23. Be careful what you say and how you say it
24. Don't be upset by moderate grousing
25. Use every opportunity to build up in a staff member a sense of their importance
26. Give your people goals, a sense of direction
27. Give staff members a chance to take part in decisions, particularly those affecting them
28. Keep your people informed on matters affecting them
29. Let your staff know where they stand

WHERE BOSSES FAIL

Some years ago, Charles F. Austin, Consultant in Executive Development, Human Relations and Organizational Behavior, discussed in his book, *Managements Self-Inflicted Wounds*[5] some definite points on "where bosses fail." Many of these points might well be studied by the athletic director as they pertain to his leadership role in interscholastic athletics.

His jobs are never completed before the deadline, he is a crisis manager.

He never passes along a memo without making changes. He is a nit-picking manager.

He never frankly tells his subordinate what he is really after. He is a hidden agenda boss.

He has an executive assistant, a right-hand man by any other name.

He is a boss with a deputy complex.

He never defends his employees in front of his superiors. He is a one-way loyalty boss.

He procrastinates decisions until they no longer are decisions. He is a no decision boss.

He feels personal contact with his employees doesn't befit his position as a manager. He is an unnecessarily lonely boss.

His door is open but he's guarded from contact with his employees by a series of complex procedures. He is a shielded boss.

He only wants to see his subordinates when he chooses to do so. He is a closed door boss.

He is often surprised by unanticipated events. He is a boss who is not ready for the unexpected.

Many of his important projects seem to get lost in the press of daily business. He is a boss who does not know what to neglect.

He has not identified his inadequacies. He is a boss who doesn't know what he doesn't know.

When he has a leadership problem, he refers to a handful of tried and true rules. He is a boss who manages by the rule book.

When something goes wrong, he wastes time wishing he hadn't. He is a boss who only wishes things were different.

Members of a committee that he appoints always seem to endorse his ideas. He is a boss who sabotages his committee.

He does not know the detailed characteristics of highly effective groups. He is an unaware-of-groups boss.

He frequently vetoes a younger man's suggestion to substitute his own with words, "Experience is the best teacher." He is a handicapped-by-experience boss.

He really believes that all problems can be solved by mathematical equations. He is a slide rule manager.

He can never catch up with the work load. He is an after-the-fact manager.

He wants to take credit for all work done in his department. He is a grab-the-credit boss.

He doen't feel that a subordinate deserves praise "just for doing his job." He is a slow-to-praise boss.

He thinks that the onlyr eason that a job gets done is because of the threat of punsihment he uses in line of authority. He is a boss who leans on the crutch of authority boss.

He uses the written disapproval because he doesn't have the nerve to do it face to face. He is a boss who lacks courage.

His secretay takes care of those letters of anniversary congratulations and even signs his name. He is an insincere boss.

He doesn't believe that anyone can effectively carry out his plans unless the person agrees with them. He is a brainwasher boss.

He keeps his official rating of his staff a secret from them. He is a secret performance appraisal boss.

He will dismiss any disapproval of his actions with the words, "I'm not running any popularity contest." He is an unpopular boss.

He doesn't care who does the job as long as it gets done. He is a boss who allocates the work unfairly.

He thinks looking busy is being busy; he thinks being busy is looking busy. He is a don't-let-me-catch-you-thinking boss.

He thinks that pinning the blame on someone will prevent future mistakes by his subordinates. He is a witch-hunter boss.

He uses memos for orders rather than face-to-face discussion. He is a one-way communication boss.

He makes up for his small physical stature by belittling others. He is a runt-complex boss.

He is intent on proving that every man has a breaking point. He is a human-erosion boss.

He is reluctant to promote anyone on the grounds that he's not ready for the job. He is a boss who neglects the development of his subordinates.

He always uses profanity in talking to his employees because he feels it's more effective. He is a vulgar boss.

He believes that disagreement among his staff is unhealthy business. He is a boss who doesn't want conflicts.

Anything that he does is right because he's the boss. He is a boss who is drunk with power.

He doesn't contribute as much effort as he should to his organization. He is a lazy boss.

He believes the only time anything gets done is when he's around. He is a breathe-down-the-neck boss.

He believes threats and fear are the only way to get the job done. He is a manage through fear boss.

Every project that he gives out has equal importance at any given time. He is a horizontal priority boss.

He knows how to do the work but he doesn't know how to get it done. he is a boss who doesn't use his staff.

He believes that as long as he gets rid of a symptiom the illness will desappear with it. He is a boss who treats the symptom and ignores the real cause of the problem.

His employees know that whatever proposal they offer, it will be watered down by everyone elses proposal. He is a boss who manages by compromise.

The loneliest man in his organization is the man with the new idea. He is a boss who stifles creativity.

He feels that all problems can be solved according to standard policies he's set up. He is a policy manager.

He believes that, if you concentrate on the smallest details, the whole will take care of itself. He is a boss who strains at gnats but swallows camels.

He believes that intangible rewards are hardly important in a corporate system. He is a boss who misuses recognition and awards.

He demands flattery and deference from the employees, even in a social situation. He is a boss whose boots must be licked.

There is no doubt that he can solve any problem before anyone can say "think." He is a solve the wrong problem boss.

He knows that his decisions are often retractable because he often makes decisions just to pacify one subordinate. He is a yo-yo boss.

There is no such thing as an honest mistake in his organization. He is a no-freedom-to-fail boss.

He wants all his people to act and think alike. He is a boss who craves conformity.

All he is interested in is results. He doesn't care what methods his subordinates use to get them. He is a result-at-any-price boss.

He surrounds himself with many assistants with no thought of his effect on the organization. He is a high-overhead boss.

He believes that it is better to make a wrong decision than no decision at all. He is an often-in-error, never-in-doubt boss.

Supervision is an absolute; it cannot vary in kind with different organizations. He is a boss who worships the unity of command concept.

He tries to solve the problems by reshaping his organization. He is a reorganizer boss.

He's the first one to say that informal personnel relationships have no bearing on the job he's doing. He is a boss who ignores the informal organization.

What his organization does it its problem, he declares himself innocent of any action by higher-ups. He is a boss who does not carry the conscience of his organization.

HOW TO DESTROY IDEAS

In their seminars of Positive Image Building, The Pacific Institute of Seattle, Washington[6] list what they call "Killer Phrases," statements leaders make that destroy ideas and chloroform creative thinking. Some of the more common statements are:

A swell idea, but....
We've never done it that way before....
Too modern....
Too old fashion....
We haven't the time....
It's not in the budget....
Too expensive....
We've tried that before....
Good idea, but our school is different....
All right in theory, but can you put it in practice....
Too academic....
Too much paperwork....
It's not good enough....
There are better ways that that....
Who do you think you are....
Let's not step on their toes....
Let's discuss it at some other time....
Let's form a committee....
Let's shelve it for the time being....
Not ready for it yet....
Too hard to administer....
Too early....
It needs more study....
It's against school policy....
You haven't considered....
Somebody would have suggested it before if it were any good....

POSITIVE APPROACH TO LEADERSHIP

On the other side of the coin, the Pacific Institute lists what they call "Igniter Phrases," positive approach to leadership. Some of the more common igniter phrases are:

I agree....
That's really neat....
I made a mistake, I'm sorry....
You're doing better....

Super....
I looked at this last night and really like it....
That's good....
Good job....
Let's go....
That's a great idea....
I'm glad you brought that up....
I like the way you came in today and got the job done....
That would be interesting to try....
Things are beginning to pop....
Good work....
I couldn't do that well myself....
You're on the right track....
Great idea, I know it will work....

THE MASLOW THEORY

Psychologists recognize that a person's primary and secondary needs must be satisfied first. As the more basic needs are mets, a person seeks to satisfy higher needs. If the basic needs are not met, they claim priority, and efforts to satisfy higher needs must be postponed. A need priority of five levels is explained by A. H. Maslow[7 and 8] as follows:

1. Basic physiological needs.
2. Safety and security.
3. Belonging and social activity.
4. Esteem and status.
5. Self-realization and fulfullment.

Although a detailed discussion of Dr. Maslow's human needs priority is outside the scope of this book, any discussion on motivation must include at least a few comments on his theory. Briefly, the first two levels are primary human needs dealing with survival and are primarily satisfied through economic behavior. The other three levels are human needs of the mind and spirit and are primarily satisfied through symbolic behavior of psychic and social content.

What significance does Maslow's human needs theory have for the athletic director, both personally and professionally, who is in a leadership position in middle management? Succinctly, the athletic director must motivate by trying to aid subordinates and coassociates to move to satisfy higher order needs. When lower order needs are satisfied, it becomes one's wish to satisfy higher level needs. Although it is some time argued that third level needs of belonging, affection, and social activity may be met away from work, many hours are spent on the job. For one involved in athletic administration and coaching, a 60-hour work week is not uncommon. Therefore, some of the individual's belonging needs are met at work. We need to have, receive, and to give esteem and status to satisfy the fourth level of basic needs. We need to feel inside ourselves that we are worthy, to feel also that others think we are worthy (status), and to believe that they likewise are worthy. Much of this depends on how we view human dignity and our fellowman.

The fifth basic need is self-realization, which means to become all that one is capable of becoming. This need is less apparent than the others because many persons have not unleashed it. Though self-realization dominates few people, it influences nearly all persons. To those who are operating on this top priority need level and to those seeking this level, work satisfaction is tremendously important. They find their work a challenge and the result is inner satisfaction.

The athletic director who deals with faculty members and coaches in today's society will find that Maslow's first two level needs have been moderately well met. However, there is increasing emphasis on third priority social needs; the third need as well as other two higher order needs all heavily involve human relations. What the need priority model essentially says is that gratified needs are no longer strongly motivating. Faculty members and coaches, as well as many other employees, are enthusiastically motivated by what they are seeking, more than by what they already have. Any leader trying to motivate employees, including an athletic director working with associates and subordinates, should emphasize ways to meet and satisfy high priority human needs, including helping individuals to actualize their potential.

Questions

1. Discuss the statement, "Others are more likely to follow a leader who leads by example, rather than one who leads by merely telling others what to do." Does this mean an athletic director

leads by doing the tasks and chores himself rather than asking or directing others to do them?

2. Enumerate and discuss ways a leader can motivate others, such as an athletic director motivating the coaching and supportive staff members.

3. What are some personal guidelines one could follow in assuming a position of leadership, such as a person being named athletic director for the first time in his career?

4. Since the athletic director is in a leadership role, that person is often identified as "the boss" even though this may not be his leadership style. Enumerate and discuss some undesirable leadership charactistics that could contribute to "where 'bosses' fail."

5. Does A.H. Maslow's "order of priority of human needs" theory apply to motivation and the human relations aspect of the athletics director's position? How?

REFERENCES

1. Lyle, Kurby, Supervisor of Athletics for the Cherry Creek Schools, Englewood, Colorado, November-December *Staff Management* (Part 2) Interscholastic Athletic Administration, Summer 1975, Vol. 1, No. 3, p. 32, adapted from "Management Time: Who's Got the Monkey," *Harvard Business Review*, 1974. Original article was written by William Onchen, Jr. and Donald L. Wass.

2. Ibid.

3. Tingey, Sherman and Vibber, Van R., "Creativity in Management," from Management Services 5:44 July & August, 1968, Ch. 4. By permission of Dr. Sherman Tingey, Associate Professor of Management, Arizona State University, Tempe, Arizona 85281.

4. Sabock, Ralph J., *The Coach*, W.B. Saunders, Philadelphia, 1973, p. 203. By permission. Originally appeared in Air Force R.O.T.C. Air University Leadership Training, 1968, p. 32.

5. Austin, Charles F., "Where Bosses Fail." Reprinted by permission from *Nations Business*, October 1966, Copyright 1966 by *Nation's Business*, Chamber of Commerce of the united States. Tokuma Shoten Publishing Company Tokyo, Japan—By permission.

6. Goforth, Jeff, The Pacific Institute, Pacific Institute Seminar, 1975, Seattle, Washington. By permission.

7. Maslow, A.H., "A Theory of Human Motivation," *Psychological Review*, Vol. 50, pp. 370-396, 1943.

8. Maslow, A.H., *Motivation and Personality*, Harper and Row, New York, 1954.

SUGGESTED READINGS

Davis, Keith, *Human Relations at Work: Human Relations and Organizational Behavior* 4th edition McGraw-Hill, New York, 1972, Ch. 2, Leadership, pp. 100-117 and Ch. 3, Mainsprings of Motivation, pp. 42-62.

Dubin, R., *Human Relations in Administration* 3rd edition, Prentice-Hall, Englewood Cliffs, N.J., 1968.

Goble, Frank, *The Third Force, The Psychology of Abraham Maslow*, Pocket Books, A Division of Simon and Schuster, New York, 1970.

Maslow, A.H., *Toward A Psychology of Being* 2nd edition, Van Nostrand-Reinhold, New York, 1970.

PART VII
MANAGEMENT FUNCTION: REPRESENTING

403

Chapter 28

The Controlling Force
of the National
and State Associations

In the final analysis, the superintendent of schools, acting as executive officer for the board of education, is responsible for the athletic activities of the school system. The superintendent, who undoubtedly will delegate many duties to subordinate personnel, relies heavily on the national and state athletic associations for leadership in planning, directing, and controlling the high school interscholastic athletic program in his school district.

State interscholastic athletics or activities associations have been important factors in improving and maintaining high standards for the administrative control of interscholastic athletics. Each state association establishes the responsibility for the administration of interscholastic athletics in order to increase the educational value of the programs throughout the state and to establish a feasible plan for conducting play and determining championships.

State associations do not interfere in any manner whatsoever with the local autonomy of schools, but rather devote themselves to the elimination of excesses and abuses of overenthusiastic promotion that accompanies athletic activities.

State associations also promote the acceptance of the Cardinal Principles and Code of Ethics as set up by the National Federation of State High School Athletic Associations. It should be understood that state athletic associations have quasi-official status in most cases in that schools voluntarily affiliate and that the state association is primarily a regulatory body. Throught the state association affiliation with the national federation, interstate uniformity is maintained.

PURPOSES OF THE STATE ASSOCIATIONS

State associations assist in setting the regulations of competition so that the athletic program fits into the total school curriculum and guides the interscholastic athletic program so as to safeguard the physical welfare of the students participating.

State athletic associations provide assistance to schools in planning and developing a better athletic program by supervision of athletic contests and advising schools on athletic problems. Standards of competition are established pertaining to age, semesters in school, scholarship, residence, transfers, and amateur standing to prevent proselyting of high school athletes and to eliminate the exploitation of high school students because of their athletic prowess.

State Associations Serve the Schools

Although the state association's specific functions are concerned largely with eligibility regulations and other administrative details, they also serve the high school in other ways.

Insurance Benefits. State associations provide supplementary insurance at nominal nonprofit cost for medical care, hospitalization, and accidental death coverage as required by the education code.

Coaching Clinics. Rules meetings and clinics for coaches and officials in the various sports are conducted yearly. In conjunction with other organizations, meetings and clinics are conducted on crowd accommodation, new methods and techniques of coaching, injury prevention, conditioning and training, and the medical aspects of athletics.

Resource Materials. Printed materials such as eligibility forms, contracts, handbooks, and sports rule books are distributed to member schools. Monthly bulletins provide up-to-date material and minutes of the state association meetings.

Cooperation with Professional Associations. The state association works with professional associations such as the school administrators, medical associations, state and national associations for health, physical education and recreation, and state coaches and athletic directors associations in coordinating appropriate activities.

Consultant Services. The state association provides, upon request, consultant services for athletic programs.

The state association allies itself with the National Federation of State High School Athletic Associations to attain uniformity and mutual benefits of cooperative action. Interstate competition is regulated through the cooperation of the officials of the two groups.

The state association is divided in sections and leagues. Each section and league is coordinated by a commissioner who is responsible to the state commissioner. In most of the large states, the executive board of the state association is made up of high school principals who then become the governing force of interscholastic athletics. A very desirable recent trend is to have members of the State Athletic Directors Association and the State Coaches Associations on the governing boards. In earlier days, state athletic associations were superintendent and principal oriented.

PURPOSES OF THE NATIONAL FEDERATION OF STATE HIGH SCHOOL ASSOCIATIONS

The National Federation of State High School Associations was organized primarily to secure proper adherence to the eligibility rules of the various state association during interstate contests and meets. As the prestige of the national organization grew, the program for the sanctioning of interstate meets was developed. The latter led to definite action relative to national and sectional athletic events. The scope of the National Federation work has broadened so that all high school athletic and nonathletic groups profit through an exchange of experience and a pooling of interests.

The National Federation maintains a relationship with such professional educational organizations as the National Education Association, the United States Office of Education, the Amateur Athletic Union, The American Alliance for Health, Psysical Education and Recreation, and the National Association of Secondary School Principals. The National Federation has a close working relationship with the National Collegiate Athletic Association (NCAA) especially in the area of televising professional football games, recruitment, and all-star games to insure they are not detrimental or have a negative effect on interscholastic athletics.

To a lesser extent the NFSHSAA coordinates matters of mutual interest with the National Association of Interscholastic Athletics (NAIA) and the National Junior College Athletic Association

(NJCAA). The National Federation supplies reprints of position papers dealing with everyday problems of the athletic director, philosophical articles, information on trends in modern-day athletics, information, and help on legislative matters and legal aid. The National Federation subsidizes the National Conference of High School Directors of Athletics and distributes 12,000 copies of their proceedings annually at no cost to athletic directors and school administrators throughout the country.

Basic Belief

The activities of the National Federation are based on the belief that strong state and national high school athletics organizations are necessary to protect the activity and athletic interest of high schools, to promote an ever-increasing growth of the type of interscholastic athletics that is educational in both objectives and method and that can be justified as an integral part of the high school curriculum, and to protect high school students from exploitation for purposes with little educational implication.

Services of the National Federation.[1] "The growth of size and influence of the state high school associations and their National Federation insure some degree of teamwork on the part of more than 22,000 high schools and more than five (5) million participants and this teamwork has enabled them to formulate policies and plans for improving high school athletic conditions and to make these plans function."

The National Federation Serves the State Associations. The National Federation has been a service organization since its inception. It was founded on the premise that it would provide service to individual state associations. Adapting sports to the high school program is necessary if the best interests of the high school student are to be served. Secondary school youth have needs different from athletes at other levels and, therefore, sports activities must be tailored to satisfy these needs if they are to best serve their purpose. This has been done through scientific study of the relationship of these sports to the high school program and the establishment of machinery whereby the nature of the game is influenced by the people in direct charge of high school athletics and by a system of experimentation and observation.

Among the services provided by the National Federation are a nationwide program of athletic experimentation and testing and authorized experimentation of rule variation. National Federation publications encourage uniformity and increased efficiency in contest management. The rules writing program was inaugurated by the National Federation in order to insure that high schools would have a voice in developing playing rules that govern interscholastic competition.

The various federation publications include an edition of the official basketball rules, baseball rules, Alliance track and field rules, and records; these publication have a circulation of more than 2,000,000 copies, which are distributed to member schools and associations. Other publications currently being printed include girls' basketball, boys' and girls' gymnastics and soccer.

NATIONAL OPERATING COMMITTEE FOR SAFETY IN ATHLETIC EQUIPMENT

Research programs have been developed and maintained for the purpose of safety and comfort in athletic equipment. The research committee, consisting of representatives from the Athletic Goods Manufacturers Association, the American College Health Association, the National Collegiate Athletic Association, and many other groups has authorized in-depth experimentations of protective equipment.

The NOCSAE Has Stated Its Objectives as Follows:[2]

1. To promote, conduct and foster research, study and analyze the collection of data and statistics relating to athletic equipment with a view to encouraging the establishment of standards in the manufacture and use thereof for the benefit of amateurs.

2. To disseminate information and promote, conduct and foster other activities designed to increase knowledge and understanding of the safety, comfort, utility and legal aspects of athletic equipment.

3. To provide a forum in which individuals and organizations may consult and cooperate in considering problems relating to athletic equipment.

4. To do all of the foregoing exclusively for charitable, educational and scientific purposes.

NOCSAE was formed in answer to the need for high quality standards for any athletic equipment in which safety is involved in its use. [See Chapter 22, "Safety Considerations in Interscholastic Athletics."] This is an on-going committee which intends to investigate all aspects of all school sports so they may be made as safe as possible for the participants.

CARDINAL ATHLETIC PRINCIPLES

These principles, as stated in the *National Federation of State High School Associations Official Handbook*,[3] were drawn up by a joint committee representing the National Federation and the American Alliance for Health, Physical Education and Recreation.

Schools provide opportunity for each individual to develop himself to the limit of his capacity in the skills, appreciations and health concepts which engender personal satisfaction and civic usefulness. A good school program includes the means for exploring many fields of activity. One such field is that which involves athletic performance. Participation in and appreciation of the skills in a sports contest is a part of enjoyable living. Ability to recognize degrees of proficiency in these skills is one important attribute of the well balanced individual. The perfectly timed and coordinated activities by which an individual or a team strives to achieve a definite objective is an exemplification of cooperation and efficiency. A good school program provides a mixture of benevolent restrictions and freedoms, of mental growth and physical development, of liberties and restraints. Developing and maintaining a physically fit nation is one of its important aims. For developing endurance, strength, alertness and coordination, contests and conditioning exercises have been made a part of the school program.

Nature wisely insured a degree of physical development and social adjustment by endowing the individual with a desire to play. Around this desire as a nucleus, can be built a complete program of beneficial exercises in which healthful and satisfying habits and attitudes are stressed.

To Be of Maximum Effectiveness, the Athletic Program Should

1. Be closely coordinated with the general instructional program and properly articulated with other departments of the school.
2. Be sure that the number of students accommodated and the educational aims achieved justify the use of tax funds for its support and also justify use of other sources of income, provided the time and attention which is given to the collection of such funds is not such as to interfere with the efficiency of the athletic program or of any other department of the school.
3. Be based on the spirit of non-professionalism so that participation is regarded as a privilege to be won by training and proficiency and to be valued highly enough to eliminate any need for excessive use of adulatory demonstrations or of expensive prizes or awards.

4. Confine the school athletic activity to events which are sponsored and supervised by the proper school authorities so that exploitation or improper use of prestige built up by school teams, or members of such teams, may be avoided.
5. Be planned so as to result in opportunity for many individuals to explore a wide variety of sports, and in reasonable season limits for each sport.
6. Be controlled so as to avoid the elements of professionalism and commercialism which tend to grow up in connection with widely publicized "bowl" contests, barnstorming trips and interstate or intersectional contests which require excessive travel expense or loss of school time or which are bracketed with educational travel claims in an attempt to justify privileges for a few at the expense of decreased opportunity for many.
7. Be kept free of the type of contest which involves a gathering of so-called "all stars" from different schools to participate in contests for the benefit of colleges or professional organizations who are interested in soliciting athletic talent.
8. Include training in conduct and games ethics to reach all non-participating students and community followers of the school teams in order to insure a proper understanding and appreciation of the sports skills and the need for adherence to principles of fair play and right prejudices.
9. Encourage a balanced program of intramural activity in grades below the ninth grade to make it unnecessary to sponsor contest of championship nature in these grades.
10. Engender respect for the local, state and national rules and policies under which the school program is conducted.

To promote and stimulate safe and healthful participation among a high percentage of secondary school boys and girls in a wide variety of wholesome athletic activities and after careful study of the problems that have been created by certain types of interscholastic contests (including meets, tournaments, national championships, contests that require distant travel, contests that are sponsored by individuals or organizations other than a high school or group of high schools, and contest between teams of high school all-stars), the Joint Committee makes the following recommendations.

The Joint Committee urges that all of the organizations represented adopt these major interpretations and place them in the form of policies, standards or regulations in accordance with the established practice of each organization.

1. The program of athletics should be developed with due regard for health and safety standards as set forth in *Suggested School Health Policies* of the American Medical Association.

2. Good citizenship must result from all coaching and from all interschool competition. The education of the youth of the nation fails unless it creates the proper ideals and attitudes both in the game and off the field.

3. The ten "Cardinal Athletic Principles" are accepted as expressing the policies of our organization, and it is urged that these be displayed in the literature of our organizations.

4. All schools shall use reasonable care in avoiding any participation in a contact sport between participants of normal high school age and participants who are appreciably above or below normal high school age.

5. All schools shall fully observe and abide by the spirit and letter of established eligibility requirements which have been democratically developed by each of the state athletic associations.

6. Each state athletic association should attempt to secure the cooperation which would provide a plan of continuous eligibility from high school to college.

7. For competition in which only one state is involved, no school shall participate in a meet or tournament involving more than two schools unless such contest has been approved by its state high school association or its delegated constituent or allied divisions.

8. The use of school facilities or members of the school staff shall not be permitted in connection with any post-season or all-star contest unless such contest has been sanctioned by the state athletic association.

9. A school shall not permit any employee or official to encourage or collaborate in any negotiations which may lead a high school athlete to lost his eligibility through the signing of a professional contract.

10. The solicitation of athletes through try-outs and competitive bidding by higher institutions is unethical and unprofessional. It destroys the amateur nature of athletics, tends to commercialize the individual and the program, promotes the use of athletic skill for gain, and takes an unfair and unjust advantage of competitors.

11. In all interstate athletic contests, each athlete shall compete under eligibility rules which are at least as restrictive as those adopted by the state high school athletic association of his state, except in the case of schools which are not eligible for membership in their state associations.

12. No school shall compete in any of the following contests unless

such contest has been sanctioned by each of the interested state high school athletic associations through the National Federation: (a) any interstate tournament or meet in which three or more schools participate; (b) any interstate two-school contest which involves a round trip exceeding 600 miles; (c) any interstate two school contest (regardless of the distance to be traveled), which is sponsored by an individual or an organization other than a member high school.

13. No basketball tournament which is purported to be for a interstate high school championship will be sanctioned, and no basketball tournament involving schools or more than one state shall be sanctioned unless the tournament is purely community in character.

14. No contest which is purported to be for a National High School Championship in any sport shall be sanctioned.

RELATIONSHIPS WITH OTHER ORGANIZATIONS[4]

The National Federation and the state associations have a working relationship with many other organizations, for example:

□ American Alliance for Health, Physical Education and Recreation
□ National Association of School Administrators
□ National Association for Sport and Physical Education of AAHPER
□ National Association for Girls and Women in Sport of AAHPER
□ Association of Intercollegiate Athletics for Women (AIAW)
□ The Athletic Institute
□ Amateur Basketball Association of the USA
□ National Collegiate Athletic Association
□ National Association of Intercollegiate Athletics (NAIA)
□ Amateur Basketball Association of the USA
□ National Collegiate Athletic Association
□ National Recreation and Parks Association
□ National Council of Secondary School Athletic Directors
□ National Junior College Athletic Association (NJCAA)
□ The President's Council on Physical Fitness and Sports
□ United States Olympic Committee
□ United States Collegiate Sports Council
□ United States Track and Field Federation

NATIONAL COUNCIL OF SECONDARY SCHOOL ATHLETIC DIRECTORS

The operating code for this council was established in 1969 with the following statement, "The name of this Council shall be the National Council of Secondary School Athletic Directors of the National Association for Sport and Physical Education of the American Alliance for Health, Physical Education and Recreation."

Purposes of the Council

The purpose of this Council shall be:

1. To improve the educational aspects and articulation of interscholastic athletics in the total educational program.
2. To foster high standards of professional proficiency and ethics.
3. To improve athletic understanding and relationship throughout the nation.
4. To establish closer working relationships with related professional groups.
5. To promote greater unity, good will and fellowship among all members.
6. To provide for an exchange of ideas.
7. To assist and cooperate with state athletic directors organization.
8. To assist in the organization of state athletic directors' councils.
9. To provide a national forum for the exchange of current practices and the discussion of evolving trends in the administration of athletics.
10. To make available to members special resource materials through publications, conferences, and consultant services.

Membership. Membership shall be open to all members of AAHPER who have the primary responsibility for directing, administering, or coordinating the interscholastic athletic program at the junior or senior high school level.

Membership will also be open to directors of athletics who administer or coordinate interscholastic athletic programs for a school district.

Memberships with other Organizations. The relationship of the NCSSAD with other organizations:

□ National Association for Sport and Physical Education
□ National Intramural Sports Council of AAHPER (NISC)
□ National Council of State High School Coaches Associations of AAHPER
□ The National Association of Secondary School Principals
□ The American Association of School Administrators
□ United States Collegiate Sports Council (NCAA, NAIA, NJCAA, NACDA, AAHPER)
□ United States Olympic Committee
□ President's Council on Physical Fitness and Sports

NATIONAL HIGH SCHOOL ATHLETIC COACHES ASSOCIATION[5]

The NHS/ACA was organized in 1965 for the following purposes:

1. To give greater national prestige and professional status to high school coaching.
2. To conduct a convention and clinic in different parts of the nation each year, providing coaches with an opportunity to meet coaches from other areas and exchange ideas on coaching problems.
3. To honor members of the profession.
4. To provide a medium for projecting the high school coaches' views and interests at the national level.

Dwight Keith, Atlanta, Georgia, was truly the founder and architect of the national organization and executive secretary for the first pioneering years of the National High School Athletic Coaches Association. From a beginning membership of a few hundred, the membership grew to 20,000 in 1975 and 45 states were represented at the annual convention. Seventeen states enroll their entire membership while seven other states and several colleges and manufacturers have sponsoring memberships. The projected membership for the coming decade is 50,000. The potential for service to athletics is tremendous. Carey McDonald, Orlando, Florida has assumed the executive director's position.

The outgoing president of the NHS/ACA, Jimmie Bryan, who is

also secretary of the Virginia High School Coaches Association, stated at the 1975 convention, "I believe that the NHS/ACA is becoming the potent force in high school athletics in America, a guiding light. It has established leadership among high school coaches and is recognized by most local, state and national athletic organizations. Its possibilities are boundless, the first ten years have just been the beginning."

STATE ATHLETIC DIRECTORS ASSOCIATIONS

There has been a rapid growth of state athletic directors associations throughout the nation. At the present time there are 35 state athletic directors associations: California, Colorado, Florida, Hawaii, Idaho, Illinois, Indiana, Iowa, Kansas, Kentucky, Louisiana, Maine, Massachusetts, Michigan, Minnesota, Mississippi, Missouri, Montana, Nebraska, New Hampshire, New Jersey, North Carolina, North Dakota, Ohio, Oklahoma, Oregon, Pennsylvania, Rhode Island, South Dakota, Tennessee, Texas, Vermont, Virginia, Washington, and Wisconsin.

In addition to yearly state conferences, athletic directors have the opportunity to attend regional conferences and the National Conferences and the National Conference of High School Directors of Athletics sponsored by the National Federation of State High School Associations.

STATE COACHES ASSOCIATIONS

Each state has a coaches' association that furthers cooperation between the high school interscholastic program and the state athletic association. Most coaches associations have representation on the board of the state athletic association, which brings about a closer relationship with the coaching profession and the administration. Each state organization is a member of the National Federation of State High School Associations and operates under its own constitution for the welfare of the athletic activities in its state.

Purpose of State Coaches Associations

Each state association is charged with a purpose, some of the more common are:

1. To develop within the coaches a deeper sense of responsibility in developing, maintaining, and conducting interscholastic athletics.
2. To foster and encourage the playing of athletics in accordance with the highest traditions of interscholastic competition.
3. To correlate the athletic program with the general objectives of education.
4. To encourage and promote better teaching conditions and standards.
5. To maintain a membership group, representative of various sections of the state.

In general, the philosophy of State Coaches Associations is to provide a professional organization, uniting all coaches of the state, dedicated to the maintaining of the highest standards for athletic competition and coaching conditions in the state.

Questions

1. What are the advantages of a coach or athletic director affiliating with the state coaches association and state athletic directors association?
2. Explain what is meant by the title of this chapter, "The Controlling Force of National and State Associations." What are the purposes of the National Federation of State High School Athletic Associations?
3. Discuss how the objectives of the National Operating Committee for Safety in Athletic Equipment are designed to protect the student-athlete and the school's administrators, including the coach, athletic director, and members of the board of education.
4. A promotor wants to stage an "all-star" football game in early August with the game's financial proceeds reputedly going to a worthwhile charity. He wants to use "stars" who graduated from high school the previous June and have local high school coaches handle the coaching duties. Can any sanctions be imposed on the "stars" and by whom? Can any sanctions be imposed on the coaches to prohibit them from accepting such coaching assignments, even though they are on vacation and not under contract at their respective high schools during the summer months? Can any promoter merely organize and stage such an "all-star" game or must the promoter first get a sanction to do so? If your answer.

is affirmative, what is the procedure and to whom would the promoter apply for sanction to stage the "all-star" high school game? If your answer is negative, why would anyone object to an "all-star" high school football game where most of the graduated seniors who will be participating have probably received athletic scholarships anyway. The coaches have a chance to earn a little money and the recognition of coaching an "all-star" game. If the game is being played for a worthwhile charity, what is the harm?

REFERENCES

1. Fagan, Dr. Clifford B., Executive Secretary, *National Federation of State High School Association Handbook*, National Federation of State High School Associations, 400 Leslie St., Elgin, Ill. 60120. By permission.
2. National Operating Committee for Safety in Athletic Equipment, National Federation of State High School Association. By permission.
3. National Federation of State High School Associations and American Alliance for Health, Physical Education and Recreation Joint Committee on Standards, National Federation of State High School Association. By permission.
4. Merrick, Dr. Ross, National Council of Secondary School Athletic Directors, American Alliance for Health, Physical Education and Recreation, Washington D.C. 20036. By permission.
5. McDonald, Carey E., Executive Director, National High School Athletic Coaches Association, P.O. Box 16042, Orlando, Florida 32811.

Chapter 29

Counseling and Guidance for the Student-Athlete

A recent survey by the National Federation of State High School Associations revealed that only 1 out of 29 high school football players received full grant-in-aid scholarships. This statistic is mentioned only to assure the reader that the main goal is not and should not be to develop college or professional athletes. Nor does the board of education dictate that it is the role of the coach or the athletic director to assure a high school athlete of a college scholarship.

However, because the grant-in-aid (athletic scholarships) make up 20 percent of all aid given to students, it should be one of the functions of the high school athletic director and the high school coach to offer assistance as counselor to the student-athlete.

The athletic director or coach can be of valuable help if the student-athlete qualifies financially and athletically for a grant-in-aid scholarship. College recruiting is a highly competitive business and because of the counselor's experience in such matters, he can give positive direction if it is desired.

CRITICAL FACTORS IN RECRUITING

Drs. P.E. Allsen and Elmo Roundy of Brigham Young University[1] in an effort to study the factors that influence a star high school athlete to select a particular college, selected 64 football and 51 basketball players from colleges who were representative of NCAA geographical districts and who had records of excellence in basketball and football. The players contacted were the three best freshman basketball prospects and the five best freshman football prospects as selected by the head coaches of the respective sports.

Reason for Selecting a School

On a scale of 1 to 10, with 1 being the highest and 10 being the lowest, the football players listed the following reasons for selecting a school:

1. Football tradition (3.2)
2. Coaching staff (3.4)
3. Educational Opportunities (3.7)
4. Campus facilities (4.9)

The basketball players listed the following reasons:

1. Coaching staff (2.3)
2. Basketball tradition (3.0)
3. Educational opportunities (4.4)
4. Style of ball played (4.8)

The obvious results of the survey point out that a coach's personality has a lot to do with his recruiting success or failure and that a winning tradition rates very high on the scale when it comes to the recruit's final decision.

Drs. Allsen and Roundy came up with some other noteworthy results in their survey. Basketball players are more heavily recruited than football players because one "superstar" in basketball can turn an entire program into a success whereas in football, it is hardly possible for one athlete to turn a program around, regardless of his potential.

The study by Drs. Allsen and Roundy should by regarded as only a beginning in determining why high school athletes select a particular college.

GRANT-IN-AID SCHOLARSHIPS

Grant-in-aid scholarships are limited in amount by the National Collegiate Athletic Association and the National Association of Intercollegiate Athletics. A full grant-in-aid scholarship includes room and board, tuition, and books. The financial aid for incidental expenses was eliminated in 1975.

Partial grants-in-aid that cover any portion of the total college expenses are also awarded. Most often these just cover tuition. Most of the scholarships go to football and basketball but they may be awarded for any sport, regardless of sex, that the college chooses. Colleges and universities follow general guidelines relevant to the number of scholarships that may be awarded in any given sport.

Athletic scholarships in the United States have traditionally been awarded to men and for the most part, still are. Dramatic changes are taking place under the leadership of the Association of Intercollegiate Athletics for Women (AIAW) and under the provisions of Title IX. The law demands that women be given equal opportunities for athletic scholarships. Progress has already been made in this regard. For example, at Stanford University, scholarships were recently awarded $32,147 to nine women on the swimming, golf and tennis teams. At UCLA, $57,000 in scholarship assistance is being awarded to 49 women in nine sports. At Penn State, scholarships for women athletes have been raised form 18 a year ago to 30 this year.

Of college respondents to an AIAW survey, 173 institutions give financial assistance in basketball, 132 give aid in volleyball, 125 in tennis, 82 in swimming and diving, 74 in track and field, 65 in gymnastics, 49 in softball, 45 in field hockey, 38 in golf, and 14 in badminton. Some institutions also offer scholarships to women in fencing, lacrosse, bowling, skiing, archery, riflery, and crew. Cross-country and soccer are being considered.

At its third Delegate Assembly in Scottsdale, Arizona, this year, the AIAW worked on a restructuring plan called "Women's Athletics—A Search for Sanity," which would treat intercollegiate athletics as an educational activity subject to the same standards as other college-sponsored activities. The Assembly also passed a resolution calling on male-dominated athletic groups that govern intercollegiate athletics to join the AIAW in limiting scholarships to tuition and fees and eliminating free room, board, and books.

Right now it is a recruiter's market. There are more qualified high school athletes than there are college scholarships. With the high cost of tuition and other soaring expenses in attending college plus the limited number of scholarships being offered, it has become more difficult for the student-athlete to select a college of his choice and receive aid based on athletic ability. This is not the case in women's athletics where colleges are actually searching for girls with the proper qualifications.

THE COLLEGE BOUND ATHLETE

Most high school athletes who have the talent to continue their athletic career in college would like to attend a college or university that has a winning tradition. This is neither feasible nor practical for all athletes. George E. Killian, Executive Director, National Junior College Athletic Association,[2] states,

> We see, all too often the by-products of this system within six to twelve months after the youngster is sent on his way to fame and fortune. Each year, we get a large number of superior athletes coming back to their community junior college and enrolling and waiting to resume their athletic careers. Most of them have done well athletically, but present little or nothing on their transcripts in the way of academic accomplishments. Unfortunately, if a youngster does not complete ten hours of transfer credit in his last quarter or semester at the four year college, he must sit out a probationary period of eighteen weeks before he can play. This wipes out the full fall season and the winter season of his available time to participate, all because he got started on the wrong foot.
>
> Even more tragic is the case of the youngster who somehow manages to last through the first year and into the beginning of the second. If he is forced to leave the four year college, he has no athletic life left at the community college level at all.

The athletic director must use the utmost discretion in offering advice because most parents and high school coaches tend to overrate the high school athlete's potential for success in college athletics.

Student-Athlete Questionnaire

The athletic director and coach of the sport should prepare a quest-ionnaire for all athletes as a first step in helping them formulate college plans. The questionnaire, as illustrated in *The Coach*,[3] written by Ralph J. Sabock, includes the following questions:

1. Name, height, weight, address, phone
2. Grade point average
3. Class standing
4. College board scores
5. Do you plan to go to college?

6. Are you interested in playing college sports?
7. Preference of school: large; small; four year; community college
8. What course of study do you plan to follow?
9. Will your parents need financial aid to send you to college?
10. Have your parents or guardian filled out a financial statement?
11. If you can, list your first three choices of colleges you would like to attend
12. Do you want any assistance from the athletic department in making your choice?
13. Have you been contacted by any college?
14. Would you like to have a conference with a member of the athletic department that would include your parents?
15. Have you checked with the counseling department for advice on what colleges offer a curriculum in your major interest area?

The main purpose of the questionnaire is to determine if any of the student-athletes plan on attending college, if they plan on furthering their athletic careers, and if they want any help from the athletic department.

Parent-Athlete Conference

If the athlete desires a conference with the athletic director or coach acting as counselor, a meeting should be set up at the end of the season. The following ideas should be offered at the outset of the meeting. The importance of choosing a college that would best suit the individual, carefully discussing the appropriate level of competition for the athlete. This is a very delicate subject and must be handled with care. If asked, the athletic director or coach might offer several suggestions as to what level of competition they think the athlete would be best suited for. Neither the athletic director nor coach should attempt to influence the athlete, but rather give information based on factual knowledge.

Then the counselor might discuss the pros and cons of attending the local community college. There are many junior or community colleges (over 900) with outstanding academic and athletic programs. Many students at these colleges successfully transfer to large and small four-year institutions.

If the college of the athlete's choice is in a location in another section of the country, the counselor might call to the athlete's attention the cost of transportation for trips home during the year.

If the athlete has been contacted by a college recruiter, the athletic director should point out the various rules regarding visitations, trips, and the signing of letters of intent. Many schools have a form that indicates the National Collegiate Athletic Association and the National Association of Intercollegiate Athletics rule relevant to recruitment; these aid the student-athlete and his parents in intelligently conversing with the college and university representatives.

At the conclusion of the conference, the athletic director or coach should offer his services, if desired, in contacting the college of the athlete's choice.

If the athlete has been offered a scholarship and is ready to sign a letter of intent, he should realize that this is a contract. An athletic scholarship is worth thousands of dollars and the athlete is obligated to the institution if he accepts their grant-in-aid. It should also be pointed out to the athlete and to the parents that the NCAA now permits only a one year grant-in-aid and that it is based on the athlete remaining academically eligible.

The College Recruiter

Most high schools have definite rules pertaining to all school visitors and should have a policy pertaining to college recruiters. The college recruiter will normally make arrangements prior to his visit either by telephoning or writing the coach or athletic director. The following letter (Form 29-1) was formulated by the North Puget Sound League Schools and is sent to the athletic directors of the colleges and universities that recruit the North Puget Sound League Schools. It clearly defines the recruiter's reason for visiting.

The Athletic Director's Position

The athletic director should inform his coaching staff of the following responsibilities of working with the college recruiter. Murney Lazier, Evanston Township High School, Illinois[4] lists the most important points the "contact with the college."

1. Coaches must fill out any questionnaire they receive from colleges and universities.
2. The college recruiter is told not to contact the player before the season is completed.
3. All phone calls from the college recruiter must be answered and returned.
4. Requests for films must be complied with, but colleges must request

RECURITING BY COLLEGES AND UNIVERSITIES

TO: Athletic Directors   FROM: Principals Association
     Colleges and Universities   North Puget Sound League
     Recruiting North Puget Sound League

SUBJECT: Athletic Recruiting Practices

We are quite pleased with the relationships we have had with your representatives and hope that we can continue to have our athletes considered for possible scholarships.

Some years back, our league requested that recruiters come to our schools by appointment. The response by most of you was very good and the situation was as we had hoped. However, we seem to have drifted back into the old pattern, and there has been some problems.

What we are asking, then, is that we now apply the "Recruiting Code of Good Conduct", approved and adopted by the National Collegiate Athletic Association and the National Federation of State High School Athletic Associations. Specifically, the section that states:

"It is the institution's obligation to:

3. Demand that persons recruiting on behalf of its athletic interests cooperate at all times with school officials as follows:

    (a) Request and obtain permission from the principal to contact a prospective student-athlete on school premises or during school time.

    (b) Arrange meeting times with prospective student-athlete so that there will be no interference with his class program or any other high school academic or athletic responsibility.

    (c) Under no circumstances contact a high school athlete before, during, or after a game or practice without the expressed consent of the Principal or coach.

    (d) Arrange college campus visits at a time which does not interfere with the high school athlete's academic or athletic responsibilities."

Your cooperation in this matter will be greatly appreciated.

Sincerely,

North Puget Sound League Principals

Representing the following high schools:

Evergreen	Kent Meridian	Renton
Glacier	Kentridge	Tyee
Hazen	Lindbergh	
Highline	Mt. Rainier	

FORM 29-1 Form letter athletic recruiting practices. (North Puget Sound League, Washington. By permission.)

the film by letter so that a record may be kept as to the whereabouts of the film.

5. The college recruiter must have an appointment to visit the school.

Form 29-2, designed by the Kent High School Athletic Department, Washington, has all of the pertinent information regarding an appointment request.

Advice to the Student-Athlete

Bron Bacevich, recently retired former head football coach at Roger Bacon High School, Cincinnati, Ohio[4] in his clinic presentation that appeared in the summer manual of the American Football Coaches Association, offered the following advice to the student-athlete contemplating his college career.

"Every student athlete arrives at the moment of his career when he must narrow the field of schools that he would like to attend. The task is seldom easy, and is often viewed with more than just a little apprehension. If the student-athlete knows what he wants to study in college, it makes the choice of colleges a lot easier."

Coach Bacevich outlines a method of screening prospective colleges and universities.

1. Consult all available sources that describe college curriculums and athletic programs.
2. Measure your criteria and goals against the offerings of any school that you are considering.
3. The student-athlete must obtain a clear and realistic idea of exactly what life at the college or on the team will be like. To succeed in this, the student-athlete ought to be prepared to ask the questions which will enable him to know which school is best suited for and will best meet his needs. To obtain answers to all such questions, he must consult with as many individuals and groups as possible.
4. Both the athlete and, if possible, his parents, should visit the schools that are being seriously considered. Whenever the athlete eliminates a school, the school should be informed immediately.
5. It is best to narrow the field to three or five schools. Any more than that brings on a confusing and cumbersome situation which only impedes the decision making process.
6. Once the student-athlete decides on the colleges he wishes to visit, it is imperative to make his visitations meaningful. While on campus, he should visit potential professors, especially those in his major field, the academic dean of student affairs. The student-athlete should take advantage of the opportunity to eat on campus and stay in one of the residence halls overnight.
7. It is important for the student-athlete and his parents to realize that

KENT HIGH SCHOOLS
COLLEGE RECRUITER VISITATION RECORD

Appointment request (as required by NCAA rules)

NAME_____

COLLEGE_____

DATE_____ TIME_____

To meet with:

COACH_____

ATHLETES_____
_____
_____
_____

APPROVED_____
(Athletic Director or Principal)

— —

Athletic Director or Principal send this form to Coach to be visited, if approved, Coach completes and sends to Athletic Director.

— —

School records checked_____

Game films viewed_____

Parents to be visited_____

College visitation by Athletes_____

COACHES COMMENTS:

Probability of success_____

Probability of graduating_____

_____

Other_____

_____
_____
_____

FORM 29-2 College recruiter visitation record. (Kent School District, King County, Washington. By permission.)

recruiting is a two-way street. They should be aware that the recruiter has a job to do, that is "selling" his school, his programs and himself, and he is bound by rules and regualtions laid down by the NCAA or NAIA. It will be most beneficial to all concerned if there is mutual honesty, sincerity and a spirit of cooperation between the recruiter, the student-athlete and the parents.

Questions for the Student-Athlete to Ask the Recruiter

The athlete and his parents must be cognizant of many general areas of concern about recruiting. Coach Bron Bacevich says,[5]

1. Accreditation
2. Reputation of the school
3. Academic curriculum
4. Role of athletics
5. Calibre of competition
6. Scholarship grants-in-aid
7. Player-coach relationships
8. Geographical location
9. Size and type of school
10. Facilities, equipment and medical care
11. Food and lodging
12. Spiritual, cultural, social and recreational opportunities

In addition, the question of accommodations and racial opportunities for minority athletes should be realistically dealt with. Also the types of remedial programs that are available and the question of the placement of graduates should be answered.

FUNDAMENTAL RECRUITING POLICY

Information pertaining to rules and regulations governing recruiting, eligibility, and financial aid may be obtained from any of the athletic associations. Pamphlets are also prepared by each athletic conference with information to prevent an institution's representatives, a student-athlet, or his family from jeopardizing the prospective collegiate career of the athlete.

For information regarding any of the following, consult the local collegiate athletic conference: amateur student-athlete status; financial aid; recruiting in regard to transportation, entertainment, visitations, tryouts, publicity, sports camps; academic entrance requirements for high school students, community college students, and transfer students.

RULES/REGULATIONS SHEET

PART II (To be read by each new incoming student-athlete prior to his completing the NCAA Student-Athlete Statement the first time.)

During the recruitment of a prospective student-athlete, a member institution, its athletic staff members of a representative of its athletic interests SHALL NOT:

1. Offer, promise or provide any special arrangements, extra benefits, or like improper inducements to a prospect, his relatives or other friends. (Bylaw 1-1-(a))

2. Permit a prospect to appear on a radio or television program conducted by a college coach, a program in which the coach is participating, or a program for which a member of the athletic staff of a collegiate institution has been instrumental in arranging the prospect's appearance or related program material. (Bylaw 1-1-(a)-O.I. 109)

3. Contact a prospect in-person, off-campus for recruiting purposes except during specified periods and on the number of occasions set forth in NCAA Bylaws 1-1-(b) and (c). (Bylaws 1-1-(b) and (c))

4. Contact a prospect at his school (high school, preparatory school or junior college) without permission from the school's executive officer or authorized representative. (Bylaw 1-1-(c))

5. Contact a prospect at the site of his school's (high school, preparatory school or junior college) athletic competition when the prospect is a participant therein. (Bylaw 1-1-(d))

6. Publicize or arrange the publicity of the commitment of a prospect to attend an institution or accept its tender of financial assistance other than through the institution's normal media outlets. (Press conferences, receptions, dinners or similar meetings held for the purpose of making such announcements are prohibited.) (Bylaw 1-1-(e))

7. Publicize the visit of a prospect to its campus. (Bylaw 1-1-(e))

8. Permit company funds to be used to pay expenses (including the provision of a company airplane) incurred in transporting a prospect to visit a campus or for any other recruiting expenses. (Bylaw 1-2-O.I. 108)

9. Permit any agency, group of individuals or organization outside the institution to administer or expend funds for recruiting prospects in any way in behalf of the institution, including the transportation and entertainment of and the giving of gifts or services to a prospect, his relatives or friends. (Bylaw 1-2-(b))

10. Permit two or more persons to pool resources for the recruitment of a prospect. (Bylaw 1-2-(c))

11. Conduct or have conducted in its behalf on its campus or elsewhere, any athletic practice session, tryout or test in which the prospect demonstrates or displays his athletic ability. (Bylaw 1-3)

12. Conduct or participate in any coaching school or sports camp which includes as a participant any prospect who is eligible for admission to a member institution or has started classes for his senior year in high school. (Bylaw 1-3-O.I. 112)

FORM 29-3 Eligibility information. (National Collegiate Athletic Association, Shawnee Mission, Kansas.)

13. Permit a prospect to receive more than one expense-paid visit to the institution's campus. (Such a visit may not exceed 48 hours or occur until after the prospect begins classes for his senior year in high school, and a prospect may not accept such a visit to more than six NCAA member institutions.) (Bylaws 1-5-(a), (b) and (c))

14. Pay or arrange payment of transportation costs incurred by relatives or friends of a prospect to visit an institution's campus or elsewhere. (Bylaw 1-5-(d))

15. Permit the relatives or friends of a prospect to be transported by an athletic representative of the institution in his own vehicle to visit the campus or elsewhere. (Bylaw 1-5-(d)-(2))

16. Entertain a prospect or his parents anywhere except one time on the institution's campus at a scale comparable to that of normal student life. (Bylaws 1-5-(d)-(3); 1-5-(e))

17. Entertain the friends of a prospect at any site. (Bylaw 1-5-(e))

18. Provide a prospect cash or the use of an automobile during a campus visit. (Bylaws 1-5-(e))

19. Entertain a prospect or his relatives in an excessive manner during a campus visit or at any other time. (Bylaw 1-5-(e))

20. Provide free admission to its away-from-home athletic contests to prospects, their friends or relatives. (Bylaws 1-1-(a); 1-5-(e))

21. Expend any funds for a prospect, his family or friends while visiting with them, excluding the prospect's official campus visit. (Bylaw 1-5-(f))

22. Pay any costs incurred by an athletic talent scout or representative of the institution's athletic interests in studying or recruiting a prospect. (Bylaw 1-5-(h))

23. Reimburse the coach of a prospect for expenses incurred in transporting a prospect to visit the campus. (Bylaw 1-5-(h))

24. Entertain high school, preparatory school or junior college coaches at any location except on the institution's campus. (Such permissible entertainment is limited to providing a maximum of two complimentary tickets to home athletic contests held on the institution's campus, and does not include food and refreshments, room expenses or the cost of transportation to and from the institution.) (Bylaw 1-5-(i))

25. Offer, provide or arrange financial assistance for a prospect to pay in whole or in part the costs of his educational or other expenses for any period prior to his regular enrollment or to obtain a post-graduate degree. (Bylaw 1-6)

26. Permit a high school, preparatory school or junior college athletic award winner to be employed or receive free or reduced-cost admission to any sports camp operated by the institution or a member of its athletic staff. (Bylaw 1-8)

# # #

The National Collegiate Athletic Association
December 1, 1975/1mm

COMPUTERIZED COUNSELING FOR
HIGH SCHOOL ATHLETES[6]

Student-athletes now have much of the guesswork removed from finding just the right college because of a program called Computer Share Time.

> With the use of a computer terminal that resembles an oversized type-writer, a student-athlete can find out in seconds where he or she can study and have his or sports, too.
>
> The computer system, developed by qualified professional counselors, is acknowledged to be one of the most up-to-date, comprehensive and useful sources of occupational and educational information available to students and counselors in the United States.
>
> The System permits the students to explore large data files stored in a computer and to examine the ways in which their personal criteria for selecting colleges affect their range of opportunities.
>
> The high school counselors and coaches like the computerized guidance system because it frees them from searching for catalogs and files. They can spend their time on discussing the finer points of decision-making and dealing with the personal and academic problems of the student-athlete.

A student-athlete and his parents would do well to read recruiting literature and become familiar with recruiting methods and procedures by talking with the high school coach or athletic director, rather than trying to make an important decision without prior consultation. Recruiting is a two-way street and, when the student-athlete accepts the athletic scholarship, he must then perform athletically in return.

The athlete and his parents may lose sight of the fact that the selection of a college should not be based on the pleasing personalities of the coaches, whose jobs are to "sell" their school, nor the warm climate, nor the nice buildings and friendly campus. The choice should be made on the basis of the course of study to be pursured and where the athlete can get the best education possible.

Questions

1. Why is it not advisable for a high school coach or athletic director to make the choice of colleges for a student-athlete, even though they may be requested to do so by the athlete and the parents? Discuss.

2. A player's mother telephones you, the athletic director, informing

you her son is very much confused as to which college he wants to attend because of conflicting information he has received from you and the basketball coach. Discuss the situation and how you would go about resolving the dilemma and hopefully aiding the confused athlete.

3. A college recruiter employs the tactic of "knocking" other colleges and their athletic programs, rather than "selling" his institution and its athletic program. Do you consider this acceptable or unethical? Do you feel it is your obligation to comment on his methods of recruiting, even though the recruiter is making his remarks to the student-athlete and his parents and you have been invited to sit in during the recruiter's home visit. If your answer is affirmative, do you make the comments in the student's home in the presence of the recruiter? To the parents and the student after the recruiter departs?; Or to the recruiter after he and you have departed? Why? Discuss.

REFERENCES

1. Allsen, Dr. P.E. and Roundy, Dr. Elmo, Brigham Young University, *Where the "Blue Chip" Athletes Go and Why*, Provo, Utah 84601. By permission.
2. Killian, George, E., "Don't Sell the Jucos Short," *Kendall Sports Trail Magazine*, 1974, p.6., The Kendall Company, Sports Division, 20 Walnut Street, Wellesley Hills, Massachusetts 02181. By permission.
3. Sabock, Ralph J., *The Coach*, W. B. Saunders, Philadelphia, 1973, Ch. 8, p. 209-210. By permission.
4. Lazier, Murney, Evanston Township High School Evanston, Ill., *Counseling the College Bound Athlete*, 4th Annual National Federation Conference of High School Athletics Directors, December 1973, Marriott Hotel, Chicago, Illinois, p. 21. By permission of the author.
5. Bacevich, Bron, Roger Bacon High School, Cincinnati, Ohio, "The Area of Successful and Satisfying Recruiting," Published by the *Summer Manual*, The American Football Coaches Association, 1974. By permission of the author.
6. Warner, Dave, "Computerized Counseling for High School Athletes," *Kendall Sports Trail Magazine*, Vol 29, No. 4, p. 11, 1975. The Kendall Company, Sports Division, 20 Walnut Street, Wellesley Hills, Massachusetts 02181. By permission.

Chapter 30
Public and Community Relations

It is difficult to accurately measure the effect of public relations on the interscholastic athletic program. We do know it plays an important role in the opinions the community has of the school.

The athletic director must establish harmony with the school administration, students, school faculty and community and make it clear that interscholastic athletics are a viable part of the educational program. Because of the nature of interscholastic athletics, all athletic department activities and programs are scrutinized carefully by students, faculty, administration, community, and alumni. The problem of public relations is compounded by the emotional aspect that surrounds athletics in general, brought about by the news media and other means of communication. Whether we admit it or not, upon obtaining a newspaper, many people scan the front page headlines first, then turn directly to the sports section. This being so, athletic directors and coaches have a means of informing the public since they already have the vehicle and a captive audience. The athletic director and coaches should make available to the press sports news items for inclusion in dailies. If this material is not available, the space, which would go to the local schools, will be filled by colleges and professional sports with their ever-present releases. Therefore, an athletic director and coaches must adopt a certain philosophy toward the press, such as, furnish worthy, favorable sports items to the press regularly and gain support for the program.

Public relations is a means of promoting goodwill between the school and the community. The public is more apt to support an average-to-poor program about which it is well informed than a good-to-excellent program about which it knows very little. It may be planned or accidental in so far as the actual happenings of the school are concerned. Any form of communication that is initiated at the school and becomes public knowledge is in essence public relations.

The Development of an Athletic Code

The development of an athletic code was discussed in Chapter 4. It is an excellent device to show the school administration and the community that athletics are a part of the total educational program. Jack Burrell, Athletic Director, Kent Schools, Washington[1] recommends that

> the code be structured to inform the athlete what is expected of him and what is to be accomplished and to give the parents, administration and community a summary of your program position. The code should state objectives clearly, have educational validity, rationale, and should promote the defensibility of the objectives, as well as the rules and regulations. The rules and regulations should be: (1) clearly stated, (2) necessary for promotion of objectives, (3) be supplemented by follow-up procedures for enforcement, and (4) designed in a manner that recognizes the coach as the key figure. Once the athletic program position has been determined (via an Athletic Code, or some similar means) the task becomes one of promoting status and acceptance. Seek official adoption by the school board; inform the community through the press, service clubs and PTA; inform the faculty and parents and enlist their support.

Most athletic department handbooks or manuals contain athletic codes and may be used as an effective tool in the promotion of the program. The handbook or manual should not lay on the shelf or be buried in a file cabinet, but should be in the hands of all parties concerned with the interscholastic atheltic program. If people realize what the athletic department is trying to accomplish, they will be more receptive and cooperative in aiding the department to reach its goals.

Many times the athletes themselves do not know what is expected of them or the philosophy of the athletic department; this makes it difficult for them to aid in the public relations aspect of the interscholastic athletic program. The athletes can be ambassadors of goodwill for the departmen', for they are the ones who move into the community after each school day. As public relations is an ongoing process, these ambassadors carry with them the doctrine of the school and especially the athletic department.

Daily Relationships

Dick Karlgaard, Director of Athletics, Bismark, North Dakota,[2] says, "The coaches on your athletic staff must also be made aware of their responsibilities in the area of public relations. They should realize that the measure of their positive relationships with the patrons of the community is directly proportional to the relationships that they have with their athletes. Honesty and fairness should describe their position as they attempt to provide a sports education for the boys and girls in their program."

Public Relations is Getting People Involved. Probably the most important phase of public relations is getting people involved in the program. This begins with the students themselves. The entire school community should be encouraged to get involved in one form of athletics or another. Every student should be encouraged to participate in some form of sports, whether it be in physical education, intramural, or interscholastic athletics. A good physical education program is the base of the pyramid that produces a good sound intramural and interscholastic athletic program. It is an old axiom that if there is good morale in the physical education department, there is good morale in the total school program.

Most parents are more familiar with the athletic program at the school than any other part of the curriculum, mainly because of their participation or exposure to athletics when they were in school and partly because of the nature of athletics in general. Most parents mirror the reactions of their children. If the child is having a healthy, worthwhile experience in some form of athletics in school, the parents generally hold the school program in high esteem.

Total involvement through members of the band, song leaders, yell leaders, dance groups, and any organization connected with the athletic program—people who will share the same spirit and emotions of a well-rounded interscholastic athletics program—is all part of public relations.

People want to belong to or be indentified with a group and then more people involved or identified with athletics, the better. This will promote good school and community spirit.

The athletic director should make a concentrated effort to get the faculty and coaches involved. The coaches should be encouraged to join the faculty for their noon meal, to participate on school committees, and to get involved in school activities. A warm, friendly, cordial school atmosphere and environment permeate the entire community. The result is that everyone wants to get involved in the program.

Coach-Athlete Relations. As mentioned previously, public relations is on ongoing process. The coach has respect for the athlete and the athlete has respect for the coach, and both respect each other as human beings.

In addition to the daily tasks of communicating with athletes on the technical skills of a sport, the treatment of injuries, and game strategies, the coach must be interested in helping the young student-athlete become a good citizen. Part of the coach's commitment is encouraging respect for authority, living up to the traditions of athletics, following the rules and regulations as set forth by the athletic council, study habits, improving grades, counseling athletes as to future education, and "words of wisdom" that will perhaps set the athlete on the right course in life.

Athletics are more than x's and o's games won or lost. The athletic field is probably the best classroom in the school when it comes to preparing a student-athlete for adulthood. The athletes of today will be the citizens of the community of tomorrow and with this in mind, it is not hard to realize that public relations begin at an early stage as far as human relations are concerned.

METHODS OF DEVELOPING PUBLIC RELATIONS

A common method of establishing public relations is to develop an athletic department prospectus or brochure to be distributed to students, faculty, parents, selected community members, booster club members, and any or all people involved in the interscholastic athletic program.

This prospectus does not have to be an elaborate or expensive item. It can be duplicated or mimeographed with a cover designed by the art department or donated by the booster club. The purpose is to keep the community aware of what is happening, which is part of good public relations. The material included in the prospectus should include schedules, rosters of teams, biographical sketches of players, coaches, athletic director, principal, faculty members or members of the community who were former athletes, records of past season, team and individual statistics, information about former athletes, sketches of song leaders, yell leads, band director, or other items that may be of interest to the public. Other items of interest to be included in the prospectus might be a hall of fame column to include former captains, former MVPs, special award winners, or anything that would get a person's name in the prospectus. Public relations are people relations. People like to see their name in print and this would be one method of doing so.

In addition, it is the custom of many high schools to publish (for the media and for opponents) a brochure or prospectus for each sport or sports season. These can be duplicated, printed, or lithographed and are a valuable public relations and communications tool. The athletic director should take an active role in putting together the publication, not with the idea of controlling the flow of information on athletics, but to eliminate conflict and to positively and effectively inform the public and promote the athletic program.

Establishing Relationship with the Media

The local newspaper is obviously the best means of communications between the school and public. The athletic director must establish a good relationship with the local paper.

The procedures and instructions for releasing or disseminating information to the media should be spelled out. Essentially releases and official information should flow through a central point or public relations representative. This should be done prior to the opening of school at a luncheon for the local prep writer and the coaching staff. Here the athletic director should be prepared to distribute pertinent information to the local press, such as the prospectus, pictures, and any information that may be used by the media. A copy of the *Athletic Department Handbook* should also be given to the press to communicate the philosophy of the department.

At this luncheon meeting, details should be outlined for the pre- and postgame coverage. In the case of many small towns. the local sportswriter will have to cover many schools and many sports; since he cannot do this personally, he will have to rely on other sources for his information.

The ideal situation would be to have a faculty person assigned to act as the public relations representative. A person who is trained and qualified in this area, such as the journalism teacher, would be a good representative. Qualified students, working under the supervision of the journalism advisor or a faculty representative, can be very effective in assisting with the public relations of the school. Students can help cover athletic events and work as liaison between the school and local paper. As mentioned previously, the local paper generally has a limited staff and cannot possibly cover all athletic events, it welcomes any help it can get, especially the reporting of the results of night games.

Journalism students can also submit human interest stories to the local papers, such as homecoming queen nominations and results, stories of interest about song leaders, yell leaders, honors and awards bestowed upon any student-athlete, or faculty members.

Pregame Information. Another method of keeping the public aware of the local interscholastic athletic program is to announce pregame information. In addition to being a service to the community, it also serves as a good form of public relations. Ticket prices, places where tickets may be purchased, box office hours, suggested routes, parking plans, starting time of the game, and any or all information concerning the contest should be included in the pregame information.

Picture Days. Local camera days, similar to those conducted by college teams, provide an opportunity for the local press to take pictures of the players, coaches, and the administration. The athletic director should encourage his coaches to devote part of an early season practice session to photographers and should arrange to have the players in their game uniforms. This is an excellent time to take the pictures of the song leaders, yell leaders, and members of the band. This time will be well spent since pictures are one of the most effective means of publicity.

Local merchants should be encouraged to place pictures of the athletes in their store windows along with a schedule. This creates a great community interest in the athletic program.

News Releases. If time and resources permit, publicity releases and weekly statistics reports are of great value to members of the press. They also indicate that the athletic director is interested in assisting with and promoting the coverage of your school's activities. Because everything that happens in the athletic department is news, the athletic department must take the time to tell the right people about it, at the right time and most important, in the right way. Most schools make a practice of mailing out weekly "Sports Bulletins." These bulletins list all the sports activities that will take place the following week and highlight some of the more important events. Basically, the news bulletins are brief and should include names, titles, accomplishments, and quotations if time and space permit. The basic principles of a news story still hold true: it must cover who, what, where, and when. These sports bulletins are mailed to the media, not only the local press, but to papers in towns and areas that games are scheduled. The bulletins are also mailed to members of the community.

Daniel J. Scherer[3] writing in the *School Management Magazine* lists some do's and don'ts for press releases:

1. Do be sure your information is current.
2. Don't send an article marked "hold for release" to the editor more than two or three days ahead of the release date.
3. Do type the release, double spaced, on one side of the paper only.
4. Do put your name, organization name, address and telephone number at the top of the left-hand side of the first sheet of paper.
5. Don't write a headline for the article.
6. Don't start the article at the top of the page. Put your first paragraph one third of the way down to leave room for a headline.
7. Do write "more" at the bottom of the page if the article continues to another sheet of paper.
8. Do put an end mark (−30) at the end of the article.
9. Don't expect your article to be printed exactly as you wrote it.
10. Do be accurate. Make certain names are spelled correctly. Get all the facts right.

Responsibility and Procedures for Publicity. The athletic director who has assumed the responsibility for the weekly news releases must have the full cooperation of coaching staff. The coach, realizing that publicity for his team has a direct effect on team spirit and morale, must make it his responsibility to get the information to the athletic director at a specified time. This information should include data about the preseason, pregame, postgame, and postseason, as well as any personal items that might be of interest to the community.

The athletic director must develop a form for this information and educate the staff in its use. Form 30-1 shows two examples of forms that can be used to provide local public relations agencies with knowledge about teams, games, and any other items of interest.

Form 30-2 is another sample of a press and radio information form that is used by University High School, Benton, Colorado.

Form 30-3 shows the weekly activities, "This Week in Sports" as used by Ron Davis, Athletic Director, Corona del Mar High School, Newport Beach, California.

The following are examples of types of forms that can be used to provide local public relations agencies with information about teams, games, etc.

TEAM INFORMATION AND PUBLICITY SHEET

School _____ Sport _____ Date _____

Coach _____ Telephone _____

Name	Number	Position	Ht.	Wt.	Varsity Exp.	Yr. in School

I. TEAM INFORMATION AND PUBLICITY SHEET

II. FOOTBALL SQUAD LIST FOR RADIO AND NEWSPAPER PERSONAL
ATLANTA CITY SCHOOLS

School _____ Date _____

No. L.E.	No. L.T.	No. L.G.	No. C	No. R.G	No. R.T.	No. R.E.

No. QB

No. L.H.B	No. F.B	No. R.N.B.

Coach _____ Co-Captains _____

Source: Unknown

FORM 30-1 Team information and publicity sheet. (Atlanta City Schools.)

439

III. PRESS AND RADIO INFORMATION SHEET

University High School
N. University Ave.
Benton, Colorado

INFORMATION FOR PRESS AND RADIO PERSONAL

Basketball: University High vs._____

Date:_____   Time of Contest:_____

School Colors: Visitors:_____ and _____

University High: Green   and   Gold

Team Information	Visitors	University
Head Coach	_____	Jim Cousy
Asst's	_____	Jack Jones, Bob Ford
Trainer	_____	Dave Benton
Athletic Director	_____	Dr. Donald Hoos
Principle	_____	Frank Johnson

Coaching Record of Jim Cousy —   Varsity Coach 2 years.
Won 39 lost 5
City Champions 3 years
Graduate Sacramento State College

Seating Capacity University High Gym — 4,5000

Parking Facilities for Press and Radio —   reserved spaces at southwest
end of parking lot. Please
enter on Sixth St. entrance.

University High School Band Director — John Mills

Team Cheer Leaders: Jill Jones, Bertha Busby, Sue Sims, Cindy Clout

For other information please contact;   Bruce Patton
University High School
444- 4444

Source Unknown

FORM 30-2 Press and radio information sheet. (University High School, Benton, Colorado.)

"THIS WEEK IN SPORTS"

Monday_____thru Saturday _____

Sport	Class			Where	Time

MONDAY_____

_____	_____ vs. _____	_____	_____
_____	_____ vs. _____	_____	_____
_____	_____ vs. _____	_____	_____
_____	_____ vs, _____	_____	_____
_____	_____ vs, _____	_____	_____

TUESDAY_____

_____	_____ vs. _____	_____	_____
_____	_____ vs. _____	_____	_____
_____	_____ vs. _____	_____	_____
_____	_____ vs. _____	_____	_____
_____	_____ vs. _____	_____	_____

WEDNESDAY_____

_____	_____ vs. _____	_____	_____
_____	_____ vs. _____	_____	_____
_____	_____ vs. _____		
_____	_____ vs. _____	_____	_____
_____	_____ vs. _____	_____	_____

THURSDAY_____

_____	_____ vs, _____	_____	_____
_____	_____ vs. _____	_____	_____
_____	_____ vs. _____	_____	_____
_____	_____ vs, _____	_____	_____
_____	_____ vs. _____	_____	_____

FRIDAY_____

_____	_____ vs. _____	_____	_____
_____	_____ vs. _____	_____	_____
_____	_____ vs. _____	_____	_____
_____	_____ vs, _____	_____	_____
_____	_____ vs. _____	_____	_____

SATURDAY_____

_____	_____ vs. _____	_____	_____
_____	_____ vs, _____	_____	_____
_____	_____ vs. _____	_____	_____
_____	_____ vs. _____	_____	_____
_____	_____ vs. _____	_____	_____

By permission: Ron Davis

FORM 30-3 This week in sports. (Corona del Mar High School, Newport Beach, California. By permission.)

Game Program

The game program should be used to promote and publicize the activities of the school. In addition to the necessary information in a game program, possible items to be included are feature articles on new buildings, projects, outstanding faculty members, history of the school's mascot, the local booster club or any item that will have an influence on the general public that is interested in the school and especially, the interscholastic athletic program.

Home Athletic Contests

The administration of athletic contests was discussed in Chapter 17 and crowd accommodation and management for interscholastic athletics is the topic of Chapter 31. However, it is important to mention the public relations aspects of both phases of the interscholastic athletic program at this point.

It is imperative that the comfort of the spectators be given paramount consideration regarding parking, routes to the stadium, purchase of tickets, and seating arrangements.

It is also important to have an effective public address announcer, one who knows the activity, has good voice control, and is experienced enough to realize what the job is, that of keeping the people informed and to be descriptive without acting as a radio announcer. He must realize that the people he is talking to are also at the game.

The Press Box[4]

It is obvious that a well-organized press box is essential for good public relations. If possible, a paid adult supervisor should be in charge of the press box, and he should be responsible for the cleanliness and organization of this area. He must make certain that the telephones, scoreboard, public address system, and the field phones are all in operating order.

Press box seats should be preassigned. The first priority should go to the members of the working press, public address announcer, and spotters and should not be filled with faculty members and alumni. The number of persons that should have access to the press box should be limited to avoid confusion during the contest.

The supervisor of the press box should provide as many services as feasible to members of the working press. The services should include programs, game statistics, alphabetical and numerical rosters of each team, and refreshments during halftime. There should also be a press parking area, on with easy access to the press box.

Visiting Scouts

Scouting has become a recognized part of interscholastic athletics, and every effort should be made to treat visiting scouts with the same courtesies and services your scouts would expect to receive when they visit an opposing school. An area for visiting scouts should be established in the press box. If there is insufficient room, a row should be reserved directly in front of the press box for the scouts.

Scouting requests made in advance to the athletic director of the home school should be honored in an efficient manner to avoid any confusion at the gate at the time of the game. Credentials should be available for pickup by the scouts at "will call" or a designated ticket booth. The pass gate attendant and ushers should be aware of where to direct scouts for their seating assignments. They should be given programs and game statistics.

Demonstration Night

Still another method of keeping the public involved and informed is a parent's night or demonstration night to explain various points of interest to the parents and interested members of the community. The athletic director or members of the staff can inform the parents on such areas as equipment, insurance, conditioning, training regulations, eligibility rules, discipline, and other appropriate information regarding participating in the interscholastic athletic program.

A clinic or demonstration is also a popular item with parents and members of the community. In this type of program, the coach could have the players go through basic drills and techniques as well as an explanation of the offense and defense that will be used during the season. This is a good time to introduce team members and members of the coaching staff.

OFFICE OF THE ATHLETIC DIRECTOR   EAST CAMPUS   SEPTEMBER 8, 1964

TO: ADMIMISTRATIVE STAFF, FACULTY, STUDENTS, AND CITIZENS OF WAUKEGAN

FROM: MR. LEO L. SINGER, DIRECTOR OF ATHLETICS

RE: KICK-OFF NIGHT — SPONSORED BY THE PARENTS' CLUB OF WTHS

DATE: SATURDAY, SEPTEMBER 12, 1964

TIME: 6:00 P.M.

PLACE: WEISS FIELD

ADMISSION: 50¢ Adults — Those that join the Parents' Club for 1964-65 will be admitted free.   Membership $2.00 per family. Students free.

ORDER OF EVENTS

6:00 — 7:00 P.M.   Freshmen Inter-squad Game

7:00 — 8:00 P.M.   Sophomore Inter-squad Game

8:00 — 8:10 P.M.   Welcoming Remarks   — Mr. John Alden
    President Parents' Club
    P.A. Announcer   — Mr. Sam Filippo
    Assistant Principal West Campus

8:10 — 8:25 P.M.   Flag Raising   — ROTC M/Sgt. LeRoy Woodard
    National Anthem   — Band

8:30 — 9:30 P.M.   Varsity Inter-squad Game

NOTE: Parent's Club will sell memberships at two entrances.

Band will take part in the program under the direction of Mr. Les Gilkey.

Cheerleaders will take part in the directing of cheers under the supervision of Miss Joanne Wooldridge.

ROTC will act as ushers under the direction of Captain Herndon Godfrey, Jr.

The Concessions will be operated by the "W" Club under the supervision of Mr. George Harro.

Officials will be furnished by the Northern Officials Association.

PLEASE READ AND POST

FORM 30-4   Parents day. (Waukegan Township High School, Waukegan, Illinois.)

THE ATHLETIC DIRECTOR AND THE COACHING STAFF

The athletic director should work with his staff to assure they are aware of their responsibilities in the area of public relations. The staff must realize that their relationships with members of the community is in direct proportion to the relationships they have with their athletes.

The coach is in a better position to have an influence for good upon the young of a community than any other member of the faculty. The coach has an obligation to develop a personality and character that is above reproach. Most coaches are admired and imitated by young people. The example set by the coach is of extreme importance. During a contest, the coach is on center stage. The attitudes demonstrated by his players are a direct reflection on the coach. The attitide and opinions formed by the spectators and members of the community during a contest will go a long way in establishing good public relations between the school and community. It is obvious then that everything the coach does must have the best educational interests of the athletes as a base. If the profession sincerely approaches athletics with this objective in mind, good public relations will become a reality.

The athletic director must keep the public informed with a well-planned, honest and fair relationship between himself, the staff, and the public. The basic program of public relations must include a sound program of athletic administration in which the athletic director identifies the goals and objectives of the athletic program and takes steps to implement these goals and objectives.

The coach, being a teacher first, should be in a position not only to teach the necessary skills for the activity involved, but to teach with a positive attitude so that the student-athlete will have a worthwhile experience while participating in interscholastic athletics.

BOOSTER CLUBS AND PUBLIC RELATIONS

Booster clubs should be established with the sole purpose of assisting and supporting and making possible deserved and equal recognition of all student-athletes. They can also provide means of honoring teams and athletes in all sport programs of the school. Booster clubs should be organized to further a closer understanding between the parents and their sons and daughters in their particular athletic activities, to develop closer understanding and relationship with the school coaching personnel, and to gain personal enjoyment for the school's athletic program.

The booster club should completely refrain from directly or indirectly interfering with or influencing the policy or execution of the athletic program of the school.

Membership in the organization should be open to all parents, guardians, or relatives of boys and girls enrolled in the school, together with any other persons having an interest in the association.

The athletic director, acting as the school representative, should be the liaison officer between the association and the school. He should be responsible to the president of the organization and to the principal of the school.

The president of the organization shall correlate the overall program of the association, nominate and fill all committees, call and preside over all meetings, and work in conjunction with the school representative.

The secretary's duties shall be to keep minutes of all meetings and give notice of any and all mettings. Minutes should be duplicated and distributed to the board members of the organization and to the principal.

The treasurer's duties shall be to collect and keep a record of all monies received by the association, to establish a bank account in the name of the association, and to draw from the funds to meet the needs of the organization. The treasurer should present a budget for the board's approval at the first meeting in September. The treasurer should work with the school representative who should poll the coaches of the various sports for their needs for the coming year. Any other expenditures that are necessitated during the year should be voted on by the board.

The board of directors should consist of each and all of the officers and the immediate past year's president. Ten voting members of the board should be the president, secretary, school representative, treasurer, vice president in charge of girl's sports, football, basketball, spring sports, publicity chairman, and a membership chairman. The board of directors should hold regular scheduled meetings at the call of the president of the association.

The association should be incorporated as a nonprofit organization and take out a liability insurance policy for their various activities.

Recent Survey[5]

In a recent survey conducted by the California Coaches Association as to the types of activities the booster clubs were performing, the schools that reported had very active booster clubs which contributed a great deal of time and energy to the support of athletics. The four main catagories of booster club participation were awards, banquets, supervision of events, and general financial aid.

Some groups were one-sport organizations, while others contributed to all activities. All had large memberships and charged dues. Raffles seemed to be the largest money raising activity with the proceeds going directly to the athletic program, either through equipment purchases or award programs.

One of the questions on the survey was in regard to crowd control. Some of the reactions to this question were as follows:

1. Problems of crowd control should be discussed openly with parents and booster clubs.
2. Parents should contribute ideas and manpower to support programs and activities for crowd control.
3. Preventative measures should be in operation before a major problem develops.
4. The majority of the trouble comes from drop-outs and recent graduates.
5. Wanton destruction of property after events is seen as a major issue.
6. A clearer definition should be made as to the role of administrators, teachers, students, and parents in contributing to crowd control. Too often the school tries to go it alone.
7. Strong state association enforcement is needed for institutions who are not able to control their crowds. This could give the problem schools extra leverage to deal with the matter.
8. There should be league booster club meetings to cooperate and coordinate their activities in crowd control. The "home" booster club needs assistance from the visiting school's booster club.

On the question of booster club banquets, program, and awards, these fell into three catagories:

1. Banquets for football only, sponsored by the booster club.
2. Banquets honoring all sports in the fall, winter, and spring seasons.
3. Special awards nights that do not include dinner. Other reactions to this question were as follows:
   One school has an all-male group that meets every Tuesday evening during football season. It is active only as a football group. Women attend only two nights a year and there are approximately 450 members. Raffles are on game balls and gifts donated by local merchants. This raises money for weekly awards to players. Only varsity football players are given awards.

Fund-Raising Activities

By necessity, in order to keep the program ongoing, it might be necessary to initiate some type of fund-raising activity. This is obviously not the "educational" way to fund an athletic program, however many schools have to resort to these types of activities to raise money for the program.

Some of the ideas that were successfully used, according to the survey were:

1. Fireworks stand, raised as much as $3500.00
2. Christmas tree lot
3. Operation of concession stands
4. Horse show, raised $1500.00
5. Pancake breakfast, raised $1700.00 in one day
6. All sports program
7. Season tickets
8. Harlem Clown's basketball game
9. Raffles, game ball, items donated by local merchants
10. Spring football game
11. Las Vegas night
12. Special seating tickets
13. Collect market coupons, such as blue chip stamps, etc.
14. Professional football players game
15. Donkey basketball game
16. Car wash
17. Hole-in-one golf tournament
18. Sponsor ads in program
19. Membership drive, patron membership, commercial membership, lifetime membership
20. Fourth of July parade organized by captains of each sport, prizes for best decorations, etc.

Summation

A dictionary definition of public relations is "the art and science of developing reciprocal understanding and goodwill between a person, firm or institution and the public." Individuals connected with high school athletic programs, particularly coaches and the athletic directors, should strive to accomplish this objective. Unfortunately many do not recognize or understand the value of public relations and only give lip service and cursory attention to the subject.

Questions

1. Which news items for public relations purposes are likely to be included in an interscholastic athletic department prospectus or brochure?

2. Enumerate some accepted "do's" and "don'ts" for press releases.
3. Through the course of the football season you have observed numerous inconsistencies in the statements your head football coach has given to the news media relevant to such matters as the height and weight of some of his athletes, the starting lineup, and the severity of injuries. His strategy is to cry "wolf" and "poor mouth" his situation and team. Aside from the matter that his demeanor is a violation of the code of ethics for athletic coaches and teachers, from the public relations standpoint, is the coach's strategy good or bad? Why?
4. Your high school basketball coach has an outstanding player who has attracted much attention from the press and the college recruiters. In the morning newspaper, your coach is quoted as saying, "Yes, Smitty is the best player I have ever had. To date more than 120 colleges and universities have contacted me about him. Whatever school he goes to, I'm going to coach there too." Is this good public relations for the athlete, coach, or high school? Why or why not? Explain your answer. Discuss other ramifications of the coach's statement relevant to recruiting and ethical conduct.
5. Your school's football team has committed numerous errors, played poorly, and lost a game that they should have won. To the news media, your coach "named names," fixing the blame on those who had committed obvious errors, as your coach believes in "telling it like it is." Strictly from a public relations standpoint, is this the course of action the coach should have taken? How would you have handled this situation? What is the logic of your decision?

REFERENCES

1. Burrell, Jack, "Building Interest in Your Athletic Program," pp. 10—11. *1971 Proceeding of the National Conference of High School Directors of Athletics*, National Federation of State High School Associations. By permission of the author.
2. Karlgaard, Dick, Athletic Director, Bismark Public School Bismark, North Dakota, "Public Relations for Interscholastic Athletic Programs," pp. 20-22, 1974. Proceedings of the National Conference of High School Associations. By permission of the author.
3. Scherer, Daniel J., professional publicist, "How to Keep Your District in the Public Eye," Reprinted from p. 122 of the September 1966, *School Management Magazine*, CCM Profession Magazines.
4. Crowd Control Manual, pp. 1-4 *Public Relations*, California Interscholastic

Federation, Southern Section, 1974. By permission of Tom Byrnes, Southern CIF Commissioner.
5. Dr. Richard O. Keelor, Ph.D., Director, Program Development, The Presidents Council of Physical Fitness and Sports, Washington, D.C. 20201. *Survey of Booster Clubs in California*, 1973. By permission.

SUGGESTED READINGS

Tucker, Ross N., *Postscript on Public Relations*, pp. 55-56, Secondary School Athletic Administration, American Association of Health, Physical Education and Recreation, Washington, D.C., 1969.

Purdy, R. L., *The Successful High School Athletic Program*, Parker Publishing, West Nyack, N.Y., 1973, Ch. 4, Developing Persuasive Public Relations with Parent and Community and also Ch. 14, Developing a Dynamic Cheerleading Program.

Ewing, David W., *Writing for Results in Business, Government and the Professions*, Wiley, New York, 1974, Ch. 1, Improving Written Communications, pp. 3-18; Ch. 4, Strategies of Persuasion, pp. 71-98; Ch. 5, Organizing Facts and Ideas, pp. 99-139; Ch. 10, How to Make Yourself Clear, pp. 28-330.

Cutlip, Scott M. and Center, Allen H., *Effective Public Relations* 4th edition, Prentice-Hall, Englewood Cliffs, N.J., 1971.

Capp, Glenn R., *Basic Oral Communication*, Prentice-Hall, Englewood Cliffs, N.J., 1971.

Minnick, Wayne C., *The Art of Pursuasion* 2nd edition, Riverside Press, Cambridge Mass., 1968.

Chapter 31

Crowd Accommodations
and Management
for Interscholastic Athletics

"Crowd accommodation has for many years involved providing ample parking, concession convenience, clean rest rooms, shelter from rain, drinking fountains and the provision of other conveniences. It has more and more in recent years involved providing protection for players, coaches and spectators from malcontents and vandals."[1]

As noted in *Crowd Control for High School Athletics*,[2] "There is general agreement that when properly planned, supervised and administered, interscholastic athletics have a tremendous educational value."

There is also general concern that the conduct and behavior of the players and spectators at interscholastic athletic contests have prompted many school districts to take action that has seriously limited athletic programs and in some cases has eliminated major segments of the program.

Physical attacks upon officials, players, and fans have created a complex problem in many areas. Some school districts have given up nighttime activities, and others are considering dropping the interscholastic athletic program altogether.

The lack of crowd control has imposed severe spectator restrictions in regard to scheduling athletic contests. Principals and athletic directors have sometimes been forced to schedule games on days and at hours when no spectators would be admitted. In one community, for example, the players report to their school in preparation for

451

playing a football game, get on the bus, and play the game at some unannounced site. The athletic director informs the coach where the game will be played as the bus leaves the school grounds. This is an isolated case used as an example of the need for comprehensive game management. Still another example occurs after the game when students, taking the community bus home, harass other passengers. Game times have been changed so that the end of the game does not coincide with commuter hours. The athletic program suffers because the community cannot handle these problems and puts the blame on the school.

"When contest are held under these restricted conditions, the damaging effects upon the attitudes, ideals and other attributes of citizenship detract from rather than contribute toward, the educational objectives of the schools."[3]

MANAGEMENT OF INTERSCHOLASTIC ATHLETIC EVENTS

Under the above mentioned conditions, it becomes increasingly important that attention be given to the planning, administration, and supervision of interscholastic athletic contests. Improving sportsmanship and avoiding misconduct necessitates three phases of action: education, involvement and enforcement. The total community must be educated to the philosophy, objectives, policies and standards of the school's interscholastic athletic program. Effective contest management is achieved by involving as many individuals as practical. In addition to the principal, athletic director and coaches, it is recommended that representatives of the local law enforcement agency, the pep club sponsor, selected faculty members, members of the letterman's club, booster clubs, and student body officers be included in both planning and supervision.

Proper management in the form of pre-planning and involvement of these representatives will provide an overall look at the problem and development of a plan for safe and orderly conduct at all athletic events plus greater spectator convenience and enjoyment. Once the policies have been developed they should be published and procedures for implementation must be initiated. Without appropriate procedures for implementation, policies established then become ineffective.[4]

It should be pointed out that the Board of Education has jurisdiction only on school property. Special problems arise when spectators leave the school site, such as in a public parking lot or other off-street parking sites. This must be the responsibility of the local city police and not that of the school. The off-duty officer who has been assigned to the game might not have the power to arrest unless the athletic director or some school official prefers charges. Many will not prefer charges, which tends to dissipate and eliminate an effective system of control. Responsibilities should be well defined, preferably written, and communicative channels must be established so that situations as mentioned above can be terminated before further infractions occur.

RESPONSIBILITES OF THE STATE AND NATIONAL ASSOCIATIONS

Harold Meyer, Commissioner, Ohio High School Athletic Association, strongly advocates that "each state association must adopt rules and regulations governing the conduct of athletic contests under its jurisdiction. They may be part of the association's constitution and by-laws, or be promulgated through bulletins, newsletters, or other media." In a recent article published by the *American Alliance for Health, Physical Education and Recreation,*[5] Meyer offered the following solutions for proper crowd accommodation.

> All schools must be made aware that they have certain required responsibilities as a member of the association, as a host school, or as a visiting school. The responsibility may vary in degree but not in importance.
>
> Crowd control is a problem only if there is a crowd, it must be assumed that an athletic contest is a potentially explosive situation.
>
> It is logical to establish controls and clearly state all procedures essential to smooth contest management. To insure correct behavior of student athletes it should be mandatory that a faculty member of the school accompany the coach. His duties vary with the type of activity, but primarily he is the person of responsibility.

FUNDAMENTALS OF SPORTSMANSHIP[6]

Management and crowd accommodations mean communication. All people concerned must know exactly what is expected of them. The following is a sample of the material given to all schools that enter the Ohio High School Athletic Association basketball tournaments.

Show Respect for the Opponent at all Times

The opponents should be treated as a guest, greeted cordially on arriving; given the best accommodations; and accorded the tolerance, honesty, and generosity that all human beings deserve. Good sportsmanship is the golden rule in action.

Show Respect for the Officials

The officials should be recognized as impartial arbitrators who are trained to do their job and who can be expected to do it to the best of their ability. Good sportsmanship implies the willingness to accept and abide by the decisions of the officials.

Know, Understand, and Appreciate the Rules of the Contest

A familiarity with the current rules of the game and the recognition of their necessity for a fair contest are essential. Good sportsmanship suggests the importance of conforming to the spirit as well as the letter of the rules.

Maintain Self-Control at all Times

A prerequisite of good sportsmanship requires one to understand his own bias or prejudice and to have the ability to recognize that rational behavior is more important than the desire to win. A proper perspective must be maintained if the potential educational values of athletic competition are to be realized. Good sportsmanship is concerned with the behavior of all involved in the game.

Recognize and Appreciate Skill in Performance Regardless of Affiliation

Applause for an opponent's good performance is a demonstration of generosity and goodwill that should not be looked upon as treason. The ability to recognize quality in performance and the willingness to acknowledge it without regard to team membership is one of the most highly commendable gestures of good sportsmanship. With the fundamentals of sportsmanship as the points of departure, specific responsibilities and expected modes of behavior can be defined.

RESPONSIBILITIES OF THE COACH[7]

The coach bears the greatest burden of responsibility for sportsmanship. He has the strongest influence upon the attitudes and behavior of the players, the student body, and the community. In order for good sportsmanship to become a reality, it is essential that the coach subscribe to the values of sportsmanship and teach its principles through word and deed. Specifically, it is recommended that the coach:

1. Always set good examples for others to follow.
2. Instruct the players in their sportsmanship responsibilities.
3. Discipline students who display unsportsmanlike behavior. If necessary take away their privileges of representing the school.
4. Be a good host to opponents. Treat them as guests.
5. Provide opportunities for social interaction among coaches and players.
6. Endorse or recommend only officials who have demonstrated the highest ethical standards.
7. Respect the officials' judgments and interpretations of the rules.
8. Publicly shake hands with the officials and opposing coach before and after the contest.

RESPONSIBILITIES OF THE PLAYERS[8]

The responsibility of the players for sportsmanship is second in importance only to that of the coach. Because players are admired and respected, they exert a great deal of influence over the actions and behavior of the spectators. Desirable behavior for the players includes:

1. Treating opponents with the respect that is due them as guests and fellow human beings.
2. Shaking hands with opponents and wishing them good luck before the contest.
3. Exercising self-control at all times, accepting decisions and abiding by them.
4. Respecting the officials' judgments and interpretations of the rules. Never argue or make gestures indicating a dislike for a decision.
5. Not communicating with the officials regarding the clarification of a ruling. This is a function of the captain, if necessary.
6. Congratulating the opponents in a sincere manner following either victory of defeat
7. Accepting seriously the responsibility and privilege of representing the school and community

CROWD MANAGEMENT GUIDELINES FOR
COMMUNITY ORGANIZATIONAL SUPPORT

The following crowd management guidelines were published after several years of research on crowd accommodation and crowd control problems in Southern California. They are reprinted here courtesy of Kenneth Fagans, Commissioner, California Interscholastic Federation, Southern Section.

The suggested guidelines are general in nature and, as outlined, may not be strictly applicable to all communities. Civic leaders are urged to first meet with local school administrators to precisely determine in what activities during athletic events, civic group assistance would be most helpful. The guidelines should be discussed, expanded, and revised as necessary to suit the situation.[9]

CONTROLLING THE SITUATION

Utilization of game officials at assemblies or rallies, which rules are explained and interpreted, may facilitate the crowd's understanding of the game. All too often, spectators are misinformed about the rules and interpretations made by the officials and direct their animosity toward the officials and opposing players. It seems desirable that the coach appear before the student body and discuss sportsmanship with the students. Here are a few suggestions he might make to the student body.

1. Know and demonstrate the fundamentals of sportsmanship.
2. Respect, cooperate, and respond enthusiastically to the cheerleaders.
3. Censure fellow students whose behavior is unbecoming.
4. Respect the property of the school and the authority of school officials.
5. Show respect for an injured player when he is removed from the contest.
6. Do not applaud errors by opponents or penalities inflicted upon them.
7. Do not heckle, jeer, or distract members of the opposing team.
8. Respect the judgment and strategy of the coach.
9. Avoid profane language and obnoxious behavior.

Jack E. Razor, Dean, College of Applied Science and Technology, Illinois State University, in 'his article, *Variables in Crowd Control*[10] "commends efforts by school administrators who may conduct rap sessions with students providing an opportunity for information to be exchanged in both directions. He suggests pep sessions at which coaches, teachers, school officials, as well as students, comment on and explain the need for sportsmanship in a competitive environment."

CONDUCT OF CHEERLEADERS

Cheerleaders may do a great deal to control unruly crowd behavior by performing an appropriate cheer at a key time during the contest or by not actually trying to compete with the opposing teams's cheerleaders. Their behavior and leadership can be instrumental in quelling and soothing feelings of the spectators and classmates.

LIMIT THE CROWD

Control of the crowd may take place prior to the actual contest. The sale of tickets may be limited to an established number and a specific audience. Selling tickets one or two days prior to the contest and to a select group may significantly reduce the possibility of unruly crowd behavior.

PERSONNEL ON THE FIELD

Only those individuals who are actually participating or in some manner needed on the field should be permitted on or in this vicinity.

TRANSPORTATION

Transportation to and from the game should also be studied by school administrators. Transporting students and spectators to and from a contest has been the source of considerable discussion and debate, and school administrators are urged to emply a plan that works.

UTILIZATION OF COMMUNICATION

School administrators should seek the cooperation of the news media. Utilization of various communication media such as newspaper, radio, and television to provide appropriate information relative to athletic contests may do a great deal to avoid conflict and possible injury.

SCHEDULING OF GAMES

Scheduling games at times during the day rather than in the evening is quite common in large cities and is gaining favor by schools attempting to avoid trouble. The scheduling of games Monday through Thursday is also a common practice and is on the increase. Even though gate receipts are becoming increasingly important, they should not be the basis for scheduling contests especially where riotous conduct is likely to occur.

THE GAME SITE

The physical logistics of the game site contribute to the safety and welfare of both the participants and the spectators. Providing adequate lighting both on the field and in parking lots and surrounding areas may discourage unruly behavior.

PUBLIC ADDRESS SYSTEM

Having an adequate public address system for making announcements, and having someone who is knowledgeable about the game and who recognizes the potential of appropriate and inappropriate remarks over a public address system are also important.

PARKING FACILITIES

Providing adequate parking lot attendants, lights in the parking area, numerous, adequate, and well-lighted exits for crowds and cars will also facilitate the likelihood of a safer and more controlled exit.

POST GAME EVENTS

The conduct of post game activities at the game site or in close proximity should be discouraged.

ENFORCEMENT OF THE LAW

Where unruly behavior is common and severe, it will be necessary for law enforcement officials to penalize those who are guilty of such behavior. Establishing and enforcing laws and rules, both civil and within the schools, may aid in curtailing unruly behavior.

IMPOSING SANCTIONS

Where a school, coach, or community has had a previous history of unsportsmanlike behavior, it may be necessary for sanctions, such as disqualification from competition for a period of time, be imposed by league and state officials.

GAME OFFICIALS

Game officials should be conscious that they also play an important role in preventing riots and lessening an already emotionally charge enviornment. The athletes and their play should be the focus of attention at all contests, not the officials. Officials should arrive at the game site together and appear and disappear from the field or court in as unobtrusive a manner as possible."

CROWD MANAGEMENT PROCEDURES FOR HIGH SCHOOL ATHLETIC CONTESTS

The following material has been compiled by members of the California Interscholastic Federation, Southern Section, Crowd Management Committee and is reprinted, in part, by permission of Kenneth Fagans, Commissioner.[1]

GAME SITE PREPARATION AND PLANNING

Planning Responsibilities

Detailed procedures should be developed to bring people into the stadium or gymnasium comfortably and to dispatch them quickly and safely at the conclusion of the event. Insist on adequate sites and facilities for large attendance events such as playoffs to aid with you planning responsibilities.

Police Services

Cooperation of your local police officials is essential to insure successful planning for crowd accommodation. The following guidelines may be useful to prepare for and secure their assistance.

A. Establish a working relationship plan of coordination at the district superintendent-chief of police level. Continued communication at this level is important in order to insure that adequate police protection will be available.

B. Development of a human relations program with the local police force is vital.

C. Pre-Game Organization:
1. A written philosophy of duties relating to police services should be established.
2. A specific school official should be assigned to contact and arrange details of police services.
3. A school official should be assigned to supervise and act as liaison for officers while on duty.
4. A meeting site at a game facility should be established for all police personnel.
5. A map of the game site should be provided, indicating control points with a description of duties for each point.

D. Recommendations:
1. One teacher should be assigned to each police officer if possible.
2. A student might also be assigned to each officer.
3. Arrange for a suitable location to detain anyone arrested by police until they can be taken away with the least amount of confusion.
4. An instruction list should be provided for each officer. [See Forms 31-1a and 31-1b.]

SAMPLE

LONG BEACH UNIFIED SCHOOL DISTRICT
LONG BEACH COUNCIL OF P.T.A.

Police Supervision of PTA Football Carnival
Long Beach Veterans' Memorial Stadium

TO POLICE OFFICERS:

For many years we have had excellent police supervision at our Football Carnival. Only through your fine work have we been able to keep the number of incidents at this affair to a minimum. We all appreciate your fine contribution to the children of this community.

WEST SIDE BLEACHERS

Assignment #1 — Entrance of Ramps (5-10 Officers)

Post #1 — Ramp 1	Post #5 — Ramp 5
Post #2 — Ramp 2	Post #6 — Ramp 6
Post #3 — Ramp 3	Post #7 — Ramp 7
Post #4 — Ramp 4	Post #8 — Tunnel entrance

Duties

1. Assist school personnel in maintaining control and admitting people to proper sections.
2. Actively supervise area around ramp entrances and admittance gates.
3. Make regular inspections of rest rooms.
4. Supervise tunnel entrance — admit only authorized personnel.

Assignment #2 — Top of Bleachers in Aisles (7 Officers)

Post #1 — Top of aisle 1	Post #5 — Top of aisle 5 and Press Box
Post #2 — Top of aisle 2	Post #6 — Top of aisle 6
Post #3 — Top of aisle 3	Post #7 — Top of aisle 7
Post #4 — Top of aisle 4	

Duties

1. Actively supervise your area.
2. Keep the aisles free and traffic moving.
3. Officer assigned to Press Box should admit only people with Press Box passes and scouts.
4. Prevent crowd from throwing any objects.
5. The use or possession of alcoholic beverages by students and adults is not allowed.
6. Discourage rowdyism of any type.
7. Standing or sitting is not allowed in the top row; this provides supervisors with an opportunity for lateral movement.

FORM 31-1 Police supervision—plans and instructions. (Long Beach Unified School District, California. By permission.)

Assignment #3 — Front Aisle at Ramp Entrance to Stands (7-10 Officers)

Post #1 — Front aisle — entrance to stands — Ramp 1
Post #2 —   ”   ”   ”   ”   ”   — Ramp 2
Post #3 —   ”   ”   ”   ”   ”   — Ramp 3
Post #4 —   ”   ”   ”   ”   ”   — Ramp 4
Post #5 —   ”   ”   ”   ”   ”   — Ramp 5
Post #6 —   ”   ”   ”   ”   ”   — Ramp 6
Post #7 —   ”   ”   ”   ”   ”   — Ramp 7

Duties

1. Keep crowd moving — prevent "ganging up" at ramps.
2. Keep aisles free.
3. Prevent crowd from throwing objects.
4. The use or possession of alcoholic beverages by students and adults is not allowed.
5. Discourage rowdyism of any type.
6. Help supervise and control track area.

SOUTH BLEACHERS

Assignment #4 — South Bleachers (2-4 Officers)

Post #1 — On track area west of South Bleachers.
Post #2 and #3 — In front and behind South Bleachers.
Post #4 — On track area east of South Bleachers.

Duties

1. Actively supervise South Bleacher area in front and behind bleachers — circulate.
2. Prevent students from standing in top row or jumping from bleachers.
3. Prevent east side and south side spectators from coming to west side.
4. Guard gates entering field from parking lots.

EAST BLEACHERS

Assignment #5 — East Bleachers (4-6 Officers)

Post #1 — South of East Bleachers near entrance gate.
Post #2 — #5 — In front and behind bleachers.
Post #6 — North side of East Bleachers near entrance gate.

Duties

1. Actively supervise area in front and behind bleachers — circulate.
2. Prevent junior high school students from crossing field to west side.
3. Supervise east side spectator entrance.
4. Keep aisles free.
5. Supervise east side entrance — bands, song girls, etc.

SAMPLE

5. It is highly recommended that officers with previous juvenile and crowd control experience be assigned whenever possible.
6. Be aware of the effect police behavior can have on crowd behavioral pattern—emphasize crowd accommodation.

E. Parking Sites: Parking sites should be administered in such a way as to provide optimum entrance and exit routes.
   1. Critical streets should be blocked prior to the game.
   2. An effort should be made to secure permission for street parking on game nights.
   3. Publicity should be disseminated regarding recommended parking sites.
   4. Specific responsibility should be established for policing parking sites before, during, and after the contest.
   5. Provide a reserved parking area for game officials, press, doctor, and VIP's.

F. Auto Traffic Control: Careful planning should provide for free flow of traffic to and from the game site.
   Most problems occur when people are not moving.
   1. A definite plan for parking and dispatching of buses should be established. Buses should be headed toward the exit at the game's conclusion, ready to load and leave immediately.
   2. Parking facilities for home and visitors should be separated.
   3. It is highly desirable to have uniformed parking attendants.

G. Control Points: Potential problem areas surrounding the game site should be idintified and given a high priority for supervision.
   1. Rest rooms should be clean and well supervised by police or faculty.
      a. It is highly recommended that separate rest rooms facilities be provided for the visiting school.
   2. Concession areas should be supervised and prices for each item clearly posted. Provide prompt service and keep customers satisfied.
   3. Guidelines for booster club activities during the contest should be established in advance.
   4. Ushers and ticket takers should be well schooled in how to accommodate the public as guests of the host school.
   5. Specific responsibilities should be designated to the maintenance staff.

H. Spectator Conduct and Education: Special care should be taken to provide a comfortable atmosphere for spectators to enjoy the athletic contest.
   1. Inform students of CIF, league, and school rules regarding conduct and sportsmanship through bulletins, assemblies, physical education classes, and school newspaper.
   2. Involve the student council, service organizations, coaches, and teams in fostering proper attitudes toward opponents and officials.

3. Non-Students
   a. Send bulletins to junior high and elementary schools in the district outlining spectator rules and regulations for each sport.
   b. Visit lower schools and speak to students in assembly.
   c. Print philosophy of athletic program in game program.
   d. Communicate philosophy of athletic program effectively to local and school newspapers and other news media.
   e. Prepare written statement for public address announcer to read just prior to flag raising ceremony.

I. Faculty
   1. Prepare and distribute synthesis of materials described above to faculty.

J. Education of Partipants
   1. Distribute to the participants listed below a carefully prepared bulletin which describes the philosophy of interscholastic athletics, the responsibility of game management participants, and the responsibility each has to the goals and objectives of the contest. Include this bulletin with the check list of duties of each group and individual has been assigned.
      a. Faculty supervisors.
      b. Volunteer supervisors.
      c. Coaches and athletes.
      d. Pep squads, bands, drill teams, service clubs, and ROTC.
      e. Police supervisors.
      f. Game officials.
      g. Public address announcer.
      h. Maintenance staff.

K. Spectator Seating
   1. All special seating areas should be clearly marked and supervised to assure spectators and special groups adequate seating.
   2. Supervision of seating areas should continue throughout the contest to insure acceptable crowd behavior.
   3. To reduce the possibility of confrontation of students and adults, provide reserved sections for the following groups:
      a. Visiting school students and adults, keep separate.
      b. Home school students and adults, keep separate.
      c. Junior high students.

L. Ticket Booth Planning: Ticket booth operation should be of such a nature to insure easy access and agress. The following plans of action are suggested.
   1. Have sufficient number of booths open and adequate lighting.
   2. Booths should be placed at least 100 feet or more away from turnstile gates to eliminate congestion.
   3. Sellers and takers should have sense of humor, but be efficient.
   4. Signs should be made for ticket prices and entrances readable and

clear.
5. Establish gates for both general public and ASB and have a separate pass gate.
6. Keep ticket booths open to end of game and keep ticket sellers at gate until end of game. (This will discourage late comers who are only there to cause trouble.)
7. Have children and junior high students pay adult prices at gate.
8. Study flow pattern of cars, buses and spectators arriving and leaving game to determine most effective placement of ticket booths and entrance and exit gates.
9. Be flexible, open another gate immediately if the need arises.
10. Assign a supervisor in charge of the ticket takers, pay extra, and have him check all gates throughout the evening.
M. Concession Planning: For the convenience of the public and as a possible money raising project, the following suggestions should be helpful in planning for concessions.
1. Have concession stands for each side of the field, keep separate.
2. Encourage selling concessions in the grandstands, this cuts down the amount of traffic in the areas of the concession stands.
3. Evaluate in advance what people will buy.
4. Have a commerical company handle the concessions and take a percentage, or have the booster club or PTA in charge, or hire one faculty supervisor and let each class rotate with providing help and participate in the sharing of the profits. Do whatever would be best for your situation.
5. Do not sell beverages in cans to the public, use software.
6. Basketball concessions
   a. Keep liquid food out of the gymnasium proper.
   b. Use trailer in back of gym or provide vending trucks at halftime.

FACILITIES-SITE MANAGEMENT

Management Responsibilities

Preplanning and preparation of the facilities and site are vitally necessary to the successful conduct of an event in order to assure their readiness prior to the arrival of spectators.

1. Stadium Checklist:
   a. Separate facilities need to be provided for home and visitors, i.e. bleachers, rest tooms, concession stands, parking, etc.
   b. Special reserved seating areas should be roped off or designated in advance. These areas must be properly marked, directional signs posted, and ushers and ticket takers informed of the locations.
   c. Have separate entrance gates for general admission and ASB card

holders and, in addition, a separate pass gate; all stadium gates should be locked prior to scheduled opening time.

d. Perimeter gates, interior gates, and roped areas should be posted with directional and identifying signs.

e. Check ticket booths to make sure that all lights work, area is clean, necessary supplies are available and price signs are posted. These booths should be located at least 100 feet or more away from entrance gates.

f. The locker rooms for teams and game officials must be clean and adequately equipped for guests (chalk boards, chalk, erasers, towels, soap, training table area, etc.). Separate dressing facilities should be provided for the officials, preferably away from the teams.

g. Check all rest rooms to make certain that they are clean and lights and equipment are in working order, and that they are adequately supplied with toilet paper, paper towels, soap, and trash cans.

h. Concession stands should be fully supplied, properly lighted, water source available and operating, fire extinguishers available, and delivery vehicle ready (gas tack full and battery charged). Price signs should be hung high enough to be easily visible to all people standing in line, and trash cans should be empty and strategically placed.

i. Set up press box with clean facilities, adequate seating for the space you have available, game programs, phones, and proper lighting.

j. Have a site map available for guests prior to game day. This map should show the traffic flow, locations of ticket booths, entrance gates, rest rooms, and concession stands, designated seating areas, and automobile and bus parking.

2. Field Checklist:

a. Field properly worked and marked, or floor swept.

b. Adequate team benches and related supply items in place. Remember the field phones.

c. Down markers, chains, and game ball available.

d. Timer's bench in place, including towels for officials and safe location for them to store jackets during game.

e. Check scoreboard to make certain it is in operating order and replace any burned out bulbs. Use the designation "guest" rather than opponent for visiting team on scoreboard.

f. First aid supplies and stretcher available at sideline.

g. Make arrangement to secure sidelines for unauthorized persons.

3. Traffic Control

a. Automobile

(1) Work with police to develop plan for free flow of traffic.

(2) Parking lots must be well lighted.

(3) Keep home and visitors parking separate, if at all possible.

(4) Arrange for team bus loading and unloading in separate areas

and away from spectators.
(5) Provide adequate area for band and rooters buses, with entry at auxilary gate.
(6) It is highly desirable to have uniformed parking attendants.
b. Pedestrian
(1) Every available gate should be open immediately prior to the conclusion of game to provide for rapid exit of spectators.
(2) Work with the police and ushers to develop plan to keep crowd moving after game.
(3) Load rooter's buses at separate gates, if possible.
(4) Flood light all exit gates, sidewalks, and parking areas.
c. Public Address Announcer
(1) Announcements regarding egress and exit traffic patterns should be made at games' end.
(2) Announcements can direct stadium leavers to tune in a certain radio station that will have traffic information.

GAME MANAGEMENT

Game management responsibilities for facilities and personal services should be accomplished in a manner which will contribute to the utmost comfort, convenience and safety of students, spectators, and players.
1. Police Supervision
a. A meeting with the officer who will be in charge of the police detail should be scheduled prior to the first home game in order to review plans for crowd control.
(1) The school administrator in charge should give specific instructions and recommendations and note specific areas that need constant supervision.
(2) Develop a plan to make the police officers feel a part of the educational goals and objectives of the contest as well as part of game.
(3) The number of police will vary with crowd size and anticipation of potential difficulties.
b. Police officers hired should be given specific instructions concerning their responsibilities and to whom they can look for direction, and a map of the game site indicating the location of all facilities.
c. The administrator in charge should meet with the members of the detail as they arrive in order to review last minute instructions. Police officers should arrive at least one half hour prior to the starting time of the contest.
d. A police car should be made available at the site in order that spectators involved in serious problems can be removed from the area immediately.

e. The public address announcer should make it perfectly clear before the contest that spectators not following established crowd control policies will be asked to leave the premises.

f. Some means of communication (i.e., walkie-talkie) should be made available between the home and visiting school administration and the police officer in charge.

g. Arrangements should be made for a police escort of rooter and team buses from the area

2. Home School Supervision

a. Faculty supervisors should be ones who are as familiar as possible with members of the student body in order to facilitate identification of students whenever necessary.

b. Develop a supervision chart of duties and lines of responsibility for faculty.

c. Some means of staff identification should be used.

3. Visiting School Supervision

a. The home school should make arrangements with the visiting school administrator in charge to meet immediately prior to the contest in order to review crowd control procedures and introduce him to officers on duty.

b. The visiting school should assign a sufficient number of supervisors in order that adequate crowd control can be accomplished.

c. Some means of staff indentfication should be used.

4. Ticket Booths

a. Ticket booths should be easily recognizable and accessible, and manned by adults.

b. There should be a sufficient number of booths available and open to easily handle the anticipated crowd.

c. Have adequate lighting and police supervision in the area of the ticket booths.

d. All booths should have a ticket price sign posted.

e. Booths should open at a pre-announced time, far enough in advance of the start of the game to allow for easy accommodation of spectators.

(1) Notify the visiting school of the opening time for the ticket booths.

f. Booths should remain open and ticket takers remain on duty until the end of the game.

(1) Free entry to the stadium or gymnasium at halftime is discouraged.

(2) Passout checks are definitely discouraged.

(3) No unchaperoned childern under the age of 12 should be admitted to the contest.

g. Inform the visiting school of any special gate arrangements so that students and other fans may be advised in advance.

   h. Have a visiting school administrator at the entrance to the visitor's gate.

   i. Ticket takers should have samples of all tickets honored for admission, including press, faculty, league, and CIF passes.

5. Banking

   a. Concern for protection of gate receipts and organization of the ticket selling operation is vital. The following plans of action are suggested.

     (1) Have sufficient change (coins and $1.00 bills) on hand.

     (2) Have separate money bags for each booth.

     (3) Deposit money in bank immediately after game is over. Have police escort you to bank.

     (4) Pay your ticket sellers and ticket takers; they will be more responsible than volunteer help.

6. Spectator Seating

   a. All special seating areas should be clearly marked and supervised to assure spectators and special groups adequate seating.

   b. Provide separate seating areas for visitors.

   c. Rapid entrance and exit areas should be provided for student body rooter buses, and if possible, arrange for entrance to stadium through auxiliary gate so as to not congest main gate area.

   d. Schools should notify rooters to remain in their assigned areas at all times except for trips to rest rooms and concession stands.

     (1) Students should not be allowed to sit in opponent's rooting section.

     (2) Discourage students from leaving and returning to the game.

   e. Adequate supervision must be provided by both schools in their respective seating areas.

7. Rooter buses

   a. Provision should be made for pre-sale of game tickets for all rooter bus riders, if school or league policy permits such.

   b. Students should be assigned to a specific bus and passenger lists compiled.

   c. Faculty supervision should be arranged for each bus.

   d. Bus driver should be directed as to route taken.

   e. Faculty supervisor should be provided with a roster of bus riders and a description of his duties as supervisor.

   f. Decision should be made about time cut-off sale of rooter bus tickets and announced to students.

   g. Specific instructions should be given to rooters on buses arriving at and departing from game sites, about conduct on buses which could lead to confrontations with home school spectators.

8. Public Address System and Announcer

   a. The public address system should be checked thoroughly prior to the game to make certain that it is in proper working order.

b. It is recommended that schools have an adult as their public address announcer and that he be paid.

c. [Refer to Forms 31-2 *a, b, c* for "Football Public Address Announcer Guidelines."]

9. Printing of Programs

   a. Have some type of program, even if it has to be mimeographed.

   b. Responsibility for publication should rest with the journalism advisor, who should be paid.

   c. Have a class or club sell the programs and retain a percentage of the profits.

   d. Circulate program sellers through the stands during the first half.

   e. Have specific place assigned for programs to be checked out and money turned in.

   f. Utilize advertiser if this will help to defray the cost of printing.

10. Press Box

    A plan should be developed in order to accommodate all necessary persons in the press box [see Form 31-3] and an adult supervisor should be hired to be responsible for press box security.

11. Rest Rooms

    Separate rest room facilities should be provided for each school and be under constant supervision.

12. Concession Stands

    a. Arrangements should be made for separate refreshment stands whenever possible.

    b. Encourage selling concessions in the grandstands; this cuts down the amount of traffic in the areas of the concession stands.

    c. An adult supervisor must be responsible for each concession stand.

13. Dressing Rooms

    a. The athletic director or his representative should meet the visiting teams upon arrival, direct them to the dressing room, and assist with any last minute requests or needs.

    b. Security arrangements must be made to protect valuables, clothing, and equipment.

    c. All unauthorized persons must be kept out of the dressing room areas.

14. Field Supervision

    a. Police officers or faculty supervisors should be assigned to keep the field clear of unauthorized persons and to protect the equipment in the areas of the benches.

15. Scoreboard Operation

    a. The scoreboard operator should be a paid adult, and he should be located in the most advantageous position in order to have an unobstructed view of the entire field of play.

       (1) A faculty member from the visiting school should be requested to sit with the scoreboard operator.

16. First Aid: It is recommended that a licensed physician and a stand-by

APPENDIX A: *FOOTBALL PUBLIC ADDRESS ANNOUNCER GUIDELINES*

The following information should be of assistance to your public address announcer at your home football games. This material has been prepared by John T. McDonough, Consultant, Physical Education, County Superintendent of Schools office, Orange County.

Pregame Preparation

(1) Go to the officials' dressing room, or see the officials on the field. Get the proper pronounciation of their names and the positions they will work.

(2) Go over the referee's signals with him and ask him for any instructions he might have. It is up to you to interpret his signals to the crowd. If you have a person on the sidelines relaying information to you, explain this to the officials so they can forward information about unusual rulings to you.

(3) Go to each team and be sure you have the correct numbers and names of all the players.

(4) Be sure you have the proper starting line-up for each team.

(5) Check the accuracy of any information about the visiting team you plan on using before the game, or at halftime, with someone from that team. You should have done this for your own team during the week.

(6) Always start your program by welcoming the crowd and introducing yourself. For example: "Good evening, ladies and gentlemen, welcome to the Rose Bowl; this is Earl Ricker, your Game Announcer."

(7) Give the line-ups at a moderate pace — not too fast, but especially not too slow. Start with the left end and go across the line, then the left half, right half, fullback and quarterback.

(8) After you give the line-ups, give the names of the officials in this order — Referee, Umpire, Head Linesman, Field Judge.

(9) Give the winner of the toss and the options the captains choose.

(10) If the National Anthem is used, invite the crowd to sing. For example: "Ladies and gentlemen, would you please rise and join our director John Boudrou and the Ram Band in singing our National Anthem."

FORM 31-2   Football public address announcer guidelines. (County Superintendent of Schools Office, Orange County, California. John T. McDonough, Consultant. By permission.)

Game Suggestions

(1) Remember, you are NOT a radio announcer and should not give a play-by-play account of the game. This is an insult to the intelligence of the spectators. In a normal game you will be speaking about 25% of the time and be QUIET about 75% of the time. The crowd came to *see* the game, not to hear your opinions about it.

(2) Give the down and distance before each play. Simply say, "Third and eight on the USC 42."

(3) When the ball is snapped, do not say "Jones has the ball and is going around left end." Again, you are insulting the intelligence of the spectators. Merely give his name — "Jones is the ball carrier."

(4) When the play is over, give the name of the man or men who made the tackle and set up the down and distance again.

(5) After a long run, pass, or kick, give the total yardage, but make no comment. Such comments as "What a beautiful run" or "A great kick" are in bad taste. The crowd can see that it was a good run or kick, and as a PA announcer you must be 100% impartial and objective.

(6) *NEVER* try to outguess the officials. If you think you see a foul, don't mention it. The chances are you will be wrong. If one of the officials throws a red foul marker, simply say, "There's a flag on the play." *Then wait* — don't try to explain the foul. When the referee gives his signal, interpret to the crowd. Get a copy of the rule book or a program which has the signals. If it is an unusual play, the arrangements you made prior to the game will get this information to you for you to pass on to the spectators.

Give the nature of the foul — whether accepted or declined — and the new down and yardage situation. For example: "The foul is 15 yards for holding. It is now first and twenty-five." Or, "The offsides penalty is declined by UCLA. It is now second and eight."

(7) Never use the names of officials during the game. You should read their names prior to the game. But *do not say*, "The foul was called by Head Linesman Jones," or "Referee Smith is explaining the foul to Captain Brown."

(8) Never comment on the fouls that are called or the work of the officials, whether you think it is good or bad. This is a good way to start a riot.

(9) Never comment on the sportsmanship of play of either team or either coach. This, too, is a good way to start a riot.

(10) Never designate the player who committed a foul. You probably will be wrong anyway, and this type of announcement tends to make the game get out of hand.

(11) If a player is injured, give his name. You are not a doctor, so do not try to diagnose his injuries from the press box. If you get a later report on the player's condition, give it with no comment.

Never try to explain how a player was injured. This can easily be misconstrued by the crowd as an unsportsmanlike act on the part of an opponent and cause an unfortunate situation.

(12) If the crowd starts to boo the visiting team or the officials to an extreme degree, say, "Ladies and gentlemen, these people are our guests tonight, let's treat them as such."

(13) A few minutes before the end of the game — preferably during a time out — thank the people for coming, announce convenient routes for leaving the stadium, and remind them to drive carefully on the way home.

In summary, the public address announcer just covers the facts of the game as impartially and objectively as possible. You should not give opinions of your own because the spectators are present and should be left free to form their own opinions. A radio announcer gives his opinions because the listener is seeing the game through his description, but you are a public address announcer and this is a totally different art.

471

PRESS BOX SECURITY INSTRUCTION SHEET

<u>SAMPLE</u>

Football Press Box Instructions
Victor Valley High School

I. *PERSONS AUTHORIZED IN AND ON PRESS BOX;*

    A. *ON TOP OF PRESS BOX:*
        1. Our cameraman plus one assistant.
        2. Our coach and one assistant.
        3. Visiting team's cameraman.

    B. *INSIDE PRESS BOX:*
        1. KAVR Radio — 2 men, north end. Door must be locked when they go in.
        2. Public Address announcer — Walt Swain.
        3. Visiting team's coach — phones.
        4. Our statistician.
        5. Our spotter.
        6. Visiting team's spotter.
        7. Visiting team's radio personnel (2).
        8. Daily Press Sports Writer.

II. *ALL PERSONS WILL HAVE PASSES:*
        1. Visitors' passes will be picked up when they go into the press box.
        2. Remember — some people lose passes, some never get them. But: Try to keep a "no pass, no entry" rule enforced.

III. We are going to have the table marked with names and seats assigned. Please show them their seats.

IV. Mr. Robert McNaught is in charge of press box security.

                      Rick Novack, Director of Activities

<u>SAMPLE</u>

FORM 31-3 Football press box instructions. (Victor Valley High School, California. By permission.)

ambulance by available for the home and visiting teams.

    a. If a physician or ambulance is not available, options for emergency medical care should be clearly outlined for the teams and for the in case of a spectator emergency.

    b. Emergency facilities should be available for spectators with qualified attendant

17. Game Officials

    a. Adequate dressing facilities are necessary to insure comfotable and safe preparation by the game officials.

      (1) These facilities should be located away from either team and no one should be allowed to enter the area even if they are using the coaches' dressing room.

      (2) The athletic director or his representative should meet the officials upon arrival to direct them to their dressing room.

    b. Officials should be sent a courtesy letter in advance of the game. This letter should include a time schedule for the game, directions to the game site, location of parking and dressing room facilities, and complimentary game tickets.

      (1) Be sure to notify the officials of any changes in the time schedule, such as extended halftime, etc.

    c. Check to pay the officials should be prepared in advance and payment should be made prior to the game to allow the officials to leave the field immediately after the contest.

    d. The athletic director should pay the officials; under no circumstances should this responsibility be assigned to one of the coaches.

    e. The game ball should be delivered to the officials well in advance of the start of the contest.

18. Pre-Game and Halftime Ceremonies

    a. Arrangements should be made and coordinated in advance for any pre-game or halftime ceremonies.

      (1) All affected parties should be notified of the plans and time schedules, including both teams, coaches, officials, announcer, participating bands, drill teams, etc.

      (2) Participating units must be advised of the need for strict adherence to the announced time schedule; delays in the start of games or lengthy halftimes are sources of potential crowd control problems.

19. Visiting Team Information

    a. The visiting school should be supplied with an informational bulletin [Forms 31-4 *a, b, c.*]

APPENDIX C: *VISITING TEAM INFORMATION*

<u>SAMPLE</u>

Letter sent to Vice Principal or Athletic Director of visiting school:

Dear Sir:

Here is a map of the Victor Valley High School athletic facility, also a time schedule and three passes to the press box. These passes will be picked up by our press box attendant when presented for admission.

Please show this information to your coach, especially the field diagram (not all schools divide the field this way).

The passes are for your cameraman, spotter, and the assistant coach who uses the phones. We will have phones for your coaches. The cameraman must go on top of the press box — all others will stay inside.

A custodian will be on duty in your locker room when you are out of it during the game.

A letterman will meet your team and act as runner should you need anything.

If you have any questions, please feel free to call.

Good luck.

Sincerely,

_____

Rick Novack
Director of Activities

Enclosures

<u>SAMPLE</u>

474

<u>SAMPLE</u>

DIRECTIONS TO VICTOR VALLEY HIGH SCHOOL FOOTBALL FIELD:

Barstow Freeway to Mojave Drive exit, east on Mojave past stoplight to the first stop sign, corner of Sixth and Mojave, left on Sixth Street one block to driveway, up driveway to first large gate on driver's left (approximately 3/4 block).

Mr. Blaser will meet you. He will direct you to the unloading and parking zone.

Mr. Shea is our stadium supervisor. If you have any questions, see Mr. Shea. He will meet your bus as you unload.

These directions are for rooters' busses only.

TIME SCHEDULE — FOOTBALL GAMES

1. Varsity teams — On field as Sophomores leave field.
2. Coin toss during warm up.
3. Off field at 7:45 p.m.
4. Band takes field at 7:45 p.m.
5. Teams return at 7:57 p.m.
6. National Anthem at 7:58 p.m.
7. Kickoff at 8:00 p.m.

If the Sophomore game is longer than normal, the Varsity game time will be set back. Teams will still leave the field fifteen minutes before game time.

FORM 31-4 Visiting team information. (Victor Valley High School, California. By permission.)

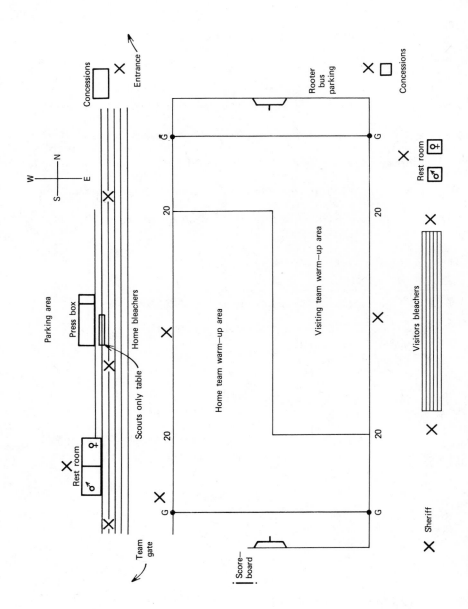

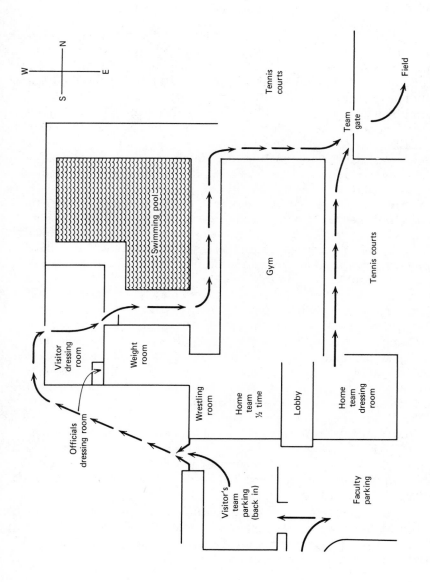

477

Questions

1. Give some illustrations of how an athletic coach, by his sideline conduct, or lack of bench control, could incite and "fire up" the spectators so that crowd control could become a problem.
2. Enumerate the responsibilities of the athletic coach and the student-athlete during the athletic contest.
3. Unknown to you, the athletic director, a comical drunk joins your school's cheerleaders behind the players' bench and is assisting the cheerleaders with their yells. You note that the spectators have come to life and are encouraging the antics of the drunk. It appears that no harm is being done by the drunk's unauthorized appearance behind the players' bench. As athletic director, you must decide whether to permit the drunk to remain with the cheerleaders or have him removed from the stadium. What is your decision? Is there a time element involved? What is the rationale of your decision? What should you as the athletic director have done in your pregame planning in the first place so that you would not be in this dilemma now?
4. The lights in your stadium where you play your night football games have been malfunctioning, despite the fact you have had the lighting checked out by an electrician the day before the game for the past two weeks. To this point of time only a single bank of lights has malfunctioned, one side of the field or the other, and the football games have progressed without interruption. In anticipation of the fact that all lights may malfunction at once and/or electrical power is not available for any lights or the public address system in the stadium, what plan or procedures should you set up *in advance* to be operable should this emergency arise the night of a contest when the entire stadium is thrown into darkness? Enumerate and discuss the procedural steps to be followed should you as athletic director be confronted with such a situation.
5. Since managment and crowd accommodations means communication, what type of information should be included under the subject of "Fundamentals óf Sportsmanship" for a printed basketball program you are having prepared?

REFERENCES

1. *Coaches Manual*, National Association for Sport and Physical Education, American Alliance for Health, Physical Education and Recreation, Washington D.C. By permission.

2, 3, and 4. Keller, Irvin, "Tolerating Misconduct Can Jeopardize Interscholastics," *Crowd Control for High School Athletics*, 1970, p. 4, prepared by the National Council of Secondary School Athletic Directors, American Alliance for Health, Physical Education and Recreation, Washington D.C. By permission.

5, 6, 7, and 8. Meyer, Harold, "Responsibilities of State and National Associations," *Crowd Control for High School Athletics*, pp. 9-12, 1970, prepared by the National Council of Secondary School Athletic Directors, American Alliance for Health Physical Education and Recreation, Washington D.C. By permission.

9. Fagans, Kenneth, *Crowd Management Guidelines for Community Organization Support and Management Procedures for High School Athletic Contests*, California Interscholastic Federation, Southern Section, 1971. Reprinted by permission.

10. Razor, Jack E., "Variables in Crowd Control," *Athletic Journal*, Vol. 71, No. 3. November 1971, p. 30. Evanston, Illinois.

11. Fagans, Kenneth, *Crowd Management Guidelines*. Interscholastic Federation, California Southern Section, 1971. Reprinted by Permission.

PART VIII
IMPLICATIONS FOR THE FUTURE

Chapter 32
Implications
for the Future

Although no one can predict future happenings with any degree of certainty and accuracy, as in the business world, one can make certain assumptions based on current trends.

GREATER PARTICIPATION

There is every indication greater numbers of athletics will be participating at the secondary school level although the trend may be away from some of the traditional sports such as football, basketball, baseball, and track. There is much interest today in the lifetime sports activities of tennis, golf, swimming, cycling, backpacking, karate, judo, and skiing. Presently activities such as golf, tennis, and swimming are included in the interscholastic programs of many schools. This is not to say that students will not want to participate in cycling, backpacking, karate, or judo, for example, on a competitive interscholastic basis in the future. If their recreational interests are in these activities and if funds are available, it is likely these sports will be made available to students.

Coeducation Participation

With the implementation and enforcement of Title IX, July 21, 1975, not only will girls' participation in their own sports become more prevalent, but most of the athletic programs, including interscholastic athletics, are unlikely to be catagorized according to sex. Girls participating in athletics at the high school and collegiate levels is no longer a novelty. Although they have participated previously on their own teams, boys and girls participating on the same athletic teams is now commonplace. There appear to be few problems when girls are treated as team members, which is what they want. Until recently most males felt they were expected to treat females differently from the way they treated other males. This may be the situation in other social activities; this certainly isn't the situation in athletic participation when competing together in coeducational activities. The girls do not expect any preferential treatment when competing in athletic contests. The programs are becoming truly asexual in nature.

Justification of Program

Athletic directors and coaches find that having to constantly justify athletic programs, for funding purposes, a source of irritation. This trend is likely to continue. The financial crunch is not only likely to prevail for some time, but constant scrutiny of the activities in the program and of the conduct and administration of the program will continue. As pointed out, traditional sports are likely to be scrutinized and some of them are likely to be replaced by other sports and activities that are now run by clubs at this time. Values and interests of students and the community will continue to change and will dictate the types of activities that will be carried on under the sanction of interscholastic athletics.

Medical, Safety, and Legal Aspects

Without a doubt, administrators and coaches will continue to provide the best training and medical services and equipment possible for the participants. Although these aspects not only aid the participant to improve his performance, coaches, administrators, and school personnel want to protect themselves against lawsuits. Everyone will continue to be liable for personal negligence, but the possibility of lawsuits can be alleviated by providing medical services and safe equipment for the participants.

Coaching and Trainer Certification

The future will see universal certification standards adopted for coaches and trainers so they will truly move into the realm of a professional. By necessity this may occur because of the threat of lawsuits. There is likely to be inservice training dealing with such areas as law and care and prevention of injuries for those already coaching. Such courses will probably be required before new teachers coming into the coaching profession can be certified.

Athletic Director Certification and Management of Programs

There will be a pronounced change in the administration of athletic programs and those who administer such programs. Gone are the days of retiring the old coach upward to the position of athletic director. This individual must be a professional in every sense of the word. Athletic director certification will be necessary, which will mean pursuing a course of study similar to the one outlined in Chapter 9, in order to qualify for such a position.

In the future the athletic director will move into the role of middle manager on a full-time basis, assuming an administrative role on the same level as the dean of students or vice principal and on a commensurate salary level with other administrators. The individuals in the position of athletic directors will be performing the management functions as identified and discussed throughout the book. However, such an individual will have to be innovative and creative in order to retain ongoing, viable programs since not only must the expenditure of funds be justified but outside funds must be secured.

Physical education has been dropped as a mandatory course in the curriculum in a number of states and is available to students on an elective and voluntary basis. Athletics, although considered extra-curricular activities by many people were supported in the high schools by general funds allocated to physical education activities. In schools that once enjoyed this relationship, athletics no longer are afforded this protection. All school athletics are now vulnerable to being placed on an extracurricular basis. The danger is not the title affixed to athletics; it is that funds, once available to physical education, of which athletics were a part, may no longer be available to physical education, much less to athletics.

Summation

The real challenge to the administrators of interscholastic athletic programs is to leave themselves open to new ideas and concepts, to welcome change if it is good and not view it as a threat, and to find ways to retain ongoing, viable programs. The experienced athletic director's faith in the future of school athletics is not likely to be shaken nor is he likely to doubt his ability to carry on the program adhering to valid management principles and concepts. The individual who couldn't comprehend and accept change in the past, will have little chance to survive in the future. Although such an individual is apt to fall by the wayside because of managerial obsolescence, the future of interscholastic athletics continues to look bright.

SUGGESTED READINGS

Annotated Bibliography—General Administration and Management

American Association of School Administrators, *Staff Relations in School Administrators*, National Education Association, Washington, D.C., 1955.

Barr, A.S., Burton, Willian, Brueckner, Leo J., *Supervision*, Appleton-Century-Croft, New York, 1947.

Bennis, Warren, G., Benne, Kenneth D., Chin, Robert. *The Planning of Change*. Holt, Rinehart and Winston, New York, 1969.

Colardarci, Arthur P. and Getzels, Jacob W., *The Use of Theory in Educational Administration*, Stanford University Press, 1955.

Drucker, Peter F., *The Effective Executive*, Harper and Row, New York, 1967.

Feinberg, Mortimer R., *Effective Psychology for Managers*, Prentice-Hall, Englewood Cliffs, N.J., 1965.

Griffiths, Daniel E., *Human Relations in School Administration*, Appleton-Century-Crofts, New York, 1956.

Getzels, Jacob W., Lipham, James M., and Campbell, Ronald F., *Educational Administration as a Social Process*, Harper and Row, New York, 1968.

Halpin, Andrew W., *Theory and Research in Administration*, Macmillan, New York, 1966.

Hampton, David R., Summer, Charles E., and Webber, Ross A., *Organizational Behavior and the Practive of Management*, Scott, Foresman, Glenview, Ill., 1968.

Hersey, Paul, and Blanchard, Kenneth H., *Management of Organizational Behavior*, Prentice-Hall, Englewood Cliffs, N.J., 1972.

Knowles, Henry P. and Saxberg, Borje O., *Personality and Leadership Behavior*, Addison-Wesley, Reading, Mass., 1971.

Leavitt, Harlod J., *Managerial Psychology*, University of Chicago Press, 1972.

McCay, James T., *The Management of Time*, Prentice-Hall, Englewood Cliffs, N.J., 1959.

Newman, William H., Summer, Charles E., and Warren, E. Kirby, *The Process of Management*, Prentice-Hall, Englewood Cliffs, N.J., 1972.

Nolte, M. Chester (ed.), *An Introduction to School Administration*, Macmillan, 1966.

Peter, Laurence and Hull, Raymond, *The Peter Principle*, Morrow, New York, 1969.

Selznick, Philip, *Leadership in Administration*, Harper and Row, New York, 1957.

Simon, Hervert A., *Administrative Behavior*, The Free Press, New York, 1965.

Strauss, George and Sayles, Leonard P., *Personnel: The Human Problems of Management*, Prentice-Hall, Englewood Cliffs, N.J., 1972.

Index

GV
346
F86
20,065

CAMROSE LUTHERAN COLLEGE
LIBRARY

Date Due

BJJJ

PRINTED IN U.S.A.   CAT. NO. 24 161   BRO DART